The ECONOMICS *of* ELECTRONIC COMMERCE

Soon-Yong Choi

Dale O. Stahl

Andrew B. Whinston

MACMILLAN
TECHNICAL
PUBLISHING
U·S·A

Macmillan Technical Publishing, Indianapolis, Indiana

The Economics of Electronic Commerce

By Soon-Yong Choi, Dale O. Stahl, and Andrew B. Whinston

Published by:
Macmillan Technical Publishing
201 West 103rd Street
Indianapolis, IN 46290 USA

Copyright © 1997 by Macmillan Technical Publishing

Printed in the United States of America   4 5 6 7 8 9 0

Library of Congress Cataloging-in-Publication Number 96-80466

ISBN 1-57870-014-0

Warning and Disclaimer

Publisher Don Fowley

Publisher's Assistant Rosemary Lewis

Publishing Manager Tom Stone

Marketing Manager Mary Foote

Managing Editor Carla Hall

About the Authors

Soon-Yong Choi is Economist and Assistant Director of the Center for Research in Electronic Commerce at the University of Texas at Austin, where he received his Ph.D. in Economics. He has worked as economist and computer and statistics consultant for various research, public, and private organizations. His areas of research include cable service pricing, quality differentiation, antitrust, and the economics of electronic commerce. His e-mail address is soon@mail.utexas.edu.

Dale O. Stahl is the Malcolm Forsman Centennial Professor of Economics at the University of Texas at Austin. In 1969 and 1970, he received B.S., M.S., and Engineering degrees from the Massachusetts Institute of Technology in the field of Electrical Engineering with research experience in computer science and neural nets. In 1981, he received his Ph.D. from the University of California at Berkeley in the field of Economics with a focus on mathematical economics. Since then he has held positions at Duke University, M.I.T., Boston University, Tilburg University in the Netherlands, and Oxford University. He has published on a wide range of topics including benefit-cost analysis methods, the stability of quantity and price adjustment processes, strategic merchant price setting, consumer search and firm advertising, political effects on tariff policy, game theory and bargaining theory, experimental investigations of bounded rationality, and network pricing. His e-mail address is stahl@eco.utexas.edu.

Andrew B. Whinston is the Cullen Chair Professor of Information Systems, Computer Science and Economics, IC^2 Fellow, and Director of the Center for Research in Electronic Commerce at the University of Texas at Austin. He received his Ph.D. in Management from Carnegie Mellon University in 1962, and held positions at Yale University, University of Virginia, and Purdue University. He is the Editor in Chief of the journals "Decision Support Systems" and the "Journal of Organizational Computing and Electronic

Commerce". His recent research interests are Internet pricing and application of client/server computing to support groups working collaboratively. His e-mail address is abw@uts.cc.utexas.edu.

Trademark Acknowledgments

Acquisitions Editor
Tom Stone

Senior Editors
Sarah Kearns
Suzanne Snyder

Project Editor
Brad Herriman

Copy Editors
Margo Catts
Keith Cline
Malinda McCain
John Sleeva
Sharon Wilke

Assistant Marketing Manager
Gretchen Schlesinger

Acquisitions Coordinators
Amy Lewis
Tim Micheli

Cover Designer
Gary Adair

Cover Production
Aren Howell

Book Designer
Glenn Larsen

Manufacturing Coordinator
Brook Farling

Director of Production
Larry Klein

Production Team Supervisors
Laurie Casey
Joe Millay

Graphics Image Specialists
Sadie Crawford, Wil Cruz

Production Analyst
Erich Richter

Production Team
Tricia Flodder, Aleata Howard,
Malinda Kuhn, Rowena Rappaport,
Pamela Woolf,

Indexer
Virginia Bess

Contents at a Glance

Table of Contents

2 Characteristics of Digital Products and Processes   59

4 Quality Uncertainty and Market Efficiency   137

11 Business and Policy Implications of Electronic Commerce   463

PREFACE

This book is written in the belief that the tenets and teachings of economics are vital to an insightful analysis of the broad spectrum of issues affecting commercial uses of the Internet and the next-generation information infrastructure. Our digital future is being decided on the Internet, where prototypical products and services have been test-driven by an odd collection of individuals. Just a few years ago, commercial uses of this somewhat chaotic and decentralized network of networks seemed highly unrealistic. Today, while the government and large corporations are grappling with proposals on how to build the national information infrastructure, major components of commercial use of the Internet (users, technologies, and digital contents) are already converging, aided by the rapid acceptance of the user friendly World Wide Web. What *The Economist* called an "accidental superhighway" has become the hottest commercial medium. While there is considerable uncertainty about who will be the winners and what products and technological standards will dominate this new arena, the basic foundation for a totally unique competitive market has been set and so has the stage for a fundamental market analysis using economics.

Defining Electronic Commerce as a Market

Electronic commerce goes far beyond simply "doing business electronically." Doing business electronically means that many conventional business processes, such as advertising and product ordering, are being digitized and conducted on the Internet. However, the Internet is not a mere alternative channel for marketing or selling products online, for instance, the most recent alternatives to mail-order business, catalog shopping, home shopping networks, and direct marketing. Instead, the electronic marketplace enables sellers to innovate whole business processes from production to customer service—which were said to occur in stages—by integrating them in a seamless whole, where, for example, product choices and prices are updated according to consumer information in real-time on web stores. These process-related changes will significantly impact intra-business organization, business-to-business relationships, and business-to-consumer interactions.

On top of all this, old and new products alike are being released from their physical constraints and are being converted into digital products that can be delivered via the global network and paid for using digital currency. With digitization and digital payment systems, the electronic marketplace becomes a separate and independent market needing no physical presence for stores, products, market institutions, or sellers and buyers. New technologies such as the World Wide Web, digital signatures and encryption, and electronic currencies are tools of the trade in the nascent world of electronic commerce. From an economics perspective, our interest in this world lies in analyzing how these tools are used, how the products are chosen, what level of prices and competition will prevail, and ultimately whether a market exists or fails.

About this Book

This book is not about how to use the web or how to set up a web page for a successful business. Instead of presenting a user's guide for electronic commerce tools, this book will introduce readers to the underlying economic aspects of electronic commerce. Electronic commerce clearly crowns the list of technology-related media topics, as evidenced by the abundance of literature covering the technical and legal aspects. Specific subjects span a wide spectrum from fundamental design and implementation prerequisites, such as copyright protection and privacy in transactions, to discussions on whether the electronic marketplace will materialize at all! However, in virtually all of these publications, the economic aspects have largely been neglected.

This book is about electronic commerce as a market. At the core of electronic commerce is the meeting of sellers and buyers to trade digital products using digital processes. Production, product delivery, and payments are all handled electronically as are marketing and consumer searches—the electronic equivalent of shopping. Except for online delivery, non-digital product sellers also will be affected by the Internet's unique business processes in such areas as disseminating product information, tracking sales, and collecting customer information, application engineering, and customer service.

Given this market setting, electronic commerce is a suitable candidate for microeconomic market analysis. However, existing literature on the Internet is limited to teaching readers how to use the Internet. Topical literature dealing with digital copyrights, online marketing, and electronic payments, on the other hand, is usually geared toward the technical and legal aspects of these new technologies. In this book, while paying attention to the current status of some of the intertwined issues of electronic commerce in technology, standards, policy, and legal issues, the focus will be on many economic issues and aspects of electronic commerce that other existing literature does not cover. Six major issues are identified: quality and the role of intermediaries; digital copyrights; advertising; consumer searches for product information; product selection and pricing strategies; and electronic financial and payment services. As the market has not yet consolidated around one solution in most cases, for each of these issues an understanding of the short- and long-term implications and economic ramifications of various proposals and guidelines under consideration are provided.

Applying standard economic analyses to an entirely new industry will lay the foundation for the development of radically new business models. Given the urgency of the issues and the immediate applicability of the economic analysis, our primary focus will be to provide detailed analysis for those involved in the actual production, marketing, and distribution as well as for professionals doing business in the electronic marketplace. As electronic commerce progresses toward a full-fledged marketplace, economic analysis will take on increasingly greater importance. It is already clear that those businesses that achieve early success from applying these theories will enjoy a distinct comparative advantage in this newly defined world of business. Given this, the audience this book is directed at is not limited to professionals and students of the world of economics but also includes business professionals and casual readers. The economic topics we explore are related to the basic aspects of doing business electronically and are relevant to anyone interested in entering the realm of electronic commerce—be it as an entrepreneur, an investor, or an established business.

How Is This Book Organized?

The first three chapters set the general framework necessary for later in-depth analysis of the issues. In a concise and succinct manner, Chapter 1 defines electronic commerce as a market, and discusses the characteristics of the electronic marketplace and its sellers and buyers, and presents an overview of current issues and research activities. Chapter 2 defines the "raison d'etre" of the electronic marketplace—digital products. Although digital products are often equated with online information products, a much broader definition is given. Digital products include not only software and online contents but also advertisements and product information, payment information, digitized processes, and communication. Many physical products are also digitized, for example, digitized house keys, concert tickets, currencies, and smart products. Finally, Chapter 3 presents an overview of the Internet network and technology, concluding with an in-depth review of various pricing strategies for the network.

The next seven chapters revisit each of these issues in depth. Each chapter presents a summary of the issue, a brief review of relevant literature in economics, and an analysis focusing on the economic perspectives. Each of the seven chapters can be read separately if readers are interested in a specific topic. Each chapter provides a summary of economic models and issues sufficient to allow readers to follow later discussions. In Chapter 4, an analysis of the critical problems of quality uncertainty and a discussion of the role of intermediaries in preventing market failure are given. Chapter 5 focuses on the need for copyright protection as a means to promote market efficiency and product quality in electronic commerce. Chapter 6 analyzes how sellers can signal product quality to their buyers using advertising and other marketing strategies. Looking at quality from the other side, Chapter 7 evaluates how electronic commerce is affected by buyer initiatives to find about product quality and prices. Three related topics in product selection strategy—product choice and customization, the use of information about consumer preferences, and discriminatory pricing—are explained in Chapter 8. Finally, Chapters 9 and 10 are concerned with the financial and monetary effects of doing business electronically. Chapter 9 focuses on online financial services while Chapter 10 is devoted to electronic payment systems, especially those systems based on digital currency and their impact on the monetary system and policy.

The final two chapters summarize our conclusions, adding a strategic perspective. We also point out areas in this emerging marketplace deserving future research.

At the end of each chapter, we provide a list of academic and technical literature for advanced economic study. Although it is not our intention to produce a reference or a user's manual for Internet users, we do provide information, in sidebars, on technically advanced topics and terms. In addition, we include examples whenever possible to make our discussion more concrete and specific. The online references to these and other related sites and documents found at the end of each chapter will allow readers to further explore these and other examples on their own.

Acknowledgments

This book is a result of collaboration among the authors but many thanks are due to our colleagues who provided us with interesting materials, read the manuscript, and made invaluable suggestions. For their help, we would like to thank John Allison, Valerie Bencivenga, Scott Freeman, Mark Lemley, R. Preston McAfee, David Sibley, and Bruce Smith as well as anonymous reviewers. Alok Gupta's collaboration for the section on the infrastructure pricing is specially acknowledged. Susan Kutor suffered most while reading and editing often incomplete chapters, and we are indebted to her for her suggestions and corrections. We'd also like to thank our editor Thomas Stone, who tirelessly worked to make this project perfect, and Amy Lewis, Tim Micheli and the staff at Macmillan Technical Publishing. Finally, we would like to acknowledge financial support from the Information Technology and Organizations program at the National Science Foundation and the program managers, Drs. Su Shing Chen and Les Gasser, and the support from the Texas Higher Education Coordinating Board through its Advanced Technology Program grant.

CHAPTER 1

Electronic Commerce and the Internet

Our objective in this and the next two chapters is to provide you with a framework for understanding the economic impact of the new business medium by defining electronic commerce and the nature of digital products. Opinions regarding the future of the Internet and electronic commerce may vary widely, but the general consensus is that commercial uses of the Internet will have an immense effect on businesses, governments, and consumers. The question is, "In exactly what areas and in what ways will they be affected?" A shared definition of electronic commerce is the first step toward presenting the answers.

In this chapter, we discuss the characteristics of computing environments that have made the Internet the infrastructure for electronic commerce. Presented in section 1.1 is an overview of how computing and networking environments have evolved into the Internet. The objective here is to highlight differences between the Internet and previous computing and communications environments in order to give a clearer understanding of the importance of the Internet as a commercial medium.

Section 1.2 reviews commercial and noncommercial uses of computing and communication technologies, and defines what electronic commerce is within the context of changing technologies. It will be evident that conventional distinctions between commercial and noncommercial uses of the Internet are no longer valid. Section 1.3 discusses the market characteristics of electronic commerce, pointing out the differences from traditional, physical product markets as well as issues arising from the novice nature of electronic commerce. Finally, in section 1.4, key issues in electronic commerce are discussed along with a look at how economic analysis may help to resolve many uncertainties. While these snapshots put the issues in perspective, later chapters will deal with each in depth.

1.1.   Developments in Internetworking

The Internet is a network of networks. Each network is comprised of computers connected by wire or wireless mediums, such as radio signals, that enable component computers to "talk" to each other. Once computers are networked, files on one computer can be accessed from any other computer on the network; messages can be exchanged, and limited resources such as printers can be shared. Large or small, each network is owned and managed by a company or a single group with the exception of the Internet.

The Internet is not owned or managed by any single entity, although its component networks are independent units managed and usually paid for by the network's owners. (Chapter 3, section 3.6, covers Internet technology and infrastructure in detail; in this chapter, we focus on general characteristics of the Internet as a market infrastructure.) Computers on these component networks became a part of the larger Internet when they used the same standard for cross-communication—the TCP/IP protocol—known as the language of the Internet. Therefore, any computer "speaking" TCP/IP protocol is Internet-enabled in terms of connectivity.

The Internet is clearly the largest network of computers in existence today. There are, however, many non-Internet networks such as commercial online services that are quite large in their own right. The sudden dominance of the

Internet as a model mechanism for information transfers and commercial transactions may seem accidental in view of these large networks. However, the Internet or Internet-like networks have two overriding factors in their favor to become a market infrastructure: distributed computing and openness.

Distributed and Networked Computing

A distributed computing environment consists of multiple sites (or computers) that are capable of performing the same type of functions or executing a portion of a task. This is in contrast to a mainframe computer environment in which shared users send commands and receive results via dumb terminals connected to the computer. In a mainframe environment, all of the computing necessary to process a task is done at the central computer (the host), whereas terminals are used only for inputting instructions and displaying results. The Internet, on the other hand, is an example of distributed computing in which host and client computers are each capable of independent computing.

The distinction between a host and a client is based on which machine (or program) provides content and service. A client machine typically establishes a connection to a host—known also as a server—and initiates a request for a service, such as to download a file. A web browser, for example, is a program that runs on a client machine, whereas an httpd, which sends out HTML files (web pages) upon request by a browser, is a program that runs on a server.

However, this distinction between a server and a client is only arbitrary. In a distributed computer network, each connected computer can act as either a server or a client. This potential is not obvious to many Internet initiates who use their computers as clients only. But the strength of a distributed computer network such as the Internet is its connectivity that supports peer-to-peer relationships. What this means in terms of a market is that each computer or user connected to a peer-to-peer network is a potential provider of contents, for instance, a seller as well as a buyer. Any personal computer connected to the Internet is capable of hosting a web site or sending a file instead of simply acting as a tool to visit web sites and download files. The traditional division between corporations as content providers and consumers as buyers is still evident in the way some commercial online services organize their services so that subscribers are targeted only as readers or customers. Such customers are assumed to be "surfing" the net just like television viewers and newspaper readers are passively consuming the contents provided by the sellers.

On the contrary, the strength of the Internet lies in the potentially interactive environment in which consumers regard themselves also as the content providers. The proliferation of personal homepages, which is often dismissed as a transitory fad, indicates that the Internet users understand the power of the medium in providing content. Nevertheless, the majority of Internet users are assumed to remain passive. To surf the net, it may be adequate to have a passive communication device which connects and downloads files without the capability to act as a host. A stripped-down network computer—a web-browsing machine with limited processing power—resembles a television receiver, or a dumb terminal of the bygone era.

Even when consumers are not selling contents on the Internet, the medium's interactivity enables sellers to collect information about consumers' tastes and their preferences for product quality, price, and customer service using the medium itself. Unlike the broadcasting media, the Internet facilitates two-way interactions between sellers and buyers, the result of which can also be fed seamlessly into production, marketing, transaction, and consumption processes. In short, a network means a worldwide system of interaction, whether for business or for communication, in which computers connected to the network are simply points of presence.

As the conventional distinction between a seller and a buyer is lost in a distributed network such as the Internet, transactional processes undergo a similar transformation. A typical commercial transaction involves many agents and processes. Each of these processes performs a specific function—production, assembly, marketing, delivery, payment clearance, insurance, certification, and so on, which typically occur in stages. Different intermediaries have evolved to fulfill one or more of these functions in the physical market. Intermediaries are now evolving to fulfill these functions in a distributed computer network, where they may be processed simultaneously by different agents. The scope of market activities undertaken by these agents will be defined as the commerce on the Internet matures. However, the organization of agents in electronic commerce will be sufficiently different from physical markets. For example, the traditional difference between a wholesaler and a retailer is lost in the digital marketplace because a producer only needs to transmit one copy to an intermediary. An efficient market organization is more likely because activities of each agent involved in a transaction, from production to payment and consumption, may be monitored and evaluated more efficiently, and new product strategies and pricing can be implemented rapidly and concurrently. Such changes in market organization are the subject matter of later chapters.

Open Networks

Distributed computing presupposes a network. Large corporations, governments, and research organizations have maintained extremely large networks of computers often made up of several layers. For internal communication and computing needs, computers are typically connected in local area networks (LANs) using physical connections such as cables. These LANs can then be interconnected into wide area networks (WANs) via telephone lines or satellite links. And private value-added networks (VANs) have been in operation for over two decades to facilitate company-to-company transactions using electronic data interchange (EDI). The disillusioning truth in this image of an interconnecting system of cogs is that not all LANs and WANs can communicate with each other, because of both technical and policy choices made by network owners. VANs, in particular, are limited to paying members and use proprietary communication standards. A need exists for a means to bridge the gaps between the different sized cogs that will enable them to communicate. The Internet is one such means.

The Internet is unique as a networking environment in that it is based on open standards which enable any computer or network to connect to it using TCP/IP protocols. Internet Protocol (IP) is the most basic layer in communication protocols for the Internet and handles addressing and delivery, whereas the Transmission Control Protocol (TCP) maintains message integrity. Being an open network is similar to postal communication systems. Once you have a mailing address you can send and receive messages using the postal service. There is no restriction to become a mail user, and the use of mail is not limited to specific types of messages. Similarly, once you obtain an Internet address for your computer—an IP address or a domain name—linking to the rest of the computers on the Internet is a matter of connecting a cable or dialing through a modem.

The openness of the Internet facilitates interoperability between different computer platforms and supports the exchange of human-readable messages. Because of this, the potential of electronic commerce over the Internet far surpasses that of EDI or private VANs. The use of EDI was projected to be one of the most important business developments that would have made paper-based business transactions obsolete. Through the use of EDI, businesses have obtained significant cost savings and gains in efficiency and competitiveness. Nevertheless, actual use of EDI has fallen far short of projections.

The primary reason for the limited use of EDI is its requirement for asset-specific investments. A large amount of capital investment is necessary to construct an EDI system because EDI transactions depend on proprietary software. Each time interaction with a new EDI system becomes necessary, new hardware and software must first be developed. But perhaps, most significantly, EDI transactions are limited to machine-to-machine communications based on machine-readable forms. Due to these factors, EDI is limited to a small set of predetermined transaction data, whereas normal communications between companies are conducted via paper, telephone, fax, and other conventional methods.

The Internet, in contrast, offers a very different medium of communication. The strength of the Internet lies in its versatility in transmitting various file formats and the nature of open-end networking. Using a wide variety of application software, users of the Internet can conduct many activities that EDI simply does not support. The rapid growth of the World Wide Web, for example, has demonstrated the importance of communicating multimedia contents and user-friendly interfaces. At the same time, the ease in using web browsers and authoring software, such as HyperText Markup Language (HTML), has enabled all computers that are connected to the Internet to become content providers instead of being simply receivers of information. These advantages have spurred the use of the Internet as a tool for communications and commercial transactions. Electronic commerce based on an open Internet will affect all aspects of a market instead of duplicating traditional seller-to-buyer market relationships, yielding a whole new area of economic research.

The Internet, despite such advantages, has a series of potential problems. Although the openness of the TCP/IP protocol suite is the reason why the Internet is growing so fast, it also poses a serious problem as a commercial medium due to the fundamental lack of security measures in TCP/IP (Bhimani, 1996). Compared to private VANs, the Internet has many weaknesses in this respect. Messages can easily be wiretapped and eavesdropped during transmission. The messages could then be altered and sent to another party. Because of this, the receiving party cannot be assured of the identity of the original sender. Challenges exist to meeting many essential security requirements for computer transactions: confidentiality, authentication, data integrity, and repudiation.

How serious are these security problems when the Internet is used for commerce? After all, access control for any computer on the Internet can be achieved by using access passwords, firewalls, or by simply disconnecting from the network when not in use. In general, only those files designated for sharing by owners can be transferred. To secure confidential and authenticated messages, encryption and digital signature technologies that provide content-level security are already being adopted. Such security measures are applied to each message being transmitted just as a secure envelope with a tamper-resistant seal protects a message within. Alternatively, the transfer medium may be secured, such as the communication line itself. The next generation Internet protocols will incorporate security measures on TCP/IP layers thereby securing the transfer conduit itself (Hinden, 1996). In short, with adequate access control and content security, via encryption, today's Internet offers a rather robust, albeit imperfect, security.

While the level of performance guarantee for the Internet is lower than that for private networks, the chance for a catastrophic failure is lower for the Internet compared to a private network that is controlled and administered by a central authority. A message traveling on the Internet will be rerouted if a part of the Internet fails. At the same time, eavesdropping on the Internet is not targeted or specific, as in the case of private networks. Since private networks carry designated information over the same network, the result of a security breach will be more severe than on the Internet, where message packets travel in mixed jumbles. When the next generation of Internet standards are implemented along with content-level encryption, the security of the Internet may become a concern in mostly isolated instances.

While security and reliability will significantly increase in the next generation Internet, its ever-increasing traffic due to multimedia, real-time, and broadcasting applications may not result in any noticeable improvement in terms of network congestion. More efficient compression technologies, faster modems, and larger pipelines will certainly increase the absolute size of the Internet bandwidth. However, cheaper and more abundant integrated circuits and powerful microprocessors have been overwhelmed by concurrent, or outpacing, increases in the demand for computational power. Similarly, congestion may become a more critical issue in electronic commerce than network security problems that have worried many prospective online marketers.

Who Controls the Internet?

From its beginning in 1969 as ARPAnet (Advanced Research Projects Agency of the U.S. Defense Department), connections to the Internet have been based on open standards to provide flexibility and robustness in order to maintain communications capability even under a catastrophic disaster or a serious system failure in some of the network's component computers.

As the Internet grew into a network of networks, no single computer or network acted as a central authority. However, as in other social organizations, there are certain groups whose opinions matter.

At the top of these groups is the Internet Society or ISOC (http://info.isoc.org/index.html), shown in figure 1.1. The Internet Society is a volunteer membership organization that appoints the Internet Architecture Board, or the IAB (http://www.iab.org/iab/). The IAB is responsible for maintaining interoperable standards for communications as well as Internet addressing.

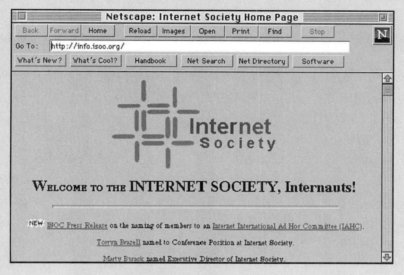

Figure 1.1 The Internet Society home page.

The Internet Engineering Task Force or IETF (http://www.ietf.cnri.reston.va.us/) is another volunteer organization that sets up working groups to deal with operational and short-term technical problems. Anyone can participate in these working groups. Their reports are recommendations for voluntary adoption or may be sent to the IAB for more official treatment. As a participant and a user of the Internet, any network needs to follow both IAB and IETF decisions and reports. Ignoring the recommendations by these bodies often leaves no choice but to disconnect from the Internet.

Two-way Communications and the Web

The Internet can be thought of as a two-way broadcast system with the capacity to send targeted messages to individuals. It combines the characteristics of two-way communications, such as telephone and fax (one-to-one communications), with those of broadcast media, such as radio and television (one-to-many communications). It is not an exaggerated prediction that the Internet, spurred on by the World Wide Web (WWW or the web), will someday supersede all these communication mediums.

The significance of the World Wide Web cannot be overemphasized in the development of the Internet and electronic commerce. The web has been touted as a multimedia presentation tool that is capable of enticing more attention from viewers through interactive activities as opposed to earlier text-based file transfer programs (see "Predecessors of the Web," p.11). But the even greater significance of the web lies in its capability for two-way, many-to-many communication. Today's Internet marketers concentrate on developing colorful and jazzy web pages to elicit visitors' attention. The premise of this advertising, which is based on broadcast media, is to maximize the number of "eyeballs" and their attention span using the most common denominators, such as sex and violence. But Internet marketers have discovered that advertising methods based on one-to-many broadcasting attracts responses, often negative, from the viewers. And unlike over-the-air commercials or mass-mail advertising, users of email can simply click a reply button to express their opinion, and their messages travel back over the same medium to the source of those advertisements.

A two-way broadcast system that gives the same level of reach, at a low cost, to everyone connected to the network also means that large corporations and companies do not necessarily dominate the marketing and distribution in the market. If wordprocessors have made desktop publishing possible, the web and its authoring language (HTML) have made everyone a potential publisher. And with e-mail, these potential publishers have access to the same marketing medium as large corporations.

Increasingly, web browsers are becoming web publishers. As the number of web surfers grows, more and more of these net-travelers are putting up their own web pages to establish their points of presence. Subscribers to America Online, Inc. (http://www.aol.com), can now make their own personal web pages on the access provider's web server. Today, web servers usually reside on expensive workstations because of their system requirements. But within a few years, web servers will be as simple as web browsers and as easily installed and maintained on small computers. Personal web servers and the personal web contents residing on these servers will establish a truly two-way communication and will be a significant factor in growing Internet communication and commerce.

Predecessors of the Web

The World Wide Web is only the most recent development designed to simplify the user interface for file transfer by automating transfers and enriching content presentation. Until very recently, the most frequently used method for transferring files was the File Transfer Protocol (FTP), which requires a remote login and allows only authorized users to connect. If you don't want to limit access, an anonymous FTP can be set up that allows guest logins by virtually anyone on the Internet. Automated anonymous FTP programs were the next step in presenting nontechnical connections to users, but users still had to log out and log in whenever they wanted to connect to another site. The next development following the automated FTP programs was Gopher service, which enabled users to log into many sites in one session. Simple and consistent, a Gopher client presents users with a series of menus in a hierarchy. FTP reached the pinnacle of its popularity in 1993, and Gopher service was rapidly increasing in 1994.

Conversely, the World Wide Web has reversed the growth of both. It has replaced FTP as the easiest and most popular way to transfer files, and has replaced Gopher as the preferred method for presenting files and information. Similar to Gopher, the web allows users to browse different sites in one session, but instead of hierarchical menus it uses jumps via hypertexted links to other web pages. Each web page is essentially a different connection, which admittedly slows down data access. But unlike previous methods, the web has an added feature of being able to transmit and display nontext files. This capability to present digitized audio and video files compensates in many cases for the loss in speed. Perhaps the most important feature, however, is the authoring program, HTML, which is easy enough for nontechnical people to construct their own web pages. This enables them to be content providers as well as content receivers. This combination of advantages is fast eclipsing its Internet counterparts. While the web transmission grew from almost zero to over 30 percent of the total data sent over the National Science Foundation NET (NSFNET)—the Internet's backbone until 1995—the share of FTP transactions has fallen by a third (see figure 1.2). Many files previously designated for public access under anonymous FTP and Gopher servers are now being moved to web servers and eventually the web may replace all other file transfer methods.

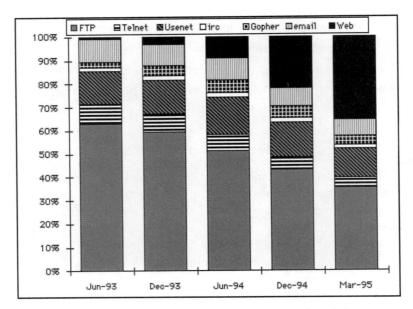

Figure 1.2 Types of data sent over the NSFNET backbone.

Source: Data from http://www.mit.edu:8001/people/mkgray/net/web-growth-summary.html.

1.2.   Electronic Commerce

In this section, electronic commerce is defined. This is not as simple as it sounds, because electronic commerce is a fast-moving target. The definition is ever-changing and expanding to include more and more sectors of the economy, as the influence of electronic communications extends. A conventional definition emphasizes technological aspects in an attempt to provide a lasting concept. The following sections stress economic aspects and define electronic commerce as a new market offering a new type of commodity, such as digital products through digital processes. Sellers of physical products are affected as well by digital processes—online ordering, market research, and payment settlement—and are part of this new market.

Electronic Commerce Examples

Technology is transforming many aspects of business and market activities. In its broadest sense, electronic commerce refers to the use of electronic means and technologies to conduct commerce, including within-business, business-to-business, and business-to-consumer interactions. The enabling technologies, of course, are also used for noncommercial activities such as entertainment, communication, filing and paying taxes, managing personal finance, research, and education, which may still include the services of online companies. As a result, it is somewhat difficult—and sometimes arbitrary—to separate electronic commerce areas from noncommercial applications of the same technologies and infrastructure.

Nevertheless, what characterizes electronic commerce is the pervasiveness of technology. For example, Mobil (http://www.mobil.com) gas stations in St. Louis are testing a windshield-mounted radio device, by which customers can get credit card approval and activate a gas pump by the time they get out of their cars. Customer preferences are also recorded in the device so that a cup of coffee or a newspaper can be delivered to their cars while they are pumping gas. Office Max (http://www.officemax.com) plans to install kiosks in banks and malls, which offer access to the company's full inventory of products and enable customers to order and pay for products to be delivered. Personal services for those pressed for time are moving from telephone to the Internet, with easy customization for product selection, payment, and delivery. In Boston, several online grocery shopping businesses (notably Peapod at http://www.pea-pod.com) deliver groceries, while Streamline (http://www.stream-lined.com) adds dry cleaning and video rental services.

Although these may be cutting-edge applications, conventional electronic commerce areas include:

- Searching for product information
- Ordering products
- Paying for goods and services
- Customer service

All are conducted online. The use of the Internet to support marketing and customer-interface is only part of electronic innovations that are changing the way firms do business. With intranets, corporations distribute internal memos and announcements to their employees, and knowledge exchange and scheduling communications flow worldwide in a timely fashion. With direct connection to suppliers (for instance, an extended intranet), the same technology is used for manufacturing and supply-chain management. 3M (http://www.mmm.com), for example, expanded its EDI service to the Internet, allowing its over 2,000 suppliers and customers access to its EDI transactions via any way they choose—private VANs, phones, and faxes, as well as the Internet. To sum up, for within-business, business-to-consumer, and business-to-business applications, electronic commerce includes:

- Internal electronic mail and messaging
- Online publishing of corporate documents
- Online searches for documents, projects, and peer knowledge
- Distributing critical and timely information to employees
- Managing corporate finance and personnel systems
- Manufacturing logistics management
- Supply chain management for inventory, distribution, and warehousing
- Sending order processing information and reports to suppliers and customers
- Tracking orders and shipments

and countless other business activities. More important than the mere number of areas being affected by electronic commerce is the fact that these activities can be integrated into a holistic business process. Thus, all the areas mentioned above are not really a separate application, but rather, one aspect of the whole electronic commerce process. For example, inventory and supply management is tied to production as well as to the demand data collected from consumers ordering via web stores. In short, the business potential of electronic commerce is the capability to innovate and integrate business and market processes. The most obvious and immediate use is achieving transactional efficiency.

Electronic Commerce as a Communications Network

At the core of traditional electronic commerce is the use of electronic means to expedite commercial transactions and improve efficiencies in business processes and organizations. In this vein, electronic commerce on the Internet means online ordering and payments. The narrowest definition of what electronic commerce is holds that electronic commerce on the Internet is a networked electronic data interchange (EDI) with a more flexible messaging system. Traditional EDIs are limited to signals that only computers can read and that correspond to information on electronic forms used in standard business transactions, such as ordering, invoicing, and shipping. An open EDI using the Internet means that EDI messages may be sent and received via email. On the next level of sophistication, EDI can use electronic forms made available on web pages for customers to order. This view considers electronic commerce and the use of the Internet as merely improving business and communication, especially in business-to-business transactions. Accordingly, issues in doing business on the Internet are mainly organizational and operational, ranging from security, competitive advantages in product development, and R&D (research and development), to efficiencies from automating purchasing functions, EDIs, point of sale information, and other interorganizational transactions.

To many familiar with EDIs, doing commerce on the Internet is not entirely advantageous compared to traditional EDIs. A clear tradeoff is made between secure, but limited VANs using traditional EDIs and an insecure, but far more flexible network with messaging and remote login possibilities over the Internet. For example, Chevron Corp. of San Francisco pays over $1,200 each time it sends an EDI report to the U.S. government via a private VAN. In comparison, it pays about $2,000 per month for unlimited access to the Internet (Radosevich, 1996). However, many consider the Internet to be inferior to EDIs because of the perceived lack of security and reliability, even though they are adjusting their EDI strategies to include the Internet. Already, Internet-oriented EDI applications, such as EDI/Open and Templar by Premonos Corp. (http://www.premonos.com), have reduced EDI prices and afforded small and medium size companies to take advantage of electronic transactions.

However, many interactions between sellers and buyers happen before they are ready to exchange orders and bills. A somewhat broader view of electronic commerce includes these interactions between businesses and consumers. Consumer services and product announcements have been routinely released to the Internet by computer companies for many years. And increasingly, firms are gearing up for Internet advertising and marketing. Going even further down the digital road, electronic shops and malls are springing up that offer electronic versions of catalog shopping in which consumers can search and order products using web browsers, bypassing traditional paper and phone-based merchandising. Organizations devoted to commercial uses of the Internet such as CommerceNet (http://ww.commerce.net) and government agencies such as the National Telecommunications and Information Administration (NTIA) (http://www.ntia.doc.gov) have encouraged doing business electronically by virtue of their presence on the Internet. As recently as September, 1996, Yahoo!'s list of online malls contained over 700 shops (http://www.yahoo. com/text/Business_and_Economy/Companies/Shopping_Centers/Online_Malls) and Open Market's Commercial Sites Index contained 41,731 listings of commercial web sites in October, 1996 (http://www.directory.net/dir/statistics.html).

Electronic Commerce of Digital Products

Despite the broadening view on electronic commerce, the commercial Internet is still seen primarily as a new medium of communication, like an open and interactive version of a magazine, television, or telephone. As an efficient communications medium, the Internet can be used to facilitate marketing, advertising, ordering, and customer service functions of the business organizations, lessening their dependence on traditional media. With the development of digital currency, many aspects of payment clearing procedures will also change significantly, particularly in terms of per-transaction cost and speed. Such changes in marketing, payment, and customer service will affect the markets for both physical and digital products—for example an online furniture dealer as well as an electronic magazine distributor. However, even more fundamental changes will accompany the online sale of digital products since they, unlike physical products, can be both produced and delivered over the network, transforming the very tenets of the manufacturing and distribution functions.

This business of digital products is radically advanced from conventional electronic commerce areas, and requires further developments in communications infrastructure, electronic payment systems, appropriate laws regarding copyright and sales taxes, liability and consumer protection laws, and so on. It is no longer doing the same business electronically, but instead, demands new business models and processes to take full advantage of the enabling technologies in the multimedia industry. This core of electronic commerce, as distinguished from conventional electronic commerce areas, is referred to as a "fully-digital business."

Figure 1.3 shows the difference between the core of electronic commerce and conventional electronic areas. A market is composed of three components: players (or agents), products, and processes. Market players are sellers, buyers, intermediaries, and other third parties, such as governments and consumer advocacy groups. Products are the commodities being exchanged. The interactions between market agents regarding products and other market activities are processes, which include product selection, production, market research, searches, ordering, payment, delivery, and consumption. These three components of a market may be either physical (offline) or digital (online). The horizontal axis in figure 1.3 represents whether market players are digital or physical. For example, a web store is digital; a department store is physical. Online shoppers are digital; shoppers in a mall are physical. Similarly, the vertical axis represents the degree to which a product is digitized. For example, a printed newspaper is physical, whereas its online version is digital. CD-ROMs are in-between because their contents are digital products but packaged in physical containers. Finally, the third axis shows whether a process is digital. Visiting a store is a physical process, whereas searching on the web is a digital process.

The traditional commerce—the lower-left cube in the figure—is where all three components are physical. In contrast, these components are all digital at the core of electronic commerce, where not only production, but also delivery, payment, and consumption (reading online or processing by a computer program) occur online. The remaining white areas are part of conventional electronic commerce, in which some of the components are digital. For example, products may be physical, but marketing and payment may be conducted online; products may be digital, but payments could be made via checks, or buyers may be reading printouts instead of screen outputs. The growing use of digital processes for business-to-business transactions and consumer marketing is evident in the figure, which shows that electronic commerce dominates the traditional market.

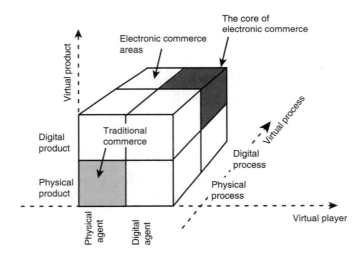

Figure 1.3 Electronic commerce areas.

Most of current electronic commerce applications and issues fall within the white areas of figure 1.3, dealing with one aspect on a particular axis, for example, setting up a web store, content digitization, electronic payments, online marketing, and so on. Later chapters in this book also tackle these issues one by one, and consumers are not limited to digital product sellers. However, in each chapter, every effort to analyze an issue in a broader context that includes all three components of a market is made. Therefore, product digitization (of the product axis) is discussed in connection with online consumption and digital marketing (of the process axis) and the role of web store sales representatives (of the player axis).

Market activities, from production to consumption, occurring online, bypassing all paper-based transactions and traditional communications media, represent the future of electronic commerce. The Internet becomes not only an alternative communication medium, but a microcosm, or an electronic version, of physical markets with characteristics that are fundamentally different from physical markets. This digital world of business, in which market institutions, agents, and products are becoming "virtual" and native to the Internet, is also at the core of electronic commerce economics.

The main difference between the digital world of business and the traditional, physical business world stems from the very nature of digitized products, which is discussed in Chapter 2. However, there are many reasons why consumers too will behave differently in a networked market. For example, access to product information via the network using sophisticated computer programs will certainly affect the way consumers compare prices. In turn, efficient shopping will affect product choices, pricing strategies, and competitive efforts among sellers. Business organizations and relationships will also be affected as spatial and temporal limitations of the market are removed and replaced by different considerations of costs, efficiencies, and the mode of interaction on a network. In other words, the market environment, enabled by the open distributed Internet, resembles no other physical market. The physical distance and geographical topology of a market are replaced with network architectures and preference-based market territories. Thus, the objective is to investigate the economic aspects of this newly emerging market of electronic commerce by applying standard economic tools and by evaluating qualitative differences in economic efficiencies and organizational changes.

This analysis of the electronic commerce market is timelier than you might think. The scope of digital products, and correspondingly, the scope of electronic commerce, will be much wider than we imagine today, and broaden much sooner. Although digitized information products are only a small portion of Internet-traded goods today, suitable online payment systems, especially for small value items, will spur an explosive growth in digital products trading. In the immediate future, CD-ROM and disk-based sales will be conducted online as the transmission speed bottleneck is removed. And digital products are not limited to information or "infotainment" products. All paper-based products, like posters, calendars, and all sorts of tickets, and all other products comprised of graphics, images, and sound can be converted into or replaced by digital counterparts. Even some products representing value may take a digital form, as in digital currency and electronic checks, stocks, and bonds. Some purely physical products are made into smart products that allow digital interfaces for monitoring and control—smart cars, smart boilers, and home security systems. Users will be able to interact with these products via email, exchange personal settings online, or download trouble-shooting programs. Essentially, all types of business services and processes have the potential to become digital products exchanged on a digital network, expanding the core of electronic commerce (see figure 1.4). Whether directly, through their own businesses, or through the businesses of their competitors, the producers of both digital and physical products will be affected by the trends in electronic commerce.

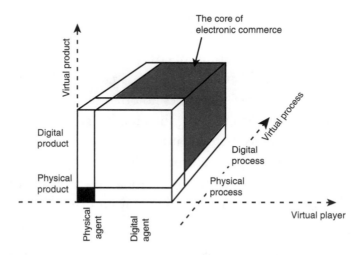

Figure 1.4 The growth of electronic commerce areas.

Commercial Potential of the Internet

Businesses need to place electronic commerce within the context of broader uses of the Internet than the traditional commercial framework. As a market, electronic commerce impacts not only marketing but also production and consumption. Information collected through web stores is used to customize products, to forecast future demand, and to formulate business strategies. Consumers not only order and pay for products online, but also search for product information, reveal their preferences, negotiate with sellers, exchange information about products and firms, and use products online by filtering, processing, and linking them with other computer programs. Likewise, supply chain relationships among businesses and competitive strategies need to aim at increasing the overall market efficiency, not just transactional efficiency.

The Internet can certainly be used as an alternative marketing channel, selling existing products online, but the future of electronic commerce will be guided by innovative digital products and services that will emerge in the electronic marketplace. But from where are these products and processes coming? The explosive growth of the Internet gives a partial answer. The core of digital commerce comes from selling digital products, but no one is certain how big the digital product market will become. To get an idea, one only needs to list products that can be digitized: all paper-based information products such as newspapers, magazines, books, journals, and databases; computer software, and games; audio products, including music, and speeches; video and multimedia products, such as movies and television programs; other information products, such as weather reports, stock quotes, government information, consumer information, and even personal information; and digital counterparts for existing products, such as room keys, digital currency, digital checks and other financial instruments, airline and concert tickets, and so on.

Many business professionals dismiss the commercial potential of the Internet, pointing out that the most common uses of the Internet and the web are browsing and entertainment. In turn, the most promising use of the Internet technology is found in intranets and other within-business and business-to-business applications, in which EDIs and corporate networking are already familiar. A survey found that only about one in ten uses the Internet for shopping (GVU Web Survey (http://www.cc.gatech.edu/gvu/user_surveys)). However, shopping here is very narrowly defined. Internet users seeking information are, in fact, in search of products, and thus, network uses commonly categorized as informational and entertainment activities need not be viewed separately from commercial activities. Unlike television entertainment in which commercial advertising and noncommercial entertainment are alternatively presented, commercial uses of the Internet encompass all aspects of user activities. Even e-mail messages can be thought of as digital products, for instance digitized information, which can be sold directly as a product or used as a component of business transactions. All so-called non-commercial activities on the Internet are indeed commercial, an important realization for digital product sellers. In a truly informational age, the immense amount of human knowledge already accumulated and linked via the Internet will be the product being exchanged. As Christopher Anderson of *The Economist* argued, "In the audacious uselessness of millions of personal fish tanks (web pages) lie the seeds of the Internet revolution" (1995). These fish tanks are displayed side by side with products marketed by America's corporate giants.

1.3.   Market Characteristics of Electronic Commerce

As mentioned earlier, electronic commerce today consists of two interrelated strands of network computing: 1) an expanded use of open networks by traditional EDIs to interconnect private networks with the Internet; and 2) an entirely new marketplace on the Internet using the World Wide Web technology. While large businesses and information management professionals are familiar with EDIs, the public and consumers, unaware of existing electronic business transactions, see electronic commerce on the Internet as a completely new market. In this section, the status of this new market is reviewed, detailing the pattern of usage, the characteristics of its users and market institutions, as well as the relevant legal environment.

Current Commercial Uses of the Internet

The size of the market, judged by the number of agents or domain names, is growing rapidly on the Internet. The growth rate in the number of Internet hosts is exponential; it grew from about 300,000 in 1990 to over 12 million by the end of 1996 (see figure 1.5). Admittedly, most of these Internet sites are only potentially commercial. But the awareness of its commercial use among businesses is growing. According to the O'Reilly & Associates' Internet Survey (http://www.ora.com), almost half of all large companies with 1000 or more employees surveyed in 1995 have created an Internet presence through publicly accessible World Wide Web pages (http://www.ora.com/gnn/bus/ora/survey/index.html). Medium-size companies (between 101 and 999 employees) show a weaker presence at 35 percent. Although the relatively lower cost and larger reach of Internet-based marketing and commerce is very well suited to small and medium companies, large companies seem to have more experience from EDIs and better recognize the need for establishing their presence.

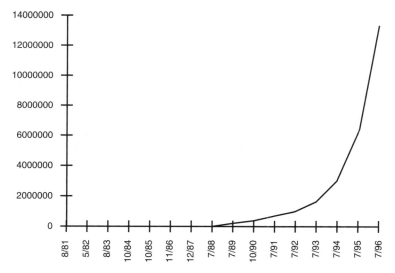

Figure 1.5 The growth of the Internet Hosts (1981–1996).

Source: Internet Domain Survey (http://www.nw.com/zone/host-count-history).

The same survey reports that many of these companies are not entirely convinced that the Internet has improved the business environment significantly. At present, most Internet-savvy companies are content to provide company and product information for public access, and to augment electronic messaging capabilities for intrabusiness communications by adding intranets into their corporate networks. While the interest for commercial use of the Internet is growing, there seems to be a widespread skepticism and uncertainty about the potential of Internet commerce. A more willing acceptance for doing business online depends on these companies gaining a better understanding of how electronic commerce applies to their line of business as well as learning business and marketing strategies appropriate for the Internet. The first step toward this is to define clearly how and what kinds of commercial activities are being conducted electronically.

Primary commercial uses on the Internet, other than EDIs, are advertising and customer services. Online advertising has generated about $150-$200 million dollars, up significantly from $10-$15 million in 1995 (Nua Internet Survey (http://www.nua.ie)). This advertising revenue is the amount Internet marketers received for their services, such as Internet billboards now common in search sites, targeted emailing, and customized web advertising. However, establishing a web storefront accounts for a significant portion of Internet advertising activities, which is not fully reflected when we calculate advertising revenues in a traditional way.

Through web presence and emailing, companies are establishing consumer contacts as well as providing after-sale consumer services online and new product and update announcements. For example, Apple Computers, Inc. (http://www.info.apple.com) maintains over 20 mailing lists that send out new hardware and software information, dispatch press releases, and hold open discussions among users.

Transactions, such as payments and delivery, are conducted via traditional communications media. One sector of business that actually delivers products online is the online publishing industry that offers digitized products, such as electronic databases, newspapers, magazines, and journals. It is also increasingly common for companies to deliver freeware, shareware, or demo version software online. Even in these cases, however, payments are still made by traditional means. While credit card information is transmitted online, actual payment and clearance are done offline.

Electronic commerce as a marketplace still lacks many components. First, despite increasing investments to upgrade and widen the bandwidth, many bottlenecks exist, especially at the last mile that connects individual users to the Internet—the ramp to the information highway. The long-run prospect is not optimistic either. With the increase in the multimedia contents of web pages and increasing uses of broadcasting and real-time applications, the network has become highly congested. Some humorously contend that WWW stands for the World Wide Wait. Second, data transmission must be made secure from tampering. While encryption technologies secure messages transmitted on an insecure pipeline, protocol level security measures are undergoing considerations to be implemented in the next generation Internet Protocol (IPng). Third, secure and reliable online payment systems must be effective and widespread. With developments in these areas, all aspects of business transactions may be conducted electronically. More importantly, solving these problems will enable the trading of digital products, making the Internet a true electronic market.

User Characteristics

Despite the constraints listed above, between ten and twenty million users are already connected to the Internet according to various surveys conducted in 1995 and 1996. We can get an idea of the latest potential for an increase by comparing this with the 95 million television households in the U.S. and about 50 to 60 million households that subscribe to cable television service. Already, the Internet's reach is almost half that of cable television, which, for comparison, was launched in the late 1940s as community antenna television (CATV) and took off during the 1970s with the help of cable-only networks. Still, Internet users—being technically savvy, relatively wealthy, educated, males—are quite unlike the general population.

One limiting factor for more widespread Internet use is the cost. To connect to the Internet a typical home-based user needs a computer, a modem, a telephone line, and an account with an Internet service provider. Even more desirable is a faster direct connection using Ethernet or ISDN instead of modem-based phone dialing, but because of costs associated with direct connections, most home-based users suffer from slow and unreliable connections via ordinary phone lines. While the telephone companies and cable companies have proposed to set up an information superhighway that will solve the transmission bottleneck for many years, their willingness to invest in this has been limited by the current use of the Internet, which is more informational than commercial, and thus reduces consumers' willingness to pay for upgraded services.

In the meantime, reduced personal computer prices are leading to a rapid increase in the number of home PCs, another prerequisite to Internet hookup. According to a 1996 survey by Computer Intelligence Infocorp., almost 40 percent of all U.S. homes now have one or more PCs (*Wall Street Journal,* 21 May, 1996), and this increase is still growing. The number of homes with PCs in 1995 was 16 percent. Growth is also seen among low to middle income families as well as among the over 60 population. Some key demographic figures of Internet users were revealed by the 5th World Wide Web survey done by the Graphic, Visualization & Usability Center of Georgia Tech University. In 1996, the average user was 33-years-old with a mean household income of $59,000. Over half of the respondents had either educational occupations or computer-related jobs (60 percent). Among the rest, 30 percent belonged to professional or management occupations. Of all the respondents about 32 percent were female. Even though this survey has a clear sample selection bias (based on voluntary participation), it generally confirms that Internet users are young, male professionals with higher than average income. Nevertheless, the trend from the last two years shows that the percentage of female Internet users and users in other age groups has been increasing.

The same survey also polled users on how willing they were to pay for access to web sites. Interestingly, a full 65 percent said they would not pay, a higher percentage than found in previous surveys. The authors attributed this to the fact that people primarily used the WWW for entertainment and browsing and that they already paid connection charges. About 12 percent said that they were willing to pay some fees on a subscription model, while another 11 percent would agree to pay on a pay-per-view basis. Although different payment systems would likely be based on the type of information sold rather than on consumer preference—a subscription model would be relevant for large databases or newspapers that offer updated information, whereas for one-time use information, pay-per-view would be appropriate—the survey findings raise the important question of how access charges and payment for contents will be managed in the future.

Competition and Market Organization

Today's Internet users may be different from the general population in many ways, until the majority of the populations participate in the market. However, electronic commerce as a marketplace differs fundamentally from other physical markets in many respects. For example, the size of a firm is not a significant factor in establishing one's presence in the virtual marketplace. Big and small companies can be located side by side with no difference in shop floors or interior decorations. Consumers can search for product information and compare prices over the whole Internet where geographical distance plays no role. From an economics perspective, electronic commerce has many characteristics of a perfectly competitive market. Although perfect competition has been the basis of most economic studies by which we evaluate economic efficiency, it is far more an exception in real life than the norm. Electronic commerce presents an experimental stage to further realize the economic efficiency of a competitive market.

Both economists and government regulators use perfect competition as a benchmark against which market efficiency is judged. In a perfectly competitive market, a commodity is produced for which the consumer's willingness to pay equals the marginal cost of producing the commodity, and neither sellers nor buyers can influence supply or demand conditions individually or collectively. A society cannot improve its economic welfare by deviating from competitive markets. However, perfect competition is seldom evident in real markets because it requires that several assumptions be met. Among the assumptions are:

- Many potential buyers and sellers must be able to enter and exit the market at no cost (no barriers to entry)
- There are many sellers and buyers who cannot individually influence the market (price takers)
- Products are homogeneous (no product differentiation)
- Buyers and sellers both know the price and quality of the product (perfect information).

Although wholesale agricultural markets are often cited as one example of a perfectly competitive market, in most other markets one of the above assumptions, and often all four, will not be met. Heavy investment requirements in manufacturing facilities and R&D often limit free entry by competitors. Advertising also influences consumer behavior by changing demand preferences or establishing reputation, which gives sellers a degree of market power. To exploit taste differences among buyers, firms sell differentiated products by brands or by quality, which as a result limits the competitive effects on prices. Finally, both sellers and buyers have limited information about demand and product quality given that it is costly to learn about product quality, prices, and even the location of shops. Indeed, if sellers and buyers were perfectly informed, there would be no need for advertising, marketing, or sales efforts.

Even at a quick glance, the electronic marketplace better resembles the abstract market of many sellers and buyers in which prices are determined efficiently by supply and demand. The most important differences are lowered barriers to entry (low overhead costs) and the opportunity to search and obtain perfect information about products and demand.

The Internet is supposed to be the great equalizer, where big corporations will have no inherent advantage over small vendors. In physical markets, bigness has certain advantages, helping firms to command a larger presence in physical form, market share, and reputation. The importance of this 'big' presence to consumers is that it presents a signal of the quality of a firm's products. We know that products sold by big firms are not necessarily of higher quality, but it is one viable signal available in the physical market. A similar correlation between bigness and assumed quality does not exist in electronic commerce, lowering the barriers to entry.

Another characteristic of the ephemeral perfectly competitive market, the availability of perfect information, is typically undermined in physical markets by the consumers' inability to search completely or at a cost that reflects the value of searched information. In electronic markets, automated indexing and cataloging technologies that gather and present information at low cost aid a complete search. The search for information is then as efficient as is allowed by search services. Using conventional economic reasoning, however, a complete indexing of the entire digital universe may not be economical, although desirable. Nevertheless, indexing and cataloging have been the most important Internet-based activities. Along with search services, they provide means to advertise web pages and to direct browsers to specific sites. Because of their importance, search services may be the first to be commercialized with access fees, but it will be essential to maintain search fees as low as possible, perhaps through competition, in order to minimize transactions costs.

Contrary to intuition, not only buyers benefit from perfect information, but so can sellers. Electronic transmissions generally leave a trail of information about consumer demand and tastes, which has a high value in its own right. Refined demand information is useful in reducing wastes due to demand uncertainty. Also, it leads to greater product diversity, enabling consumers to obtain customized products that better match their preferences instead of products that represent the average tastes of consumers. The flip-side effect of this is the ability for sellers to charge the maximum price consumers are willing to pay, which is discussed in Chapter 8, increasing sellers' market power rather than reducing it.

Despite the benefits to both sides, informational efficiency in electronic commerce is not guaranteed. The consumers' need to know about products and the seller's desire to gain more knowledge about consumers' preferences have to be balanced to avoid one taking advantage of the other. Clearly, complete product information will be available only if sellers are willing to provide that information just as consumer information is limited by the willingness of consumers to reveal their preferences. Fully customized products may increase the total social welfare but transfer benefits from consumers to firms. It remains important, however, to recognize the unique potential for perfectly informed sellers and buyers that electronic commerce presents.

Business Organization and Virtual Firms

When the World Wide Web first gained in popularity, many firms created web pages and initiated direct contact with consumers. Increasingly, however, web page development is contracted out to professionals, and many Internet-based marketing activities are handled by intermediaries. Even sales in electronic malls may be delegated to intermediary merchants, with the firms having no direct contact with the buyers. Since physical distance is not a barrier to business transactions, the electronic marketplace may resemble the face-to-face business of the old tradition, making such intermediaries unnecessary. On the other hand, market intermediaries have traditionally played other functions designed to enhance efficiency. The new electronic marketplace will necessitate new innovative models of firm organization, production, delivery, and overall market institutions, including a close examination of the role of intermediaries. Chapter 4 discusses this fundamental issue in detail.

Other time-tested, basic business assumptions can no longer be presumed to hold true in this new world. In the electronic age, firms no longer are based in a single location because all functions need not be operated in one locale. Going beyond even decentralization, a firm on the Internet becomes a distributed company, or a virtual firm, where any operation can be anywhere. A company like First Virtual (http://www.fv.com), for example, exists only on a network (Borenstein et al., 1996). The critical difference between this and a multi-office corporation is that a virtual firm's day-to-day operation is also conducted on a network. The mundane aspects of managing a company—administrative tasks, scheduling meetings, supervision of remotely located employees, and so on—appear to be the greatest challenge of a virtual company because coordinating such matters most often depends on traditional means of communication.

A promising application of electronic commerce for a virtual firm is to use the web technology for within-business and business-to-business interactions. Business logistics including supplier management, inventory, warehousing, and invoicing can be integrated in a corporation-wide intranet, or intraweb, which is defined as "a secure corporate network with rich functional features of Local Area Networks interconnected by the Internet or its technologies and applications" (Chellappa et al., 1997). Suppliers and customers are given appropriate levels of access to intranets so that employees, suppliers, and customers can be integrated in the firm's production and sales functions in a network rather than a physical locale.

Another still unanswered question is whether interfirm relationships of virtual firms will be different in electronic commerce. Economists have argued that a firm is an organization by which producers can internalize transaction costs, which are costs incurred in transacting business such as writing, monitoring, and enforcing contracts. For example, if the cost of contracting book-keeping and accounting with an outside CPA (Certified Public Accounting) firm is high, a firm may reduce costs by establishing an accounting department of its own to handle the tasks. In an extreme case, a firm may find it efficient to handle all activities from production, marketing, and payment to delivery. When transaction costs are low, on the other hand, many functions done within a firm may be contracted out in a market (see section 4.3). To the extent that electronic commerce reduces transaction costs, firms will contract out or delegate many of their functions to other agents in the market.

Increasing use of contracting implies a more fluid interfirm relationship and a more decentralized, nonhierarchical organization. However, Steinfeld et al. (1995) have examined the buyer-seller relationships between firms on a network, and concluded, based on case studies, that the use of an electronic network between firms tends to lock out other firms. They present this as evidence that networked businesses tend to promote hierarchical organizations (such as corporations) instead of markets. In other words, doing commerce on a network increases interdependence between existing partners, and has not encouraged firms to seek new suppliers or buyers in an open trading market. Such a trend is clearly observed when new firms have to invest in hardware and software to participate in bidding and contracting. The open Internet, however, lowers such investment requirements, and will facilitate a more market-like organization among networked companies.

Legal Environment

The unique nature of the Internet brings it into uncharted legal and political territory in regards to a number of different issues, among which copyright is just one. Because the Internet is not constrained by political boundaries, electronic commerce is not adequately defined by existing laws or regulated by one government entity. For example, as commerce over the Internet increases, city and state governments are seeking ways to collect and remit sales taxes on Internet transactions (*BusinessWeek,* 1996). But a 1992 court case (*Quill Corp. vs. North Dakota*) held that for a state to collect taxes on sales, the vendor must have significant sales operations within the state. Because many Internet operations have highly dispersed personnel, little inventory, and no showrooms, at this time it is not clear whether states and local governments have a legal right to collect taxes on their sales.

The issue regarding retail sales taxes in the electronic marketplace, while just one of many, illustrates how the legal and economic systems must evolve to accommodate the new electronic medium. Because authorities can control points of sales through requirements and permits, sales taxes are a reasonable method used to augment local revenues. But this practice becomes untenable in a boundless marketplace. The same problem is foreseen with tariffs and international trade. The question is whether governments should impose control measures such as permits, requirements, and regulations so that they can extend their locus of control over Internet commerce, or they should give special treatment to electronic commerce and look for other venues for tax. Each choice will have a substantially different effect on the future development of electronic commerce. A more detailed discussion of taxation issues can be found in Chapter 11.

Internet Sales Tax Permit?

To open a business of any kind, one needs to obtain a sales tax permit and register business names with counties in which one intends to operate. Necessary permits must be obtained depending on the type of product handled. Financial and accounting records must be kept and sales taxes must be reported periodically.

To open an Internet business, however, one only needs to get an Internet account through an ISP (Internet Service Provider), and open up a web page announcing business. Although one can register a domain name, a sort of store name, it is not required. In fact, Internet domain names have been given out on a "first-come, first-served" basis. Legal issues in terms of trademarks are just beginning to be contested. And what are the procedures for recording and reporting sales and accounting figures? How do accounting firms audit electronic transaction records? For such aspects of business, public policymaking, as well as private entrepreneurial solutions, need to be explored.

The nature of Internet communication also compounds many legislative and legal efforts going on at the national and international level to adapt to the new electronic environment. For example, one contentious issue taken up in Chapter 5 is how copyrights of content owners should be protected in the digital age. The primary concern about copyrights is linked to the sellers' and buyers' access to the same production technologies that enable mass reproduction and mass distribution of any digital product without quality degradation. Prohibiting or limiting the use of the technology is clearly not the solution. Rather, every aspect of production, sales, and distribution has to be analyzed and redefined before a proper and effective legal framework can be created.

The challenge is very real. Detecting pirate copies of books or sound recordings is relatively easy compared to discerning digital copying and distribution over an open network. Besides many difficulties in copyright enforcement, there is substantial difficulty in defining what constitutes a legitimate copy. Traditionally, copy is protected if a work is fixed in a substantially permanent medium. Is a screen display or a CD-ROM cache permanent enough to merit copyright control? And because viewing a file on-screen involves transferring of the file, should all file browsing be regarded as copyright infringement? How different is web browsing from browsing a book in a bookstore? These and a long list of other questions remain to be resolved.

For example, at the international level, differences in copyright laws across countries and even between two international copyright conventions, the Berne Convention and the UCC, must be reconciled. While illegal piracy may be dealt with using trade sanctions authorized under General Agreement on Tariffs and Trade (GATT) and other trade agreements, the Internet simply supercedes all political jurisdictions, making it harder to cope with through traditional trade negotiations, which are often lengthy and ineffective. On another note, the Organization for Economic Cooperation and Development (OECD) raises the issue of maintaining linguistic and cultural diversity in the face of dominant use of English as the Internet language. But by using a different language, one community may end up isolating itself from a variety of information that will negate many of the benefits of information exchange.

Although there is a definite void in terms of adequate legal protection in electronic commerce, hasty legislation is not the answer. Take, for example, the consequences of one attempted solution. The problem is that it is possible for hackers to set up their computers to impersonate other sites receiving and sending messages, while their correspondents are not aware of the true identity of their partners. To prevent this kind of fraud, called *spoofing*, on the Internet, a new Georgia law makes it a crime to falsely identify oneself or to direct others to unintended sites. Poorly worded, the law may also prohibit any links on a web page. While the zeal of public officials to use legislation to address open network problems is understandable, any effort to apply legal control blindly to the digital medium is misguided unless law makers understand how the Internet communication works and consider all the ramifications of simply incriminating network activities.

Recent controversies over the public availability of highly uncrackable encryption technology such as Pretty Good Privacy (PGP) (http://web.mit.edu/network/pgp.html) and the Communications Decency Act (Title V of the Telecommunications Act of 1996) for the Internet have shown how difficult it is to impose control over the digital network. However, it is prudent to remember that proactive laws are seldom effective when the environment they intend to regulate is continuously evolving. In fact, they often have detrimental effects on its development. The Internet and the electronic marketplace have many strengths, but require understanding and nurturing instead of control and regulation.

1.4. Current Issues in Electronic Commerce

Now that we have defined electronic commerce as a market and examined its characteristics of the marketplace, you may be enjoying a sense that it is smooth sailing from here to harnessing the enormous potential of this new world. However, basic questions remain regarding how the commodity, sellers, and buyers will actually come together in a market that still lacks many essential features necessary for secure commercial transactions. While current debates on electronic commerce issues focus on legal or technological aspects, our goal in this section is to review and highlight the economic aspects of these and other issues.

Contents and Quality

In any market, traditional or electronic, uncertainty regarding the quality of products can lead to the collapse of that market. Although the Internet provides a wide variety of services and is used by millions, there is still a noticeably wide gap between the number of commercial products and services that could easily be digitized and those that are currently offered on the Internet. Some see this as a sign of the reluctance of content owners to participate in electronic commerce and a signal of a reduction in the overall quality of what is available on the Internet. For physical products, consumers may prefer to inspect products and actually try them out instead of looking at a picture or reading a description. Lacking a proper means to verify quality, commercial opportunities may be limited to a few whose quality consumers already know about or can easily learn online. Online banking and travel services are two examples for which consumers are already familiar with electronic processing and purchasing. For others, online markets may not materialize at all.

Although copyright protection is an important legal issue, and one that is doubtlessly connected with product quality, there is a more fundamental reason drawn from economics that helps to explain why products of high quality may not be offered on the Internet: uncertainty about product quality stemming from asymmetric information. Quite simply, when consumers do not have adequate information about product quality, their willingness to pay depends on the expected level of quality. For example, if there is an equal chance of getting a good product worth $100 or a bad product worth $50, buyers are willing to pay, on average, $75. Being an average, consumers break even in the long run by paying $75 for this product. To put it differently, $25 benefits the consumers who get a good product and evens out with $25 losses by those who receive a bad product.

Consumers may be persuaded to pay more than $75 if sellers are able to convince them that their products are indeed of high quality. Without such information or guarantee, a seller cannot charge more than $75. If the cost of producing a good product exceeds $75—the expected price in the market— then a seller of a high-quality product will do better not to sell the product. Further, if the number of bad products exceeds the number of good products, consumers' willingness to pay diminishes as the expected—average—level of quality decreases. If there are only bad products in the market, the only possible market price will be $50. As high-quality products withdraw from the market, this leaves the market with low-quality goods, that is, *lemons.*

The so-called lemons problem occurs in most markets when it is difficult to know product quality prior to purchase (Akerlof, 1970), which is a prominent aspect of electronic commerce for at least two reasons. The first is that digital products are more than just a digitized version of paper-based products. Instead, digital products incorporate the unique advantages of the electronic medium. Newspapers, for example, are personalized, searchable, and updated instantly. The value and quality of a digitized newspaper, then, cannot be adequately estimated based solely on the experience and practice in paper-based counterparts. Furthermore, when products are highly customized and their contents vary greatly, assessing quality becomes increasingly subjective and personal.

Another reason for heightened uncertainty—and increased potential for the lemons problem to arise—is the diversity of producers. Unlike physical products, digital products are produced and sold by virtually anyone on the Internet. Through today's personal homepages and web servers running on every personal computer in the future, every user will be a producer and a potential seller as well. Even for physical products, the worldwide market will provide consumers with a considerably greater number of vendor choices that may not be as familiar as local sellers. Conventional means to convey product quality, such as reputation and brand name, are less useful in this type of market with a vast array of sellers who may be in the market only for a short time. Relatively small overhead costs to enter the electronic marketplace will certainly lower the barrier to entry and will increase the level of competition and choice, but consumers face many difficulties in selecting reliable, suitable vendors.

Will an exhaustive and technically useful digital catalog be enough to persuade consumers to trust online vendors about the quality of their products? Seller-provided product information is useful if the products in question are search goods; to judge quality, one only needs a picture or a product specification. For experience goods, which must be consumed to learn the quality, no amount of information will suffice.

One typical means of resolving the quality uncertainty in similar situations in physical markets is through the use of a trusted third party. For example,

- A used-car buyer can take the car to a trusted mechanic for evaluation
- Consumer advocacy groups publish product evaluation reports
- Governments and industry groups also typically set standards for quality and issue licenses to qualified producers in certain industries.

All these mechanisms depend on the neutrality and trustworthiness of the parties who provide the supposedly objective information. The neutrality of these parties is often in doubt, or otherwise their information is limited due to various reasons—the lack of adequate funding, the vast number of products to be evaluated, or the diversity in product specifications. In electronic commerce, the number and diversity of digital products and their producers may prove to be too costly to engage in complete and objective product evaluations. An alternative is to rely on the market mechanism, in which an intermediary reseller provides its customers with product information. An efficient intermediary could economize costs in evaluating and guaranteeing product quality. At the same time, the intermediary's need to maintain or guarantee quality lies in its profit motive, not in its commitment to public service. In Chapter 4, an evaluation of the role of intermediaries as a mechanism to resolve quality uncertainty in a distributed network environment is examined in more detail.

Copyrights versus Users Rights

While quality uncertainty is one reason why good quality products withdraw from the market, inadequate copyright protection also discourages content owners from offering their products. The surging trends merging computer and communications technologies has vastly increased the amount of information and entertainment resources shared over the network—the areas which most often include copyrighted materials. Efforts to protect copyrights on the Internet have evoked legal as well as emotional responses and have clearly revealed the inadequacy of current copyright legislation. Without resolving this issue, selling online may not be the future in distributing contents.

Copyright and the Freedom of Speech

The case commonly referred to as "*Church of Scientology vs. the Net*" has been at the center of copyright and censorship debates, and legal and net attacks, and counter-attacks between the Church of Scientology (the Church) and "netizens" who oppose any restriction on the use of the Internet. (See Electronic Frontier Foundation archive at (http://www.eff. org/pub/Censorship/ CoS_v_the_Net/).) The case started in 1994 when a part of the Church's Operating Thetan (OT) materials, considered by the Church to be secret and copyrighted, appeared in the alt.religion.scientology UseNet newsgroup via an anonymous mailer. OT materials are a major source of revenue for the Church, which charges substantial amounts of money for its members to view and study them. As the Church was unable to identify the original anonymous mailer, it brought a copyright infringement suit against one who reposted the same material on the newsgroup. As the Internet buzzed about the incident, more participants in the newsgroup joined in related attacks at the copyrighted materials and the Church itself. The Church not only sued other users and the Internet service providers, it tried to shut down the newsgroup and cancel messages posted to it. As the Church's effort expanded, those concerned with censorship intensified their counter-efforts in protest against the Church.

To date, the legal and nonlegal measures taken by the Church have not been effective in protecting its documents and its reputation. However, the incident serves as an illustrative example of how difficult it is to enforce copyright control in cyberspace. The Church could prove that the materials had economic value to them, but the alleged had no economic motives—no one sold the material—and considered their actions to be within the boundaries allowed by the fair use doctrine of copyright law. In contrast with pirate book publishers, whose economic motives are easy to prove because they have loci of operation and traceable accounts of sales and profits, public exchanges on public networks are hard to track and even harder to control.

Legal and Economic Considerations of Copyrights

The current debate on digital copyrights focuses on the ambiguities in legal definitions and the technical means of control that must be modified to accommodate digital products. For example, since copyright protection is extended only to fixed physical expressions, not to the idea itself, copyright enforcement is linked to the physical forms that are used to express these ideas. But is a flickering image on a computer screen a "fixed expression" of an idea protected by copyright law? If so, there will be two copies of a document when a stored file is viewed on the screen, one on the screen and the other in the hard drive. Is the user required to pay for two copies? Ambiguities such as this have convinced most participants in the debate that the digital medium and the transfer conduit of networked computers necessitate a completely new approach to copyrights and other intellectual property rights. Although the problems are well debated, what is still lacking for a solution is the economic arguments as to why and how copyrights should be applied to digital products and electronic commerce.

From an economics point of view, the new approach is based on market analysis, which evaluates property rights of content owners as well as the public's interest in protecting certain products. The term "public's interest" does not cover extreme positions such as absolute free speech or the opinion that ideas must be freely available, but economic aspects that are not so apparent from legal analysis. For example, in the well-known *Lotus vs. Borland* case, Borland argued that the user interface used by Lotus was not copyrightable. The interface in question was the way Lotus 1-2-3 arranged its command hierarchy for its menus. Borland copied the command structure so that its users could use macros written for Lotus 1-2-3. The legal question was whether the user interface was copyrightable or simply constituted a series of commands as do buttons on a VCR remote control. The Supreme Court let stand the 1st Circuit Court of Appeal's decision in favor of Borland in January, 1996 without written explanation.

In arguments, regarding protecting Lotus 1-2-3's command structure, many economists focused on its network externalities and user switching costs.

The availability of third-party macros written for 1-2-3 constitutes an added benefit for its users. This kind of indirect advantage is a positive network externality, or more correctly, a positive network effect. Also, when users switch to a different product, they have to learn new features, such as keystrokes, which is costly. Thus, to maximize network effects and to minimize switching costs, users tend to stick with a popular software package. If Borland were prohibited from using 1-2-3's user interface, Lotus would enjoy extra market protection from indirect economic effects secondary to Lotus's own product.

Whether user interfaces should be protected is still being argued. Regardless of the ultimate decision, this case illustrates that market analysis in a copyright infringement case involves much more detailed study on specific product characteristics and the market. For digital products, copyright schemes based on economic analysis may prove more valuable than legal and technical solutions. Current copyright laws and enforcement methods have evolved in the context of printing presses, and their offspring, such as photocopiers, and the way consumers use printed copies. The scope of the law has also expanded to cover new forms of intellectual products—books and manuscripts, musical scores, paintings, photographs, sound recordings, movies, performance arts, and architectural works. Digitized files and their distribution through computer networks could be considered, as yet, another form of intellectual product to be included. The effort to redefine what constitutes a reproduction and a distribution on the Internet certainly harks back to the days of printing presses. An alternative is to recognize the digital age as the second-coming of the printing press, and to formulate a new framework which underscores the ways consumers and markets operate in this so-called knowledge-based economy. Chapter 5 presents an in-depth discussion of this topic.

Interactive Advertising and the Use of Consumer Information

One area of explosive growth and considerable skepticism is Internet advertising and marketing. In adapting marketing and advertising strategies for the Internet, the emphasis has typically been on the behavioral and cultural characteristics of Internet users and the radical difference in the communication environment compared to traditional broadcasting media. Current Internet marketing guidelines summarize the behavioral idiosyncrasies of Internet dwellers in two broadly accepted traits:

- Consumers react vigorously, unlike TV and newspaper audiences, to unwarranted messages. Even a rudimentary understanding of the Internet culture makes it clear that active broadcasting of advertising messages will not work.

- In the electronic marketplace, consumers come to the sellers. An interactive advertisement works by providing these consumers with relevant information on the sellers' web site.

- Implications of the above are that Internet advertising needs to be two-way, interactive communications that offer some values to consumers. Does this mean advertisers on the Internet lose their traditional means to push their messages? While the debate regarding push versus pull models of online advertising rages on, what is gaining the support of both advertisers and consumers is actually a mixture of the two.

Push or Pull Advertising

A *push* advertising actively seeks out audiences and sends unwanted messages, a familiar sight in physical markets. On the Internet, however, a *pull* model advises advertisers to passively receive consumers who are in search of product information. For example, Internet marketers are strongly warned against sending unsolicited emails to lists, newsgroups, and individuals. *Spammers,* who disregard this common netiquette, are listed in the Blacklist of Internet Advertisers (http://math-www.uni-paderborn.de/~axel/BL/). Although the list is not exhaustive in any sense, group and individual efforts to warn against spammers and fraudulent advertisers continue.

To counter the passive nature of waiting for visitors to patronize their web sites, Internet advertisers rely on interactivity—the buzz word of Internet marketing. Interactivity is the Internet's counterpart for sex and violence that entice television viewers. But unlike advertising models based on broadcasting media, not only contents on web sites are eye-catching and jazzy, but also Internet advertising uses a novel form of two-way communications in which customer participation is encouraged. An active participation is desired in part because it increases the chance that the viewer will remember the advertising content. As a result, the model for web advertising and product delivery is no longer one of push or pull. Instead, customers specify what products they want, for example, *pull,* and sellers *push* these products to consumers following prearranged agreements.

Measuring the Impact of Online Advertising

The actual impact of advertising is hard to track and quantify for both mass media and the Internet, although interactive technology presents new possibilities for the entire advertising industry. In the case of mass media, there are companies that measure the size of the audience per commercial message, for instance Nielson TV and radio ratings, and efforts are underway to further evaluate the economic impacts of advertising by correlating advertising and an increase in sales. But broadcast advertising is fundamentally inefficient because of its redundancy. It sends messages regardless of whether people are interested, receptive, or relevant to the product. In comparison, selecting an audience and verifying the number of people who received a message is relatively easy on the Internet. However, the advertiser still does not know whether the receiver actually read the message or not.

Refined measures and methods are being proposed for the Internet. Proctor & Gamble (http://www.pg.com), for example, limits payment for its ads on the Yahoo! search engine (http://www.yahoo.com) to the number of people who actually request more information by clicking on their advertisement rather than paying based on the number of Yahoo! customers to whom its advertisement is presented on their search pages. This is in contrast with the traditional method of measuring viewer-ship, and payment—based on "eyeballs," equivalent to the number of connections to Yahoo!, or the "hit rate." As more and more sellers begin to doubt the effectiveness of broadcast advertising on the Internet that simply flashes banner advertisements, many advertiser-based services have to rely on different revenue sources, for instance, subscription fees. As a result, there will be reduced outlets for broadcast-based advertising in the future. An alternative is targeted advertising.

Targeted Advertising and Privacy

The essence of targeted advertising lies in the Internet's interactivity via two-way communication. For example, when a web user types the keywords "French wine," the response page displays not only the search results but also advertising messages by wine sellers. Although advertisers may send mass mails based on consumer profiles obtained through third-party information sellers, web advertising allows a more integrated, real-time targeting, which is then linked to market research, production, and sales efforts.

Interaction between advertisers and buyers brings up a highly sensitive issue in Internet advertising, for example, the use of consumer information. Electronic transactions leave a trail of information, which can be used to generate powerful personal profiles for prospective consumers. Yahoo!, for example, openly admits that the company is not in the business of selling a search service but of selling consumer information collected by the web server that monitors and records a wide range of information about its visitors. Consumer surveys and market research has always been an intrinsic part of a successful advertising campaign. Now, extensive data on consumers are being gathered from various sources, like telephone records, credit card usage, and web browsing. Computers can easily cross-reference this data to generate databases for specific advertising purposes. This cross-referenced information about users is sometimes called metainformation—metainformation originally meant the information about information—and has become the most valuable information generated by the Internet. As it becomes more common, advertising and marketing based on consumer metainformation collected via the net will become a contentious issue, which is discussed in Chapter 6.

The economic implications of the use and misuse of this consumer information cannot be ignored. First, sellers are able to offer customized products instead of one of average tastes. Also, in many cases, consumers are willing to reveal their preferences to get better quality in the way of customized products.

From another perspective, refined demand information can reduce waste, such as over-production resulting from market uncertainty. The use of consumer information in terms of product selection and pricing will be discussed in Chapter 8.

Internet Intermediaries

Intermediaries play a far more important economic role in physical markets than might at first be apparent. For example, retailers provide consumers with access to goods produced by remote sellers. Beyond this distribution function, however, they also act as insurers of product quality and diversity, and provide product information. Even so, intermediaries are often perceived to add unnecessary costs to consumers. An efficient market is defined as one that reduces the number of intermediaries, or the number of intermediary steps necessary for a market transaction.

It follows then that an efficient market such as the electronic market should do without intermediaries, and instead, consumers should buy products directly from producers. In the physical market, if someone living in Texas wants to buy a product from a firm in California, the cost of flying to that store will be prohibitive for most products. This is in fact a prime example of how intermediaries such as wholesalers and a retailer in the customer's location in Texas actually help to reduce transaction costs. However, it is true that one can order some products via mail order, which reduces the number of intermediaries and cuts transaction costs further. Similarly, the growth of a global commerce network such as the Internet may further reduce the number of intermediary steps necessary for trade. In this vein, some argue that the Internet resembles a preindustrial market where sellers and buyers meet at one place at the same time. When the network serves as a market, buyers and sellers may exchange goods directly instead of through intermediaries (Benjamin and Wigand, 1995), creating a more efficient market.

However, retailers perform functions other than distribution. When an intermediary has superior experience, knowledge, and authority in evaluating product quality, the need for its service will persist. Also, customers will incur increased costs if they have to deal with as many sellers as needed to purchase goods. Thus, there will remain a need for intermediaries and brokers in electronic commerce. Retail shops, for example, perform various functions such as transporting and distributing goods, evaluating and displaying related products, and providing their expertise in matching a certain good of a certain quality with the need of a consumer. As these functions might not be provided by one, or even most producers, there is a continuing need in the electronic marketplace as well as in physical markets for an intermediary that increases efficiency by reducing various types of transaction costs.

Intermediaries will come in all different sizes and shapes and serve different functions in electronic commerce. The informational role of an intermediary is discussed in Chapter 4 when the question of quality uncertainty is taken up. Search intermediaries will take part in consumer searches for product information (Chapter 7) and financial intermediaries will play a role in investment payment efficiencies (Chapters 9 and 10). But a functioning market needs other intermediary services as well, such as insurance, accounting services, brokers, financial services, regulators, network service providers, and so on. Even UseNet newsgroups depend on the services of various groups who advise on group creation during the request for discussions (RFD) and call for votes (CFV) stages, volunteer vote takers, administrators of news-servers, anonymous remailers, and users, as well as self-appointed net patrollers. All these services are necessary and are currently done on a voluntary basis. However, they all hold the potential to become paid intermediaries.

Security and Privacy of Internet Transactions

Unsecured transmission on the Internet is often cited as the main deterrent for a rapid growth of electronic commerce. Although much progress is being made in terms of security, the net is still considered to pose a risk for commercial transactions. Although the Internet's lack of security stems from the fundamental design of the basic protocol suite (Bellovin, 1989), security measures can be implemented at various levels of Internet communications. Network level security secures the conduit, while encryption secures the content traveling through the conduit. Security takes on added importance when we look at the special case of financial payment mechanisms.

While payment security usually means protecting sensitive information from eavesdropping and theft, a secure transaction has a broader set of requirements, including nonrepudiation, authentication, integrity, and confidentiality. *Nonrepudiation* means that the parties in a transaction cannot deny it after the fact. *Authentication* refers to the ability to verify the identity of persons involved in transactions, while *integrity* means that the data transferred should not be modified in transit or in storage. Finally, *confidentiality* refers to privacy, in other words, that the transaction is only between participants. A strong form of privacy is *anonymity*, where the identities of one or more of the participants is not known to the other parties of the transaction.

Nonrepudiation and authentication are aspects that have not been explored fully and require further developments in certification technologies and services. As in notary services, a market mechanism for nonrepudiation and authentication involves a trusted third party (Froomkin, 1997). The U.S. Postal Service has recently identified its electronic commerce opportunities to be a service provider as a trusted certification authority. Although discussion on this topic usually entails the legal implications of certifying actions and liabilities, it is another area where intermediaries play an important role in electronic commerce.

Data integrity and confidentiality issues have been dramatically addressed by advanced encryption and digital signature technologies. There is a large body of literature on the use of these technologies, that typically invokes constitutional rights to privacy and the protection of free speech. Our focus, instead, is on the economic implications of integrity and confidentiality. Integrity, for example, relates to the derivative right guaranteed by copyright law. Also, maintaining the integrity of a digital document will be tantamount if that document in question is a digital currency or a digital financial document. The concern for confidentiality turns into an economic issue when transactional data are used or sold by sellers for other purposes. Such issues related to the use of consumer information are discussed in Chapter 8. The desire, as well as technologies, to conceal such information has resulted in anonymous payment systems. The issues of transaction security and payment mechanisms are explored in Chapter 10.

Pricing Strategies for Digital Products

Little has been written on product pricing in electronic commerce. Traditional marginal-cost pricing is regarded as inappropriate for digital products, which have almost zero marginal costs. On the other hand, the marginal cost of a digital product may be substantial because of copyright payments, which will apply to most digital products. Treating the cost of developing a first copy of a digital product as fixed cost, the appropriate price based on marginal cost pricing appears to be per-copy copyright payments. However, when a firm has market power, which will be most likely if products are differentiated, digital products may be priced based on a consumer's willingness to pay and the pattern of usage rather than on the cost of production. In this kind of pricing scheme, pricing strategies become a complex exercise in customization, bundling, and unbundling of products. The following discussions on pricing strategies are expanded upon in Chapter 8.

In most markets, firms have discretionary power over product pricing. This will be even more prominent in electronic commerce due to product differentiation. Consumers are often charged differently even for the same physical product. For example, many services are priced differently for children, students, or senior citizens. A motion picture is distributed first in theaters, then to pay-cable channels, video sales, rental videos, and network television. At each distribution channel, prices for the same motion picture are differentiated based on consumers' eagerness to view it. Products are often differentiated by quality with different prices not necessarily corresponding to the quality level. In all these cases, the product prices are influenced more by factors other than the basic cost of production. It can be expected that a similar situation will hold true for electronic commerce. But which factors will influence prices the most is still an open question.

Electronic commerce is radically changing the way products are distributed. Prices for electronic newspapers, for example, may differ from those for printed newspapers. Should we expect products ordered through web pages to be priced lower because the process seems equivalent to direct-from-factory merchandising? For personalized digital products, the cost of production may vary for each consumer. Cost differences warrant different prices, and the nature of network computing may enable sellers to implement complex pricing strategies, which have been impractical in physical markets.

Research into these and other issues related to product pricing in electronic commerce is just emerging. Most attention has been paid to software pricing. With the durability problem in digital products, research is focusing on renting, licensing, and leasing strategies. But there are non-conventional methods of price discrimination which will be prevalent in electronic commerce and which will have peculiar economic effects. Deneckere and McAfee (1996) show an example where a lower quality product may cost more than a higher quality one, and both sellers and buyers are better off. An example of price discrimination of this sort is commonly observed where some functions of computer hardware or software are disabled for specific markets.

A variant version of renting and licensing is subscription-based pricing. An initial cost of producing a database is large but the cost of extracting and selling a portion is minimal. The price for a database, therefore, cannot be based on the cost of production or the marginal cost of serving a customer. A break-even price will depend on the total number of subscribers, who vary widely in their usage. Thus, optimal pricing will reflect differential usage. Such a nonlinear optimal pricing strategy has been developed for natural monopoly industries such as electric utilities, natural gas, and telecommunications. In a way, the digital product industry is similar to them because of the relatively high proportion of fixed costs to variable costs. The problem is how to measure individual usage and associate the usage to price. Usage-based pricing has been discussed in terms of network infrastructure, but its application to product or service pricing is still not clear. Some argue that pricing based on bundling and subscription will entirely circumvent the problem of measuring usage and individual valuations, although measuring usage is rather convenient on the Internet. But a more efficient allocation can be achieved if consumers are allowed to purchase unbundled products using micropayments. This and other subjects regarding digital product pricing will be discussed in Chapter 8.

Online Taxation, Regulation, and Other Legal Issues

As the number of Internet users grows and many areas of commerce begin to feel the effects of electronic commerce activities, legal and regulatory environments for the electronic marketplace are increasingly scrutinized by the media and the legislators in a growing number of areas including:

- Taxation for online sales
- Income taxes for worldwide online activities
- Anonymity and criminal activities
- Global framework to deal with copyright infringements and electronic crimes
- Money laundering and online banking regulation
- Digital currency regulation and monetary policies
- Consumer protection in online transactions
- Consumer privacy measures for identifiable information
- Deregulatory policies in telecommunications and ISP services
- Anti-competitive behaviors in software and digital products

While many of these issues deserve an in-depth analysis in separate volumes, their legal aspects are discussed in Chapter 11, while we examine those related to copyrights (Chapter 5), consumer information (Chapter 8), digital currency and monetary policies (Chapter 10 in section 2).

Of particular importance to today's growing online commerce is to have a uniform and global commercial environment. If we were to treat online commerce simply as an extension of physical markets, taxing online sales of physical products would be relatively straightforward except the fact that the taxing jurisdiction is often difficult to establish for the sellers, who may be located anywhere in the world. Digital contents distributed online, on the other hand, may be taxed as a sale or a royalty income depending on how we define the product or service—as a sellable item or a renting and leasing of a copyrighted material. If each taxing jurisdiction applies a different definition, an online seller may be subject to a long-term uncertainty or even to a double taxation. The globalized online market highlights the need to cooperate among governments to streamline different commercial laws and regulations prevalent in physical markets.

For many issues listed above, encryption and certification services play an important role in establishing digital identity, preventing money laundering and anonymous crimes, digital currency and consumer privacy. Not surprisingly, the security and reliability of online commerce also depends on how these services evolve and are accepted, not only by businesses and consumers, but also by international governments. For digital product sellers, encryption technologies are critical in maintaining control over their contents. These technologies and certification authorities, who are intermediaries, are discussed in Chapter 9.

1.5. Summary

The development of the Internet represents a fundamental change in networked communication. Commercial enterprises on the Internet and the next-generation networks must be adapted to the new environment of open, distributed, peer-to-peer communication. At the same time, because of its capability to use various file formats and support all kinds of communications activities and its growing reach, the Internet will subsume many aspects of business activities and organization. Already, electronic commerce has expanded to include digital, as well as physical products, and informational, as well as noninformational products. More importantly, as business processes and noncommercial activities themselves are digitized, new products and intermediary opportunities are springing up. Electronic commerce will change not only the way firms do business but will also transform intra- and interfirm organizations, and in the process, the economics of the market. Understanding the Internet in all its ramifications will be critical to developing proper business strategies and seizing new opportunities that the Internet will generate. At the same time, policy-makers and legislators need to broaden their understanding of the nature of electronic commerce in order to make it a viable economic sector by setting up proper policies and legislation.

Snapshots have also been provided of major issues and attempts to show why they are of relevance and concern to the world of electronic commerce have been explained. Subsequent chapters will add color and depth to each of these topics, always stressing the economic perspective. Free speech versus absolute author rights will not be explored further. Instead, emphasis on the need for a market analysis of copyrights is given. Similarly, this book will refrain from fueling the security concerns of potential commercial uses of the Internet, which are no more severe than those posed by traditional media. Rather, we explore the economic issues of who will control the revealed consumer information and the payment systems.

References

Akerlof, G., 1970. "The Market for Lemons: Quality Uncertainty and the Market Mechanism." *Quarterly Journal of Economics*, 84: 488–500.

Anderson, C., 1995. "The Accidental Superhighway." *The Economist.* July 1, 1995. Available at http://www.economist.com/surveys/internet/intro.html.

Bellovin, S.M. 1989. " Security Problems in the TCP/IP Protocol Suite." *Comput. Commun. Review*, 19(2): 32–48.

Benjamin R., and R. Wigand, 1995. "Electronic Markets and Virtual Value Chains on the Information Highway." *Sloan Management Review.* Winter: 62–72.

Bhimani, A., 1996. "Securing the Commercial Internet." *Communications of the ACM*, June 1996, 39(6): 29–35.

Borenstein, N.S., et al., 1996. "Perils and Pitfalls of Practical Cybercommerce." *Communications of the ACM*, June 1996, 39(6): 36–44.

Business Week, 1996. "New Tolls on the Info Highway?" Feb. 12, 1996.

Chellappa, R., A. Barua and A.B. Whinston, 1997. "Intranets: Looking Beyond Internal Corporate Web Servers" In R. Kalakota and A.B. Whinston, eds., *Readings in Electronic Commerce*, pp. 311–321. Reading, Mass.: Addison-Wesley.

Deneckere, R., and R.P. McAfee, 1996. "Damaged Goods." *Journal of Economics and Management Strategy*, 5(2): 149–174.

Froomkin, A.M., 1997. "The Essential Role of Trusted Third Parties in Electronic Commerce." In *Readings in Electronic Commerce*, Chapter 6, pp. 119–176. Reading, Mass.: Addison-Wesley Longman, Inc.

Hinden, R.M., 1996. "IP Next Generation: Overview." *Communications of the ACM*, June 1996, 39(6): 61–71.

Radosevich, L., 1996. "The Once and Future EDI." *CIO* (http://www.cio.com), December 15, 1996/January 1, 1997, pp. 67–77.

Steinfeld, C., R. Kraut, and A. Plummer, 1995. "The Impact of Interorganizational Networks on Buyer-Seller Relationships." *Journal of Computer-Mediated Communication (JCMC)*, vol.1, No. 3. Available at http://jcmc.huji.ac.il/vol1/issue3/steinfld.html.

Suggested Readings and Notes

History of the Internet

D. Lynch and M. Rose, 1993. *Internet System Handbook*. Reading, Mass.: Addison-Wesley.

See also MacKie-Mason, J.K., and H.R. Varian, 1994, "Economics FAQs about the Internet.," *Journal of Economic Perspective*, 8(3): 75–96.

Firms and Markets

There are various ways to define a firm. Economic definitions are mainly concerned with potential gains in efficiency, for example reduction in production or transactions costs.

In "The Nature of the Firm." *Economica*, 4:386–405 (1937), R. Coase views the firm as a means to economize transaction costs. (Reprinted in *Readings in Price Theory*, G. Stigler and K. Boulding, eds., 1952. Homewood, Ill:

Irwin.) Depending on which minimizes transaction costs, a market-like organization or a centralized firm is preferred. O. Williamson further elaborated the concept of transaction costs in terms of the uncertainty in long-term relationships such as future switching costs or investments in his *Markets and Hierachies: Analysis and Antitrust Implications.* (New York: Free Press) in 1975.

A concise summary on the role of a firm in a market is found in Jean Tirole's *The Theory of Industrial Organization*, 1989, pp. 15–60. Cambridge, Mass.: The MIT Press.

Electronic Data Interchange (EDI)

Phyllis K. Sokol, 1995. *From EDI to Electronic Commerce: A Business Initiative.* New York: McGraw-Hill, Inc. Sokol's view of electronic commerce is limited to an "open-EDI," which means a more flexible business-to-business EDI. Nevertheless, it contains good information about the traditional EDI.

A detailed discussion on EDI and electronic commerce can be found in Kalakota, R., and A.B. Whinston, 1996, *Frontiers of Electronic Commerce*, Chapters 9 and 10, Addison-Wesley.

In additiona to Radosevich (1996) cited in the reference, see also a short article by Davis, J., and M. Parsons, "EDI Vendors Adjust Strategies in Face of Growing Internet," *Infoworld*, December 25, 1995.

Internet Resources

Implications of Digital Process

A wide range of thought-provoking articles regarding the impacts of the digital process are available, appropriately enough, online.

George Gilder is the author of *Life After Television*, 1992, New York, W. W. Norton & Company, and discusses the effects of digital technologies on a variety of social and economic spheres. Some of his articles are available at http://www.seas.upenn.edu/~gaj1/ggindex.html.

Nicholas Negroponte is the author of *being digital*, 1996, New York, Alfred A. Knopf, whose introduction and excerpts are available at http://www.obs-us.com/obs/english/books/nn/bdintro.htm.

Jeffrey Rayport and John Sviokla teach Managing in the Marketspace at Harvard Business School. The "marketspace" is where business is conducted via information-based products, services or markets. Their course material is available at http://www.hbs.edu/smig/marketspace.

The Internet Society (ISOC)

To contact ISOC, use email: isoc@isoc.org. ISOC holds annual INET conference and publishes "Internet Society News." For more information, visit ISOC web site at http://info.isoc.org/index.html.

Related web sites for IETF: http://www.ietf.cnri.reston.va.us/.

Related web sites for IAB: http://www.iab.org/iab/.

Statistics and Surveys on Internet Usage

Nua Internet Survey: An extensive list of Internet survey companies and sites can be found at Nua's "Internet Survey Companies and Consultancies" page: http://www.nua.ie/choice/Surveys/SurveyLinks.html.

Nua also sends out monthly updates via email. To subscribe, send an e-mail to: surveys-request@nua.ie with the word "subscribe" in the body of the message. The 1996 year-end review issue is available at http://www.nua.ie/surveys/1996review.html.

GVU Web Survey:

http://www.cc.gatech.edu/gvu/user_surveys

O'Reilly & Associates/Trish Information Services:

http://www.ora.com/gnn/bus/ora/survey/index.html

Church of Scientology v. the Net:

Alison Frankel, 1996. "Making Law, Making Enemies." An article appeared in *The American Lawyer*, March, 1996, available at:

http://www.counsel.com/spotlight/scient.html.

Ron Newman's Scientology page:

http://www.cybercom.net/~rnewman/scientology/home.html

Lotus Development Corporation v. Borland International, Inc.

Lotus vs. Borland resources at Berkeley HTLJ:

http://server.berkeley.edu/HTLJ/lvb/lvbindex.html

Economics professors' amicus brief in support of Borland:

http://www.SoftwareIndustry.og/issues/docs-htm/brf-econ.html

CHAPTER 2

Characteristics of Digital Products and Processes

As the Internet progresses beyond merely being an efficient communications medium and truly expands the opportunity for trading goods, the very definition and basic characteristics of products will change in this electronic marketplace. Information is commonly thought of as the new commodity for electronic commerce. Information, which is often loosely defined to include software and so-called "edutainment" products as well as other knowledge-based products that can be digitized and delivered via networks, has received the most attention in the public press. However, information, even in its broadest sense, is far from the only product that can be digitized. Many physical products can be made "smart" by adding an electronic interface to monitor and control their functions, for example, smart cars and smart appliances, which become hybrid digital products. Other examples are electronic currencies and various forms of financial instruments and securities. Even market processes are being digitized. For example, instead of driving to stores, consumers visit web stores. Messages containing price quotes and orders sent over the Internet can, indeed, be considered to be digital products which perform the same functions as advertising and ordering in physical markets.

In light of this far broader scope of possibilities, in this chapter, properties and characteristics of digital products are defined. Various types of digital products in terms of usage and valuation are discussed. Next, an examination of three physical characteristics of digital products that distinguish them from their non-digital counterparts and that define the unique opportunities (and challenges) of electronic commerce is given. Finally, a new taxonomy of digital product types based on user-product interactions is presented. This taxonomy will facilitate production and marketing decisions for the sellers, as will become apparent throughout our analyses in later chapters.

2.1.   What Are Digital Products?

Even a few random examples illustrate that virtually any product can be sold electronically using the Internet as an advanced communications medium for marketing and advertising, purchasing, and payments. Large corporations to family-owned and neighborhood shops have set up online storefronts selling everything from flowers (Virtual Flowers (http://www.virtualflowers.com/)) to salsa (Bueno Foods (http://www.buenofoods.com/)). In fact, a full range of easy-to-use software has been available for some time through vendors like Open Market (http://www.openmarket.com/) that help businesses to set up an electronic shop. Electronic shopping can offer more than just convenient ordering. For example, when shopping groceries online through *Peapod* (http://www.peapod.com), shown in figure 2.1, you can search, compare, substitute, sort, and categorize your purchases using information on brands, prices, nutritional contents, and size. *Peapod* takes advantage of the computational power of the electronic marketplace to offer its customers convenience as well as personalized, planned, economic shopping. Once a customer's product choices are recorded and analyzed over a period of time, online shopping services can offer inventory and automated refill recommendations, as well as targeted advertisements and promotions. Such an integrated shopping experience is indeed a digital service made possible in the electronic marketplace.

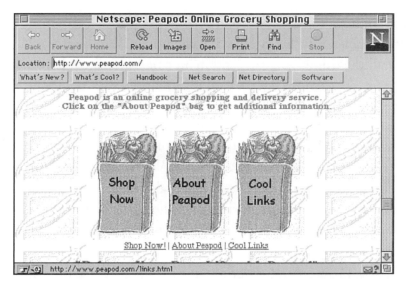

Figure 2.1 Peapod Homepage (http://www.peapod.com/)

Although selling physical products on the Internet is the main goal of *Peapod* and many online businesses, their process innovations are at the core of electronic commerce. For businesses selling physical products online, their focus has been on improving the efficiency of business transactions or on enhancing their services to improve market share, but innovative thinking can transform many physical products and processes into digital products.

Information is a primary example of a digital product, for example knowledge-based goods that can be digitized and transferred over a digital network. Information goods include a wide range of traditionally paper-based products such as books, magazines, newspapers, journals, photographs, maps, and other graphics. Most of these products are first produced in digital format and then printed on paper. Some information products such as databases, computer software, and computer games are distributed and used in digital format. Since video and audio signals can now be digitized, multimedia products, such as movies, television programs, and sound recordings can be combined with information products or sold separately as entertainment products. Clearly, these are all transparent examples of products that exist as physical products but that can easily be digitized for the electronic marketplace.

We can, however, take this process one step further. Anything that one can send and receive over the Internet has the potential to be a digital product. Just think of all the things you can send in an email message—letters and postcards, news, instructions, credit card information, product inquiries, and so on. Paper-based products of all kinds can become digital products by scanning or by changing, conceptually, the way we use those products. For example, airline, concert or baseball tickets need not be printed on paper. Instead, a ticket—or the authorization for entry—can be assigned, transferred, and stored digitally in a person's ID card. To make a reservation, one can log on to a web site, and make payments digitally. The ticket is then downloaded into the customer's storing device, which is scanned when boarding an airplane or entering a sports venue.

Similarly, business and government forms that we fill out every day can be digitized in their entirety. Instead of simply viewing information about a government service on web pages, you could easily fill out a request form for public assistance and receive, for example, welfare payments deposited digitally on an electronic card or hard drive. Tax returns may be disbursed electronically, completely digitizing the whole process—maintaining expense records, calculating tax liabilities, submitting electronic filing, and paying taxes or getting refunds. Some non-paper objects can also be digitized. Museums routinely collect, describe, and catalog their collection using databases, photographs, and sounds. Virtual museums could digitize these materials and offer them on the Internet, reaching a far larger population (see Internet Resources at the end of this chapter for an example). When art objects themselves are digital pictures and photographs, museums may be more virtual than physical, and the commerce of such objects includes the right to digitize them, and thus the ability to control the content of the Internet for which Microsoft and other companies are prepared to pay a large sum of money.

Some products or services do not have a corresponding physical form but exist as a knowledge base or a process. This does not mean they cannot be turned into digital products. Take, for example, a salesperson in a clothing store who has considerable expertise and knowledge of fabrics, sizes, and fashion acquired through years of training and experience. This valuable knowledge base could be digitized into a file or a program and made available to customers.

Similarly, any process involving multiple human interactions and communications can be organized as a digital process or an electronic market. For example, a news clipping service searches newspapers and magazines every day to locate and collect articles for a client based on specified preferences. A computer program could do the same information filtering of digitized news articles. Auctions for virtually all products could be organized as electronic markets where auction items are viewed online, and bids and payments are taken electronically. *Christie's* (http:// www.specialcar.com/christies) publishes its auction catalog online, but it may well have to adapt its auctioning process itself to respond to its electronic competitors in the future. The government and corporations may also use electronic markets to send out requests for proposals. They may also receive and evaluate them in digital form, not only improving efficiency but expanding the number of participants. If a TV or radio station conducts a viewer response session using phones, faxes, or letters, a few hundred responses may strain its human and material resources. Conducted on a web page, it can easily accommodate tens of thousands of responses, analyze them and respond in real-time. Innovative digitizing may also change the way we woo. Although some occasions may demand real flowers, a virtual flower (a graphic file of a flower) is an example of digitizing a physical product whose main purpose is symbolic. A flower sent over the network could embody the gesture of greeting, consolation, affection, or any other emotion.

The list of digital products is bounded only by human imagination. Still, they share a number of common traits. Besides the apparent physical quality of being a stream of bits, they have no physical bounds in production and use. They can, however, be grouped in the three broad categories shown in table 2.1. As concert tickets demonstrate, many products are simply a token or a symbol whose physical form is not an essential requirement. Paper money is another example of a product which needs not necessarily be printed on paper. It is merely a symbol, in fact, a concept of value that can be digitized.

Table 2.1   Examples of Digital Products

1. **Information and entertainment products:**
   - Paper-based information products: newspapers, magazines, journals, books
   - Product information: product specifications, user manuals, sales training manuals
   - Graphics: photographs, postcards, calendars, maps, posters
   - Audio: music recordings, speeches
   - Video: movies, television programs

2. **Symbols, tokens and concepts:**
   - Tickets and reservations: airline, hotels, concerts, sport events
   - Financial instruments: checks, electronic currencies, credit cards, securities

3. **Processes and services:**
   - Government services: forms, welfare payments
   - Electronic messaging: letters, faxes, telephone calls
   - Business value creation processes: ordering, bookkeeping, inventorying, contracting
   - Auctions and electronic market
   - Remote education, telemedicine, and other interactive services
   - Cybercafés and interactive entertainment

2.2. Characteristics of Information Products

In the electronic marketplace of today, digital goods consist primarily of information products. An information or knowledge good is a peculiar kind of commodity. It needs no physical presence and the same idea or information can be conveyed in many ways. As the virtual cyberspace exists in the minds of the users, the idea or information—as the product of the mind—is said to be the native dweller of the cyberspace. Its economic significance, however, should be analyzed as a consumable commodity for which a market is organized and a price is determined based on its usefulness. In this section, some economic aspects of information products in terms of their usage by consumers is highlighted. These aspects apply to both digital and non-digital information products.

Dependence on Individual Preference

As conceptual embodiments of human ideas, knowledge, and intelligence, information products do not have physical form or structure that can be physically consumed. So information products are not "consumable" goods in a conventional sense. What is being "consumed" is the idea represented by the information and the use to which the information is put—something that varies greatly among consumers. Although the demand for any good varies according to the heterogeneity inherent in consumer tastes, the demand for information is likely to be more variable than that for other products. The main reason for the difference is that knowledge or information has many uses that often cross the boundary of established product categories. Consequently, information product sellers need to rely more on the signals consumers send in order to group consumers according to preferences. As a result, product customization and discriminatory pricing based on consumer types or other identifiable information become essential for digital products because their uses and values are relatively heterogeneous. With differentiated products, pricing strategies will be based on consumers' valuations or their marginal willingness to pay rather than on the marginal costs of production.

Transitory or Cumulative Utility

Many information products are time-dependent. For example, weather information is used to forecast an output level of crops. For this year's crops, last year's weather information has no relevancy as long as we assume that the weather conditions in each year are determined by a random process (that is, we discount the possibility to forecast this year's weather based on last year's). In this sense, some information, like time-dependent, outdated, or outmoded information, may be transitory and perishable. Yesterday's weather information or news is no longer needed except for archiving and referencing purposes. But, archiving and referencing of transitory information has value in its own right. This means that the utility of information is really cumulative. A portion of any information file can be recycled and reused to produce different products. In contrast to most other types of products, even "consumed" goods can have value for information products.

Interestingly enough, not only the consumption, but the creation of information is also a cumulative, and often collaborative, process. John Perry Barlow (1993) has argued that "information is conveyed by propagation, not distribution." His point is to emphasize that information propagates like a plant and that both, transferer and transferee, have the same information. Often, information evolves as it is transferred through accumulation, modification, addition, and improvement. The process of schooling and learning begins with reading texts of accumulated knowledge and continues with improvements made by successive generations. In an age of digital products, changes can be made at an exponential rate. Due to this continuous, cumulative process of creation, given an information product, delineating and protecting a author's rights is no simple matter. Whether a work is copyrightable will depend on a close examination of all legal requirements, which will be discussed in Chapter 5. It suffices to say that cumulative consumption and production of digital products significantly complicates product pricing strategies.

Externalities of Information Products

Externalities are economic consequences that are not fully accounted for by the price or market system. These could be either unaccounted benefits or harmful effects. Automobiles pollute the air but its cost on environment is not reflected in the price of the automobile—an example of a negative externality. If your neighbor's tree gives you shade, it is a positive externality for you. A new agricultural technique—the use of fallows in the Middle Ages, developed by one, has benefited all other farmers. The use of the new technique by others does not prevent the inventor from using it on his land. Therefore, the technique has a positive externality.

Many products have network externalities, which means that the value of a product increases as more people use it. Network externality is one example of a positive externality. The benefit of network externality may come directly from the increasing number of users, as in the case of the telephone. The value of the telephone is low if few people have a telephone, but much higher if you can reach almost anyone. Congestion is a negative externality that can offset positive network externalities. You benefit if many people have a telephone, but are hurt if they use it so much that you get a frequent busy signal. Another example of a network externality is the software industry, where more companies develop programs for users of a popular operating system, for instance Windows, than for less popular operating systems. Other digital products have network externalities. For example, some computer games are more enjoyable when there are more people to play with. A communications network such as email or newsgroup messaging clearly enjoys network externality similar to the telephone as well as negative externalities, such as congestion.

Sharing of information, computer software, and other digital products is often encouraged by the fact that the gains from sharing are substantial due to network externalities and often exceed the potential cost of sharing if caught and levied copyright infringement fines. When information products have network externalities, the control over reproduction and sharing has been the primary objective of copyright protection. Copyright control has been effective as long as infringers are easily located. Copies of books and audio tapes, for example, are usually pirated by those who have access to mass production facilities. As the number of potential pirates is limited and the investment necessary for such an operation is relatively high, most serious copyright infringement by pirates has been by overseas publishers operating beyond the reach of territorial copyright enforcement. However, digital products are highly vulnerable to copying by consumers who have the very same technology as the producers. The stakes are raised even higher when we consider the possibility of pirate copies of digital currencies and electronic financial instruments.

Appropriate technologies and effective legal means must clearly be established to adapt to this new environment, the topic of Chapter 5. A more proactive strategy, however, can be found in the very nature of digital products. Some information is inherently more valuable if fewer people have it. In these cases, the information has a harmful, or negative, externality if someone else has the same information. Although a basic tenet of economics observation holds that the value of a good is higher if it is more scarce, in the case of information, the opposite is often true due to network externality. Nevertheless, there are numerous instances where exclusive information is more valuable because its exclusivity renders the owner benefits. A primary example would be market information that can be used for investment or speculative purposes. The profitability of insider trading, although illegal, depends on the exclusivity of the information.

For digital products with negative externalities, it is not easy to guarantee maximum value to a buyer. Value assurance is comparatively easy in the case of physical products. If one owns an item, it is physically impossible for others to own the same object at the same time, and the fewer similar items that exist, the higher the value of each. In a digital world, however, products can be reproduced and redistributed at will and the exclusivity of information products is not due to physical impossibility. Rather, exclusivity is artificially imposed through control of ownership. Hoarding a physical product to create an artificial scarity and to corner a market may be illegal, but there is no such constraint placed on hoarding an idea. Preferably, if sellers want to guarantee the value of information to their customers, information should be hoarded, or its access be limited. In terms of copyright protection, information sharing by consumers is never a problem for a seller when there is negative externality since sharing would mean lowering its value. However, sellers of information products need to provide stronger evidence of their guarantee or trustworthiness to customers than do sellers of non-digital products.

Intrinsic Values of Digital Products

Exclusivity in production can be just as valuable as exclusivity in consumption. This is akin to the reputation built by high-quality good producers of physical goods. When many versions of information, software, news analysis, or commentary are available, exclusivity depends on the originality and creativity of producers. An exclusive news coverage or carriage of a syndicated column distinguishes one newspaper from another. In the world market for digital products, it will be the individuality or point of view of the authors, and the relevancy to the customers' needs that give one producer an edge over the other. By producing unique and customized products (exclusive products) sellers will be able to compete successfully regardless of size.

As an intermediary distributing products of many producers, the exclusivity or uniqueness also applies to the selection or bundling of these products. For example, retail outlets in physical markets offer a distinctive selection that attracts targeted customers, just as a magazine or a newspaper distinguishes itself from the rest through the selection of particular articles and features. Implementing such a unique selection or a "point of view" becomes easier because of the physical nature of digital products, especially their transmutability, which is discussed in the next section.

2.3.   The Physical Nature of Digital Products

Whereas the nature and use of information discussed previously applies to both digital and non-digital forms of knowledge-based products, there are some characteristics of digital products that are fundamental or unique to the medium. Because there are concerns over commercial aspects of delivery and transmission over digital networks, here are three such fundamental and unique features: indestructibility, transmutability (easy to modify), and reproducibility. Some non-digital products share these characteristics, but only to a limited degree. For example, pictures can last for many decades with proper care; parts of a song can be copied and changed; and whole books can be photocopied. Despite these similarities, a digital file is the first medium of expression that takes all these characteristics to an infinite degree of perfection.

Indestructibility

Once created, a digital product maintains its form and quality ad infinitum because of the lack of normal wear and tear. While some durable goods such as automobiles or buildings may have a long life, they still suffer from usage, and initial quality differences are further accentuated by consumer usage behaviors. But the quality of a digital product does not degrade no matter how long or how often it is used. Therefore, no distinction can be made between durable and non-durable goods in the case of digital products. In other words, for most purposes, a product sold by a producer is equivalent to one offered in the second-hand market. This alone has significant ramifications on the market.

Like any durable good, a producer of a digital product competes with its own past sales since consumers purchase a digital product, at most, once during the product's life. As a result, the producer is often forced to charge a very competitive price—the lowest possible price—for its product even when it has no competitor. Suppose that Alice sells a complete database of Medieval English names. As the list is complete and no new names can be added, the database is most durable. Suppose that those with English heritage are willing to pay $100 for such a database, while non-English persons will pay only $10. On the first market day, Alice can maximize her profit by selling only to English descendants at $100 each. After all the sales are made, if Alice wants to sell more she must lower the price to $10 because that is all the potential buyers are willing to pay. However, if Alice lowers the price to $10 on the second day, consumers who know the market demand could have predicted the price change. Knowing that price will be lowered on the second day, no buyers will pay the initial high price. Therefore, Alice can only price her product at $10 at any time.

This peculiar market behavior is due to the shrinking market size as the durable good producer makes sales. The loss of market power for durable goods is known as the *Coase conjecture* and affects all digital product sellers (Coase, 1972). Several measures are available to avoid lowering prices. For example, Alice may announce that she will not lower her price below $100 on the first day, or issue a buy-back guarantee if the price is lowered, but their effectiveness depends on her credibility (Bulow, 1982). Alternatively, she may sell to the same number of customers in each market period with different, or 'updated' products. That is, a supposedly 'complete' database is continuously updated based on 'newly found' data—a strategy of planned obsolescence.

Frequent updating and licensing are two popular strategies of durable good sellers having a significant impact on digital product marketing and pricing. Frequent updates make old versions of software obsolete, thereby enabling the seller to continue to sell durable goods to the same buyers. While updated versions may be used to introduce new and more efficient features, the underlying profit motive in updates often increases inefficiency. Software manufacturers often make changes in the user interface, to differentiate new products sufficiently from old ones, so that users need to relearn the software, resulting in waste. And in some cases, it is not clear whether new versions are of superior quality to old ones. After many years of updates, some computer programs have become exaggerated in size and complicated with unnecessary and useless features.

Licensing is another way to continue to sell. By renting instead of selling a durable good, consumers are charged for the usage in each period, whereby the market for the seller continues to exist. When renting, consumers are not affected by their expectations about the future sales and prices, and the firm has no incentive to produce any additional units or to lower prices in the future. Thus, licensing software will achieve the same goal in maximizing profit as the practice of frequent updating.

The indestructibility of digital products is another factor why digital product sellers would prefer licensing or leasing to direct sales. The life of a digital product is not only comparably longer than that of most durable goods, but it also has to compete with "used" products that are indistinguishable from new products. When products in second-hand markets resemble the products in new product markets in every aspect, revenue protection for producers will depend on how successfully they can discourage second-hand sales, especially when the life of a product is longer than the product's usefulness to each consumer. Consequently, certain products like books and musical CDs may need special protection against reselling. Despite the obvious rationale from the producers' perspective, it is still uncertain whether second-hand markets can be legally prohibited.

Transmutability

A paradox to the above claim is that the content of digital products can be changed instantly. They are extremely customizable and, indeed, seem to be changing constantly. Changes, whether accidental, intended, or fraudulent, can be irreversible. Hence, by the nature of digital products, producers lose some control over the integrity of their products. Although most free documents on the Internet state that they allow distribution only for unmodified copies, in a world composed of ones and zeros, this is a stipulation that is virtually impossible to enforce. This does not prevent producers from employing a wide variety of mechanisms in their attempts to quail this behavior. Certain technologies, for example, prevent easy modification. For example, a document such as a PDF file can be viewed or printed with Adobe's Acrobat Reader, but users cannot save the file in digital format. Therefore, any casual digital modification will be prevented although unlimited printing is allowed. Acrobat Reader is platform independent and used to disseminate technical papers that contain graphics and equations. Despite these advantages, the program is extremely large for its limited function and has spread very slowly.

While it is difficult to control content integrity at the user level once a digital file is downloaded, there are mechanisms that can verify whether a document has been modified. Encryption technologies (Data Encryption Standard and RSA—public key encryption scheme patented by RSA Data

Security, Inc. (http://www.rsa.com)) provide privacy and protection against modification, but only in transmission. Other authentication technologies have been developed primarily for checking authenticity or whether a document's content has been altered. These technologies are useful if buyers are concerned about corrupted copies but will not provide sellers with effective control against unauthorized modifications or copies.

The strategic implication of transmutability is that rather than trying to protect content integrity, producers need to differentiate their products by customizing and updating, and by selling them as interactive services, not as standard shrink-wrapped products. This product differentiation is not only a possibility but should be the overall business strategy adopted by companies producing digital products. Component texts, graphics, audios, and videos, or an overall look and format cannot be adequately protected. On the other hand, consumer updates can be a natural process in the evolution of information and digital products increasing the value of unmodified new products. This is underscored by the third and final attribute of digital products—reproducibility.

Reproducibility

The beauty and the bone of all digital products is that they can be reproduced, stored, and transferred at ease. This means, quite simply, that after the initial fixed investment cost, the marginal cost of production is almost zero. However, if the producer cannot appropriate even the fixed cost from the market, product quality may be lowered, or the product may disappear altogether. Given a set market price, the level of fixed costs determines the minimum number of sales or market share needed to break even. Consequently, advocates for intellectual property rights have centered on preventing improper duplication and reselling of digital products. Whether reproduction can be prevented via technology remains to be seen, but there is great skepticism that this can be achieved. Rather, producers must strive to make reproduction less valuable or irrelevant by continuously changing and improving their products.

For an obvious reason, the marginal cost of a digital product is assumed to be zero. In terms of production, or reproduction, costs, this assertion would be reasonable enough. However, the copyright payment would be applied to each copy or reproduction, and a non-zero, per-unit cost is added. Once we include such variable costs in the total production costs, digital products no longer have zero marginal costs. Theoretical conclusions of some pricing models critically depend on the assumption regarding marginal costs because they play an important role in economic analyses. In Chapter 8, pricing strategies for digital products are investigated. Here, we emphasize that, although digital products may be reproduced at a minimum or no additional cost, this in no way implies that their marginal costs will be zero.

Physical Nature and Economic Issues

The unique characteristics of digital products are all related in different ways to the key issues in electronic commerce. The indestructibility raises the concern regarding the effects of durability on market shares as well as the product choices which producers of durable products must employ to counter these effects. The first sales doctrine—allowing buyers to resell or lend purchased products—may destroy the market completely unless an information seller, for example, can restrict its customers from reselling.

On the other hand, the transmutability of digital products lends itself to product differentiation and customization, perhaps to a much heightened degree than any other physical products. Due to more flexible production technologies, consumers are increasingly enjoying products which match their tastes far better than mass-produced products that cater to average tastes. In electronic commerce, each consumer would be able to purchase a product based on his or her individual preference. The transmutability raises the whole issue of customized products, individualized pricing, and the proper use of consumer-revealed information.

Among the three characteristics, reproducibility has been widely recognized as the most problematic aspect of digital commerce. Participants in the international copyright convention held in Geneva in December, 1996 spent an extraordinary amount of time debating whether the temporary copies made by computers when browsing, backing-up, and displaying on screen, being reproductions, technically violate the copyrights. When copyright laws apply to paper-based products, a simple act of photocopying is undoubtedly an area of concern. For digital products, however, transmitting and reading a document on a computer involve a different set of user behaviors. Transmitting a file, for example, is based on the reproducibility of the file—a file transfer program always sends a copy rather than the file itself. Such routines are embedded in all aspects of computer file operations, but only now became a serious issue.

How digital copyrights should evolve—through redefining copyright terms or through adapting to the new usage pattern of digital products—will be discussed in Chapter 5. But the three characteristics of digital products discussed earlier clarify many aspects of digital copyrights. Resale prohibition, for example, stems from the producer's concern about the infinite life span of the product—indestructibility. Content control is necessary because of the product's transmutability, and duplication prohibition is motivated by the ease of reproducibility. Of these three, only transmutability can be countered by producers through business strategies, frequent updating and customization. Correspondingly, product differentiation and price discrimination based on consumer tastes will be the main economic concerns in the electronic commerce. The other two characteristics of digital products appear to work in the consumers' favor, and producers have high incentives to prevent reproduction and resale.

Digitized products can be composed of text, data, graphics, video, or audio. Technologies are also making it possible to convey "feelings" in addition to sights and sounds. For example, when a cursor passes over a surface described as "rough" on the computer screen, a joystick or a mouse shakes and jolts. Because of the ease and speed with which these components can be reorganized, digital products are innately heterogeneous, making it difficult to derive marketing or pricing strategies that can be used for a wide variety of products. In this section, we develop a taxonomy by which digital products can be grouped into a few major categories around common features and that is meaningful in analyzing economic issues and developing business strategies.

A number of alternative schemes have been used to categorize digital products. For example, file components have been used to characterize a product as either a text file, a graphic or a data file. With the increasing use of multimedia formats, however, this distinction is no longer useful. Categorizing digital products into databases, information products, entertainment, software, and so on, is both descriptive and subjective. Although useful, this practice is inadequate and gives the false impression that electronic commerce simply mirrors other product markets. Furthermore, it is loosely based on the usage of a product which, as we discussed, may differ among consumers. In light of this, we propose to categorize digital products based on user-product interactions. Once converted into digital format, all products are essentially the same. What determines the type of product is how it is acquired and how it is used by consumers.

The first criterion we can use to classify digital products is the transfer mode. Products that are downloaded at once or in piecemeal fashion, such as through daily updates, can be called *delivered products. Interactive products*, on the other hand, are products or services, such as remote-diagnosis, interactive games, and tele-education. A simple communication between a server and a client, such as a request for a search that is accomplished by sending information and receiving a reply, is usually defined as interactive. In this definition, however, all two-way communications are interactive. Video-on-demand is regarded as an interactive service; a movie that allows viewers to select different plots and endings is called an interactive movie. But they simply operate under an automated process of the delivered transfer mode.

To characterize a transfer as interactive requires the use of a real-time application and the need to interact in successive requests and responses. For example, a requested search information may be delivered in seconds or in hours depending on the status of network congestion. But once delivered, there is no more need to interact. Sending another request will be a different service. TCP (Transfer Control Protocol) is well suited for delivered products where transfer integrity and reliability are of primary concern. The TCP waits until all packets of a message are collected before reassembling and presenting the message (see Chapter 3 for protocols). An interactive product or service, on the other hand, consists of a stream of requests and responses in a session that defines an objective such as a search, a game, or a consultation with a doctor. A live or real-time communication requires an orderly transfer of data, for example, you would not want to hear words backward. Other protocols than TCP are in use for interactive services on the Internet, which we discuss in Chapter 3.

At present, the vast majority of digital products on the Internet are delivered, not interactive. Information products such as databases and electronic versions of all printed media, including books, journals, newspapers, and magazines dominate the commercial offerings in today's Internet commerce, and most are delivered. Even web browsing is a delivered product, it depends on a sequential transfer of files which does not require a continuous connection or a real-time coordination with other users or processes. Similarly, a subscription service to a database is not an interactive product even though it involves periodic deliveries. Piecemeal access or delivery is the common mode of transferring files when periodic updates are needed, or if the whole database is not needed at once, or too expensive to buy. In any case, these updates do not require real time interaction between sellers and subscribers, and despite that, such products are called *interactive editions*, as they are delivered products.

A conventional definition of interactivity often includes search activities. For example, forms and queries submitted to and processed by World Wide Web servers are often considered to be interactive. However, search, catalog, and directory services can be considered to be equivalent to a subscription service with a large database (indexes), a portion of which is accessed by a buyer. Thus, searches are delivered, not interactive, products. What does seem to be an interactive process in the case of search services is in fact the process of customization. That is, a search service customizes the product on the basis of a customer's requested criteria. However, once produced in this way, the product is simply delivered to the customer. Many online services use consumers' requests as an input to their production processes. These involve producer-consumer interactions, but they are not interactive services in terms of transfer mode.

True interactive products are becoming more common on the Internet. One area of expanding business is online consumer services, including health services such as telemedicine, remote diagnostics, and tele-education. Other types of interactive products are based on real-time video and audio communications, such as video conferencing, Internet telephony, and the real-time Internet broadcasting or multicasting (see Chapter 3 for Internet infrastructure), and entertainment, such as Internet Relay Chat groups or games played in MUDs (Multi-User Dungeons or Domains). While the latter may appear to be a frivolous use of this valuable resource, it is often the place where new technologies and uses have been test-driven, in this case, a truly interactive service. Such interactive digital products may actually be the most profitable services in electronic commerce because they are less prone to personal arbitrage and reselling. Interactive services are fundamentally personalized products which have consumption value for only the targeted individual. To maximize such benefits, sellers can also prevent copyright violations by converting delivered products into interactive products, an alternative strategy to a costly, technology-based, control mechanism.

The second criterion for our taxonomy is timeliness. Time-dependent products lose value rapidly, which may be a deterrent to offering them for resale or distributing without authorization. Timeliness is critical to daily news, stock quotes, and other information needed for quick decision-making. The timely value of these products can be maintained by periodic updates and sold as subscription goods whereby sellers retain some control. Examples are stock quotes, government-issued economic data, and journal abstracts.

Time-dependent products become obsolete and worthless when they are out-of-date. Artificially created time-dependence, however, can be useful. For example, it can convert time-independent, durable goods into non-durable goods. Considering the indestructibility of digital products, this is the most important aspect which firms can exploit in marketing. For example, a web page providing information about a resort town may be visited once. To entice revisits, the content of the web page should be updated periodically. Updating in this regard is an arbitrary means to make old products obsolete and open new marketing opportunities. When a digital product is time-independent, sellers tend to use such strategies to transform it into a time-dependent product.

While timeliness refers to the nature of digital products, exogenous factors may confound the ability to provide timely service. If the network is congested, even timely information may become obsolete by the time it reaches consumers. Congestion at the seller's server is, in principle, controllable by the system via capacity and pricing, but congestion elsewhere in the network is outside the control of the seller. When the delivery network performs poorly, controlling a product's timeliness involves both an endogenous production decision and an exogenous factor that may require cooperation and integration with service providers.

Time-dependence may be specific to the individual or may be applied to all consumers. The timeliness of news and stock quotes, for example, is general to all consumers. The freshness and the value of the information diminishes at the same rate for everybody. When such products are offered the next day, their prices would reflect their reduced valuation across the market. However, the result of searches and queries made by a consumer for a specific decision-making is time-dependent to that consumer only. Suppose Alice wants to buy information on the sales figures of a firm in which she is considering investing. This information is time-dependent for Alice because it is useful for her decision. But after the decision is made, the information is no longer needed.

However, it may still be of considerable value to Bob who compiles a table of sales revenues. In such a case, Alice will be able to use the information and still sell it to Bob at the full price.

In keeping with this, time-dependent products can be further divided into two subgroups. Most databases, including indexes and directories, are time-dependent specific to individuals, while news and stock quotes are time-dependent general to all buyers. This difference is apparent if we consider a similar distinction in TV programs. Producers of many programs, in particular of sitcoms and TV movies, depend on revenues from reruns and syndication. These programs find audiences who missed the first time. In contrast, news and sports programs, in general, are not rebroadcast because of their time-dependence across all consumers. Magazine-format news programs have been popular despite this disadvantage because of low production costs. More to the point, these programs often deal with time-insensitive topics, and they recycle old programs, for example, features about "This Day in History" and update segments. Similar adaptive strategies may be applicable to digital product marketing.

To sum up, time-dependence may or may not be advantageous to marketers. Since time-dependent products lose their value rapidly, there is a limited window for marketing. But on the other hand, time-dependence discourages reproduction and reselling, and avoids the problem of a durable good—competing with its own past sales. When consumer reselling is not a concern, products may be more valuable if they are made time-independent. Bundling information into large databases, archives, and references helps to reduce time-dependence. When the durable goods problem is present, sellers increase time-dependence. Software, including computer programs and games, is generally time-independent. Here, software vendors use updates quite often, as discussed earlier, to force people to buy new products.

The third criterion against which to distinguish product categories is the intensity in use. In this respect, single-use products resemble conventional non-durable goods, and multiple-use products may correlate with durable goods. As with traditional durable goods, consumers get benefits from a multiple-use product over time, unlike a single-use product. An example for a single-use product is a search result which is no longer needed once it serves its intended purpose. In contrast, software programs and most games can be used repeatedly.

By definition, the total value of a multiple-use product must increase with use since the value accumulates. But its growth rate may be diminishing, constant, or increasing. In figure 2.2, graph A shows an example where a consumer's utility is increasing, for example, as he learns more about a program and becomes more efficient in its use. Graph B depicts a case of a product whose utility declines over time, for example a computer game which becomes less fun after each use. These are not the only possibilities. A different product's utility cycle may be a combination of these two, increasing for a certain duration and then decreasing, or vice versa. From time t1 to t2, the total utility or value of a product is the area under the graph bounded by the two dates.

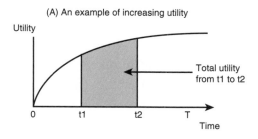

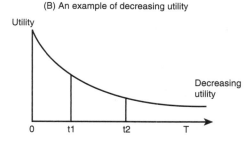

Figure 2.2 Increasing and decreasing utility.

To the extent that consumers keep multiple-use products longer than single-use products, it is in the firms' interest to prevent a resale of single-use products. Since a "consumed" product in this case is still equivalent to a new product, reselling by consumers directly competes with the product's original seller. Literary works and other forms of electronic publishing appear to be most severely affected by reselling. For these products, prohibiting resale as well as reproduction may be needed. Another way of countering this ill effect is to individualize products, thereby discouraging consumer arbitrage. For example, query information from a specific search is individualized (by the choice of the buyer). Therefore, reselling this information is not usually feasible unless two people happen to look for the same information. For single-use products, accommodating buyer choices is not only a good customer service but also a requirement for survival. This is important for most subscription-based database services.

Another criterion in our taxonomy is operational usage. Operational usage refers to whether a product is an executable program or a fixed document. This distinction is meaningful not only because of the prevalence of computer software, but also because producers can add control over consumer usage by converting any product into an executable program. Interactive CDs, for example, present materials, like documents, in a controlled environment prescribed by programmers.

Today, executable programs tend to be multiple-use products, although not all multiple-use products are executable, such as music or speech products. But a growing number of executable products will be found in single-use products. Instead of delivering a document, for example, sellers may incorporate it within an executable program which controls such aspects as viewing and printing. Increasing use of Java-based applets will help producers to deliver their products in an executable program that can be pre-programmed only for a certain function. Many application programs such as word processing can be downloaded as a Java-based applet and discarded after use. The increasing use of applets then signals the unbundling of unwieldy programs, which today's word processors have become.

Similarly, the growing interest in NCs (network computers) instead of PCs as the Internet appliance points to the future when most programs and documents are delivered as executable programs on an as-needed basis rather than pre-packaging all functions in shrink-wrapped products. Furthermore, executable programs may be tailored to take advantage of the Internet's distributed computing environment. The strength of the Java programming language (http://www.javasoft. com/) lies in that a Java-based program can be used in different platforms by using only an interpreter. That, in turn, implies that duplicative efforts and wastes inherent in today's multiplatform environment can be reduced. In view of these advantages, executable products may become dominant over fixed products in the near future.

One final criterion of product categorization focuses on externalities. Positive-externality products are those that increase (average) consumer valuation if more people buy them. Examples of this are interactive services, such as chat lines and games. Negative-externality products, on the other hand, have a congestion effect if more people buy them. Negative externality can be thought of as "wear and tear." If I resell (or duplicate and sell) a product, its value declines as if it has suffered from wear and tear, except that this lowered value affects the seller as well as the buyer. Most entertainment and information products can be consumed without negative externality. A primary example of negative externality is when information is used for gain in a zero-sum game. For example, stock market investors benefit from exclusive information. If there were more people who had the same information, its value, or the profit-making opportunity from that information, would be less than if the information were to be exclusive. When there is negative externality as in this example, consumer arbitrage, reselling and exchanging information, is less of a concern than the faith in the exclusivity. For these products, buyers themselves place a stricter control over reproduction. We have discussed the externality of information products in section 2.2.

Externalities of digital products affect pricing and marketing decisions, as well as the level of competition. Freeware, shareware, and demo versions of software are given out to increase the market share, especially when a wide-spread use and acceptance by consumers opens other venues of marketing, that is, when products have positive externalities. Many software firms, including Netscape (http://www.netscape.com), have used this strategy to establish dominance in their market. Once a computer software becomes dominant, sellers of similar products often depend on the compatibility between their products and the dominant software. Due to the positive externality enjoyed by the users of compatible products, they often command a higher price than non-compatible products (Gandal, 1994).

The dominant software firm, furthermore, enjoys a significant market power from controlling the standards in its software. The following example illustrates the importance of externalities in pricing and market competition. Lotus Development Corporation, the maker of the Lotus 1-2-3 spreadsheet program, claimed that Borland's Quattro Pro infringed its copyright by replicating 1-2-3's user interface—menus and command structure—which affords Borland's customers to run macros written for 1-2-3 (Lotus v. Borland, 1996). Equally divided (Justice Stevens absent), the Supreme Court let stand the lower court's decision denying Lotus' claim. Although Lotus' claim was denied, the nature of the decision clearly underscores the divided opinions of the court and the continuing debate on the merits of externalities.

Product Selection Strategies Based on the Taxonomy

The taxonomy presented here will give readers a means to categorize and compare different products being sold online. In each of the five criteria discussed, a product can be changed from one characteristic to another, for instance a time-independent product can be made time-dependent. One reason for doing so may be to shorten the life of the product even though it physically has almost an infinite life. Producers can also deal with digital products' reproducibility and transmutability by changing product characteristics. A few examples of how such a change can counter the problems arising from the physical nature of digital products are given in the following sections. A product may change in any of the five criteria we discussed.

Changing Time Dependence

First in terms of timeliness, the indestructibility of a digital product means a long life, and a time-independent product, just like durable goods, may limit the number of sales because consumers simply make fewer purchases in their lifetime or second-hand products are always available. In this case, the size of the market shrinks as more products are sold, for example, a seller competes with his or her own previous sales. A time-dependent product, on the other hand, has a short product life and, like consumption goods, such as toothpaste or soap, sellers find new markets or sales as long as there is a need for consumption. Sellers also worry less about the negative effect of consumers sharing products because an outdated product, in this case, is like a used notebook.

Sharing through unauthorized reproduction is a considerable deterrent to selling contents online. Thus, it is not surprising that companies who sell time-dependent information, such as news, are at the forefront of electronic commerce while copyright concerns discourage other digital product sellers. Even when products are naturally time-independent, sellers can further increase their time-dependence by putting out new, updated versions of the product. Some information services guarantee timely updates only to paid subscribers, offering outdated information freely. Besides changing the timeliness of the contents, sellers may also implement congestion-sensitive prices to reduce congestion at the local server level, and differentiate customers according to their preference for timely access. Internet-wide congestion, however, poses some problem since product sellers may not have control over delivery. Unless a seller owns their own network, product price and delivery price will have to be separated.

Changing Usage Patterns

Products may also be changed to influence the way they are used in terms of intensity and operation. A single-use product is, of course, discarded after one use, or has no value to the consumer. But it may have a value and use to other consumers, which will encourage reselling given a chance. Computer software, reference CD-ROMs and compilations, such as movie databases, are multiple-use products, whose value stream may be longer than their update cycles. A book in digital form is a single-use product, but a list of books, perhaps with abstracts and reviews for each entry, becomes a useful reference tool, which is used over a longer period. Not surprisingly, references are one of the most popular digital information products. A book is also time-independent, but can be turn into a time-dependent product by emphasizing the timeliness of its content or its temporary popularity. Likewise, multiple-use products can be time-dependent, further protecting the market against reselling and reproduction.

Similarly, instead of selling an information product online, one can change it into an executable program to gain control over its consumption. For example, a table of daily average rainfall in Austin, Texas, may be sold as a table or as a program that allows users to make queries or to graph. Other information, such as a formula that calculates interest rates, can be sold as a program that does not reveal the formula itself, but only enables its users to derive desired results. A user's guide for a computer program can be made into an executable software agent, which not only offers some added functionalities, such as search, interface, and execute functions integrated into the program itself, but also provides producers an extensive control over its usage and some protection against copyright infringements. Lastly, as mentioned earlier, an executable product, if more likely to be a multiple-use product, needs an added protection against reselling.

Transfer Mode and Externalities

In terms of transfer modes, interactive services have not yet reached their full potential for technological reasons. But they may eventually become products and services with the highest level of value added. Real-time interactive applications, such as voice on the Internet, video conferencing, and multicasting based on MBONE, will change the way we access information and interact on the Internet. To support these activities, the Internet infrastructure is being upgraded with faster modems, wider bandwidths, reliable and real-time transfer modes, such as cell relays, asynchronous transfer mode (ATM), and new protocols to support transmission (see Kalakota and Whinston, 1996, for multimedia and multicast technologies). But the critical issue is whether these engineering solutions will be able to outpace interactive services' rapidly increasing demand for bandwidths.

For products with positive externalities, like computer programs and games, we see sellers trying to create profit opportunities based on the externality. By providing freeware and shareware, programmers can create credentials and a reputation and establish a certain market position which can later be recouped from corporate sales. Similar strategies can be used for time-dependent products. For example, news companies freely distribute headline news, but charge for other services. Since free news is used to attract potential customers, its positive externality works to the seller's advantage. Such almost-free transactions seem to contradict the commercial aspirations of potential Internet merchants. However, it is important to recognize that these strategies are based on the characteristics of digital products, not an indication that the Internet marketplace lacks copyright protection or commercial opportunities.

2.4. Summary

We have defined digital products and services in terms of their usage and physical characteristics, and offered a convenient taxonomy to classify various digital products, highlighting their fundamental differences. Digital products include all goods that are already in digital format or that can be digitized. Purely physical products can also be partially digitized when they are made into smart products equipped with digital interfaces. But an equally important area of digitization is the business process itself. All aspects of digital communication and processing can be considered to be digital products. In this way, electronic commerce extends to the commerce of physical products because many business transactions involving physical products can be digitized and be a part of digital electronic commerce.

The physical characteristics of digital products are fundamental and raise contentious issues, such as digital copyrights and the use of consumer information. At the same time, they are critical in analyzing digital markets in terms of many economic issues. For example, indestructibility relates to the issues of quality degradation, personal arbitrage, and the mode of retailing—sale, renting, leasing, or subscription. Transmutability is also fundamental in understanding product development, customization, and differentiation strategies. In the process of customizing a product, firms also have to deal with the problem of consumer information and privacy. Such issues are the topics of the remaining chapters.

References

Barlow, J.P., 1993. "Selling Wine Without Bottles: The Economy of Mind on the Global Net." Available in continuously evolving editions at various sites including http://icg.stwing.upenn.edu/cis590/reading.063.html.

Bulow, J., 1982. "Durable-Goods Monopolists." *Journal of Political Economy*, 90: 314–332.

Coase, R. H., 1972. "Durability and Monopoly." *Journal of Law and Economics*, 15: 143–149.

Gandal, N., 1994. "Hedonic Price Indexes for Spreadsheets and an Empirical Test for Network Externalities." *Rand Journal of Economics*, 25(1): 160–170.

Kalakota, R. and A.B. Whinston, 1996. *Frontiers of Electronic Commerce*. Reading, Mass.: Addison-Wesley.

Lotus v. Borland, 1996. Summary of the case and court briefs can be found at http://server.berkeley.edu/HTLJ/lvb/lvbindex.html. Economics professors' amicus brief to the U.S. Supreme Court can be found at http://www.Software.Industry.org/ issues/docs-htm/brf-econ.html.

Suggested Readings and Notes

Value of Information

Lave, L.B., 1963. "The Value of Better Weather Information to the Raisin Industry." *Econometrica* 31: 151–64.

Gould, J.P., 1974. "Risk, Stochasitic Preference, and the Value of Information." *Journal of Economic Theory* 8: 64–85.

Antonovitz, F., and T. Roe, 1986. "A Theoretical and Empirical Approach to the Value of Information in Risky Markets." *Review of Economics and Statistics* 68: 105–14.

Electronic Markets

McAfee, R.P. and J. McMillan, 1997. "Electronic Markets" in *Readings in Electronic Commerce*, Addison-Wesley. The authors discuss the economic implications of using electronic markets such as the Internet for various purposes where the administrative decision-making process and market pricing can be combined. They give several examples of functioning electronic markets.

Network Externalities

Katz, M. and C. Shapiro, 1986. "Technology Adoption in the Presence of Network Externalities." *Journal of Political Economy*, 94(4): 822–841. Discusses how one technology is adopted as a standard when there is a competing incompatible technology. They point out that a less efficient technology might dominate in a free entry market.

Farrell, J. and G. Saloner, 1985. "Standardization, Compatibility, and Innovation." *Rand Journal of Economics*, 16(1): 70–83. This paper examines the case where an industry standard acquires excess inertia which prevents the adoption of new and more efficient technologies.

Gandal, N., 1994, is an empirical test of the hypothesis that a computer software with compatibility with popular industry standards commands a higher price.

Economides, N., 1996. "The Economics of Networks." *International Journal of Industrial Organization*, 16(4): 673–699. This paper on network externalities compares the economic structure of networks with the structure of vertically related industries. Prof. Economides also maintains a web site devoted to the economics of networks at http://raven.stern.nyu.edu/networks/.

Internet Resources

Java Programming Language

Java was developed by Sun Microsystems and is a favored language for applets. SUN Java site is at http://www.javasoft.com.

Java FAQ list and tutorial are at http://sunsite.unc.edu/javafaq/javafaq.html.

Commercial Sites Index

Open Market maintains, with weekly updates, a listing of commercial sites and publishes it at http://www.directory.net/dir/statistics.html.

Virtual Museums and Florist

An exhibition of 18th-century French paintings is at http://www.culture.fr/lumiere/documents/files/imaginary_exhibition.html.

Smithsonian Photographs Online (http://photo2.si.edu/) has an interactive virtual exhibition on information technology, "Information Age: People, Information & Technology" at http://photo2.si.edu/infoage.html.

You can send virtual flowers online at http://www.virtualflowers.com/.

Medical Sites on the Internet

Medical web sites often contain in-depth information about diseases, an index of physicians, and abstracts and journal articles dealing with today's health issues. Although these are not interactive services as defined in the text, an examination of the following sites will give an indication on how future interactive medical services will look like on the net.

- American Medical Association (AMA): http://www.ama-assn.org. AMA web site also contains *JAMA*, Journal of the American Medical Association (http://www.ama-assn.org/public/journals/jama/jamahome.htm) and an HIV/AIDS information center (http://www.ama-assn.org/special/hiv/hivhome.htm).
- Center for Disease Control: http://www.cdc.gov
- Go Ask Alice: http://www.columbia.edu/cu/healthwise/alice.html
- Travel Health Online: http://www.ripprep.com
- Tripod's Ask the Doctor: http://www.tripod.com/living/ask_doc
- Typing Injury Archive: http://www.cs.princeton.edu/~dwallach/tifaq
- Women's Health Specialists at San Diego: http://www.planetearth.net/SanDiego/DrRoss/submit.html

CHAPTER 3

Internet Infrastructure and Pricing

Products and services native to the Internet range from access provision to subscription-based information services. As the Internet is privatized, a large body of economic literature has grown around how to price infrastructure and connection services. By now, the general public is well aware of the congestion and subscription pricing problems experienced by America Online Inc. (http://www.aol.com). Also, the converging telecommunications infrastructure has largely eliminated once-clear boundaries between telephone, cable, satellite, wireless, and Internet service industries, which are all vying to serve Internet communication and content businesses. This chapter provides an overview of Internet communications technology—which is part of the enabling technologies of electronic commerce along with computer hardware, software, and the multimedia industry—and reviews various ways to price the infrastructure and evaluate it in terms of economic efficiency.

3.1. Internet Pipelines

The network infrastructure of the Internet is similar to that of a telephone system. In fact, most of the Internet traffic travels on the same network used for local and long-distance telephone calls, which may consist of copper wires, coaxial cables, fiber-optic cables, and wireless and satellite systems. If you consider messages as water, the Internet infrastructure is a system of pipes of varying sizes. There are four levels of networks in this traffic distribution system: end users, Local Access Networks (LANs), regional networks, and backbone networks (see fig. 3.1).

- **End users.** Consumers and businesses that initiate and receive messages using their computers, modems, and other equipment. They connect to LANs either directly (a direct Ethernet connection or a dedicated ISDN line, for example) or through dial-up service by using a telephone or cable modem. This dial-up connection establishes only a temporary connection to the network.

- **Local Access Networks.** These networks are Internet service providers, university and research institutions, local access facilities of a commercial online service provider, and corporate servers that accept remote dial-up connections.

- **Regional networks.** These networks provide a bridge between LANs and various backbone networks. A regional network may cover an area within a state, a state-wide area, or several states, collecting messages and sending them to their destinations via the backbone network. Many of these mid-level regional networks have received support from the National Science Foundation (NSF), which operated a national backbone network called NSFnet from 1984 until 1996. Examples include California Education and Research Federation Network (CERFnet), the Southeastern Universities Research Association (SURAnet), THEnet of Texas, NYSERnet of New York, and Westnet of Colorado. When the NSFnet backbone was retired in 1996, these regional networks were able to direct their traffic through commercial backbone operators.

- **Backbone networks.** These networks carry Internet traffic between regional networks and, if a connection is not present, direct it to other interconnected backbone networks that have a connection to destination regional networks. A backbone network has a very high bandwidth made up of a fiber-optic network, often capable of sending hundreds of megabits per second. Backbone networks are also linked internationally. Mexico's networks, for example, are linked to the CERFnet via a satellite, as is the System Engineering Research Institute (SERI) of Seoul, Korea. EBONE provides backbone services to a consortium of European regional networks.

As regional networks are commercialized and their traffic is routed via three major commercial backbone carriers—AT&T, Sprint, and MCI—there may not be much difference to some LANs between regional and backbone networks. Commercial backbone carriers use the same networks they use for long-distance telephone traffic. In this sense, the Internet is not much different from traditional telephone networks as far as the infrastructure is concerned. What distinguishes the Internet is the way traffic is handled.

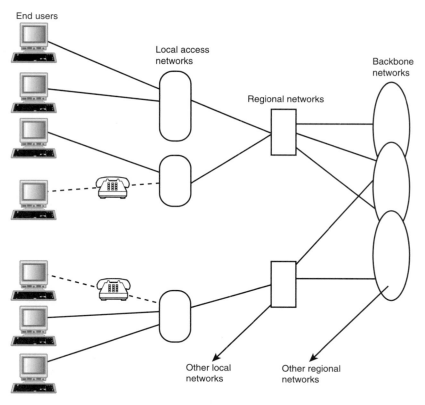

Figure 3.1 Internet network architecture.

3.2.   Traffic Control on the Internet

Messages sent through the pipeline system shown in figure 3.1—that is, the Internet—are delivered to their destination by a traffic control and distribution system called the Transmission Control Protocol/Internet Protocol (TCP/IP). In fact, the TCP/IP is a collection of protocols that include TCP and IP protocols as well as User Datagram Protocols (UDP), Internet Control Message Protocol (ICMP), and others. For purposes here, IP and TCP protocols are sufficient to understand how messages are sent and received on the Internet. This section examines three essential features of Internet traffic: packet switching, IP addresses and routing, and TCP protocol.

Packet Switching

The traditional telephone system transmits data—that is, voice—by using a circuit switching network (see fig. 3.2). When Alice (at 512-555-1122) calls Charlie (at 213-555-1212), for example, a circuit is opened via switches, connecting Alice and Charlie directly. This open circuit is maintained whether they are talking or not (that is, regardless of traffic). Note that if the switch at the area code 213 breaks down, Alice will not be able to call Charlie.

The Internet, on the other hand, uses a technology known as packet switching, which sends packets of data by way of routers. A message is broken down into many chunks of data called packets, each of which is more or less a few kilobytes long. Each packet contains necessary information such as the address for the destination—called an IP address.

Suppose, for example, that Alice sends a message to Charlie in a packet switching system where R1 through R6 represent computers and routers that check the address in each packet and forward it to the appropriate destination (see fig. 3.3). Rather than opening a circuit from Alice to Charlie, the Internet Protocol finds one route that is working on the IP network (that is, the Internet) and sends the packets through, for example, R1 to R2 to R6. If R2 or any of the component computers is unable to deliver the message or if R2's physical connection is down, Alice's packets may be routed through many alternative routes—through R4, for example (as figure 3.3 shows). This robust nature of messaging and the added bonus of economizing available physical circuits were the primary reason why ARPA (Advanced Research Projects Agency of the U.S. Defense Department) opted to use packet switching for its ARPAnet, the predecessor of the Internet.

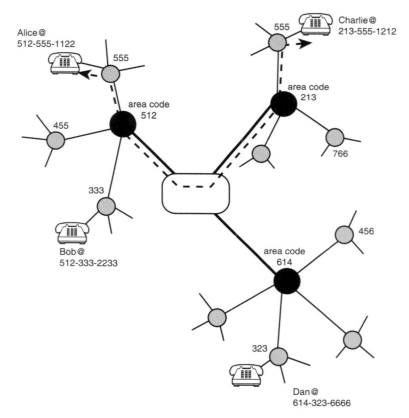

Figure 3.2 The circuit switching network of telephone technology.

Internet Protocol Addresses

Similar to telephone numbers, each Internet node or host has a unique address called an IP address, which is used to route messages. An IP address is defined by a 32-bit number—four 8-bit numbers. Each 8-bit (that is, 1 byte) number can specify 256 different sites—from 0 to 255 (or 00000000 to 11111111 in binary numbers). These four 8-bit numbers are separated by a period—for example, 128.83.124.55. The separator period represents a different class of network in a hierarchy; the computer with IP address 128.83.124.55 is connected to a higher level network with the address 128.83.124.* (class C network), which is again connected to a still higher network of 128.83.*.* (class B network). A class A network is denoted with only the first-level IP number.

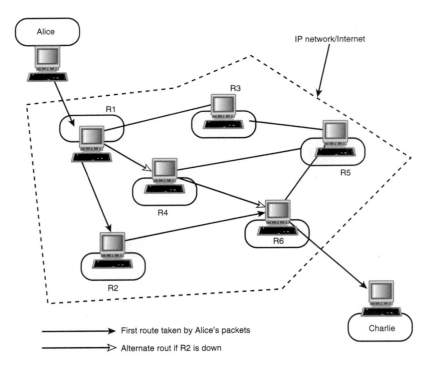

Figure 3.3 IP packet switching.

If a university network is assigned to a class B network as in 128.83, all its component sub-networks and computers share the same top two IP addresses. Its default IP address is referred to as 128.83.0.0, and its main server will typically have an IP address as 128.83.1.1. With 256 third-level and 256 fourth-level addresses, this class B network can accommodate more than

65,000 unique IP addresses in its network. A class C network can assign 256 IP addresses. Theoretically, there can be about 17 million class C networks (256 × 256 × 256) and over one trillion unique IP addresses. But many class A networks are reserved for special purposes—224 to 239 for multicasting, for example—and class B networks may not use all their assigned numbers. For these reasons, far fewer IP addresses are available.

This system of IP addresses is unique and provides a means of identifying all the component computers on the Internet. The class B network with 128.83.*.*, for example, may denote all University of Texas at Austin computers; the third level 124 may be those within the economics department; and finally the fourth level 55 may be a computer in the graduate lounge. This computer in turn may serve several graduate students by maintaining different account names, one of which may be specified as Charlie@128.83.124.55.

If Alice sends a message to Charlie, her message is broken down into several packets, each of which contains Charlie's IP address. Alice's computer searches to find out Charlie's location by sending inquiries to upper-level network servers until it locates Charlie's computer. Alice's computer also keeps a list of IP addresses, but it is usually limited to local addresses, unlike regional network servers that maintain a complete list. After Charlie's address is found, Alice's computer launches a program to send packets and monitor the progress.

Because the number-denominated IP addresses are hard to remember, domain names corresponding to each IP address are used instead. Therefore, Charlie's computer may have a domain name of eco1.utexas.edu. Each IP address is matched to a unique domain name by the Internet's Domain Name System (DNS). Domain names are also organized in a hierarchy. Typically, a working domain name consists of at least two names: a top-level domain name and a unique name. The top-level domains are *edu* for educational institutions, *com* for companies, *gov* for governments, and so on. Other top-level domains include countries such as *us* (the United States), *mx* (Mexico), *kr* (South Korea), and so forth. Seven new domains are added in 1997: *firm*, *store*, *web*, *arts*, *info*, *nom* (for individuals), and *rec* (for recreational sites). A unique domain name is added (but spelled first) to this top-level domain. The University of Texas domain name, for example, consists of utexas.edu. Computers within the utexas.edu network are also given unique names, which are called subdomains. In the preceding example, the domain name of Charlie's computer was eco1.utexas.edu.

Unlike IP addresses, there is no limit to the number of possible domain names. A single node may be known by different names as long as there is a way to map between domain names and their corresponding IP addresses. Such a database is kept in the DNS server, or nameserver, accessed by a router. A *router* is switching equipment that receives, forwards, and distributes each packet by matching IP addresses and domain names.

Transmission Control Protocol

IP takes care of addressing and finding the right destination. TCP is responsible for breaking a message into packets, sending the packets to the IP network, and reassembling them when received. TCP is actually one of many possible transmission protocols used for Internet traffic. When assembling received packets, TCP counts them and requests re-sends if some of them are missing or corrupted. On the other hand, User Datagram Protocol (UDP) is a protocol by which each packet is sent out without requiring an acknowledgment from the receiver. Unlike TCP, UDP does not check the integrity of each packet—that is, some noise is allowed—but its speed is well suited for real-time and Internet broadcasting applications. TCP is preferred for data transfers and remote applications such as Telnet.

Unicast, Broadcast, and Multicast

An efficient mechanism for resource allocation is needed to increase social welfare for limited resources such as the Internet. Such a mechanism needs to consider system-level (engineering) and economic solutions. An economic solution is based on efficient pricing strategies, discussed in the next section, that match available resources and uses. An engineering solution depends on a network's configuration and traffic control. If a telephone company were to build dedicated lines for 10 persons, for example, it would need to string 100 point-to-point lines to connect each one with everyone else. Such a system will never have a congestion problem, but will be costly and misallocate society's resources to redundant and seldom-used telephone lines. Instead, therefore, a telephone network uses a shared line and switching equipment to maximize the benefit from laying a system of wires.

The Internet network architecture is somewhat similar to the telephone network, but the Internet can support one-to-many (broadcast) distribution in addition to one-to-one (unicast) communication (the telephone system model). Unicasting is what was previously described: relaying messages from a sender to a receiver. As figure 3.4 shows, Alice can send a message to anyone who has a unique IP address. She can also broadcast the same message by sending it to multiple recipients. An automated system of broadcasting is a mailing list server that duplicates an incoming message and sends it out to all subscribers, who can then also respond to the message by broadcasting a reply. In this sense, the Internet is also used for many-to-many broadcasting. When broadcasting, however, Alice's message occupies a lot of the Internet's band-width between her and all her correspondents. When the traffic consists of heavy-duty multimedia files, the existing infrastructure suffers greatly from this unnecessary duplication.

Internet multicasting proposals are geared toward reducing the amount of traffic due to this redundancy in broadcasting by using a different method of routing messages. Suppose, for example, that Alice in Dallas wants to broad-cast her video clip on the Internet. Suppose also that there are 100 interested Internet surfers in Houston. By broadcasting, Alice's enormous video file will travel the network between Dallas and Houston 100 times, frustrating a Houston radiologist who is waiting for an X-ray file from a Dallas hospital. Alternatively, 100 Houstonians can subscribe to a multicast server in Houston, which locally distributes multicast messages. Alice then sends her file to a Dallas multicast host, which is connected to a multicast IP network (see fig. 3.4). Her file is sent over—or travels through—this network only once. Interested Houstonians connect to their local multicast server, which broadcasts the message. The term *multicasting* is used to distinguish this type of distribution from broadcasting.

One of the primary reasons for multicasting is to use the Internet infrastructure more efficiently and perhaps to prepare for the ever-increasing demand for bandwidth by real-time and multimedia applications. Although all feasible engineering and network solutions should be examined and implemented, the driving force behind a congested network is the consumer usage and preference for bandwidth. Economic research in infrastructure pricing is aimed at allocating resources by influencing consumption and investment behaviors, which the next section examines.

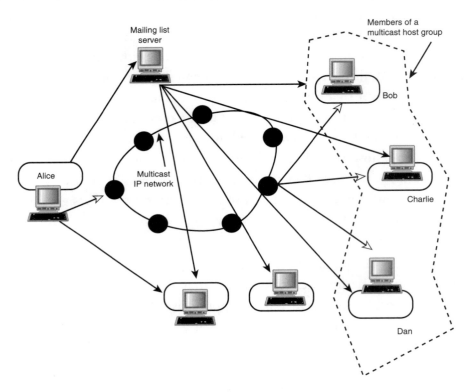

Figure 3.4 Various ways to send a message on the Internet.

3.3.   The Infrastructure Convergence

Although the TCP/IP protocol is decidedly different from circuit switching used for voice communication on telephone lines, the same physical wires and cables are used for both Internet and telephone communications. Furthermore, as voice and television signals are digitized, the same network and equipment can handle Internet, telephone, and cable data. As a result, this digital convergence is produced in the telecommunications infrastructure and the possibility of more competition and lower prices for voice, video, and Internet services. Appropriately, the Telecommunications Act of 1996 began deregulating component industries within the telecommunications sector, allowing competition in each other's turf. The major players in this convergence game include local telephone companies (Regional Bell Operating Companies or RBOCs), long distance carriers (LDCs), cable system operators (CSOs), wireless service providers, Internet service providers (ISPs), and computer hardware and software sellers. Each in this alphabet soup serves some portion of the Internet network.

The expected head-on competition between RBOCs and CSOs will be some years away, because the difference in switching technology constrains CSOs from providing one-to-one voice communications and RBOCs lack sufficient bandwidth to fully accommodate video services. Instead, competition from LDCs and Direct Broadcast Satellite (DBS) systems are proving to be more immediate to RBOCs and CSOs, respectively. In terms of Internet traffic, however, LDCs such as AT&T, Sprint, and MCI already handle a significant portion of the Internet's backbone traffic. Sprint alone carries about 50 percent of the long-haul traffic on the Internet. Likewise, RBOCs provide telephone lines for home users to dial up their ISPs. CSOs have also entered the Internet service market with high-bandwidth cable modems. Before discussing efficient Internet pricing and ownership structure in the following sections, an overview of how messages travel on the Internet is in order.

The Convergence in the Last Mile

The beginning of this chapter categorized three types of Internet service providers: Local Access Networks, regional networks, and backbone networks. LANs, typically called ISPs, are what consumers connect to from home. The number of ISPs has grown tremendously since 1991 when the U.S. government began privatizing the Internet. The Internet's backbone, which was fully funded by the National Science Foundation (NSF), has since retired; privately owned backbone networks now carry most of the Internet traffic. Also encouraged by the NSF, more regional networks were created. These regional networks sell ISPs access to the backbone networks. Even backbone operators and regional networks, however, may offer Internet service to consumers. For the purposes here, then, only two types of services need to be distinguished: the last mile service from a computer to an access point to the Internet, and the remaining long-haul service. The latter may involve a layer of service providers, including a dial-up ISP reseller, a regional network service, and a backbone operator. Of concern is the way consumers first gain access to any of these Internet network services, distinguishing it from the rest of Internet networks.

To use the highway analogy, the last mile consists of your driveway from the street and the streets in the neighborhood. Major city streets are ISPs and regional networks; highways are Internet backbones. An Internet user has multiple options to establish a connection to the Internet, including the following:

- Dial-up connection through plain, old copper wires (via RBOCs)
- Dial-up connection based on faster Integrated Services Digital Network (ISDN) service (via RBOCs)
- Direct connection through Local Area Network (LAN) and Ethernet (via ISPs)
- Coaxial connection using a cable modem (via CSOs)

Most home users rely on the first option—involving a RBOC and an ISP to complete the connection, with a maximum connection speed of less than 50 kbps (kilobits per second). An ISDN service is somewhat faster, ranging from

64 to 128 kbps. A direct LAN/Ethernet connection, usually available in workplaces and on university campuses, can range from 1 to 10 mbps (megabits per second). This speed is possible because a LAN is directly connected to a system—a firm, a university, or an ISP.

The first two (slow) options are based on traditional twisted pair copper wires, which are akin to one-lane driveways. The ISDN and more recent Asymmetrical Digital Subscriber Line (ADSL) increase the capacity of existing wires by compressing messages, achieving the rate of 1.5 to 3 mbps with ADSL. Coaxial cables used by CSOs can carry much more traffic; and using cable modems, they offer a much faster speed of 10 mbps or more. Unfortunately, faster options are available in limited areas and require significant investments in additional equipment.

A faster, direct connection today requires a physical connection to an ISP. But the next generation Internet traffic may very well bypass traditional telephone or cable networks and connect users via satellites, offering still another option to access the Internet. Primarily targeted for mobile computing, low earth orbital satellites (LEOS) can interact with transponders in personal computers, which can send and receive data without involving RBOCs or CSOs. Such wireless communications begin to dominate many business sectors. Cable subscribers, through Direct Broadcast Satellites, currently account for less than 10 percent of the cable television market, but the share is growing rapidly. Similarly, long-distance telephone companies may use satellite links to bypass local access exchanges. Even local exchanges can be constructed entirely with cell phone networks. Some predict that wireless networks will be used for voice communication, while wired—coaxial and fiber—networks will be carrying multimedia contents.

ISPs, RBOCs, and CSOs are the major players in Internet connection services for end users. An ISP typically leases a line from a larger ISP or a regional network provider to transport Internet messages, for which it pays about 25 to 40 percent of total costs (Srinagesh, 1995). This connection ranges from a 56 kbps line to a 1.5 mbps (T1) connection to a very high T3 at 45 mbps. Remaining costs include equipment such as servers, modems and routers, leased telephone lines from an RBOC, and customer service expenses. According to an estimate by *Forbes* (as quoted in Srinagesh, 1995), a small ISP provider in 1993 needed to invest about $30,000 for equipment—representing sunk costs—and $1,000 per month for telephone connections. Larger ISPs have larger sunk costs because they often have their own backbone networks and equipment. These ISPs are intermediaries that pay long-haul carriers for IP transport and offer individuals access to the Internet at a price. A dial-up connection usually costs from $10 to $30 a month, in addition to any charge for telephone connection. In comparison, cable companies charge about $40 a month for Internet access using cable modems.

The simple fact that a consumer can connect to the Internet via telephone, television cable, wireless, or a direct connection highlights the nature of infrastructure convergence. In terms of bandwidth, CSOs are in a superior position over their competitors. If voice, video, and data transports were to be handled by a single connection to a home, coaxial cables would offer the best capacity for the necessary last mile. In other words, when cars are bigger than 18-wheelers, a much larger driveway will be needed even when trips are made only occasionally. But telephone companies are meeting the bandwidth challenge through compression technologies and by rewiring homes from curbs. CSOs on the other hand seem to focus on the plain, old television broadcasting.

Today's infrastructure convergence will change the economics of the last mile—that is, the way consumers connect to the infrastructure, be it for the Internet, telephone, or television. As market boundaries fall, the same converging force has the potential to produce a few firms with significant market power across many industries. Perhaps, only one pipeline—a telecommunication monopoly—may handle all types of data transfers from home. A raging debate about who will be that monopolist has already begun. Some argue that CSOs have the advantage in bandwidth because their coaxial cables can carry more data than telephone's twisted copper wires. RBOCs, however, are more familiar with switching technologies and two-way communications, and as a result they are well positioned to expand their business into the Internet service provider market and cable television. Cable operators face a significant amount of investment before they can compete in voice and Internet data transfers (Benerofe and Kissane, 1996). Unlike the horizontal market monopolization of a century ago, however, today's convergence is not recognized as a potentially anticompetitive threat. Telecommunications research and policy must focus on anticompetitive issues such as vertical and inter-industry integration by telecommunications firms, which Chapter 11 discusses in more detail.

The increasing intensity in the debate about access charges and tax policies mirrors the high stake in the battle for the last mile fought among RBOCs, ISPs, and LDCs. The peculiar pricing structure of the Internet, or the lack of it, has prompted a necessary debate about Internet access prices both among academics, as discussed in the previous section, and in courts and the Congress. Especially poignant is the conflict between local ISPs and RBOCs. Although RBOCs have traditionally relied on a complicated fee schedule—distinguishing type of usage, time, and distance—to recover their fixed costs, the Internet traffic on their local loop is neither distinguished from voice nor priced according to usage. Efficient prices, however, have to be applied not only to telephone calls to an ISP but also to the Internet traffic itself (that is, IP transport on the backbone). RBOCs themselves have entered into backbone business along with LDCs and large regional ISPs. (Chapter 11 elaborates on the issue of Internet access charges involving the FCC and other taxation topics.)

Long-Haul Traffic

Three LDCs—AT&T, Sprint, and MCI—carry most of the Internet long-haul traffic. As mentioned earlier, Sprint, which is growing faster than AT&T or MCI, alone accounts for about half of all Internet backbone traffic (Bernier 1996). LDCs' backbone networks are the same fiber-optic networks that carry long distance telephone calls. The data travels through fiber networks at a hyper-fast rate of 52 mbps to 2.5 gbps (gigabits per second) based on Synchronous Optical Network (SONET) standards. Faster and more reliable communications are possible as new technologies and standards are implemented, such as frame relay technology and cell relay based on switched multimegabit data service (SMDS) and asynchronous transfer mode (ATM) (see "Internet Resources" at the end of this chapter).

Other commercial services that offer national and international connectivity with their own backbones include UUNET, AlterNet, and PSINet in the U.S., and Datalink (Finland), EUNET (Europe), SWIPnet (Sweden), and so on, and commercial online services such as America Online, CompuServe, and Microsoft Network. These networks are interconnected and accessible through access points known as Commercial Internet Exchange (CIX, pronounced "kicks"). Many regional and smaller local networks are also connected to the Internet through CIX. The interconnection arrangement among CIX members—and with commercial carriers—is just an agreement to honor each other's traffic without an elaborate system of metering and pricing usage. Again, efficient prices are not implemented.

Increasingly, it is the case that a backbone operator may offer Internet services directly to consumers. AT&T's Worldnet, InternetMCI, and SprintLink, for example, offer Internet services at a monthly fee comparable to that of local ISPs. Still, consumers must go through local RBOCs to dial up. But unlike long distance calls, for which they pay RBOCs metered usage charges, LDCs pay only fixed monthly fees for their telephone connections. Suppose that AT&T offers Internet long distance calls through its Internet service. These calls go through the same networks as if made by a telephone (from a local interchange through AT&T and to a destination interchange, and vice versa). RBOCs, however, do not collect usage fees that they need to recover fixed costs for their local infrastructure. As a result of the Telecommunications Act of 1996, RBOCs themselves are merging and establishing national networks, potentially duplicating existing infrastructure owned by LDCs and national ISPs. In this battle of giants, local ISPs will find it hard to survive. And if a telephone network were a natural monopoly, the Internet infrastructure would have to be another, for which efficient prices and regulations would have to be implemented to ensure its growth and to maximize social benefits. The future information infrastructure may consist of many networks, each specializing in one type of data—wireless for voice, coaxial cables for multimedia, and fiber-optic cables for long hauls, for example. Of course, efficient prices will also facilitate in allocating resources to their most efficient uses.

3.4.   Congestion and Infrastructure Pricing

We have been witnessing the transformation of the Internet from being an academic and research network into a medium for fun, education, exploration, communication, propaganda, and, most of all, for doing business, aided by the spread of the World Wide Web, networked computing, and electronic commerce. Congestion is beginning to cripple network performance, however, substantially diminishing the net benefits of users and service providers. To witness, Dan Rather on the CBS television news on the election night, November 5, 1996, reported the near collapse of the Internet due to people trying to access election results nationwide. America Online instituted a monthly flat-rate, only to be inundated by complaints (and lawsuits) from its members being frustrated by congestion. The Internet, in the short time it received spotlight in the popular press, has acquired its ignominious nickname: the World Wide Wait.

These problems are inherent in the current Internet infrastructure and are likely to grow worse for at least the following three reasons:

- The number of people who have acquired Internet connectivity is doubling every year. Further, the bandwidth requirements of future multimedia applications such as video conferencing and movies-on-demand are orders of magnitude greater than current uses (which are predominantly text-based). Although bandwidth capacity is increasing dramatically (from 56 kbps a decade ago to 45 mbps currently and 1 gbps in the near future), it is doubtful that capacity growth can keep up with demand growth, and in any event serious bottlenecks will remain at the connection pipelines to the backbone. Hence, key resources are and will remain scarce for the foreseeable future.

- The pricing strategies of infrastructure owners and access providers complicate the issue. Infrastructure owners charge flat fees for access, and access providers use either a price based on time of usage, or, as recent trends indicate, a flat monthly fee. Neither takes the level of congestion into account. A "tragedy of the commons" emerges in which the social value generated by the Internet is diminished by overuse and inefficient use.

- The system rations resources according to user patience rather than social value. Although impatient users will voluntarily leave a congested network, they are not necessarily the low-value users. Without incentive-compatible priorities, mission critical applications have no guarantee of precedence over others, or any expected level of performance. A teenager with idle time can download tetrabytes of entertaining video clips, blocking a cardiac surgeon from receiving vital X-ray data from a distant hospital in time to save a patient.

The challenge is how to manage the traffic and resources in a manner that permits the full realization of the potential of the Internet. Current efforts to manage network resources fall into two basic categories:

- Engineering fixes, and
- Non-incentive-compatible priority schemes

The engineering fixes involve substantial increases in capacity at bottlenecks—which are overloaded routers, regional networks, Internet access points, modem banks, and local telephone lines. This approach may work in the short term; however, it is expensive and is doomed to fail in the long-run because bandwidth use will always expand to fill the available capacity. There is no apparent upper limit on bandwidth uses. If capacity is expanded to handle real-time video, 3-D imaging will demand more bandwidth, and after that virtual reality, and so on. Further, the congestion that arises from the current inefficient pricing schemes can lead to inappropriate and ineffective infrastructure investments.

The next generation Internet Protocol IPv6 (Deering and Hinden, 1995) is trying to address the performance issue by moving away from a best-effort, first-come first-serve approach to one of differentiating traffic based on priority classes and associating priorities with different application classes. Such solutions, however, still do not consider the criticality of the usage context and are prone to misuse. Just because a video stream requires better response time, for example, it does not mean a recreational video should be preferred over a simple text stream being used for a stock purchase. Moreover, the priority selection in IPv6 is non-incentive-compatible: Nothing prevents a user or application from artificially boosting its priority to achieve better performance.

Recent research in computer science has been increasingly drawing from economic theory to design resource allocation schemes, otherwise referred to as load balancing schemes. Economics, being the study of resource allocation problems, can provide answers, and the standard economic answer is to create markets and let prices allocate the scarce resources. The economic answer for the Internet, however, is a bit more complicated. First, because most of the costs are sunk into infrastructure, the marginal cost of Internet data transport is essentially zero, so if Internet resources were private goods prices should be zero. Note that this discussion separates the process of data transport from the process of producing the information content of the packet being transported, and focuses now on the former. Second, Internet resources are public goods and consequently congestion is a potential negative externality. Marginal-cost pricing of public goods can lead to a "tragedy of the commons," in which the common resource is overutilized, causing avoidable losses for the whole society. When negative externalities are real possibilities, prices should exceed the marginal cost of production by the marginal social cost of the congestion, in which case a consumer uses the resource if and only if his or her private benefit from use exceeds the social cost of that usage. This is the theoretical economic argument underpinning virtually all proposals for usage-based pricing of Internet resources. Differences in how to implement this theoretical ideal separate the different proposals.

One potential barrier to the adoption of a more rational, economics-based approach toward resource allocation is social. People have become accustomed to thinking of computing resources as "free," and may find even a nominal charge objectionable. Users should recognize that the current system does not make limited resources "free," however, but instead exacts its pound of flesh for using a congested web site in terms of *time* (one of our most precious limited resources). Because time is valuable, every user should be willing to pay something if that will significantly reduce his or her waiting for web sites. Economic theory suggests that, if properly structured, rationing resources by price rather than by having people wait in queues will, on balance, leave people more satisfied. Further, during uncongested off-peak times the optimal congestion prices will be zero, so users with very low values of time can reallocate their usage in a manner that avoids monetary charges.

The following subsections provide a critical survey of a number of proposals for pricing Internet transport services. As a benchmark for comparing these proposals, the discussion begins with the theoretical ideal of optimal dynamic priority pricing. Then auctions (or smart markets), flat-rate pricing, and voluntary declaration schemes are considered.

Ideal Economic Pricing Proposals

The economic foundations for optimal congestion pricing are deeply routed, going back at least to Pigou (1928) and Vickrey (1969). To illustrate, consider the classic case of a congested highway. The travel time between city A and city B depends on the total volume of traffic. For simplicity, suppose each citizen makes one trip per morning, but that some people have the option of making their trip at non-congested times. Typically, travel time is an increasing function of traffic volume and increases at a rapid rate as the traffic volume nears the capacity of the highway. In deciding whether to travel during the congested period, a citizen compares the incremental benefit of travel to this incremental private time cost, and makes the trip if and only if the former exceeds the latter.

From the point of view of the entire community, however, the social cost of travel time is the sum of every citizen's private time costs. If some citizen decides to make an extra trip, the additional social cost is the extra travel time born by all citizens, not just the citizen making the extra trip. Only those citizens whose incremental benefit from traveling during the congested period exceeds the incremental social cost should do so, and the others should postpone their travel to uncongested periods.

Hence, if the price of highway access is zero at all times, too many citizens will decide to travel during the congested period, because they are not facing the full social costs. The theoretical economic solution is to set the price of highway access during the congested period equal to the incremental social cost—called the optimal congestion toll. Then, by comparing the incremental benefit of travel with the total cost (congestion toll + private time cost), each citizen will voluntarily make the socially optimal decision.

In addition to achieving a socially optimal resource allocation for the existing highway, socially optimal pricing provides correct signals for evaluating capital investment decisions. Without optimal pricing, there is a bias toward inefficient capacity. To see this, simply observe that, starting from a free access policy, social benefits can be increased by implementing optimal pricing without any additional capital investment, while under free access the same increase in gross social benefits would require costly capital investment. Further, with free access an additional million dollars of capacity will generate fewer social benefits for two main reasons. First, the social benefits are diminished by the congestion that accompanies increased demand. And second, the distribution of the new capacity over the highway network will very likely be inefficient. To see the last point, consider two bottlenecks, one near an industrial site and the other near a shopping center. Because shopping trips can be more easily spread over time, optimal congestion tolls could virtually eliminate the congestion near the shopping center. Because of the relative inflexibility of work schedules, however, considerable congestion would remain at the industrial site. With optimal congestion tolls, the new capacity would be concentrated near the industrial site, and with free access the new capacity would be spread over both sites, thereby producing less total benefits for the entire community.

A major impediment to congestion tolls for physical highways has been the cost of administering such a system. Toll booths add considerable delay costs to travelers, thereby negating the congestion-reducing benefits of the tolls. Even when technologies are introduced to physical highways, costs of setting up remote sensors in cars and roadway check points are substantial. When addressing electronic highways, however, it is technologically feasible to compute and assess charges with negligible administrative cost. Thus, the Information Superhighway may be the first real-world instance in which congestion tolls are practical.

Dynamic Optimal Pricing

This economic theory was first applied to computing environments by Naor (1969), Mendelson (1985), and Pick and Whinston (1989). Stahl and Whinston (1991, 1992) and Gupta, Stahl, and Whinston [GSW] (1996) extended these single-server models to network computing environments and investigated its practicality by using simulation. Subsequently, GSW (1995a-c) applied their network models to the Internet.

At the center of the GSW approach is a general mathematical representation of a computing network, a model of price- and time-sensitive user demand for services, and a stochastic model of traffic flows and buffers. It shows that a socially optimal allocation of scarce network resources can be achieved by imposing optimal priority pricing at each site of potential congestion. The optimal prices depend on the traffic flow at the site, the size of the packets, the priority class, and the social cost of time. The latter can be econometrically estimated from the sensitivity of traffic to actual price and throughput time fluctuations at the site. Gupta et al. (1997), for example, present a new nonparametric technique for estimating users' value of time from usage data in real time, and show that these real-time estimates are sufficiently accurate to cause no significant loss in the social benefits of optimal pricing (using these estimates) as compared to the benchmark case with perfect information. In GSW, a practical decentralized method of determining optimal prices in real time is proposed. A simulation model is constructed that demonstrates the feasibility of this proposal.

In GSW (1995a-c), the simulation model is calibrated to represent the Internet and to compare the historical free-access policy with the theoretical optimal pricing (see fig. 3.5). This calibrated simulation suggests that without effective management of the Internet (as provided by efficient pricing), congestion and misallocation of resources could cost the economy tens of billions of dollars of lost benefits per year. This same simulation also demonstrates that the potential social gains of optimal pricing, if sought solely from capacity expansion, could have a capital investment cost exceeding the social gains. Thus, they argue that congestion is a very real concern and not just a theoretical fine point.

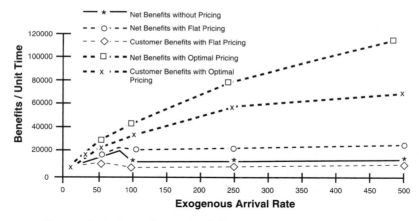

Figure 3.5 Benefits with different pricing strategies.

In the GSW vision, a typical user deciding whether and when to access an Internet service would be presented with a menu of options including the monetary cost and (when relevant) expected throughput time for each option. The options would specify a priority class, and could also include a security/anonymity level, minimum guaranteed qualities, and contingency options such as "submit the service request when the cost falls below $b." The user would then select the most preferred option. A personalized smart agent could automate the user's decision process based on previously specified user preferences. Frequently updated price and time information would come from the user's access provider. Smart agent software could serve this function also, gathering information from posted prices of transport providers and network congestion status reports.

The user would not receive a bill from each node and link of the network, but would rather receive one bill from his access provider for the posted price of that access provider for the service requested. * In turn, the access provider would receive a bill from the transport providers to which it is connected based on posted prices and actual usage. Each network transport provider needs to keep accounts only for the adjacent providers to which it is connected, not the individual users. In the vertical direction, each telecommunication carrier (such as AT&T, MCI, Sprint) need to keep accounts only for the networks (such as PSI, AlterNet, ANS, and so forth) to which it provides IP transport. This disaggregated pricing and billing approach mirrors the wholesale pricing practices in most industries. Ultimately it is the responsibility of the access providers to charge the user and to cover its costs vis-a-vis the transport providers.

Capital investment decisions can be greatly improved by the imposition of optimal priority pricing. First, as demonstrated in GSW (1995), imposition of priority pricing alone may generate more benefits at much less cost than the cost of capacity expansion. Second, without priority pricing—because the physical resource allocation is inefficient—the observed congestion can be a bad signal about which parts of the infrastructure should be expanded first. By imposing optimal pricing first, the distribution of network traffic can change significantly, revealing a different ranking of the bottlenecks. Thus with optimal pricing, capital investment can be focused on projects that will produce the greatest benefits.

Although the general model deals with potential congestion anywhere in a computing network, in practice the most likely sites of congestion are the 56-or-less kbps pipelines and modems to information content providers, their LANs, and servers. Thus in the near term, while there is still excess capacity on

---

* Recall that we are dealing with network transport services only. The user might well receive bills for the content of the data transported from many independent content providers.

the backbone, optimal congestion pricing will be most effective for these bottlenecks. As data-intensive real-time video uses grow, however, congestion could very likely become a serious problem on the backbone as well, in which case optimal priority pricing will become a valuable tool for resource allocation throughout the Internet.

Static Priority Pricing

Cocchi, Shenker, Estrin, and Zhang—CSEZ—(1993) pose the general problem of designing a service discipline and a pricing scheme that maximizes time-averaged user benefits. A *service discipline* is a mechanism implemented by the network operators to assign jobs to specific service classes (such as best-effort, virtual connection, guaranteed minimum delay, and so forth), and a pricing scheme associates a price (by bandwidth usage) to each service class (see also Shenker, 1995). CSEZ specifically investigate a standard two-priority service discipline. Theoretically, there is an optimal allocation of user demands to each priority, and there are prices for each priority such that each user facing those prices will voluntarily select the socially optimal priority. Using a simulation model, CSEZ demonstrate that optimal priority prices can be found that significantly increase the benefits over a single priority discipline and the corresponding usage pricing. [*] CSEZ do not present a computational algorithm for these prices, so this discussion cannot assess the practical feasibility of that crucial task. From the mathematical model, it appears that a central authority would need vast amounts of proprietary information from the users about the value of each class of service, but the users have incentives to misreport that information.

These priority prices are "static" in the sense that they do not vary with the dynamic state of the network. There will be times when the network is badly congested and high-priority users will be paying too little. Moreover, in contrast with optimal dynamic pricing by facility, the CSEZ scheme effectively has a high-priority user paying a premium at every facility even if only some or none are congested.

---

[*] Unlike GSW, CSEZ model the user demands as inelastic with respect to cost; Shenker (1995) acknowledges the importance of elastic demand.

The Smart-Market Approach

MacKie-Mason and Varian (1995) have proposed a different approach to implementing optimal congestion pricing. Instead of using econometric methods to estimate the social cost of congestion, they propose a mechanism in which the users have incentives to state their true willingness to pay for faster service. This, it is claimed, can be accomplished by an incentive-compatible auction—or smart market.

Suppose that users want a fixed number of jobs processed in a given time interval. In what order should the jobs be done? Let each person submit a monetary bid for the right to have his or her job processed. Submitted bids are ordered from the largest to the smallest, and the jobs are processed in this order. The price paid by every processed job is the bid of the first job not processed during the allotted time interval. If all jobs are processed, the price is zero. It is optimal for every user to bid the true value of the job, no matter what the other users do. To see this, note that bidding more will increase your chances of having your job processed only in those cases where the price you pay turns out to be greater than the true value of your job, and bidding less will only decrease your chances of having your job processed without affecting the price you pay.

MacKie-Mason and Varian propose that the Internet operators run smart markets for packets at every potential site of congestion. Each user includes a bid in the header of every packet. The network gateways carry out the sorting at frequent periodic intervals. Under this scheme, every packet would suffer a one period delay, while packets are being queued and bids sorted, before proceeding to the normal routing and transmission function. Besides this deadweight loss of time, there are other theoretical and practical problems with this approach.

The efficiency properties of the smart market pertain to a static situation in which (1) all potential users care only about whether their job is done or when, but not both; (2) all potential users are present at the auction; and (3) the value of the job is not contingent on any other market. All these assumptions are violated in a dynamic stochastic network. First, potential users value their jobs and delay time differently, so they care about both whether and when their job is done. Second, observe that to work in real time, bidding must be confined to fixed intervals of time; hence, jobs that arrive later, even nanoseconds later, have no influence on the current price. In contrast, the fully optimal congestion prices depend on the extra delay imposed on all future arrivals. This "generational" bias will cause inefficiencies in resource allocation just as citizens in a republic may squander natural resources because the unborn cannot vote. Third, the value of having a packet transmitted is contingent on having other related packets transmitted also. No matter how a user allocates bids among the thousands of packets that comprise a single Internet transaction, ex post regret will be rampant. Sometimes almost all packets will get through without incurring any significant charge, but the last crucial few will get dropped, so the user will wish the bid had been concentrated on the packets that encountered congestion. Other times, a few crucial packets will get dropped first (but after all others have begun their journey), and the user will have wasted bids on the later, now worthless, packets. Of course, you can imagine an elaborate accounting system to ameliorate these problems, or a dynamic bidding process in which each packet could communicate with the others so as to coordinate their bids as every packet proceeds through the network. Both of these fixes, however, are clearly impractical.

Connection-Only and Flat-Rate Pricing

By far the predominant forms of pricing currently in practice are combinations of connection-only and flat-rate pricing. The connection-only fee is usually based on the bandwidth of the user's connection for a contracted period of time, with discounted rates for longer-term contracts (Srinagesh, 1995). Recently, some frame relay networks began offering a Committed Information Rate (CIR) on top of a low maximum bandwidth connection fee. Users who stay within the CIR are guaranteed uninterrupted transport service, but if they exceed the CIR, they receive best-effort service only. Many customers, to the surprise of the providers, however, set the CIR to zero (Clark, 1995). Moreover, because the users do not face the full social cost of their usage decisions, connection fees cannot induce the socially optimal reallocation of demands during congested times.

In addition to these fixed connection fees, some providers charge a variable fee based on active connection time. Online service providers usually charge hourly fees if one goes over the maximum hours allowed monthly. Some online service providers, such as Netcom, prefer to forgo flat connection fees altogether in favor of variable fees. Because there is a positive correlation between connection time and bytes transmitted, one could view connection time fees as an indirect measure of bandwidth usage. It is important to recognize that connection time is not an accurate measure of bandwidth usage, however, and it obviously does not discriminate between a real-time video session and an e-mail session. Hence it does not confront the user with the correct social cost of his specific usage.

Flat-rate pricing consists of a fee for a set bandwidth that does not vary with the level of actual bandwidth usage nor the current state of congestion. America Online offers flat-rate—a sort of "all you can eat"—pricing, and New Zealand and Chile have experimented with flat-rate pricing for their international link. The latter has had a bad experience primarily due to two disjoint competing networks, which raises the important issue of whether ideal socially optimal solutions can be implemented in privately owned competing networks (see the section entitled "Public Policy and Infrastructure").

Because flat-rate pricing is a usage-based scheme, it can potentially improve the efficiency of the resource allocation over that which would prevail under non-usage based schemes. The model of GSW could be modified to solve for the best flat-rate prices by imposing this as a feasibility constraint on the optimization problem. Alternatively, the GSW simulation model could be calibrated to represent the time-averaged stochastic flows (over say a month or a year) and then take the time-averaged optimal congestion tolls as an approximation to the optimal flat-rate prices. GSW (1995b) did this time-averaging of the dynamic prices at each server in the network, and then imposed these prices. They found that per-packet prices for each server did indeed improve the efficiency of the network, but not nearly to the extent achieved by dynamic optimal pricing (refer back to fig. 3.5).

Part of the reason for the disappointing performance of per-packet pricing by server was the lack of a component that depends of the size of the "job." Optimal pricing imposes much higher prices for large jobs than for small jobs, because large jobs would impose disproportionately longer delays for the users whose jobs arrive after large jobs. Optimal nonlinear pricing causes a reallocation away from the large jobs toward the small jobs. Within the backbone where packet sizes are standardized—for example, in a cell relay used in asynchronous transfer mode (ATM)—shouldn't optimal pricing be a single per-packet fee? The answer is that the fee should be based on the number of contiguous packets from a single user sent forward, because that is the correct measure of how much the user's demand on the system potentially delays other users. * The packet-switching technology potentially breaks up contiguous packets into smaller sets, but does not completely eliminate them (due to the tail-trop first-in-first-out (FIFO) queue discipline). Only when there is excess capacity on the backbone, will a single per-packet fee be optimal (and that fee would be zero).

Moreover, the benefits generated in the GSW simulation of per-packet pricing came from load balancing—the redirection of traffic away from congested servers toward non-congested servers due to the relevant price signals. Minimalist flat-rate pricing (for example, Anania and Soloman, 1995) would establish a single usage fee independent of the nodes and links in the network that are used, thereby undermining even these load-balancing benefits. ** If Internet traffic were fairly uniform—characterized by an average flow with a relatively small variance and standard sized non-contiguous packet streams—a well-coordinated layered regional system of flat-rate pricing might achieve much of the maximum attainable efficiency. Internet traffic is anything but uniform, however. It is characterized by frequent irregular bursts of contiguous

* Imagine you are approaching the ticket office at the entrance to a football stadium along with 30 other people. Presumably you would rather see them arriving individually rather than in buses, because if you are "second" in line there is one person ahead of you in the individual scenario while there are 30 people ahead of you in the bus scenario. In the latter, you have a larger expected waiting time and a larger variance in waiting time.

** Existing router algorithms achieve some load-balancing to the extent that they can route traffic around congested nodes and links, but they cannot change the final destinations. In contrast, pricing that depends on the destination server can induce users to redirect their demands.

packets, and the variance in flow tends to increase more than proportional to the average flow. In such an environment, there are huge potential efficiency gains from better resource allocation during and between bursty periods (Edell et al., 1994). These gains can only be realized by dynamic optimal pricing.

Voluntary User Declarations

Bohn et al. (1993) propose a classification of services and assignment of priorities to those classes, asking individual users to voluntarily choose the appropriate classification. This choice would be recorded in the Type of Service (TOS) field of the IP header, but prices would not depend on the choice. The effectiveness of this scheme would depend on each user selecting the correct category, even though he has clear incentives to always choose the class associated with the highest priority. Recognizing this incentive compatibility problem, Bohn et al. suggest that occasional inspection of the packet streams and TOS field coupled with penalties for false classification could be used to enforce compliance. It is not clear, however, how such an inspection/enforcement system would be implemented nor how effective it would be. Others (for example, Kelly, 1995) have proposed that optimal prices could be posted but not charged, and that these "virtual" prices could act as guidelines that induce users to voluntarily modify their demands to bring about an efficient allocation of network resources.

It is extremely naive to assume that individual users will act in the best interest of the whole system when that conflicts with his or her private interests. Tragedies of the commons are very real phenomena, and the Internet could become another tragedy.

Synopsis

This discussion has surveyed the range of proposals for infrastructure pricing and priorities to solve the ever present congestion problems on the Internet. The GSW proposal for dynamic congestion tolls is close to the ideal economic solution and purports to be implementable in real time, whereas the proposals based on static models and flat-rate pricing are unlikely to significantly improve the efficiency of the Internet.

There are, however, practical and political barriers to implementing the GSW proposal. First, gone are the days of the government controlled Internet. The current and future Internet is a private enterprise endeavor consisting of a large number of infrastructure owners, each in business to make money. In the presence of a negative externality (such as congestion), it is a well-known economic result that the private market outcome will not be socially optimal, and the socially optimal outcome cannot be achieved by private markets.

Just what the private market outcome will be remains an open economic question. If the current state is any indication of the future, it appears unlikely that, in a competitive outcome, the private infrastructure owners will charge anything close to optimal congestion tolls, implying that the Internet will become a "tragedy of the commons," significantly eroding the potential benefits of electronic commerce. Moreover, in the current "anti-regulatory" climate, it is unlikely that governments will step in to protect the public interest.

In the world of private intranets, however, optimal congestion tolls may come to be. *Intranets* are owned by a corporation and for the exclusive use of corporate users to ensure maximum security of sensitive corporate information. As such, the corporation has every incentive to impose optimal congestion tolls internally to achieve efficient utilization of its own resources.

3.5. Public Policy and Infrastructure

In the face of such dramatic growth of the Internet, an in-depth understanding of the ownership structure of network and service providers, the pricing policies of those entities, and public regulatory policies are critical to the realization of the potential benefits. Non-competitive structures, inefficient pricing, and misguided public policy could foster a tragedy of the commons.

The ownership structure of the network determines the kinds of public policies pertinent in the obvious sense that with public ownership pricing policies could be imposed directly, while with private ownership regulatory policies are needed to influence pricing.

One very important public policy issue is equity: Should some classes of users (such as students, teachers, the poor, and so forth) be given special treatment to ensure equitable or fair access privileges. Because pricing is seen by many as a barrier to access for deserving potential users, this issue must be addressed. Partly because the Internet has historically been a free good, and partly because everyone likes a "free lunch," there is an entrenched interest group opposed to any form of usage-based pricing. Although it may appear that there is a dilemma between equity and efficiency, there is a straightforward economic solution: Optimal pricing should be imposed, and user classes deemed by the government to warrant subsidies should be awarded grants to supplement their own budgets for Internet activities.

Public Policy for a Publicly Owned Network

Obviously the goal of public policy should be to promote the full realization of the potential benefits of the network for the society as a whole. Although easy to state, this goal could be distorted by special interest groups desiring to exploit proprietary technologies and to appropriate potential public rents for private pockets. Nevertheless, because of the extensive externalities associated with the Internet and electronic commerce, a strong case can be made for a strong public role.

In countries where the network infrastructure as well as the access providers are governmental entities, the direct approach would be to establish a legislative mandate for the efficient operation of the network for the common good by means that include appropriate pricing. Recognizing the longevity of the infrastructure (fiber optics and cables), debt-financing of the required capital investment would be necessary and justified. Bandwidth usage fees should not be used to cover fixed costs—that would induce a loss of potential benefits and retard the growth of the network community. Usage fees should be based only on variable operating costs and congestion costs. Fixed costs should be recovered via connection fees and general taxation.

The public would need to guard against the possibility that the upper-level management of the network authority might attempt to distort prices or restrict capacity in ways that increase revenues, perhaps using some of this to increase its own compensation and benefits directly and indirectly.

Even if the infrastructure is owned and operated by the government, there will undoubtedly be many cases in which access and content services are provided by private entities. Because users will interact through the access providers, the pricing policies of these providers will directly impact the performance of the network. Some access providers, for example, may attempt to attract customers by smoothing the temporal fluctuations in its costs and offering customers more stable prices. Excess smoothing, however, will undermine the capability of dynamic pricing to guide the resource allocation decisions toward the socially optimal levels. Thus, even with optimal pricing at the infrastructure level, it may be necessary to exercise regulatory oversight over the access providers. The issues involved in such oversight are discussed next.

Public Policy for a Privately Owned Network

In the presence of externalities (such as congestion), it is well known that private market outcomes are not socially optimal. Beyond this, economists know very little about how a privately owned Internet might function. The bulk of the theoretical results are confined to the unrealistic case of identical users, in which case two-part tariffs can support the social optimum. Intuitively, a monopolist who charges an access fee and a usage fee, because it can extract all the user surplus with the access fee, has the incentive to maximize user surplus by charging a usage fee equal to the optimal congestion toll (Oi, 1971). Further, even if there are several (identical) network providers (and identical consumers), they will choose a usage fee equal to the optimal congestion toll (Scotchmer, 1985).

Unfortunately, these results vanish in a world with heterogeneous users. If users differ in how they value delays, for example, the social optimum may involve segregation of users by value of time into subnetworks, but some of the subnetwork owners could have incentives to upset this optimal segregation. It is not hard to construct simple examples for which there does not exist a stable pricing equilibrium among competing firms.

Given the interoperability requirements of the Internet, the number of network competitors are likely to be finite and of non-negligible size. In other words, the classic assumption of many small price-taking suppliers will be far from true. Instead, the Internet infrastructure market will be better described as a "game" with a small number of strategic players.

One of the most productive areas of theoretical research in economics over the past 20 years has been in "game theory." Recently, Rutgers University sponsored a conference on economics, game theory and the Internet (http://dimacs.rutgers.edu/workshops/economics), to foster more applications of game theory to Internet issues.

The game among network competitors has some characteristics of "Prisoners' Dilemma" (see Note). Everyone would be better off if each network manager adopted optimal dynamic pricing, but each has a strong private incentive to lower prices to attract more customers. The outcome is that everyone over-utilizes the public resource and is much worse off.

Prisoners' Dilemma

In this classic game, two prisoners are being held in connection with a crime. The sheriff has enough evidence to get a misdemeanor conviction with a one year jail term. The sheriff puts each prisoner in isolation and proposes a deal: "If you confess and supply further evidence to implicate your accomplice, I will recommend leniency for you. If your accomplice has confessed, I will recommend a 5-year sentence rather than the 10-year sentence that goes with the felony conviction, and if your accomplice has not confessed, I will recommend probation without jail for you, while your accomplice will get the full 10-year sentence."

In the game, a prisoner is better off confessing no matter what he thinks his accomplice will do. Hence, the game outcome has both prisoners confessing and serving a 5-year sentence. Note that both would have been better off if neither confessed, but there is no way of guaranteeing this "cooperative" outcome, because each prisoner has a strong private incentive to fink on the other.

This classic "Prisoners' Dilemma" captures the critical features of many public resource problems such as grazing ranges and ocean fisheries. Each player would be better off if he restricted his use to a moderate (socially optimal) level, but each has a strong private incentive to increase his use. The result is a tragedy of the commons: the overutilization of the public resource and a loss for everyone.

Thus, game theory appears to be ideally suited to studying this market game. Unfortunately, beyond rather simplistic models such as the "Prisoners' Dilemma," classic game theory has virtually no predictive power in this complex dynamic environment. Even an extremely simplified competitive network model may have no pure-strategy non-cooperative equilibrium. On the other hand, permitting intertemporal strategies unleashes the "Folk Theorems" of game theory, which say that virtually any behavior is possible.

In this environment, an active public policy involving price regulation or Pigouvian taxes to avoid a tragedy of the commons may be necessary. In the classic common resource situation, the imposition of a public fee (or tax) equaling the marginal social cost of use will avoid the tragedy. Such a fee is equivalent to optimal congestion tolls. The simulation results of GSW suggest that the computation of optimal taxes is feasible.

Because the environment is so complex, however, the optimal public policy is not obvious. Future research needs to develop a model of the Internet that contains the essential and important characteristics of the Internet, which can serve as a test bed for conducting policy studies. How will alternative regulations or taxes affect the industry structure, the pricing schemes, the pattern of use across service and user classes, congestion, social benefits, and investment incentives? Simulation is a promising practical way to pursue these questions.

3.6. Summary

If you were to consider only physical wires and cables, the Internet would be nearly indistinguishable from existing telecommunications networks. In fact, most of the Internet traffic is routed through the same pipelines used for voice, fax, and data transmissions. Rather, the Internet's strengths as a communications medium and for electronic commerce purposes lie in the way traffic is managed or routed and in its open interfacing with disparate networks that exist and are coming into existence. Aided by computers, software, and multimedia technologies, the familiar wire, cable, and wireless networks have become the information infrastructure of the future.

However, while technologies are perfected and more cables are strung, the key issue in managing this infrastructure and maximizing its utility remains a problem of efficient resource allocation in the face of congestion. The Internet infrastructure has experienced a cycle of congestion and network upgrades: from the 56 kbps backbone in 1986 to the 1.5 mbps T1 upgrade by 1989, and to 45 mbps T3 networks by the early 1990s. Now, each fiber-optic cable network, the latest upgrade, can carry 20 or 30 times more traffic than a T3 network can. Because many fiber-optic networks are built redundantly by laying several cables side by side, many predict an end to the bandwidth scarcity. But congestion is a problem in the last mile, which represents the major portion of networking costs. For this reason, the last mile still consists of copper wires and coaxial cables. Even for fiber-optic backbones, what seems to be an unimaginably large bandwidth will cause severe bottlenecks in short time because of corresponding or outpacing growth in demand. Experience with microprocessors amply demonstrates that possibility. Efficient pricing mechanisms can present effective solutions to problems of both congestion—by distributing traffic efficiently—and upgrades—by directing investments to where they can most effectively increase social welfare.

Congestion threatens the future of electronic commerce, turning the Internet into a tragedy of the commons. The ideal economic solution is to charge optimal dynamic congestion tolls. Private infrastructure owners, interested in profits rather than social benefits, however, are unlikely to voluntarily impose optimal congestion tolls. What the private market outcome will be is uncertain. More research is needed into the impact of alternative public policies on congestion, infrastructure investment, and social benefits.

Finally, new forces are coming into play, affecting the level of competition among telecommunication service providers, with serious implications for regulatory policies and consumer protection. Foremost of these forces is the convergence in infrastructure, especially in the last mile where users gain access to the Internet, where a long list of companies—including telephone companies, cable system operators, Internet service providers, long distance carriers, wireless operators, satellite systems, and computer hardware and software vendors—face head-on competition due to the disappearing market boundaries. The effects of this convergence on market performance and government policies will be discussed in Chapter 11 along with other policy-related issues.

References

Anania, L., and R. Soloman, 1995. "Flat—The Minimalist Rate." *Journal of Electronic Publishing*, http://www.press.umich.edu:80/jep/.

Benerofe, S., and J.D. Kissane, 1996. "The Technology Wars of Digital Convergence." Available at http://roscoe.law.harvard.edu/courses/techseminar96/antitrust/thepaper/thpaper.html.

Bohn, R., H. Braun, K. Claffy, and S. Wolff, 1994. "Mitigating the Coming Internet Crunch: Multiple Service Levels via Precedence." *Technical Report*, University of California.

Bernier, P., 1996. "Sprint, Unsung Network Performer?" *Inter@ctive*, August 26, 1996, pp. 43–44.

Clark, D., 1995. "A Model for Cost Allocation and Pricing in the Internet." *Journal of Electronic Publishing*, http://www.press.umich.edu:80/jep/.

Cocchi, R., S. Shenker, D. Estrin, and L. Zhang, 1991. "Pricing in Computer Networks: Motivation, Formulation, and Example." *IEEE/ACM Transactions on Networking*, 1(6): 614–627.

Deering, S., and R. Hinden, 1995. "Internet Protocol, Version 6 (IPv6) Specification." Available at http://www.epe.cz/techinfo/rfc/rfc1883.txt.

Edell, R., N. McKeown, and P. Varaiya, 1994. "Billing Users and Pricing for TCP." Department of Electrical Engineering and Computer Sciences, University of California at Berkeley.

Gupta, A., A. Jukic, D.O. Stahl and A.B. Whinston, 1997. "Designing an Incentive Compatible Mechanism for Internet Traffic Pricing." Paper Presented at the *DIMACS Workshop on Economics, Game Theory and the Internet*, Rutgers Univ., April 18–19, 1997. Postscript version is available at http://www.opim.uconn.edu/users/alokpapers/abda_rut.ps.

Gupta, A., D.O. Stahl and A.B. Whinston, 1995a. "Pricing of Services on the Internet." In *IMPACT: How ICC Research Affects Public Policy and Business Markets, A Volume in Honor of G. Kozmetsky*, Fred Phillips and W.W. Cooper, eds., Quorum Books, CT, forthcoming.

Gupta, A., D.O. Stahl and A.B. Whinston, 1995b. "A Priority Pricing Approach to Manage Multi-Service Class Networks in Real Time." *Journal of Electronic Publishing*, http://www.press.umich.edu:80/jep/.

Gupta, A., D.O. Stahl and A.B. Whinston, 1995c. "A Stochastic Equilibrium Model of Internet Pricing." Presentation at the Seventh World Congress of the Econometric Society, Tokyo.

Gupta, A., D.O. Stahl and A.B. Whinston, 1996. "An Economic Approach to Network Computing with Priority Classes." *Journal of Organizational Computing and Electronic Commerce*, 6 (1): 71–95.

Kelly, F., 1995. "Charging and Accounting for Bursty Connections." *Journal of Electronic Publishing*, http://www.press.umich.edu:80/jep/.

MacKie-Mason, J., and H. Varian, 1994. "Pricing Congestible Network Resources," ftp://gopher.econ.lsa.unich.edu/pub/Papers/pricingcongestible.ps.Z.

MacKie-Mason, J., and H. Varian, 1995. "Pricing the Internet." In B. Kahin and J. Keller, eds., *Public Access to the Internet*, Prentice-Hall.

Mendelson, H., 1985. "Pricing Computer Services: Queuing Effects." *Communications of the ACM*, 28: 312–321.

Naor, P., 1969. "On the Regulation of Queue Size by Levying Tolls." *Econometrica*, 37: 15–24.

Oi, W., 1971. "A Disneyland Dilemma: Two-Part Tariffs for a Mickey Mouse Monopoly." *Quarterly Journal of Economics*, 85: 79–96.

Pick, R., and A.B. Whinston, 1989. "A Computer Charging Mechanism for Revealing User Preferences Within a Large Organization." *Journal of Management Information Systems*, 6 (1): 87–100.

Pigou, A., 1928. *A Study in Public Finance.* London: Macmillan

Shenker, S., 1995. "Service Models and Pricing Policies for an Integrated Services Internet." In B. Kahin and J. Kellerm, eds., *Public Access to the Internet*, Prentice-Hall.

Srinagesh, P., 1995. "Internet Cost Structure and Interconnection Agreements." *Journal of Electronic Publishing*; http://www.umich.edu:80/jep/works/SrincostSt.html.

Stahl, D., and A.B. Whinston, 1991. "A General Equilibrium Model of Distributed Computing," *Center for Economic Research Working Paper* 91–09, Department of Economics, University of Texas; also in *New Directions in Computational Economics*, W. W. Cooper and A.B. Whinston, eds., Kluwer Academic Publishers, Netherlands, pp. 175–189, 1994.

Scotchmer, S., 1985. "Two-Tier Pricing of Shared Facilities in a Free-Entry Equilibrium." *Rand Journal of Economics* (http://www.rand.org/misc/rje/), 16: 456–472.

Vickrey, W., 1969. "Congestion Theory and Transport Investment." *American Economic Review Proceedings*, 59: 251–260.

Suggested Readings and Notes

Further Readings on Game Theory

For a general introduction, see Gibbons, R., 1992, Game Theory for Applied Economists. Priceton, N.J.: Princton University Press. See also Fudenberg, D., and J. Tirole, 1989, "Noncooperative Game Theory for Industrial Organization: An Introduction and Overview," in Schmalensee, R., and R. Willig, eds., Handbook of Industrial Organization, Amsterdam: North-Holland.

Technical references to repeated games and the Folk Theorem include the following:

- Abreu, D., 1988. "Towards a Theory of Discounted Repeated Games." *Econometrica*, 56: 383–396.
- Friedman, J., 1971. "Non-Cooperative Equilibrium for Supergames." *Review of Economic Studies*, 38: 1–12.
- Fudenberg, D., and E. Maskin, 1986. "The Folk Theorem in Repeated Games with Discounting or with Incomplete Information." *Econometrica*, 54: 533–556.

Internet Resources

The Internet Networking Infrastructure

An excellent list of links related to technical and economic resources about the Internet network infrastructure is the Network Economics site of the School of Information Management and Systems, UC-Berkeley at http://www.sims.berkeley.edu/resources/infoecon/Networks.html.

The proposed high-speed Internet backbone is detailed at http://www.gov.mci.net/vBNS.

Theoretically, regional networks are connected to the backbone at various network access points (NAPs) to this high-speed Internet. NAP maps are available at http://www.cerf.net/cerfnet/about/interconnects.html.

The NSFNET backbone that began in 1987 was retired in 1995. See a final report on the NSFnet: *NSFNET: A Partnership for High-Speed Networking* by K.D. Frazer, available at http://www.merit.edu/nsfnet/final.report/. An interesting history of the NSFnet is given by S.R. Harris and E. Gerich, available at http://www.merit.edu/nsfnet/.retire.html.

Many sites related to the Internet infrastructure are listed in Telecom Information Resources on the Internet, maintained by J. MacKie-Mason, available at http://www.spp.umich.edu/telecom/telecom-info.html.

Domain Name Registration

Find instructions on how to register domain names at http://www.yahoo.com/Computers_and_Internet/Internet/Domain_Registration/.

Internic Network Solutions' Domain Name Dispute Policy proposal is available at http://rs.internic.net/domain-info/internic-domain-6.html. The National Science Foundation is currently funding the domain name registration process, but plans to leave it entirely to Network Solutions beginning in 1997.

MBONE (Multicast Backbone)

Imagine that you send a large file to 100 of your friends. The same file will travese the Internet 100 times, eating up its bandwidth. The MBONE was developed to cope with that problem, by overlaying a network that can distribute (known as mroute) live audio and video data in a way to minimize duplicating the same data while in transit.

Resources about the MBONE can be found at the MBONE Information web, available at http://www.mbone.com. It also contains an MBONE FAQ.

Recent books about the MBONE include the following:

- Kumar, V., 1995. *MBone: Interactive Multimedia On The Internet.* Macmillan Publishing.
- Savetz, K., N. Randall, and Y. Lepage, 1996. *MBone: Multicasting Tomorrow's Internet.* IDG Books. Its table of contents with some text is available at http://www.northcoast.com/savetz/mbone/toc.html.

IETF IP Multicasting Proposals

IETF working groups are developing standards to support Internet multicasting, such as Resource Reservation Protocol (RSVP) that concerns bandwidth management and Real-Time Transport Protocol (RTP) with sequencing and transport of data streams.

For the RSVP specification, see 1994 IETF draft proposal available at http://netweb.usc.edu/estrin/RSVP/rsvpspec.txt.

Various reports on RTP by IETF Audio Video Transport Working Group are available at http://www.ietf.cnri.reston.va.us/ids.by.wg/avt.html.

See also the multicast routing information page by Cisco Systems at http://www.cisco.com/warp/public/614/17.html.

Broadband Online Services

For information regarding ISDN and ADSL, see ISDN information page at http://www.alumni.caltech.edu/~dank/isdn.

Cable-based broadband online services offer a high-bandwidth connection 100 times faster than ISDN service. Time Warner Entertainment started its RoadRunner cable modem service in 1996, first in Ohio. @Home (http://www.home.net) is offered by a group of cable system operators including Tele-Communications, Inc., Comcast, and Cox communications.

For information about RoadRunner, see http://www.gayson.com/sschlos/linerunner.html. An unofficial RoadRunner FAQ is available at http://members.tripod.com/~tlarrow/rrfaq.htm.

An extensive list of resources and links about cable modem is at http://rpcp.mit.edu/~gingold/cable.

CHAPTER 4

Quality Uncertainty and Market Efficiency

The efficiency of a market critically depends on the amount and the nature of information—about products and consumer tastes—available to sellers and buyers. When market agents are not endowed with proper information, the market may be inefficient or even fail to function. When the quality of a product is unknown, for example, consumers may be unwilling to pay for it. Sellers try to convey such information by using advertising and product promotions which, however, require some knowledge about the preference and the taste of consumers to be effectively carried out. If market players have complete information about products and about each other, transactions will simply be a matter of meeting and exchanging goods. A seller announces a new product, manufactured according to consumers' specifications, on the World Wide Web, and all interested consumers will purchase instantly at the price posted—no marketing campaigns, no inventories and waste in production, no product returns by unsatisfied consumers, no intermediaries for distribution, and so on. The electronic marketplace, however, will not be such a blindingly efficient market because the uncertainty about quality will linger on despite the abundance of information. This chapter introduces readers to economic reasons why a market may fail completely due to the lack of information about products or consumer tastes. Technologies alone do not eliminate these reasons, but new and innovative market mechanisms may be available in electronic commerce to counter them.

This discussion begins with the quality uncertainty problem, because the nature of digital products makes this problem more severe in electronic commerce. Digital products are mostly experience goods, whose quality becomes known only after consumption, and many information goods are purchased only once. These characteristics leave sellers without a sure way of convincing customers about the value of their products, and consumers without the willingness to purchase. In comparison, for a broad range of products known as search goods, the lack of information may be countered by simple measures such as advertising. *Search goods* are products whose quality may be learned without actually using them. A visual inspection of a product, or an advertisement, suffices to judge its quality. For *experience goods*, however, quality is learned only from experience—from actually using the product. Many digital products are this type of experience goods, for which even an excess amount of advertising and product information is inadequate to convince buyers of quality. Consumers take the risk of trying out if the learning from experience helps future purchases. But, when a product is used only once, such risk-taking may not be justified.

The uncertainty about product quality is also confounded by network congestion. A timely information may be sent out by a seller, but its quality in terms of timeliness critically depends on how fast it reaches the buyers. Under today's Internet infrastructure and pricing, product sellers often do not have control over this important aspect of quality. Because consumers' reluctance to adopt usage-based pricing for Internet services stems partly from the uncertainty about network quality for access and delivery, efficient infrastructure pricing also depends on assuring quality.

The following section, "Economics of the Lemons Market," reviews the economic reasons behind the ramifications of quality uncertainty. This section then goes on to examine various ways in which sellers in the electronic marketplace attempt to convey product information to consumers. They range from advertising to the use of third parties such as industry organizations, government agencies, and consumer advocacy groups. The objective of section 4.2

entitled "Information Channels in Electronic Commerce" is to evaluate whether these mechanisms will be efficient—and sufficient—in electronic markets. The section entitled "Quality and Intermediaries" elaborates on the role of an intermediary as a quality guarantor. The incentive for the intermediary to be truthful is the profit opportunity. Although marketing on the Internet seems to favor a distribution channel with less and less intermediary steps, intermediaries in electronic commerce may be essential in enhancing market efficiency as they become trusted sources for product information. Finally, this chapter considers electronic resale markets as an alternative to intermediaries. Although the profit motive of an intermediary is what makes it trustworthy, a simple message exchange system, such as a computer bulletin board or a secondary marketplace, can duplicate the same incentive structure of an intermediary.

4.1. Economics of the Lemons Market

The specifics of a product are hard to judge on the Internet unless one physically connects to the web page and checks it out. Even the physical presence or the identity of a seller is difficult to verify in the electronic marketplace. An electronic store—a web storefront, for example—can be constructed in a day and could disappear the next day. Technologies for certifying and authenticating the identity of a seller on the Internet would help to lower the risk of fraud or fly-by-night operation, but the uncertainty about the seller's product itself remains. One digital product vendor, First Virtual Holdings (http://www.fv.com), offers its customers the right to refuse payment after receiving a product if they are not satisfied. But, this gentler approach is prone to abuses if one is determined not to pay. Sellers will soon exit the market—finding no customers—and for this reason, First Virtual's policy is to terminate a customer's membership if one repeatedly refuses to pay. Then, how is it possible to avoid a market failure when product quality is not known?

The severity of the problem is in general lower when purchases are repeated because consumers learn about the quality and the seller has an incentive to maintain the reputation to continue sales. But reputation is a poor guide for products with a limited life span or when a seller is not a long-run market player. Already today, a multitude of both sellers and buyers want to sell and buy digital products via web pages but cannot agree on how much a product is worth. In the wake of this type of uncertainty, the market becomes inefficient or disappears, as the following example shows.

Suppose that Alice is looking for a quotation to use as an opening line in her speech at the Joint Conference of Economists and Poets. The quotation Alice wants must be relevant to both economists and poets. Alice is willing to pay $10 for a good quotation and $1 for a bad one. Bob runs a web machine that automatically produces a good quotation, at a cost of $7, based on keywords typed by consumers. Customers must pay $10 for a quotation prior to typing the keywords. Charlie runs a similar web store, but he does not have a sophisticated search-and-generate program. Instead, his machine just gives out a quotation at random, at the average cost of $1. Nevertheless, Charlie mimics all aspects of Bob's web site, including price per quote, web site appearance, and other sales policies.

If Alice has the information about Bob and Charlie, she would just go to Bob's web site. Without the knowledge, however, Alice expects to pay $5.50 on average, given that there is an equal chance of getting either a good or a bad quotation. If many Alices are in the market for quotations, the average expected price becomes the market price. It is lower than the $7 required for Bob to survive, however. Bob folds his business, leaving only Charlie in the market. But Alice will never get a good quotation and is not willing to pay the expected price of $5.50. Instead, the market price becomes $1—the price for a bad quotation. Assuming that Charlie's cost is also $1, he breaks even and is indifferent between remaining as a quotation seller and exiting the market. This phenomenon is called the *lemons problem* because only "lemons" remain in the market when the product quality is unknown. If consumer willingness to pay for a bad quotation is zero, the market for quotation disappears completely.

The lemons problem, first discussed by Akerlof (1970), is one example of adverse selection where bad products drive out good products. Similarly, a firm insuring properties such as houses and automobiles may find that many of its clients do not take adequate measures to protect their properties against theft and accidents. But without a means to distinguish careful clients from careless clients, the insurance premium—calculated based on the average risk—will apply to all clients. "Good" clients withdraw from the insurance market because they consider the insurance premium to be too high, while 'bad' clients remain. With only careless customers, the firm will have to exit the market in the face of piling insurance claims. The problem of disappearing markets occurs because of the asymmetric nature of information—that is, both parties do not have the same information. If Alice knew who to trust or if the insurance firm had knowledge about consumer behaviors, there might be some reasonable prices to complete market transactions.

Without such knowledge, both Alice and the firm must seek the information in other ways. One important method is to send a signal: Bob may send a signal to Alice that his quotations are always good, or consumers may provide an insurance firm with some evidence—signals—proving that they are low risk. Signals, however, may not be truthful. One alternative, discussed in detail in Chapter 8, is an incentive-compatible mechanism that aims to solve this problem by devising a decentralized market design that gives participants an incentive to truthfully reveal their information. The insurance company may offer two different policies with varying amounts of deductibles and co-payments, for example, so that high-risk consumers buy a different policy from one aimed at low-risk consumers.

Price as a Signal for Quality

Consumers often think that the price of a product is a sign post of its quality. The effectiveness of price as a quality signal is limited by the fact that a low-quality firm may simply charge a high price for its product. In general, prices will convey some but not all the information on product quality. Cooper and Ross (1984) suggest that, because prices may convey information adequately, two factors may actually discourage the entry of dishonest firms. The first is the number of informed consumers versus uninformed consumers. A high-quality product commands a high price because informed consumers are willing to pay the price. Thus uninformed consumers are informed about the quality through the signal—price—sent by informed consumers. The more informed consumers there are, the more difficult it is for a dishonest firm to cheat, and therefore prices do become an efficient indicator of quality. Cooper and Ross, however, do not specify how informed consumers are informed in the first place (discussed in more detail in the section entitled "Information Channels in Electronic Commerce").

The second factor determining the signaling efficiency of prices is the cost structure. As more firms enter a market, each firm's share of the market shrinks, and if the cost of production is high at low output, dishonest firms may find it unprofitable to enter. Note that dishonest firms can sell only to uninformed consumers, while honest firms continue to sell to informed consumers. Thus there will be more cheaters if a dishonest firm can make a profit with a small number of sales. Counteracting this, the entry by dishonest firms is discouraged if a large sunk cost is required. Intuitively, this is consistent with the observation that ripoffs are more prevalent for a low-cost, small-item product than for a high-cost, large-item product such as a database. Once again, however, the Cooper and Ross model assumes that there are some informed consumers. If all consumers are uninformed, prices alone cannot convey any information about product quality.

For digital products whose fixed costs are large compared to variable costs, the preceding result implies that fly-by-night operators will be discouraged to enter the market. This certainly seems a reasonable assertion for large databases and computer software. Suppose that a word processing program costs $1 million to develop. As the number of sales increase, its average cost declines along with its break-even price. If there is only one customer, for example, its price must be $1 million plus variable costs. If there are one million customers, the firm can sell a copy at slightly over $1 and still make profits. If the product is of low quality, the number of sales declines and its price must be raised to break even. As a result, low-quality products have a lower chance to survive.

For products with low fixed costs, however, fly-by-night operations may be profitable if some consumers are not informed.

Remedies for the Lemons Problem

Because the lemons problem results from asymmetric information—that is, buyers don't have the same information as sellers—the obvious remedy is to inform, and convince, buyers about the product quality. Numerous mechanisms enable one to do this.

First, sellers can convey the information to consumers through informative advertising, by building reputation, or by offering credible guarantees or warranties. To be effective, the key element in all these methods is credibility—whether it is the credibility of advertising, reputation, or guarantees.

Second, industry groups, governments, or consumer advocacy groups can provide quality information by establishing quality standards or certifications. These third parties, however, often set only minimum quality standards. Because of this, quality standards often amount to minimum standards for compatibility and interoperability, which may indicate acceptability of a product but not the level of quality.

Third, trusted third parties, rather than setting quality standards, can provide detailed quality information by comparing each brand as does the Consumers' Union, which publishes *Consumer Reports*. Similarly, a trusted mechanic may examine a used car to determine whether it is a lemon. The common criterion is that third parties need to be neutral, trustworthy, and equipped with a necessary expertise to evaluate products. Consumers' Union is an example of public third parties that are often publicly funded non-profit organizations or behave in similar ways. A trusted mechanic is an example of private third parties who offer information service for profit. Public third parties often lack funds and organization to offer product evaluations for all products and occasions. On the other hand, private third parties may become efficient information sellers who resolve quality uncertainty. Especially, this role as an information intermediary can be carried out with minimum costs to consumers when they are also product resellers (as discussed in more detail later in this chapter).

Finally, a different type of intermediary—a resale market such as a UseNet newsgroup or a public bulletin board—may carry out essentially the same function as a product reseller. Instead of the intermediary signaling quality to consumers as a trusted third party, one can open a resale market where dissatisfied buyers would try to resell the lemons or post quality information. If this resale market is efficient, then there are no low-quality sellers masquerading as high-quality sellers. The simple existence of the "punishing" mechanism—a resale market or a forum for efficient information exchange—discourages cheaters. A thorny issue in allowing consumer reselling, however, is the debate about the *first sale doctrine*—the doctrine that allows consumers to sell, rent, or lease a product after they pay for it. For some products, preventing consumers from reselling is a pertinent issue for copyright protection because resale markets can eliminate producer's future sales (see Chapter 5, "Economic Aspects of Copyright Protection"). If just one copy is put up for resale and exchanges hands rapidly on the Internet, for example, the original producer may find no buyers the next day.

If producers or original sellers are not required to provide full refunds whenever a customer is dissatisfied, however, consumers may desire to have a similar leverage against ripoffs. A "forsale" newsgroup is an efficient mechanism to solve the lemons problem without setting up artificial regulatory restraints such as quality standards, market regulation, and various consumer-protection initiatives. To protect the producer's market, reselling may be limited to first-time buyers—those who bought a product from its producer. Buyers either sell back (that is, return) to the producer, or resell in the second-hand market, but products purchased in the resale market cannot be resold.

Technologies to limit resale to initial purchasers are readily available. Authentification technologies such as encryption, digital signature, hashing, and time stamping (see Chapter 9, "Financial Intermediaries and Electronic Commerce") enable content providers to include information about both the copyright holder and the primary purchaser. When the latter wants to resell, the document can be returned to the copyright holder or to a third party to be stamped with that information. Any further unauthorized resale can be verified by examining the sales record. Although there still is much uncertainty about whether consumers should be allowed to rent or sell a digital product—although allowed under the first sale doctrine—some products such as time-dependent goods have little resale value. In this case, buyers and sellers need a mechanism such as repeated purchases (via subscription or reputation-building) to resolve the quality uncertainty problem. For products that can be resold, reselling could be an alternative to a return policy.

4.2. Information Channels in Electronic Commerce

Information about product quality can be disseminated through three types of information channels to counter the lemons problem. The first group of channels, for example, in the form of advertising, is initiated by the sellers. The second group of channels is initiated by the consumers through, for instance, product searches and comparison shopping aimed at discovering product quality. The third group of channels is mediated by third parties such as retailers and consumer advocacy groups who evaluate products and offer their information to consumers. Although this chapter's primary focus is this third group of channels involving intermediaries—Chapters 6 and 7 focus on the first and second types of channels—this chapter briefly reviews all the various information channels and investigates their effectiveness in lowering quality uncertainty in the following sections.

Sellers Provide Product Information

The primary mechanism used by companies to provide information on their products to potential customers is the web page. Conventional advertisements are sent to consumers, for example, by using e-mail to attract them to their web sites. CommerceNet (http://www.commerce.net), a non-profit consortium, listed over 40,000 Internet storefronts in operation as of October, 1996 in its Commercial Sites Index, now out of service due to a growing number of for-profit indexes. The majority of these web storefronts were geared to make certain that the company had a presence on the Internet. A Grant Thornton survey found that 25 percent of firms surveyed had web storefronts in 1997, almost double the rate from a year ago.

But beyond mere presence, web storefronts combine advertising, marketing, and sales functions with advantages not offered by traditional advertising and marketing media. These advantages include the following:

- The incremental cost per audience for a web page can be measured in a reliable manner unlike the cost required to reach a marginal audience via printed or broadcast media.

- Unlike physical storefronts, web sites offer 24-hour continuous support for customers using computerized processes.

- All web storefronts are on a level field in terms of size and geographical reach. Both small and large firms can conduct business globally despite differences in capital and location.

- Finally, a web storefront offers an efficient conduit for customer feedback and interactions that can be managed, responded to, and analyzed with the help of sophisticated computer programs and technologies.

As the number of Internet users increases even more, these advantages will become compelling enough to force companies to refocus their marketing and advertising strategies to better capitalize on the unique opportunities.

Although most web pages simply offer a brief description about the company, personnel, and products, more sophisticated web page management strategies are being developed. Digital Equipment Corporation (DEC), for example, is one large company that has emphasized Internet commerce as an important revenue source. On its product and service information page (http://www.digital.com/info/info.home.html), DEC offers an indexed and searchable database of product descriptions as well as buyer guides, performance reports, press releases, newsletters, and information to orient new visitors (see fig. 4.1). For those whose needs are not met, DEC accepts requests for additional information, providing interactive support for consumers. DEC's web store strategy is consistent with the general notion that the "push" model of advertising based on one-to-many broadcasting is neither effective nor accepted on the Internet. Instead, to avoid being attacked by angry recipients of pushed messages, web page content must be geared to meet the needs of consumers who actively seek out product information and visit companies' web sites on their own initiative, while pushed messages are limited to offering pointers to these web pages. These disadvantages of push models, however, can be minimized by customizing pushed messages as in PointCast's personalized news service (http://www.pointcast.com). (See Chapter 8, "Product Choices and Discriminatory Pricing," for a detailed discussion on product customization.) In the end, customized messages that are "pushed" are quite similar to "pulled" messages.

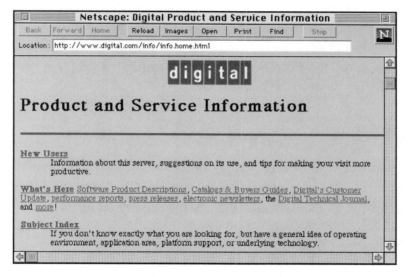

Figure 4.1 Digital's product information page.

Do firms have an incentive to provide such detailed product information to consumers? Eaton and Grossman (1986) conclude that consumers do not benefit from the information that firms reveal because competing firms end up raising prices. In their model, firms sell horizontally differentiated products (that is, different brands or colors of the same product), and are considering whether to reveal information about their products. Suppose that Alice and Bob are selling white umbrellas. Charlie, a new entrant to the umbrella market, decides to produce yellow umbrellas to cater to color-conscious or safety-minded consumers. Now that umbrellas have different colors, consumers must be informed about the product's color. By doing so, differentiated products segment the umbrella market, and consequently sellers can increase prices to extract the benefit from having products that match consumer tastes better. In this setting, sellers gain from revealing information and matching consumers with products. For search goods whose quality consumers can determine based on seller-provided information, firms will have a greater incentive to provide information.

The bottom line regarding the effectiveness of seller-provided product information in resolving quality uncertainty is whether consumers trust sellers. As mentioned earlier, for goods that consumers buy repeatedly, firms can develop a reputation for quality and trustworthiness. Offering free samples and try outs is another way. But for single purchase items such as durable goods, firms have to rely on other measures to convince consumers about their quality. One such method can be to provide consumers with "trial" products to win their trust.

Freeware, Shareware, and Other Promotions

Many products classified as "experience goods" cannot be adequately evaluated by descriptive words or pictures. For these products, a try out or a test drive is offered so that consumers can evaluate the quality themselves.

Free Products Online

Software developers commonly offer trial products in several forms. Freeware and public domain programs are ones provided free by software developers. Shareware programs are those you can use for a specified period of time for free before you decide to pay if you like the software. Often commercial programs are distributed as demo versions with some key features disabled.

These "free" programs are often archived in various sites accessible by anonymous FTP. One of the largest collections of freeware is also available via the web at Jumbo! (http:// www.jumbo.com/), as shown in figure 4.2, which offers almost 73,000 shareware and freeware programs. (See Chapter 6, "Signaling Quality and Product Information," Internet Resources section for a list of shareware sites.) Both the World Wide Web and the Internet are also used to solicit user testing. Digital Equipment Corporation in 1994, for example, allowed potential customers to test drive its applications in the Alpha AXP server for web and Internet applications. Thousands of interested customers had a chance to preview, evaluate, and make comments on the product, making the test drive a big marketing success.

Similar to software vendors, information sellers offer free products and services for consumers to try out. The reasons for offering free products and services are far from altruistic. First, unlike printed books that buyers can browse at a bookstore, in digital commerce, there is little difference between browsing and buying because files must be transferred even for browsing. Once downloaded, sellers cannot obligate consumers to pay in an effective way. Because of the quality uncertainty, buyers may not be willing to pay upfront, or the downloaded product may be of too small a value to implement a payment system other than a micropayment system being proposed. Second, digital products are susceptible to unauthorized reproduction. Hence, any product consumers are allowed to browse essentially becomes public domain. Then, how do sellers offer "browsing opportunities" for consumers who are interested but will not buy unless they have some idea about the product? Free products, excerpts, and free basic services provide the opportunity for consumers to browse, try out, and learn about the product.

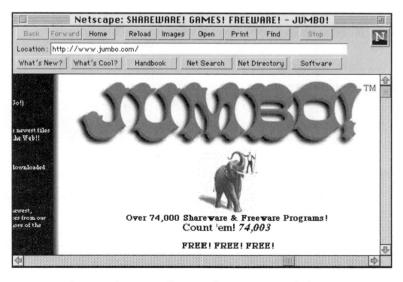

Figure 4.2 Jumbo! web site offering freeware and shareware programs.

The Economics of Try-Outs

Allowing consumers to try out a product prior to purchase is effective when true valuations become known only after consuming the product. A firm may profit from try-outs if consumers find that the product is of high value to them and thus are willing to pay a higher price. Lewis and Sappington (1994) consider a market where buyers are uncertain about their tastes (valuations) for the product offered in the market and the seller has to decide whether to allow consumers to try out.

Suppose that there are two types of consumers whose valuations for a product can be high ($1,000) or low ($500). Assume that there is an equal number of consumers—say, 500—in each type. The expected (mean) valuation of the product is $750, which is the maximum price (risk neutral) buyers are willing to pay without any information about the product. Suppose that the quality of the product is already determined (given exogenously), and the cost of the product is $600. If the firm does not allow consumers to try out the product and sells it at the expected market price of $750, all 1,000 consumers will buy. Even though consumers with low valuations are paying more than the product's worth, there is no way they can be sure of this in advance. The firm's profit is $150,000.

If, on the other hand, the firm allows consumers to try out its product, low-type consumers by definition will be unwilling to pay, after learning about the product, any price over $500 whereas high-type consumers can be charged up to $1,000. Therefore, the firm will be better off to sell its product only to high-type consumers at $1,000 and abandon all its low-type consumers. The market is naturally segmented by try-outs. As a result, the firm's profit is increased to $200,000.

Clearly, the firm's incentive to provide try-outs lies in the possibility to segment the market and charge the maximum price. Critical to this is the cost of the product. If the cost is higher than the valuation of low-type consumers, the firm abandons them and focuses on high-type consumers (see fig. 4.3). To justify high price, the firm must allow try-outs. But, if the cost is below the low-type's valuation of $500, it would be more profitable for the firm to sell it at the expected price of $750. To capture low-type consumers as well, the firm should not allow try-outs. In this case, with a cost of $400, the profit would be $350,000 without try-outs—a $350 margin for each unit sold.

In comparison, the profit is $300,000 with try outs and segmentation—a $600 margin for 500 units sold. If the firm can charge different prices, it may be able to offer its product at $500 to low-type consumers, which yields $100 per unit to bring in an additional $50,000. Then, high-type consumers may resent the fact that they are charged $1,000 for the same product, and begin to misrepresent their types. The firm needs some mechanism to distinguish consumers based on their types; otherwise it will not serve low-type consumers.

Figure 4.3 Try-out strategies and prices.

If the cost of production is higher than the expected price ($750 in this example), this try-out model is very similar to the case of the lemons problem. The firm has no choice but to offer try-outs because it cannot break even at $750, and hope to convince high-type consumers to buy. Also, if the price is higher than $750, no consumers are willing to buy the product without being sure of the its valuation. With try-outs, only high-type consumers will buy the product at the maximum valuation ($1,000). In the lemons problem of used car markets, the cost to a high-type seller is its valuation (that is, $1,000), which is higher than the expected market price. Thus, try outs, if available, can be used to resolve the quality uncertainty.

Some products are ill suited for try-outs. Suppose, for example, that Alice is selling a computer database of weather information for all major U.S. cities, and allows her customers to search for one city prior to purchase. Bob, who wants to get information about the weather in San Francisco, can get the data for San Francisco by using the try-out and then decline to buy the database. Two mechanisms may become important in such a situation. First, Alice may devise a demonstration plan, by which Bob can be convinced of the database's quality without revealing any information from the database. Such a plan is based on an algorithm known as zero-knowledge proofs. (See section 6.2 for a detailed discussion on zero-knowledge proofs). Second, micropayment methods may adequately address Bob's need, and in general support unbundled sales of digital products. Although bundling of many related products will be essential for information and digital products, microsales and microbundles are useful in allowing consumers to try out without relying on free give-aways.

For some products, consumers may not be sure of their quality even after try-outs. For others, try-outs may not be available for all features of a product, or may take time and costly effort to learn. Still others are technically too complex for consumers to evaluate their features. In these cases, an expert evaluation may be needed.

Third-Party Information

In addition to the direct seller-buyer information channels considered so far, intermediaries may be essential to resolving the issue of quality uncertainty. For some products, a certain degree of technical knowledge is needed to understand and evaluate various product specifications. Although a well-designed web page may have FAQs and links to related sites and papers for consumers to read about technical aspects of a product, not all consumers are equipped to digest this information. Therefore, someone with technical expertise is needed who can provide objective quality evaluation. And as an objective evaluation of a product often involves a comparison with competing products, a third party other than sellers and buyers is often preferred.

Third-party intermediaries can be separated into two groups: public and private. Public third parties have no profit motive and may be supported by public funds. Private third parties, on the other hand, provide information for a fee as their business.

Public third parties include a wide array of very different institutions and organizations. Newspapers, magazines, and television news programs often review and rate digital products and web sites. Personal web pages that provide assorted links by subject are in fact reviewed and evaluated by individuals. Similarly, many Internet sites are touted as being a "top 5 percent" web site, and display some kind of award. Search services maintain "What's Hot" lists that are reviewed and rated. As long as these services are offered as a public service, they may be classified as public third-party activities.

Public third parties, however, are often limited in their service because of the nature of public goods. Objective product information is a public good useful to all members of a society, but the organization or firm producing the information cannot charge those who benefit from the information. As a result, public goods tend to be undersupplied. Because of high costs, *Consumer Reports*, for example, cannot provide its valuable service for all products on the market. Third parties such as government agencies, industry organizations, and consumer advocacy groups also try to establish certain quality standards that can be applied to all products in the market. Standards set up by government or industry groups, for example, often dictate the minimum level of quality and technical capabilities such as UL sets for electric appliances and government safety standards set for automobiles. These minimum standards are often minimally useful in determining what to buy, however, because all reasonable products on the market have supposedly exceeded the minimum. As such, their usefulness is limited.

Retailers and Other Brokers

Alternatively, market organizations such as retailers and brokers who have incentives to maximize profits may offer product evaluation. A profit-motivated intermediary is a private third party who sells information as a product. As it is a long-run player, the intermediary has an incentive to review products and be truthful to consumers to maintain its reputation. Whether its information is in fact efficient and truthful will depend on the way the market rewards the intermediary's activities.

If public organizations cannot provide adequate public information, how could one expect private, profit-oriented third parties to provide objective information for the benefit of consumers? And how does one determine that their information is true? Economically, one must also be concerned with the level of information provided—that is, whether it is efficient, too much, or too little. These questions can be answered by analyzing market incentives that determine the level of services these intermediaries offer. This section first defines what these intermediaries are and then presents a detailed analysis in the next section.

For this discussion, private third parties are defined as intermediaries such as retailers who are not producers but who may convey quality information to consumers as a part of their business activities. They offer both direct and indirect quality information. Direct information is conveyed when they guarantee the quality of the product they distribute. Measures to support product guarantee such as unlimited return policy, however, may be difficult to implement in electronic commerce. First and foremost, digital products, for example, can be copied so easily that physically "returning" a product has little meaning. Second, refunds may not be feasible for items purchased with micropayments whose transaction costs may be larger than the value of those products.

Indirect information is transmitted to consumers through the identity and reputation of the third parties themselves. Building reputation is profitable when consumers repeat purchases and as long as high-quality goods command higher prices (Shapiro, 1982). When consumers are not expected to repeat purchases, however, reputable firms have little advantage over fly-by-night operators. A disadvantage of sellers in the electronic marketplace is that indirect quality signals available in conventional markets have little or no meaning. Buyers can often judge the quality of a product, for example, from the appearance of a store or the identity of a seller. A posh department store offers better quality, albeit pricey, products than a discount store. In a virtual market where physical presence has little relevance, however, these indirect information signals are not available or undergo radical changes. Clearly, the role of intermediaries and their effectiveness in conveying just such quality information in electronic commerce is a complex topic that this discussion has only begun to explore.

4.3.   Quality and Intermediaries

The need for an intermediary is often dismissed in the direct seller-to-buyer transaction model often envisioned for Internet commerce. A market-driven solution to the lemons problem, however, involves relying on an intermediary who has an incentive to provide truthful information about quality in the manner buyers can trust. When there are multiple buyers and sellers as in international cyberspace, there is even less chance of a buyer finding a seller with a recognizable name. Especially for a one-time purchase of a small document, searching and learning about all potential sellers would be far too costly. In a market where neither sellers nor public third parties are adequate in resolving quality uncertainty, an intermediary-based market clearing mechanism can achieve an efficiency similar to, or better than, any non-mediated or regulatory regime, by transmitting product information and successfully and efficiently mediating a trade.

This discussion's definition of intermediaries includes various types of market agents and institutions, besides sellers and buyers, who participate in market transactions but do not consume the product for themselves. In a typical commercial transaction, for example, a wide range of intermediaries is involved—advertising agencies, insurance companies, banks, wholesalers and retailers, delivery firms, and regulatory agencies. Each of these intermediaries adds value to the product as well as costs. The primary economic role of an intermediary is in reducing the total cost of production and delivery through transactional efficiencies, reviewed in the following section. This role, however, is of minor interest because a market will function, albeit less efficiently, without such efficiency-enhancing intermediaries. On the other hand, intermediaries perform an essential role without which a market may fail. Brokering quality information is one such instance, and for that reason, intermediaries will be as important in electronic commerce as in physical markets.

Transactional Efficiencies

Traditionally, the economic gain attributed to an intermediary—reduced costs—is largely due to organizational efficiency. Essentially, a firm can undertake the same task performed by an outside intermediary, but an intermediary is preferred because it costs less. A manufacturer, for example, could accept product orders directly from consumers and deliver them. But the firm often finds it cheaper to sell its product to a wholesaler. The cost-reducing role of intermediaries has been the subject of transactions economics of Coase (1937) and Williamson (1975). Transactions economics distinguishes production costs from other costs incurred to fulfill market transactions such as delivery, insurance, and other contractual arrangements. The efficiency of intermediaries depends on whether the total transaction or coordination cost from using an intermediary is more or less than not using it.

For a firm or a market to be efficient, production costs as well as transaction costs must be minimized. For that reason, a market with lower transaction costs is considered to be more efficient. Some see middlemen as just adding to the cost of distribution. The cost of selling to consumers in physical markets—for example, inventorying, billing, and shipping expenses—can sometimes be lowered by using intermediaries. In many cases, wholesalers and retailers provide producers with a more efficient distribution channel. Lacking these intermediaries, many firms would have to duplicate their distribution for each customer. In figure 4.4, a producer selling directly to multiple buyers incurs costs of T1 for each transaction.

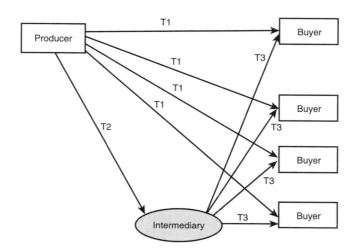

Figure 4.4 Transaction costs comparison with and without an intermediary.

In physical markets, a firm sells in bulk to an intermediary (costing T2) who is located close to consumers or has an efficient distribution system. The intermediary adds T3 as its selling cost to the final price. As a result, in an intermediated market, the total transaction cost per consumer is T2 plus T3. This may be lower than T1 because (a) the intermediary is closer to buyers, minimizing T3 and (b) the producer incurs only one T2 to deliver his product in bulk so that the per consumer cost is lower due to the economy of scale.

On the Internet, however, the firm will sell only one copy to the intermediary, who makes digital copies and sells them to buyers. Therefore, wholesaling in bulk has little meaning in digital commerce—except perhaps in "mirroring" where duplicated materials are kept in several servers—and with consumers distributed widely throughout the network, the intermediary's cost of selling to consumers (T3) might be as large as the cost of producer-to-buyer delivery (T1). In other words, the gain from retailing and distribution is not so apparent in the non-spatial environment of the Internet.

This scenario seems to indicate that there is no role for an intermediary, especially one of distribution, on the Internet. An efficient search method reduces the need to rely on someone "who knows all producers" in the market.

Therefore, the rationale for an intermediary in electronic commerce has little to do with transactional efficiencies. What then is the role of an intermediary in electronic commerce? An intermediary improves market efficiency by providing third-party information about product quality, thereby eliminating the possibility of a market failure due to quality uncertainty. The more severe the uncertainty about the quality is, the stronger the need for an efficient intermediary in electronic commerce.

In resolving the lemons problem, intermediaries may actually increase the transaction costs. The intermediary, for example, may need to invest in becoming an expert who can tell the quality of a product requiring technical knowledge. For experience goods, the intermediary may try out all the products it sells and gain knowledge. Both the expertise and experience have costs attached. Despite increased transaction costs, however, the intermediated market gains efficiency over the lemons market because the market is not foreclosed—that is, goods are available to consumers. Even an intermediary who has no expertise in evaluating quality may provide quality assurance simply by virtue of being a long-term player in the market. Again, the intermediary may add to the costs of transaction, but it does not need to invest in expertise or undergo costly testing while acting as an information source to prevent market failure. The following section discusses the informational roles of an intermediary.

Intermediaries as Experts

As mentioned previously, consumers are unable to discover the quality of a product if the quality evaluation is complicated and requires special expertise or if the product is an experience good. A gem stone or an art painting, for example, requires an expert evaluator to judge its value. Sophisticated word processing programs are often evaluated by software experts, but still leave consumers scratching their heads. For an experience good such as information, its quality can be learned only after viewing (using) the product.

Neither acquiring an expertise nor using a product is costless. An art evaluator undergoes years of training and experience to become an expert. Because an intermediary, by definition, does not derive any utility from consuming a product, he is wasting time and effort to learn the quality from usage. What then are the incentives for an intermediary to invest in acquiring evaluation skills or learning the quality of a product and to be truthful about the information? First, an intermediary makes repeated purchases of similar items, unlike consumers who may purchase a given item once or twice. Therefore, the intermediary has an incentive to acquire knowledge, a sunk cost, to be used for numerous purchases. Second, the intermediary is a long-term player and his payoff from being truthful comes from continued sales which will cease if his credibility is questioned.

Intermediaries as experts operate more frequently in certain types of markets (Biglaiser, 1993). They are common where the difference between low-quality and high-quality products is large, giving a larger profit margin from the two expected prices. Also, if there are more low-quality goods than high-quality goods, the cost to search for a high-quality good may justify the use of an expert intermediary. In contrast, experts add little value if products are in general of a high quality. A used-car market is a case in point, where products are of high value but buyers are weary about lemons. Thus a successful intermediary must assure buyers of product quality.

Aucnet USA, Inc. (http://www.aucnet.com), a new player in the wholesale used-car market, combines the role of quality guarantor with digital technologies that organize and facilitate market transactions. The idea of Aucnet originated from a Japanese used-car dealer who saw an opportunity in dealer-to-dealer trading. Used-car buyers are physically limited to visit all dealers, and as a result some dealers may have excess inventory while others may be unable to meet demand. A dealer-to-dealer exchange network, however, is also constrained by the difficulty in moving cars. Aucnet, instead, organizes a market for information on used cars trading in a satellite auction market.

Three elements distinguish Aucnet from conventional electronic malls. First, Aucnet provides detailed information on each used car put on the auction. Inspected and graded by its own trained professionals, Aucnet guarantees its quality evaluation, thereby inducing dealers to participate in remote auctions. Second, Aucnet uses auction as a price discovering mechanism instead of using posted prices. Thus, Aucnet is an electronic market that mediates excess supply and demand of its members. Finally, Aucnet also provides bulletin boards where its members trade cars before and after an auction. This secondary trading opportunity enables the market to be more active and offers a self-corrective mechanism just as options markets enable stock investors and commodity traders a chance to hedge. Aucnet members' participation in the auction depends critically on their knowledge that Aucnet guarantees the quality of each car—or the truthfulness of their information.

An Aucnet-like electronic market can be organized for any product whose supply and demand are often unmatched. Most printing shops, for example, lease expensive color copiers for which they have to make monthly payments. Depending on the rental price and the demand, the price for color copying may vary widely from week to week. A web-based intermediary market can be organized to connect all printing shops, showing jobs waiting to be finished and the status of all copiers. The service may be limited to printers or open to consumers who can comparison shop. Such an intermediary market will counter excess demand or supply problems, foster better uses of resources, and simplify the consumer search process. In a similar vein, FlyCast Communications Corp. (http://www.flycast.com) proposes to connect web advertisers (buyers) with web store owners (sellers) to leverage web space renting and advertising in a real-time dynamic exchange market. Some web sites have idle space, while there are advertisers who are willing to pay premium prices for the right mix of location, contents, and traffic. Its client/server application, AdAgent, works like a real-time stock exchange market, sending bids by advertisers and auctioning off ad spaces as well as dispatching and displaying ads in real time. Finally, as part of the effort to deregulate utility industries, electricity trading markets are being organized on the Internet, where excess power capacity is sold and bought among electricity wholesalers. To transmit electricity from a remote excess power supplier to those in need requires a complex negotiation among many transmission providers. Web-based information systems have been proposed to support such an effort through the Open Access Same-time Information Systems (OASIS) or TSIN (http://www.tsin.com). (See Chapter 11, "Business and Policy Implications of Electronic Commerce," for a detailed discussion on the utility deregulation and electronic commerce.)

Intermediaries as an Information Source

Although, in the preceding discussion, the intermediary develops a superior skill and knowledge to assess product quality, he may find it too costly to invest time and effort for small-value products. Suppose that an intermediary sells thousands of small pieces of information—literary essays and opinions on behalf of numerous individual web entrepreneurs. For such microproducts, intermediaries may have no incentive to guarantee the quality of the product. Nevertheless, the economic problem of the lemons must be dealt with for the web business to flourish. Is there an economic mechanism by which an intermediary who is not a better quality evaluator than consumers may still serve as a quality guarantor?

Such a mechanism exists when an intermediary is simply a long-term player in the market. Without heavy investment for training and experience to develop expertise, this type of intermediary provides web entrepreneurs with a sales outlet but maintains a punishment mechanism if the quality of their product declines. Because the intermediary is no better than the consumer in knowing the quality, a simple method of tracking the quality is to rely on customers' complaints. When customers complain about a product, the intermediary drops the producer from its list of sellers after reviewing the case. In this case, the role of an intermediary is similar to a bulletin-board system where consumers exchange information and blacklist cheating producers.

A critical reason why such an intermediary may resolve the lemons problem by offering quality information is that the intermediary sells products from multiple producers. Single-product intermediaries may collude with a producer, on the basis of sharing profits, to continues to sell the good despite complaints from customers. A multiproduct intermediary, however, will suffer if it colludes with one cheating producer and continues to sell a bad product, because consumers will stop buying other products from the intermediary as well. This "reputational spillover," as it is called (Biglaiser and Friedman, 1994), gives intermediaries an incentive to punish a cheating supplier by dropping its product, encouraging producers to maintain high quality. This type of simple punishment strategy works very well in a dynamic market such as the Internet because it only requires a short-term, unsophisticated contracting between the supplier and the buyer (intermediary). The section entitled "Intermediaries and Contracts" investigates the economics of short-term contracts.

Intermediaries as Producers

This section concludes by pointing out an important function of an intermediary besides that of a broker and a quality guarantor. Intermediaries in physical markets often combine or assemble several products into a new product. This activity of a retailer is in fact a production through packaging and processing existing goods to match consumer needs not met by individual producers. Consequently, intermediaries are more than a simple distributor; they are an integral part of the whole value chain from production to sales.

In electronic commerce, packaging and processing products by an intermediary will become more important because digital products are highly customizable and because producers of digital products are smaller and more numerous than in physical markets, each catering to a very specialized taste. Newspaper publishers and news organizations such as CNN, for example, are in fact intermediaries who collect, process, and distribute products authored by writers, reporters, and columnists. Consumers value articles that appear in the *New York Times* (http://www.nytimes.com) or a report on CNN because these intermediaries have reputations for high quality, whereas the quality of individual writers and reporters is hard to ascertain. Both of these companies may sell their products as a pure intermediary by just distributing articles and reports on their web pages. Instead, they act as an intermediate producer by bundling component stories into an information service. Intermediaries of this sort are pervasive in electronic commerce.

4.4.   Intermediaries and Contracts

The remaining two sections present two types of markets where the problem of quality uncertainty is solved. The first market type does it through an intermediary who, without verifying quality of each product it sells, succeeds in guaranteeing quality. The second type of market is an electronic resale market such as forsale newsgroups. In both cases, what produces the desired result is an effective punishment mechanism that encourages producers or suppliers to maintain high quality. Although both types are prevalent in electronic commerce, profit-motivated intermediaries may dominate the future marketplace because public forums such as newsgroups may not get necessary funds to support their market activities or lack an adequate means to control and sustain effective exchanges.

The mechanisms described in this and the next sections intend to show that undesirable effects of quality uncertainty can be avoided through some market arrangements. Certainly, they are not needed if consumers are well informed, and if so, the electronic marketplace offers opportunities for sellers to innovate their production, marketing, and customer-service processes. Dell Computer Corporation (http://www.dell.com) of Austin, Texas, for example, heavily relies on direct sales to its customers through its online web store, where customers can build a computer to their specification online, be informed about real-time order status, and contact service representatives (see fig. 4.5). Dell's direct marketing strategy eliminates dealer markup, costly distribution network, and physical stores. More importantly, it enables the company to be in direct contact with its customers, which not only helps to improve customer service but also enables more effective product development and marketing processes. (Chapter 8 addresses product customization and customer retention issues.)

Figure 4.5 Dell's web store.

Despite these advantages of direct marketing, consumers are wary of producers of unknown quality goods. The previous section briefly describes how an intermediary punishes cheating suppliers by refusing to accept their products in the future. But, is such a strategy sufficient to induce those suppliers to provide goods of high quality? Will it be better to institute a random but consistent procedure to verify quality, or to spell out the quality requirement in a procurement contract in the first place? Surprisingly, recent studies argue that neither a costly quality verification nor a complete contract is necessary to secure high quality. The first example comes from a study of subcontracting systems by Taylor and Wiggins (forthcoming in AER). The second example is a theoretical study by Bernheim and Whinston (forthcoming in AER) regarding incomplete contracts. In both cases, the buyers are interpreted to be the intermediary in electronic commerce.

Subcontracting Systems

Two types of subcontracting systems are in use to address the quality problem: competitive bidding and just-in-time purchasing. In the U.S. and most Western countries, a buyer offers a procurement contract to a large pool of potential subcontractors, who submit a bid to win the contract. Through this competitive bidding system, the buyer selects a subcontractor with the lowest bid. After the contract is awarded, it lasts until the quantity specified is fulfilled. Quality is checked on each delivery, and products with unsatisfactory quality are returned, but shipments continue until the contract expires. In comparison, just-in-time purchasing has been used in Japan, where a buyer deals with a relatively small number of subcontractors, and procurement contracts tend to be awarded based on past performance rather than through competitive bidding. Under the just-in-time procurement system, deliveries, which are of relatively small quantity, are seldom inspected by the buyer. The supply contract may require only a small quantity, but the length of the contract is left open-ended, lasting as long as the buyer is satisfied with the subcontractor's performance.

Neither of these two procurement systems has inherent advantages over the other, but the desirability depends on the way production is set up (Taylor and Wiggins). The competitive bidding system is well suited for mass-production facilities with intermittent production runs. Such a production facility has high set-up costs, but the unit production cost is lower due to the large scale of production. Similarly, supplies are delivered a few times in large quantity, minimizing costs for delivery as well as for quality inspection. The just-in-time delivery system, on the other hand, accommodates a more flexible production process that is run for smaller quantities. Computer-aided production systems, for example, enable producers to vary product specifications, and as a result product differentiation and customization become more important than lowering unit costs based on mass production. Correspondingly, the set-up cost or fixed cost for each production run is relatively small. Flexible production in turn requires frequent, just-in-time supplies with minimal delivery and inspection costs. In other words, the choice of a procurement system depends on how a production process is set up regarding its fixed cost.

An intermediary in electronic commerce offers an array of digital products, often assembled using parts supplied by numerous producers—for example, online newspaper publishers or CNN. For a digital product, its supply involves only one copy, and customization is more critical than minimizing the unit production cost. In this regard, the just-in-time purchasing system is more relevant than the competitive bidding system to digital-product intermediaries. This implies that intermediaries, rather than attempting to verify quality of each delivered product, will use their continued supply relationship as a means to induce suppliers to provide quality products.

The just-in-time purchasing system needs to establish a long-term relationship with suppliers because, otherwise, the threat to discontinue will have little effect on the supplier's performance. This very fact, however, limits the number of suppliers in physical markets, often foregoing the gains from a competitive supply market such as a lower price. Nevertheless, competition among suppliers may have little value in electronic commerce because digital products, unlike automobile parts, may not be standardized in any meaningful way. Furthermore, digital intermediaries need not limit the number of products they sell, and may establish a long-term relationship with all prospective suppliers as long as their products are selling.

Intermediaries in electronic commerce, then, purchase products using the just-in-time system, and offer quality products without incurring costs to learn or inspect the quality. If consumers buy directly from producers, the lack of a long-term relationship increases the chance of getting a lemon. Although consumers may refuse to pay, return the lemon, or demand a refund, such a punishment strategy based on current sale may fail to discourage cheating by fly-by-night operators, especially if payments are made prior to sale and there is no adequate means to recover them. This scenario seems to indicate that intermediaries do indeed play an important role in electronic commerce.

The key incentive for suppliers in the just-in-time procurement system is the continued profit in the future if they maintain high quality. The same sort of incentive mechanism can be implemented through short-term, incomplete contracts between suppliers and intermediaries.

Incomplete Contracts

An incomplete contract leaves certain specifications out of the contract such as the performance standard or a specific obligation, but may end up inducing the best outcome (Bernheim and Whinston, 1997). Suppose, for example, that Alice writes a contract with Bob, her son in high school, to encourage and reward his school work. Alice, being a working single mom, cannot verify how much studying Bob does each day or, more importantly, how much Bob is learning in a meaningful way. Such an intellectual activity is not verifiable—that is, in terms of business, an activity that is difficult to prove in court to be one way or the other—but his school grades, although they are an imperfect indicator for learning, are observable. Should Alice specify what grades Bob should be getting in the contract, or should she avoid specifying target grades and leave them to Bob's discretion? If the contract spells out what grades Bob should be getting—for example, all Bs—and corresponding payments, the best Alice can expect is all Bs. Even if she demands all As, that does not mean that Bob is actually learning; Bob may be cheating or just getting high grades without learning anything.

If Alice is concerned with Bob's education, she may opt to write an incomplete contract by leaving out any mention of grades or by only specifying minimum grades, but adding some discretionary payments based on her future evaluation that Bob is actually doing his best. Such an incomplete contract is common in wage negotiations: Bonus payments leave firms the ability to respond to favorable work performance by their workers. In Bob's case, under a complete contract, he has an incentive to minimize his effort to learn whether he can meet the required grades. With an incomplete contract, Bob is rewarded for all his effort, and thus doing his best is for his own advantage. The key aspect here is that Bob's and Alice's incentives work toward the same goal.

In the earlier just-in-time procurement system, the punishment—the termination of contract forever—induces the suppliers to maintain high quality. Therefore, the term of contract is left unspecified—that is, an incomplete contract. In other words, continued future contracts are the reward for high quality, although the term of contract was not specified, just as Bob's rewards are not specified by Alice. When performance is not verifiable but otherwise can be rewarded in some way—that is, if the desires or incentives of the contracting parties can be made complementary—an incomplete contract results in a better outcome than a complete contract.

Such an incomplete contract is often observed between suppliers and intermediaries, where high-quality products induce continued trading and benefit both the intermediary and its suppliers. An example of an incomplete contract is an option contract, by which an intermediary does not inspect the quality for each shipment, but has an option to terminate it at any time. Any fly-by-night operators will be excluded from the intermediary market.

Numerous online shopping malls are springing up on the Internet. See, for example, Yahoo!'s list at http://www.yahoo.com/Business_and_Economy/ Companies/Shopping_Centers/Online_Malls, the Internet Mall (http:// www.internet-mall.com), or Downtown Anywhere (http://www.awa.com). But these online marketplaces just offer hypertexted links to participating merchants' web sites or house them within their online web mall. A true online intermediary, on the other hand, must offer an integrated online shopping network, implementing a contract with its suppliers, which addresses the complaints about quality by its customers.

Such an option contract can be implemented between the intermediary and its customers as well. A complete contract, for example, is a subscription plan for an online information service, for which the seller guarantees the quality of its service and the buyer agrees to pay subscription fees for the duration of the contract. A subscriber cannot always verify the quality throughout the contract period, however, giving the service provider an incentive to shirk after the contract is signed. Customers, then, may not renew their subscription at the end of the contract, but the seller's horizon may be short enough to disregard this loss. Furthermore, unlike the competitive bidding system previously discussed, subscribers may have no satisfactory means to "return" unsatisfactory services and demand refunds or withhold payments. An incomplete contract, on the other hand, is based on microproducts and micropayments, where short-term contracts are renewed each time consumers order something. Instead of purchasing a bundled product, consumers are allowed to exercise an option to pick and choose, continuing their patronage if products turn out to be of high quality.

4.5. Summary

Although it is well understood that the Internet presents an exciting opportunity to reduce transaction costs, its future may depend on how non-technological but fundamentally economic issues such as the lemons problem are solved. A market where buyers and sellers trade goods electronically lacks many of the conventional ways to assess the quality of a product. This chapter reviewed the basic economic reason why a market fails to exist when the quality information is not available. Sellers may provide information about their products but, for some products, it is difficult for consumers to assess the quality even with detailed information. Furthermore, buyers may not trust seller-provided information. An alternative is to rely on a trusted third party who has the expertise to evaluate quality, but employing such experts may be costly. For low-value items, then, the uncertainty about quality may be the main reason why a market does not exist—witness the amount of information being stored on millions of personal web pages and the common notion that these pages are lemons. If electronic commerce were to ferment a truly informational age, any little bit of information should find a market to trade in, although a pecuniary remuneration would not be the only incentive for engaging and disseminating information and knowledge.

Intermediaries in electronic commerce may play an important role in enhancing market efficiency by providing product information even when intermediaries do not have superior knowledge and skills to evaluate quality. They act as a source of quality information by being a long-term player in the market and by carrying a range of products. Similarly, consumers are better off by having an option to buy microproducts with micropayments as well as bundling and subscription, which forces sellers to maintain high quality.

References

Akerlof, G., 1970. "The Market for Lemons: Quality Uncertainty and the Market Mechanism." *Quarterly Journal of Economics*, 84: 488–500.

Bernheim, B.D., and M.D. Whinston, forthcoming. "Incomplete Contracts and Strategic Ambiguity." Forthcoming in *American Economic Review*.

Biglaiser, G., 1993. "Middlemen as Experts." *RAND Journal of Economics*, 24(2): 212–223.

Biglaiser, G., and J.W. Friedman, 1994. "Middlemen as Guarantors of Quality." *International Journal of Industrial Organization*, 12: 509–531.

Coase, R., 1937. "The Nature of the Firm." *Economica*, 4: 386–405.

Cooper, R., and T. Ross, 1984. "Prices, Product Qualities, and Asymmetric Information: The Competitive Case." *The Review of Economic Studies*, 51: 197–207.

Lewis, T.R., and D.E.M. Sappington, 1994. "Supplying Information to Facilitate Price Discrimination." *International Economic Review*, 35(2): 309–326.

Oi, W., 1992. "Productivity in the Distributive Trades: The Shopper and the Economies of Massed Reserves." In *Output Measurement in the Service Sectors*, Zvi Griliches, ed., pp. 161–191. Chicago, IL.: The University of Chicago Press.

Rubinstein, A., and A. Wolinsky, 1987. "Middlemen." *Quarterly Journal of Economics*, 102: 581–593.

Salop, S., and J. Stiglitz, 1977. "Bargains and Ripoffs: A Model of Monopolistically Competitive Price Dispersion." *The Review of Economic Studies*, 44: 494–510.

Shapiro, C., 1982. "Consumer Information, Product Quality, and Seller Reputation." *The Bell Journal of Economics*, 13: 20–35.

Taylor, C.R., and S.N. Wiggins, forthcoming. "Competition or Compensation: Supplier Incentives Under the American and Japanese Subcontracting Systems." Forthcoming in *American Economic Review*.

Williamson, O.E., 1975. *Markets and Hierarchies: Analysis and Antitrust Implications.* New York: Free Press.

Williamson, S.D., 1987. "Recent Developments in Modeling Financial Intermediation." Federal Reserve Bank of Minneapolis, *Quarterly Review*, Summer, pp. 19–29.

Suggested Readings and Notes

Economics of the Lemons Problem

Akerlof (1970) is a classic study of the lemons problem. His model is one of pure exchange between consumers, and thus the seller's cost is the same as his valuation of the product. This implies that, in terms of Lewis and Sappington as discussed in the section entitled "Information Channels in Electronic Commerce," the cost for high-type producers is $1,000, in which case there can be no trade unless buyers are assured of quality.

Cooper and Ross (1984) is a model with informed and uninformed consumers. It analyzes the degree to which prices convey product information. In particular, they consider the shape of average cost curves: U-shaped versus constant average costs with respect to quantity.

Chan, Y. S., and H.E. Leland, 1982. "Prices and Qualities in Markets with Costly Information." *The Review of Economic Studies*, 49: 499–516. This extends the works of Akerlof, Salop, and Stiglitz (1977) in two directions: The sellers can select both the selling prices and quality levels, and the buyers can acquire price/quality information about individual sellers at a cost.

Salop and Stiglitz (1977) is a model of a market where a portion of consumers are informed, and others are not informed. This type of model is known as a "tourists versus natives" model.

Repeat Purchases and Reputation

For infinite horizon models, see the following:
- Klein, B., and K. Leffler, 1981. "The Role of Market Forces in Assuring Contractual Performance." *Journal of Political Economy*, 81: 615–641.
- Shapiro (1982) studies one mechanism that prevents deterioration of the quality: firm-specific reputation. See also Shapiro, C., 1983. "Premiums for High-Quality Products as Rents to Reputation." *Quarterly Journal of Economics*, 98: 659–680.

For limited horizon models, see the following:
- Kreps, D., and R. Wilson, 1982. "Reputation and Imperfect Information." *Journal of Economic Theory*, 27: 253–279.
- Milgrom, P., and J. Roberts, 1982. "Redation, Reputation, and Entry Deterrence." *Journal of Economic Theory*, 27: 280–312.

Internet Resources

Internet Commerce

Figure 4.6 CommerceNet logo.

CommerceNet (http://www.commerce.net) is a non-profit consortium launched in 1994 to act as an industry association for Internet commerce. It acts as the advocacy group for the use of the Internet as a commercial medium, coordinates the development of key Internet technologies, and supports their applications through pilot projects and other informational activities.

Internet and Economics

Figure 4.7 WebEC logo.

WebEc (http://www.helsinki.fi/webec/) is an exhaustive list of web resources on economics. Its mirror sites (which contain a copy) include http://netec.wustl.edu/webec.html (USA), http://netec.mcc.ac.uk/webec.html (UK), and http://netec.ier.hit-u.ac.jp/webec.html (Japan).

The List of Economics Journals (http://www.helsinki.fi/webec/journals.html) contains links to almost all economic journals published today. Some of these links have tables of contents and abstracts, and provide search facilities.

JSTOR (http://www.jstor.org) have archived articles published in *American Economic Review*, *Journal of Political Economy*, *Quarterly Journal of Economics*, *Review of Economics and Statistics*, and *Journal of Money, Credit and Banking*.

CHAPTER 5

Economic Aspects of Copyright Protection

Intellectual property laws are typically linked to a discussion of the values of intellectual creativity and society's use of information and ideas. Nevertheless, they are fundamentally economic measures and their implementation and enforcement can and indeed should be evaluated in terms of their effectiveness in achieving desired market changes. This chapter attempts to do just that. The ultimate end of intellectual property laws is to promote the creation of knowledge and useful arts. This goal, however, cannot be achieved without incentives, which most often are economic. This chapter examines the issue of digital copyright by focusing on the law's intention to protect the market for copyright owners. Therefore, any measure to enhance digital copyright has to be evaluated in terms of how well it accomplishes this. Nevertheless, far more than the use of legal and artificial market barriers, this chapter advocates the essential role of strategy in resolving the copyright debate.

The most efficient allocation of resources is obtained when markets are competitive—in other words, when prices are determined by demand and supply and fully reflect the cost of producing a good, its opportunity costs, and society's valuation for the good as well as other uses of the same resources. To achieve maximum efficiency, the market forces must not be inhibited by external measures such as taxes, artificial barriers to entry, and other measures that affect the level of market power of either sellers or buyers. Copyrights and patents seem to directly contradict this by giving authors and inventors a limited monopoly right over production and distribution of a good. Why then is there the need to give artificial monopoly rights to authors?

The need to protect intellectual properties to the extent that competitive market mechanisms are abandoned has less to do with the fact that society values creativity so highly but because ideas, once discovered and put into words and other physical forms, can be easily copied, often without incurring additional effort and time. To those who believe that human creativity belongs to humanity or society, this is an added advantage that makes disseminating ideas easier. In an age of information, however, producing ideas has become the most important economic activity, and ideas consume enormous resources and time to produce. In other words, ideas and intellectual properties have become investments that must be remunerated.

Disseminating ideas is desirable and necessary for the prosperity of a society. Teaching a new and improved farming technology to neighbors, for example, increases overall agricultural production without restricting the inventor of the new method from reaping benefits on his or her own land by using the same technology. Although ownership of physical properties such as land must be clearly defined to prevent inefficient use, intellectual properties are often more valuable if shared. After ideas are written down in physical forms that are then traded, however, the ownership right of an idea and its physical manifestations in various forms becomes an economic issue, first set forth formally in the copyright legislation of the 16th century.

5.1. Economic History of Copyright

Copyright is a by-product of the mass printing process, improved literacy, and market incentives for profits. Its statutory specifics have historically evolved in the context of the book trade, emphasizing the "property" aspects over the more "intellectual" perspective. In today's age of information and digital products, many fear that copyright laws formulated to regulate the book trade are grossly inadequate, pointing out that digital media are fundamentally different from the paper medium in both production and distribution. As the printing press forced society to re-think intellectual properties four centuries ago, the digital communication again compels a reevaluation of the purpose and practice of copyright laws.

In an effort to continue to protect authors' rights in the digital era, new technologies and tools are being developed specifically to control digital communication. The development of a comprehensive implementation scheme for digital copyright, however, must grow out of the overall purpose of such measures, and will be judged by its effectiveness in fulfilling any agreed-upon function of copyright law. To better understand the rationale for copyright protection, this discussion reviews how two strands of thought regarding intellectual properties—property rights versus authorship rights—have developed along with the modern publishing industry.

The property rights approach sees the objective of a copyright law as guaranteeing market and revenues for authors and thereby promoting a continuous supply of high-quality products. Followers of this approach regard current copyright laws to be adequate, and focus on developing new technological means of auditing, identifying, and measuring digital flows accompanied by vigorous enforcement of the laws.

On the other hand, the authorship rights approach considers the fundamental function of copyright to be protecting authors' moral rights to their creation, so a stricter mechanism is needed to control all aspects of viewing, storing, retrieving, altering, reproducing, and transmitting their creations. Whether these products are marketable is immaterial. Followers of this approach believe in redefining copyright for digital products and modifying or strengthening copyright statutes.

The Property Aspect of Copyright

An idea, knowledge, or intellectual activity as an economic property is a relatively modern invention. It is quite clear that laws governing property give an owner the exclusive right to possess, use, and transfer property and other objects connected to or derived from that property. But although physical properties such as an acre of land or a house can be clearly defined, what is an intellectual property? To establish property rights, one needs to first identify a) the owner and b) the property. The owner of an intellectual property is the author. But because of its intangible nature, ownership cannot be established over an idea, and thus property rights are awarded to the physical expression of the author's idea such as a book.

Despite being called "property," intellectual properties are obviously quite different from tangible properties, and therefore legal protection and prosecution based on copyright law are substantially different from other property laws. This difference was highlighted in the computer hacker case of *U.S. v. Riggs* in 1990 (Godwin, 1994). The prosecution tried to apply the ITSP—Interstate Transportation of Stolen Property (18 U.S.C. 2314)—statute to a computer hacker who made an unauthorized connection to a regional telephone operating system, copied its emergency 911 procedure, and distributed it, ultimately publishing it in a magazine. Instead of applying copyright or trade secret laws, the prosecution used ITSP statutes, mistakenly believing that property theft law also applied to intellectual properties. Admittedly, ITSP was wrongly applied; a law governing trade secrets—against which federal and state criminal laws have been enacted or modified to address online cases—or wire-frauds might have been better suited.

The Supreme Court had previously stated that copyrighted material does not meet the scope of ITSP, however, which applies to tangible items. In the case of copying a computer file, there is no physical seizure of an item or transport of that good. Simply put, the emergency 911 file was left on the host's computer, and only a copy was transmitted. In this way, unauthorized copying is substantially different from a theft protected by ordinary property statutes.

Even generic theft statutes are found to be irrelevant in the case of unauthorized copying. Again, theft involves physically taking an object, the remedy to which may be recovering that object. Copyright, on the other hand, does not protect the property itself, but rather the interest of the authors, especially the market or profit interests. If a book is stolen from a publisher's warehouse, for example, property laws governing theft or stolen property may apply, but pirated copies are not theft protected by generic theft statute. Instead, the violation is termed "infringement" of the publisher's interest protected by copyright. This difference is illustrated by the fact that although stolen property is recovered, pirated copies are destroyed. It is important to recognize that, economically speaking, intellectual properties are not properties—as tangible commodities—despite the misleading term, and intellectual property laws do not protect the said property, but the interests of the owners derived from the use of that property—although this interest may very well be termed as "property" in the legal sense.

When does the proprietary right to an intellectual activity and its pecuniary rewards become an issue? Stealing property, such as a theft, is an economic concern because the owner is deprived of its use by which someone else benefits. Suppose that Alice has a plow, and Bob steals that plow to plow his land. During Bob's plowing, Alice is deprived of the use of that plow, and perhaps loses her crop by missing the planting season. Bob's gain is Alice's loss. Suppose, however, that Alice invented a plow attachment that makes plowing much easier. Bob, after seeing how the attachment was made and attached, makes his own device and gains the same benefit from reduced labor. Alice in this case is not deprived of using her own idea on her own land.

Further suppose that Bob opens a business selling plow attachments. Does Bob owe some monetary remuneration to Alice? Today, the answer is a resounding yes—assuming that this plow has the same impact as it did then—but the idea of "selling ideas" did not exist until the Modern era. Protection of private property rights over intellectual activities is not an issue if there is no opportunity, now or ever, of making a profit or if there is a reasonable method of controlling reproduction and selling. During the Middle Ages, Bob or no one else would have thought of selling plow attachments as a business, and innovations of many types were copied and stolen by others without regard to intellectual property rights. (Keeping them secret was one way of controlling ideas, to deprive others of their benefits.) Some ideas, even when not kept secret, could not be copied. Even after printing presses revolutionized the book trade and brought copyright issues to the forefront, for example, the same issue was mostly irrelevant to painters and paintings, which could not be reproduced easily.

The first known copyright theft occurred when Hermodorus copied Plato's speeches and sold them overseas (Gurnsey, 1995). Was this a crime? If there was a law prohibiting speech transcription and selling, Hermodorus might have been a criminal. But the fact that there was no such law indicates that Plato and his compatriots did not recognize a potential for profit in selling the speeches. What limited the market for speeches was the lack of suitable technology for producing copies. Even during the Middle Ages, "unauthorized" hand-copying was an important part of monastic life. The primary utility of these literary works was to communicate ideas to readers. Disseminating ideas through hard-working monks was more important than any profit consideration of the authors.

When Gutenberg's printing press changed the publishing industry in the 15th century, a larger market began to appear for printed works. With mass printing, the profit potential from mass marketing was recognized and, almost immediately, some works were "popular" enough to be pirated. The idea of proprietary ownership was quickly extended to copies as well as to the original manuscript...hence the term "copyright." At this time, however, the property right was applied to bound copies of books, and publishers rather than authors controlled legal rights over publication and distribution.

This is logical if one considers that books and copies were perceived to be properties of trade, and that the first copyright laws aimed to regulate no more than the trade aspects of book publishing. The Royal Charter, for example, given to London-based Stationers' Company in 1557, granted a monopoly right to publishers. The Royal Charter was a precursor to modern copyright laws and established the "property" aspect of printed works. Once registered and printed, a book became the property of the publisher. In this way, what the Charter protected was the market, or the profit-making trade. The fact that books were based on intellectual activities was not yet a consideration. Despite the growing recognition of authorship rights and the importance of knowledge and ideas, modern copyright laws still maintain this aspect of trade regulation.

The monopoly, however, broke down as the demand for books and regional piracy increased substantially and the market regulation based on the Charter became ineffective and was abandoned. By 1710, publishing and book trading was an important profit-making activity, and interested parties demanded statutory protection of their rights to secure markets for their properties. England's Statute of Anne in 1710 laid down the first terms of copyright, limited its application to 14 years, and set out infringement penalties. Although the statute also professed to protect impoverished authors during the Age of Enlightenment by signaling the assertion of their rights, the statute met with vigorous piracy originating in Scotland and Ireland—and later in Australia and the U.S. after copyright law was expanded to Scotland and Ireland. This prompted a series of copyright laws that modified and strengthened the terms of copyright protection. The benchmarks of copyright history outlined in figure 5.1 show that a growing market and potential for rewards has always been the driving force behind the struggle for copyright protection. It is also important to remember that illegal copies became an issue only when reproduction technology became sufficiently advanced. The invention of printing presses, photocopiers, and now digital copying technologies have periodically brought the issue to the forefront. But the market environment has not changed significantly, and the digital marketplace does not present any new issues that demand a complete revision in intellectual property laws as some have argued.

Since the Statute of Anne, three major developments have occurred in modern copyright laws. First, the intrinsic rights of authors have become increasingly recognized. Although the Royal Charter and the Statute of Anne established authors' rights, they were geared more toward protecting publishing houses from pirates.

Second, the recognition that foreign market piracy is a substantial economic issue has resulted in international copyright agreements. The Berne Convention for the Protection of Literary and Artistic Works (the Berne Convention) was established in 1886 and its most recent revision (the 1971 Paris text) is administered by the World Intellectual Property Organization (WIPO) (http://www.wipo.org). A work copyrighted in one country is also protected in other countries by the Berne Convention, as long as these countries are signatories to the Convention. There are other international copyright agreements including the Universal Copyright Convention (UCC), which allows signatory countries to specify formalities such as copyright notice and registration. Although the U.S. was the primary advocate for the UCC, this and other agreements are overshadowed by the Berne Convention and the WIPO.

And third, modern laws have extended their protection to all types of intellectual properties to include paintings, musical scores, photographs, recordings, and performing arts. Since knowledge became the most important economic asset during the Industrial Revolution, the attempt to balance private property rights against public benefits to stimulate economic development have frequently resulted in clashes between the right of the author and the goal of economic progress.

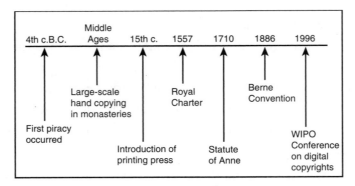

Figure 5.1 Timeline in the development of copyright.

The Authorship Aspect of Copyright

After an idea is attached to a physical object, for example when it has been set down on paper, establishing the ownership of that object is a legal question that most legal regimes are quite accustomed to dealing with. Throughout the history of copyright laws, the ownership right to an object to which an idea is attached has been a far less contentious issue than the question of authorship right to an idea. When one wrote down public speeches of Plato, for example, the manuscripts belonged to the transcriber, not the author, Plato. The former could legally duplicate and sell the speeches. Historical records do not in fact show whether the author or the government objected to this practice or recognized the issue of authorship at all. When authorship is not asserted, copying speeches could by no means be considered an act of theft.

Due to the property aspect of intellectual properties, copyright laws have evolved as a trade regulation. Intellectual properties have characteristics unlike other physical properties, however, and accordingly copyright laws are enforced differently. Damage awards for copyright theft, for example, are based on actual and potential market loss inflicted by the theft, not the recovery of the stolen property itself. In fact, as mentioned previously, stolen property— that is, unauthorized copies—is destroyed, not returned. More importantly, ideas and knowledge have so-called public goods characteristics, where the social gains may outweigh the private gains if freely available. At an extreme position are those who believe that ideas cannot be possessed, confined, or exclusively appropriated. As Thomas Jefferson said, "inventions cannot in nature be a subject of property."

As a result, the current debate on copyright protection in the electronic marketplace mainly centers on whether authors have the moral right to control every aspect of their works, or whether the public have the right to access this information. A clear understanding of this issue is needed before one can evaluate various positions on copyright protection in electronic commerce.

Modern copyright laws accept the premise that authors who provide content should be rewarded. This represents the changing view that the main emphasis in providing copyright protection is not just "protecting the market," but "creating incentives." Although the right of authors was relatively inconsequential in early copyright laws, in the 18th century countries in Continental Europe began to advocate natural and moral rights of creators as inalienable rights. In today's age when the expressive medium is no longer limited to paper and proprietary characteristics have become uncertain, authorship of an idea takes on even greater significance.

Although proponents of authorship emphasize maximizing authors' rights by controlling all aspects of intellectual properties, this goal contradicts the professed goal of intellectual property right laws to promote society's welfare, and often faces difficulties in collecting payments. A sale of a book entitles the buyer to rent, resell, and give it away as he or she sees fit, even though that will prevent the content owner from selling another copy. Because copyright in the age of printing was primarily a property law pertaining to physical books, the first sale doctrine applies to a sale of a book even though the content owner does not transfer the copyright through the sale. Even when there is no dispute regarding payments, copyright holders often lack means to monitor and control such activities. ASCAP and BMI, for example, rely on a complex formula to determine payments for copyright holders, because counting every instance of broadcast and performance of a copyrighted work is impossible. Digital technologies and the electronic marketplace give content owners means to control and monitor every aspect of consumer usage. As a result, the desire to control copyrights often coincides with the intent to maximize authors' moral rights that give content owners unrestricted control over their creations. New technical means to expand copyright control, however, face challenges from various uses of copyrighted works considered to be "fair" and a benefit society as a whole.

Public Interest

The expanding scope of copyright based on moral rights of authors is not always consistent with some purposes of copyright law. The public interest aspect of intellectual property rights, for example, was set forth in the U.S. Constitution's mandate to "promote the progress of science and useful arts," which became the basis of granting exclusive rights to inventors and authors. It reflects the recognition of the importance of authorship and intellectual activities in ensuring a society's progress. To promote this goal is to acknowledge that information and ideas have the characteristics of public goods. The transfer and dissemination of copyrightable materials—that is, change of ownership—is clearly in society's best interest. To encourage productive activity, authors do need incentives such as profits, but keeping ideas out of circulation due to an overly rigid system that is highly unproductive. Therefore, modern copyright laws have become far more than trade regulations; they also attempt to act as incentive mechanisms that balance private and social interests.

In its role as a mechanism regulating business practices, the protective and regulatory aspects of copyright law are mainly concerned with the business aspects of reproducing and distributing the physical product. As an incentive mechanism, however, copyright law carefully selects what it does and does not protect.

First, works containing no original authorship are not protected. Therefore, commonly known facts, lists, or tables cannot be copyrighted. A later section discusses the implication of this for databases, which often contain a collection of facts. Second, a fair use is not a copyright infringement. A fair use is specifically permitted to avoid a rigid application of a copyright statute if it stifles other intellectual activities such as criticism, comment, reporting, teaching, or research. A rigid application of moral rights to digital products will compromise society's need to foster intellectual activities, not to speak of the right to free speech. New copyright regimes, therefore, must continue to balance incentives for both private and social objectives. Furthermore, new copyright regimes should not be restricted to legal definitions of what copyright is and is not. To circumvent the first sale doctrine, for example, software vendors use licensing rather than sales so that the vendors rely on contractual laws rather than copyright laws for protection. Although legal ramifications of copyright and contract laws may differ, the market is the same and needs a consistent legal framework. This at the least demonstrates the need for a broader incentive mechanism that can deal with all modes of "selling" digital products.

5.2. The Nuts and Bolts of Copyrights

Anyone who creates a work covered by copyright law (see the following section) and fixes it on a substantially permanent medium automatically possesses the copyright. Under current laws, a copyright is obtained as soon as a work is created and fixed in a medium. Unlike patents, authors do not need to claim their copyright, register, publish, or give copyright notices on their work. Forms of copyright notice (for example, "C in a circle") are optional for works published on and after March 1, 1989. Through agreements such as the Berne Convention, copyright is acknowledged internationally as well, although patents have to be filed individually for each country. Unless a specific contract transferring the right is drawn up, the copyright belongs to the actual authors. Full-time employment may constitute such a contractual situation, known as "work for hire," where employers may own the copyright for the material created. For other specially commissioned works for hire, a written and signed agreement is required.

Objects Covered by Copyright

U.S. copyright law (17 U.S.C.) grants copyright protection for works of authorship in the following cases:

- Literary works including books, magazines, news articles, manuals, catalogs, advertising words, computer software, and compilations such as directories and databases
- Musical works including accompanying words
- Dramatic works including accompanying music
- Pantomimes and choreographic works
- Pictorial, graphic, and sculptural works including maps and fine arts
- Motion pictures and other audiovisual works
- Sound recordings
- Architectural works

Terms of Copyright

For works created in 1978 or later, the term of copyright is the author's life plus 50 years after the author's death. In the case of corporate-authored works, the term is 75 years after publication or 100 years from creation. Although works created before 1978 were governed by different laws, such works were given a term of 75 years from their creation.

Works That Cannot be Copyrighted

Works that do not warrant copyrights are as follows:

- Works are not protected if they are not "fixed" on a sufficiently permanent medium. This requirement is lax enough to include handwritten or typed documents as "fixed" forms of authorship.

- Only original works are protected. The "originality" requirement is also fairly flexible. Unlike patents, works dealing with the same subject or idea can be copyrighted as long as each work has a minimum degree of originality.

- When works incorporate preexisting material, only the original portion is covered by the copyright. If a journal contains articles copyrighted by individual authors, the act of collection is copyrighted as the original work.

- Facts cannot be copyrighted. Therefore, compilations of names and addresses publicly available, such as the telephone book, cannot be copyrighted. To copyright such material and databases, copyright law requires a certain originality in selection, organization, and arrangement of the data. Even then, only the original aspects are protected; the facts still are not protected. Alphabetic ordering is not considered original. Similarly, expressions that have become standard techniques for creating a particular type of work are in the public domain.

- Works in the public domain are not protected. Works can enter the public domain when their copyright expires. Due to changing copyright laws, however, a careful evaluation is needed to determine whether a work is in the public domain. Previously a failure to renew or to give proper copyright notice resulted in the loss of a copyright, for example. New laws, however, do not require copyright renewal. Also, works created after March 1, 1989, do not need to include copyright notice, registration, or deposit to be protected under copyright law. Current U.S. law still provides, however, that registration and deposit of the work with the Copyright Office is a prerequisite to the filing of an infringement suit in federal court (see fig. 5.2). Moreover, certain advantageous remedies are only available for infringements that occur after registration and deposit. Because of the Berne Convention, these formalities are not applicable to foreign nationals, and probably will have to be removed entirely from U.S. law before it is in full compliance with the Convention.

- If a work is created by the U.S. government, it is automatically in the public domain because government works cannot be copyrighted. This only applies to the federal government. State governments can copyright their documents. Laws and legislation of both federal and state governments may not be copyrighted. The only statutory exception is for data produced by the U.S. Secretary of Commerce, which are copyrighted under the Standard Reference Data Act (15 U.S.C. 290e). A gray area is when the U.S. government provides funding for independent contractors. Such works are copyrighted by contractors, but the copyright can be transferred to the government.

Figure 5.2 U.S. Copyright Office home page. Unlike patents and trademarks which are administered by U.S. Patent and Trademark Office (http:// www.uspto.gov), U.S. Copyright Office is a branch of the Library of Congress (http:// lcweb.loc.gov/copyright/resces.html).

Specific Rights of Authors Granted by Copyright

Rights of authors granted under copyright law include the following seven areas. Correspondingly, copyright infringement occurs when someone is engaged in any of these activities without authorization from the authors. The seven rights include the following:

- Reproduction right to copy, duplicate, transcribe, or imitate the work in fixed form
- Adaptive right to modify and create derivative works
- Distribution right to distribute the work by sale, rental, lease, or lending
- Performance right to perform the work in public or to transmit to the public
- Display right to show a copy of work in public

- Paternity right to claim (or disclaim) authorship
- Integrity right to prevent distorting or destroying one's work.

The last two rights—paternity and integrity—were not recognized in the U.S. when it adhered to the Universal Copyright Convention (UCC), but in 1988 the U.S. joined the Berne Convention, which recognizes all seven rights of authors. Both paternity and integrity rights pertain to the moral rights of authors discussed in the previous section. The U.S. opted out of the full moral rights provisions of the Berne Convention, except that the Congress did amend U.S. copyright law to provide limited paternity and integrity rights for the visual arts.

Fair Use Doctrine

Even when a work is fully protected by copyright law, certain uses are considered to be within the fair use rule and do not constitute an infringement of the author's exclusive rights. A fair use of a copyrighted work is allowed for purposes such as "criticism, comment, news reporting, teaching including multiple copies for classroom use, scholarship, or research."

In determining whether a particular case falls within the fair use rule, Congress has set out the following four guiding principles (17 U.S.C. 107):

1. **The purpose and character of the use.** If the use is for non-profit educational purposes, it falls within the fair use rule. Even when the use is commercial, however, a "productive" use may be allowed. A firm may use one of *Consumer Reports'* reviews (copyrighted by its publisher, Consumers Union) in its advertising as it "educates" consumers (*Consumers Union v. General Signal Corp.*, 2nd Cir. 1983). Such interpretation is used by courts to balance incentives for content providers and society's interests.

2. **The nature of the copyrighted work.** If a work is more factual than artistic, its use is more likely to be judged as a fair use. Also,

unpublished works are protected from fair use more than published works because an infringement may deprive the author of publishing in the first place and because it interferes with the author's right not to publish.

3. **The amount and substantiality of the portion used in relation to the copyrighted work as a whole.** The substantiality standard dictates that even when a small amount of a copyrighted work is used, it will be an infringement if that portion is qualitatively substantial.

4. **The effect of the use on the potential market for or value of the copyrighted work.** This is by far the most important factor to consider when evaluating the fair use rule. In short, fair use may be tolerated only if it does not interfere with the author's marketability or profits. This principle relates to a "potential," not an actual, market. Therefore, even if an author does not market a work, its potential market is protected. This also includes instances where an author markets the product only in one market—for example, in a printed form but not in a digital form, which is a potential market.

Other Intellectual Property Laws

Besides literary and artistic activities protected by copyright, other types of intellectual activities are protected by three major laws: Patent law deals with inventions that have useful functions; trademark law gives a monopoly right to any word, name, symbol, or device used to identify and distinguish one's product or service; and trade secret law protects methods, processes, formulas, and any information maintained as a secret. The difference between patent and copyright can be summarized, using the language of the U.S. Constitution, as one that distinguishes "science" from "useful arts" and "inventors" from "authors." A patentable object embodies some useful idea that results in a novel and improved function, although a copyrighted work is simply the medium for transferring an idea. The function or process described in a copyright work, therefore, cannot be protected, unless it is patented.

5.3.   Copyright Protection and Digital Products

The three primary rights of authors granted under copyright law—reproduction, distribution, and adaptive rights—are all clearly interrelated. Books, for example, are reproduced with the intent to sell or distribute. Adaptive or derivative works involve a reproduction of a portion of the original work. Essentially, all three rights are integral parts of the overall copyright protection process.

This intertwined relationship is accentuated in the case of digital products because of the way they are transmitted and used. Downloading or viewing a digital file automatically involves copying and reproducing it, just as servers and clients on the Internet often retain copies. An act of distribution on the Internet is often accomplished through reproduction. In other words, one aspect of using a digital file overlaps with other activities, affecting many of the exclusive rights simultaneously. (See Lemley, 1996a for the implications of overlapping copyrights on the Internet.) For clarity, however, this discussion distinguishes three aspects of using digital products that are relevant to copyright protection and which correspond to the three unique characteristics of digital products discussed earlier in Chapter 2: reproducibility, transmutability, and indestructibility.

Reproduction

As shown in the history of copyright law, the need for change in copyright protection has arisen historically because of increased ease of mass reproduction of an original work. With the advent of the digital world, concern has once again cropped up. Unlike earlier instances, however, the same technology is now available to both producers and consumers. When printing presses were first introduced, only entrepreneurs with significant capital would engage in reproduction. As a result, unauthorized reproduction in book publishing was mostly done by other publishers, not by consumers, and this fact often gave copyright enforcers an easy way to identify and locate infringers. Even with photocopiers, mass reproduction for the commercial market has been limited to overseas publishers. For some books, for example, it may be cheaper to buy than to photocopy. Unlike photocopying, however, digital reproduction is easy, fast, and does not result in quality degradation.

In electronic commerce, then, the issue is to what extent the reproduction technology available to consumers will erode the market to the detriment of content owners. When there is no market erosion, control over reproduction is largely meaningless. Reproduction without reselling or distributing seems harmless and appears to fall under the fair use guideline. Still, unauthorized reproduction by consumers is a complicated issue in electronic commerce. Legal experts have not yet determined whether viewing a World Wide Web page constitutes copying; after all, any connection over a network involves downloading a copy of files. If a hard copy of that file is printed, does this represent another unauthorized reproduction by the consumer? Because neither of these cases involve reselling, interpreting these activities as "unauthorized reproduction" rather than "fair use" goes too far in the interest of protecting copyrights. Extending the definition of reproduction and seeking a blanket protection against it does not reflect economic reality—the impact on the market.

On the other hand, copying files for use on other computers may or may not be considered fair use. This issue is usually dealt with via site or enterprise licensing, which specifies the number of machines and users allowed under the licensing contract. Because of the distributional aspect of licensing, the next section discusses this case.

Reproductions on the Internet

A reproduction by definition is a copy of an original work fixed on a sufficiently permanent medium. Unfortunately, there is great confusion over what constitutes a fixable and permanent medium when a digital product is transmitted over the Net. If a user makes a copy using a "copy" or "duplicate" command, the exclusive right to reproduce granted by copyright law undeniably applies. Because of the nature of the Internet and computer usage, however, many types of copies are made during transmission and display.

Depending on how one interprets the requirements of the law regarding "fixation" and "permanency," various activities of Internet communication may actually violate copyright law. Examples of these activities include the following:

- **RAM or screen copies.** When a file is displayed on a computer screen or is used by a computer program, a temporary copy is placed in the internal RAM memory of the computer.

- **Deleted but not-erased copies.** When a file is deleted from a computer hard disk, the file is not actually erased but remains until it is overwritten by the computer for some other file. Similarly, most e-mail programs may download a message from an e-mail server but leave a copy on the server. Also, sending an e-mail leaves a copy in the Out folder until it is deleted.

- **Copies in transition.** When a digital file is sent over the network, some copies may be made by intermediaries who route and forward the file for the purpose of buffering, monitoring, or record-keeping. If RAM copies are deemed to be reproductions, these copies in transition may also be considered reproductions.

- **Web cache copies.** Most web browsers automatically store accessed pages in cache for a limited period of time.

Whether these copies can be treated as reproductions that infringe any copyright depends on the way the traditional definition of copying is applied to the digital world. Several court cases suggest that these copies are not fixed and are therefore not considered to constitute copyright infringement. (For RAM copies, see *Apple Computer v. Formula International,* 594 F. Supp. 617 (C.D. Cal. 1984); for screen copies, see *NFLC, Inc. v. Devcom Mid-America, Inc.,* 33 U.S.P.Q2d 1629 (7th Cir. 1995) and *Stern Elec. v. Kaufman,* 669 F.2d 852 (2d Cir. 1982).) In recent cases—*MAI Systems Corp. v. Peak Computer,* 991 F.2d 511 (9th Cir. 1993); *Triad Systems Corp. v. Southeastern Express Co.* (9th Cir. 1995)—the court found copies in RAM to be fixed and as such constitute reproductions governed by the copyright law. Should such an interpretation prevail, all four preceding examples will violate existing copyright law.

Economic Implications of Reproduction

While clear legal definitions need to be established, the process takes time and many wrong conclusions will be reached. Instead, an economic approach toward protecting copyrights in the digital world should be based on the market. Reproduction without actual or intended distribution does not affect the size of the market for the copyrighted work. The control over reproduction therefore becomes an issue only when linked with distribution. In the paper-based world, reproduction and distribution are fundamentally related as the term "reproduction" itself is a product of the age of the printing press. In many cases, digital reproduction is required for uses other than distribution.

A pertinent question in electronic commerce is whether today's reproduction technology will lead to widespread, unauthorized distribution. If people do not distribute or transmit copies, controlling reproduction might have legal implications but be economically unnecessary. In this case, it may be sufficient to identify a copy so that when copies are circulated it is possible to verify whether they are unauthorized reproductions. Market control mechanisms discouraging unauthorized copies in this vein may be sufficient. Proposals to control every aspect of digital reproduction, using copyright arguments, will have unintended effects on other uses of digital products.

Resale and Distribution

In terms of the economic effects of copyrights, the act of making copies is irrelevant unless it is accompanied by an infringement on the owner's exclusive right to distribute copies. A person may make numerous backup copies, but this would not affect the size of the product's market if the copies are not distributed. Therefore, an act of reproduction need not be controlled by expensive technologies or preempted by copyrights and contracts when it does not have an impact on the author's market.

To determine what constitutes distribution is relatively simple although there are some issues that remain to be settled. Section 106 of the U.S. copyright law (17 U.S.C. §106) grants the right to distribute copies "to the public by sale or other transfer of ownership" to the owner. Technical issues have been raised regarding whether an Internet transmission can be considered a distribution "to the public" and whether it constitutes a "transfer of ownership." For both of these issues, Internet transmissions are considered to be subject to the copyright law with minor changes. E-mailing a message to a person, or posting it on a restricted-membership mailing list or on a limited-access intranet web page, for example, may not amount to public distribution subject to copyright law. Nevertheless, Internet distribution may be considered public by the very nature of the medium. An automatic forwarding program, for example, if used by most e-mailers, may quickly result in "public distribution." Also, the tangible object being transferred (for example, the e-mail message) consists of bits of ones and zeros that are indistinguishable, unlike pirate copies of a book, but which physically exist on the receiving end unlike over-the-air broadcasts. These differences from traditional forms of distribution may be tackled by minor changes in the definition of what constitutes distribution.

Regardless of whether an Internet transmission constitutes a public distribution, the major concern is the erosion of the owner's market due to unauthorized distribution of a copyrighted work. Whether the copy is distributed free or for a price is immaterial in deciding copyright infringement as long as the receiver of the copy is a potential customer of the copyright owner. If so, any unauthorized distribution over the Internet will deprive the owner of their customers. Resale or distribution with unauthorized duplication clearly falls within the boundary of traditional copyright protection, and can be protected through more vigorous enforcement of the law or through the use of technology without changing the existing legal framework. The problem is not so simple, however, when one resells a digital product without reproduction.

Resale and the First Sale Doctrine

Resale without reproduction, just like lending a book to a third party, is permitted under the first sale doctrine, but has profound implications in electronic commerce. The first sale doctrine allows a buyer who has purchased a copy of a copyrighted work to sell, give away, or lend it to other people.

Suppose, however, that Alice has discovered a mathematical formula that can predict the interest rate a year from now. The safest way to sell the formula would be to write it in a computer program so that Alice's customers could not know the formula but still use it to predict interest rates. But imagine that Bob buys the program, calculates next year's interest rate, and then resells the program to Charlie on the Internet. Then Charlie repeats the same process and sells the program to Dan, and so on. With the speed of the Internet, Alice may lose all her customers in a matter of days or even hours. One digital product can be resold an infinite number of times within a short time, completely destroying the market for the seller. (A separate issue may arise if Bob sells Charlie the calculated interest rate, but not the program.) Although the same problem exists with books and magazines, the far shorter transmission speed for digital products makes the problem far more significant. Consequently, the first sale doctrine will be detrimental in electronic commerce, at least theoretically.

The high transaction speed on the Internet often prompts software vendors to include a specific prohibition of resale in their copyright notices. Alternatively, vendors prefer to use licensing contracts rather than sales. Under a licensing scenario, vendors can specify designated users and prohibit any kind of transfer of the product because the terms and rights of licensing are governed by contract laws different from copyright laws.

For many digital products, resale always involves reproduction. An information product can be consumed (read) and resold, for example, because consuming the information does not affect the product physically. Requiring consumers to destroy their copy before forwarding or reselling it to another person would still leave a copy because reading and viewing information leaves an image (or knowledge) in one's mind. In such cases, reselling may be prohibited outright, abandoning the first sale doctrine granted under the current copyright law.

Whether one can legally prohibit the resale of a digital product is still uncertain. In case of a functional product—for example, a computer program—which can produce something, it is also unclear how these two products should be treated. In any case, prohibiting resale will have important implications in terms of market efficiency. When buyers are not satisfied with a product, for example, resale in the second-hand market is an alternative to returning the product to the seller, as discussed in Chapter 4, "Quality Uncertainty and Market Efficiency." If sellers do not provide an appropriate return policy or warranty, buyers should be allowed a remedy such as reselling the product.

If resale is permitted, the market erosion is still more significant for some digital products than others. Time-independent single-use products—for example, the average weather information in Austin, Texas—can find buyers all year round, making them susceptible for resale. Theoretically, the producer could only sell one copy. On the other hand, a time-dependent product loses its value rapidly, which may encourage consumers to buy the product directly from the producer instead of waiting to buy second-hand. Multiple-use products such as computer programs also resist reselling as their product life is longer than single-use products.

This indicates that one alternative to the wholesale revision of the law is for the sellers to change their product choices and marketing strategies based on consumers' uses of information products. Products, for example, could be converted into time-dependent multiple-use products. Instead of selling weather information for one city, one could sell an encyclopedic computer program about weather. Another means to avoid the economic consequences from reselling is to customize products and provide frequent updates. Personalized products, by definition, are useless for persons other than those for whom they are intended. These and other market-based solutions to copyright protection are discussed in more detail in section entitled "Market Protection Through Business Strategies."

Resale Prevention and Pricing

An important consideration in allowing consumer resale is the balance between the seller's power of discriminatory pricing and the buyer's ability to arbitrage. Consumer arbitrage refers to their buying and selling among themselves. If Alice tries to charge Bob $20 for a product that she sells for $10 to Charlie, for example, Charlie could buy two from Alice and sell one to Bob at, say, $15. The gains accrued to Bob and Charlie from such an arbitrage are what Alice could make for herself if she had a means to prevent the arbitrage. This kind of arbitrage can be prevented if Bob and Charlie live far apart, and the transportation cost does not justify arbitraging. When there is no protection against consumer arbitrage, Alice can only charge a uniform price.

Resale is one form of consumer arbitrage, and even a firm with perfect demand information cannot discriminate between consumers if buyers can transfer products among themselves. As will be discussed in Chapter 8 in connection with digital product pricing, sellers should be concerned about the lowered ability to price-discriminate when allowing resale. Therefore, there is an additional benefit from preventing consumer resale, and, depending on the size of this benefit, highly costly methods and technologies to protect copyrights might be feasible. This issue is critical if the seller wants to charge different prices for different consumer groups (for the same product). On the other hand, consumers do need to be able to preserve their leverage against sellers' discriminatory prices. Clearly, the threats and opportunities inherent in allowing or disallowing the resale of digital products involve not just copyrights but also product pricing, consumer welfare, and the efficiency of a market.

Although copyrighted products are sold at per-copy prices to consumers, they are often given away free to radio and TV stations; the latter, however, pay per-play royalties. A recorded song may be played an unlimited number of times by a consumer who purchases it on a CD. A radio station, however, must pay based on the number of times it plays the song on the airwaves. Because of practical difficulties in measuring usage, the music industry relies on the blanket license for stations and formula for distributing payments among copyright holders based on measured popularity of each song. The American Society of Composers, Authors and Publishers (ASCAP; http://www.visualradio.com/ascap) and Broadcast Musicians Incorporated (BMI; http://bmi.com) administer this complex operation. In electronic commerce, pricing and distributing payments will be technically superior and more equitable. Each use of an online article will be measured and payments can be calculated based on real—not sampled—usage or popularity. Theoretically, consumers can be required to pay per-play royalties rather than a direct sale price.

Finally, a major portion of reproduction cost for a digital product may be copyright payment. Although distribution and marketing costs will be substantial due to the increasing number of products offered in the worldwide digital market, copyright holders have means to verify actual usage for their songs and articles. If prices were to be determined by production costs and user demand, authors' rights and popularity of their products would become the most significant factors in pricing.

Content Control

Even more than reproduction and resale and distribution, content control will be the most important aspect in copyright protection for digital products. Reorganizing and modifying a digital file is much easier than altering and reproducing a non-digital work. As digital product development already emphasizes differentiation and customization, as will be discussed in Chapter 8, illegal use of copyrighted works will in all probability focus on partial copying and derivative works. Most World Wide Web users, for example, routinely select and copy a portion of a web page—for example, a graphic file or a list—to use on their own web pages. Currently, it is not clear whether these materials are copyrighted or in the public domain, although the Copyright Office routinely accepts copyright registration for web pages. Also, web documents usually consist of many sub-documents, so it is often difficult to access the whole document. Copying and downloading is done only on a portion of a work.

Preserving the integrity of a digital product becomes harder than in the case of physical intellectual properties because of the ease of changing the content of an electronic file. Exact copies are easy to identify, but changes or damages can occur either by accident or by design. Recent developments in cryptographic technologies have now made it easier to preserve the integrity of a digital product. Various authentication technologies have been developed for documenting purposes and to prevent accidental changes. Major types are encryption, hashing, and digital time-stamping.

The emphasis on cryptographic technologies stems from the fear of tampering and the desire to preserve the integrity of a digital product. But is the transmutability of digital products only a liability for sellers? To the contrary, digital products are more valuable than physical products because of their malleability. Suppose that you have completed a masterpiece painting. The copyright law gives you the right to make derivative works from the painting. To incorporate a portion of the painting, however, you need to re-draw it, which might take as much time and effort as the first time. On the other hand, a digital masterpiece can be copied effortlessly. In other words, after a product is produced, subsequent costs for derivative works could be minimal. Derivative works can be thought of as benefits of annual crops from owning an agricultural land, or annual offspring gained from owning cattle. Digital products have comparably smaller annual expenses to reap such benefits. Therefore, authors may rely on the transmutability of digital products to maximize the adaptive right granted under the copyright law by rearranging, modifying, and customizing for different markets. In this case, the primary objective as an author is to exploit the nature of digital products by changing the content rather than maintaining it by using cumbersome technologies and regulations.

In addition to the lowered cost of derivative works, differentiating products also has an added benefit of preventing copyright violations because, as discussed earlier, personalized products resist distribution. The transmutability, therefore, counters the ill effects of reproducibility and indestructibility of digital products. *Personal Journal* (http:// bis.dowjones.com/ pj.html), for example, a personalized electronic edition of *The Wall Street Journal*, consists of news and information about companies specifically chosen by a subscriber, which might not be of great value to other potential subscribers who follow different sets of companies. Without any legal maneuvering, personalizing digital products lowers the possibility of copyright infringement by discouraging consumers from sharing the product. It is a prime example of dealing with copyright problems by actively adapting to the digital product environment.

5.4. Market Protection Through Business Strategies

By granting a monopoly power in the form of copyrights, society's intention is to protect an author's market from being eroded or stolen by others. When the market is not protected from pirates who do not share the initial cost of developing the product, authors have a reduced incentive to develop a product, at least for commercial reasons. This is the same argument used to advocate that academic research has to be funded by governments if quality products are desired, because non-profit intellectual activities are not protected.

Analysis based on product characteristics, however, reveals that many types of products may actually make the copyright protection issue null and void, turning their vulnerability of easy modification into a means to increase profit through product differentiation. Clearly, a tight control over all aspects of copyrights is not always most efficient. If the result is the creation of complacent regulated monopolists, it may instead fail to give incentives to producers to update information or to develop interactive and innovative products. Also, from the consumers' point of view, personal arbitrage via reselling is an important leverage against sellers' price discrimination. A more balanced approach can only be achieved after considering all the economic implications in the market. For a practical and viable solution for copyright protection in the digital world, sellers and policymakers need to consider the unique types of products and consumer usage. Depending on its type, some products may need more protection than others.

Interactive service providers clearly represent one end of the extreme with the least concern for copyright infringement. In actual fact, these services may not have applicable copyright protection in the first place. Among non-interactive products, time-dependent products represent the bulk of the primary information products available on the Internet. For these products, digital copyright does not need to be much different from non-digital copyright because the incentive for distribution is minimal, and because, even if there is some incentive, its effect on market will not be too great. Similarly, single-use products such as search results are personalized and situation-specific, and therefore of little value to other people except the buyer. Other information products that are more valuable if few people have them will not be shared at all.

On the opposite end of the extreme are music, software, and computer games. Digital copyright protection is critical for these time-independent, multiuse products. Nevertheless, sellers can still change consumer usage of these products so that they become time-dependent. As evident in the physical product world, frequent updates and releases of new and improved versions help this process. Similarly, with some effective but not too cumbersome technologies, short-run duplication can be prevented. The current reluctance of content owners to digitize their products and sell them on the Internet has more to do with lack of technologies and security in transmission speed, payment system, and other market services, than with concern about copyright. In sum, an extensive revision of copyright laws is not warranted when product strategies based on consumer behaviors are implemented.

A separate issue exists in the case of computer software. The gist of the issue is whether copyright or patent protection is more suitable to software. In general, the consensus seems to be that copyright is the most effective means to protect software. Some software, however, has been recognized as being used to bring new and useful functions that can be protected by patents. The debate involves comparing a number of different factors. Copyright applies immediately, and a patent takes time to establish and is quite expensive to obtain. Also, a patent requires a great deal more in terms of originality than does a copyright. As a result, the protective right granted under patent law is in general stronger than that obtained under copyright law. This said, current laws are inadequate to deal with many facets of computer software, and some argue in favor of a new mechanism to protect software (Samuelson et al., 1994). The industry practices attempt to sidestep the whole issue of copyright versus patent protection for software by heavily using licensing agreements rather than sales to distribute the product. Through licensing, software vendors maintain the ownership of the product and can impose various restrictions regarding the use of their products. A proper legal protection for software would represent a legitimate instance to rethink copyright laws for electronic commerce.

5.5.   Policy Implications

The concern over protecting authors' rights in the digital marketplace has not escaped the attention of the relevant policymakers. The legislation on copyright considered by the Congress during its 1996 session (S. 1284; H.R. 2441) would have made any electronic copy of copyrighted material an infringement and also would have restricted the applicability of the fair use rule in the case of digital products. These bills reflect the position of software makers, publishers, and entertainment companies, represented by the Creative Incentive Coalition (http://www.cic.org), that favors extending copyright protection to electronic commerce. The general direction of the bill mirrors the recommendations (known as the Lehman paper; see http://www.uspto.gov/web/ipnii) made by the Working Group on Intellectual Property Rights of the Information Infrastructure Task Force, which has been widely criticized for taking the content owners' position.

Both the Working Group and the Creative Incentive Coalition maintain that content owners will not be willing to provide quality information products on the Internet unless suitable property rights are secured. Without content, the Information Superhighway will be a long, winding, and above all, empty road. And the presumed benefits from commercial use of the Information Superhighway may not ever materialize. Unlike previous copyright legislation, this will be the first time that the law is proactive, instead of reactive to the current threats to publishers' market control. The publishers' position is that an extended copyright protection is a prerequisite for their participation in the new electronic marketplace. The question to ask is whether digital markets are sufficiently different from other markets to warrant exceptional copyright protection.

This is not supported with enough evidence. On the contrary, the aspects of the digital market currently perceived as shortcomings are the very advantages it affords to the sellers. Customization and price discrimination possibilities as well as the acquisition of consumer behavioral data actually shift the balance in favor of the sellers in electronic commerce. Furthermore, the nature of digital products provide many incentives for the sellers to innovate and improve product and service selection and quality. As under any regulatory regime, overprotection of a market can result in stagnation of economic activity to the detriment of both the consumer and society.

Serious specific objections have been raised against the current proposal. Among them are the following:

- Making a new category of author's right for browsing and digital transmission
- Abolishing the first sale rule
- Limiting the scope of fair use

In each of these points, the current legislative effort seems to favor expanding publishers' rights. Debates on whether such radical changes are warranted for the digital marketplace will continue although the discussion in this chapter indicates that market-oriented solutions may well work with a minimal change in existing copyright laws.

Copyright and Antitrust Concerns

When a product has a network externality, the value of the product is increased as more people use the same product. (See Chapter 3, "Internet Infrastructure and Pricing," for a detailed discussion on the network externality.) As there are more users, more products compatible and useful to the user will be offered. In many instances, the product becomes the standard to which all other products must be compatible. A primary example is the computer operating system, for which market Microsoft's Windows and related products dominate. More computer programs are developed for Windows operating systems than Macintosh or Unix operating systems because there are more users in the Windows market.

When a product becomes a de facto standard and is protected by copyright, its producer indeed enjoys a monopoly market power. In many cases, such a monopoly is encouraged to minimize duplicative costs of having competing standards. That monopoly, however, is often regulated in exchange for its monopoly power. In today's Internet environment, where regulation is rejected from all sides, a dominant firm will have an unrestricted market power after its product becomes the standard. Copyrights for its product in turn protect its monopoly position unless other firms are allowed to license it.

Some products such as the Internet communications protocol have been developed as an industry standard which is not copyrighted. But, because of the network externality, many privately developed computer-related products exhibit the tendency to become a dominant, standard product in each market. An antitrust remedy for such a market needs to consider the role played by copyrights. To deny copyrights will certainly involve the loss of development costs and other opportunity costs for the firm. Alternatively, governments may require a kind of compulsory licensing to competitors or developers of related products. A real antitrust concern arises, however, when the dominant firm uses its position to strengthen its market power in other markets.

Antitrust remedies are notoriously slow and inadequate. In the context of network externalities, even traditional antitrust laws may prove to be ineffective (Lemley, 1996b). Section 2 of the Sherman Act, for example, prohibits any firm's monopolization through anticompetitive means. The problem, however, is to show the evidence for anticompetitive conduct when the nature of products are such that monopolization occurs seemingly as a normal course of product development, and the basis of its market power is the copyright. Similarly, Section 1 of the Sherman Act prohibits conspiratorial activities among competitors, which may have substantial adverse effect on competition. To apply the rule aggressively would mean to prevent any standard-setting initiative on the part of the firms when standardization would benefit consumers and society as a whole. On the other hand, to promote industry-wide standardization often means eliminating copyrights. Indeed, some standard-setting organizations require their members to denounce any copyright claim as a condition of participation.

Of course, being a dominant firm has its own disadvantages. A market leader can be leapfrogged, for example, by a new firm with an innovative product that becomes a new standard. The leader finds it difficult to abandon its product because of its sunk costs, or it may suffer from its own success because its product becomes unwieldy. Despite these down sides, however, monopolistic firms whose products are protected by copyrights seem to pose a significant threat to competition in electronic commerce.

5.6.   Summary

Copyright in the Digital Age has become one of the hottest issues affecting the future of electronic commerce. In the first place, the majority of digital products fall into the range of expressions protected by copyright law. An estimate by a computer software organization, although it has an obvious bias, puts the cost of piracy on and off the Internet at several billion dollars a year. An international effort to strengthen existing copyright laws was undertaken in December, 1996 in Geneva for the first time in 25 years, organized by the World Intellectual Property Organization, a United Nations agency in charge of the Berne Convention. On the other hand, the culture of the Internet as a free and unregulated communications medium has produced a strong counter-argument for increased public access to information. Consumer groups and a coalition of the free information movement warn that the new copyright laws could retard the growth of the Internet and jeopardize the very future of electronic commerce they intend to protect.

This chapter has purposely emphasized the economic significance of copyright protection. The ease in reproduction and distribution of any digital product has given rise to widespread legal and technical issues. In response, copyright laws have already been reinterpreted and revised, although sophisticated technologies are being developed to control many aspects of the transmission and usage of digital products. Because the ultimate goal of the copyright statute is to protect the market, however, and thus the remuneration, of a copyrighted work, any legal or technological solution should be evaluated in terms of how well it protects the market. Under that criteria, certain product choice strategies such as differentiation and customization naturally discourage consumers from unauthorized reproduction and distribution of a digital product. Market driven solutions such as these avoid the use of legal and artificial market barriers, a fact that is desirable in terms of market efficiency.

References

Barlow, J.P., 1993. *Selling Wine Without Bottles: The Economy of Mind on the Global Net.* Available at http://www.eff.org/pub/Intellectual_property/idea_economy.article.

Brinson, J.D. and M.F. Radcliffe, 1994. *Intellectual Property Law Primer for Multimedia Developers.* Available at http://www.eff.org/pub/CAF/law/ipprimer.

Carroll, T., 1994. *Frequently Asked Questions about Copyright.* Available via anonymous FTP to rtfm.mit.edu /pub/usenet/news.answers/law/CopyrightFAQ.

Gerovac, B., D.C. Carver and R.J. Solomon, 1996. *Electronic Commerce and Intellectual Property: Protect Revenues, Not Bits.* Available at http://far.mit.edu/Pubs /ec_ip/index.html.

Godwin, M., 1994. "When Copying Isn't Theft: How the Government Stumbled in a 'Hacker' Case." *Internet World,* Jan./Feb. 1994.

Gurnsey, John 1995. *Copyright Theft.* Aldershot, England: Aslib Gower.

Lemley, M.A., 1996a. "Dealing with Overlapping Copyrights on the Internet." Mimeo. The School of Law, the University of Texas.

Lemley, M.A., 1996b. "Antitrust and the Internet: Standardization Problem." *Connecticut Law Review,* 28(4): 1041–1094.

Losey, R., 1995. *Practical and Legal Protection of Computer Databases.* Available at http://www.eff.org/pub/Intellectual_property/database_protection.paper

Samuelson, Pamela, 1994. *Legally Speaking: The NII Intellectual Property Report.* Available at http://www.eff.org/pub/GII_NII/Govt_docs/HTML/ipwg_samuelson.html

Samuelson, P., R. Davis, M. Kapor, and J.H. Reichman, 1994. "A Manifesto Concerning Legal Protection for Computer Programs." *Columbia Law Review,* 94(8): 2308–2431.

Saunders, David 1992. *Authorship and Copyright.* London: Routledge.

Takeyama, Lisa N. 1994. "The Welfare Implications of Unauthorized Reproduction of Intellectual Property in the Presence of Demand Network Externalities." *Journal of Industrial Economics,* 17(2): 155.

Suggested Readings and Notes

Historical Development of Copyright Laws

Armstrong, E., 1990. Before Copyright: The French Book-Privilege System, 1498–1526. New York: Cambridge University Press,

Goldman, A., 1955. *The History of U.S.A. Copyright Law Revision, 1901–1954.* Washington, D.C.: Copyright Office, Library of Congress.

Bowker, R. R., 1912. *Copyright: Its History and Its Law.* Boston: Houghton Mifflin. It gives "a summary of the principles and practice of copyright with special reference to the American Code of 1909 and the British Act of 1911."

Davenport, N., 1993. *United Kingdom Copyright & Design Protection: A Brief History.* Emsworth, Hampshire (England): Mason Publications. The book follows the changes in copyright law introduced by successive acts from 1741 up to the Copyright, Designs and Patents Act 1988.

Patents and Economics

The theory of innovation studies the welfare implications of research and innovation. Within this field, most economists' attention has gone to R&D and patent races. Landes and Posner (1987) and Novos and Waldman (1984) are exceptions.

Landes, W.M., and R.A. Posner, 1987. "Trademark Law: An Economic Perspective." *Journal of Law and Economics*, 30: 265–309.

Novos, I.E., and M. Waldman, 1984. "The Effects of Increased Copyright Protection: An Analytical Approach." *Journal of Political Economy*, 92: 236–46.

Hirshleifer, J., 1971. "The Private and Social Value of Information and the Reward to Inventive Activity." *American Economic Review*, 61: 561–74.

Arrow, K.J., 1962. "Economic Welfare and the Allocation of Resources for Invention." In National Bureau of Economic Research, *The Rate and Direction of Inventive Activity*. Princeton, NJ: Princeton University Press.

Internet Resources

Articles

Okerson, A., 1996. "Who Owns Digital Works?" *Scientific American.* (http:// www.sciam.com/ WEB/ 0796issue/0796okerson.html)

Dyson, E., 1995. "Intellectual Value." *HotWired.* (http:// www.hotwired.com/ wired/3.07/features/dyson.html)

Barlow, J.P., 1996. *A Cyberspace Independence Declaration.* Barlow's reaction to the Telecommunications Reform Act of 1996. (http:// www.netusa.net/ ~jmr/decind.html)

Internet Copyright Sites

Electronic Frontier Foundation Intellectual Property Online Archive: http://www.eff.org/pub/Intellectual_property/.

The Institute for Learning Technologies (ILT) Guide to Copyright: http://www.ilt.columbia.edu/projects/copyright/index.html.

The Information Law Web: Copyright Court Cases is at http://seamless.com/rcl/things.html.

Coalition for Networked Information (CNI) Copyright Mailing List Archive: gopher://gopher.cni.org:70/11/cniwg/forums/cni-copyright

Texts of Copyright Laws

Full text of the U.S. Copyright Act (17 U.S.C.) is available at the U.S. Copyright Office at http:// lcweb.loc.gov/copyright. The Copyright Office also provides texts of the Berne Convention and the UCC.

Full text of the Berne Convention is available at http://www.law.cornell.edu/treaties/berne/ overview.html.

World Intellectual Property Organization (WIPO) Conference Resources

Report of WIPO Conference in Geneva, Dec. 2–20, 1996, by International Federation of Library Associations and Institutions (IFLA) at http://www.nlc-bnc.ca/ifla/V/press/pr970122.htm.

List and texts of preparatory documents by WIPO at http://www.wipo.org/eng/diplconf/index.htm.

CHAPTER 6

Signaling Quality and Product Information

The importance of advertising in the marketplace is evidenced by a large body of economic and business literature on that topic, and, accordingly, advertising models for the electronic marketplace have become a hot topic. Currently, however, Internet advertising and marketing literature focuses on adapting the conventional advertising framework to the peculiarities of the Internet. In other words, the Internet is seen as an alternative channel for advertising (in addition to traditional media such as newspapers, magazines, and television).

This chapter analyzes advertising and marketing activities in the broader economic context of an electronic marketplace, not just as a new channel. Selling a product is one of fundamental processes of interaction between market players. This chapter, therefore, reevaluates the nature of advertising and other types of signaling devices adopted by digital product sellers to convey product information and prices to consumers. Particular attention is paid to the problem of quality uncertainty, which can result in the "lemons" problem discussed in Chapter 4. The primary economic concern in this chapter is the effectiveness of various seller-initiated signaling devices in electronic commerce in which products are highly customized and consumers are searching for products based on their needs. Product information is provided by e-mailing, electronic billboards and banners, and product information pages on the web. Although the possibility of targeted advertising has excited many Internet advertisers, a viable strategy depends on how a product's characteristics match those of consumers, which in turn requires more detailed information about consumer tastes, technologies to process that information, and an effective means to convey it. Targeting, however, is only a procedural problem; other peculiarities arise in electronic commerce, such as the following:

- Digital products are often difficult to describe without allowing consumers to try them out.

- Product information about an information product must be detailed enough to convince buyers about the quality but should not reveal the information being offered for sale.

- Web storefronts can be used as a marketing platform but must combine other functions related to production, sales, and customer service.

This chapter's objective is to highlight these aspects of signaling in electronic commerce. Section 6.1 discusses the trends and practices of electronic advertising on the Internet and the increasing use of web storefronts as an informational channel. Section 6.2 reviews economic roles and effects of advertising and other signaling devices, and investigates how they may enhance or lower market efficiency. Section 6.3 analyzes alternative signaling mechanisms such as reputation and quality guarantee. Finally, section 6.4 evaluates some of the marketing strategies being promoted for the Internet.

The critical element in the new strategies is the participation by the buyers in developing advertising content through interactions. The importance of buyer-initiated activities will be carried over to Chapter 7, which focuses on the consumer's initiative to search for product information.

6.1. Advertising on the Internet

Because Internet advertising is a rather recent phenomenon, experts have emphasized the cultural aspects of Internet users that differ from those with whom the broadcasting and mass media world is familiar. Thus, one often hears that advertisers should rely on a "pull model" of advertising in which buyers have more say, rather than a "push model" in which sellers decide the content of advertising and select their audience. The Internet uses both push and pull models; web stores are fashioned after a pull model, whereas more refined push models take the form of targeted advertising. The following sections use specific examples to review the general trends.

Growth in Electronic Advertising

The general view of advertising and electronic commerce sees the Internet as an alternative advertising medium with consumers' awareness of the medium growing rapidly. According to a recent survey by Advertising Age (http://www.adage.com), 82 percent of consumers surveyed in 1996 are aware of the World Wide Web, almost doubling from 45 percent in 1995. Of these, 94 percent know about the Internet, compared to 82 percent in 1995.

The advertising market as a whole is a big business. The total advertising expenditure in the U.S. in 1995, for example, exceeded $100 billion (see table 6.1). Although figures for individual companies are not available, many spend a large sum of money. Proctor & Gamble, for example, spent $1.4 billion in 1986. Although firms are spending more of their dollars on the Internet, it still accounts for a tiny share of the overall advertising market. In 1995, advertising revenues on the Internet were estimated to be about $43 million (*Business Week*, September 23, 1996). Estimates for 1996 vary from $140 to $350 million dollars, hedging toward higher figures if advertising values of barters, reciprocal ads, and others are included. Even the largest estimate, however, is still less than 1 percent of the total advertising revenues in the U.S. In comparison, non-U.S. online advertising revenues in 1996 were estimated at $6.1 million, according to Jupiter Communications (http://www.jup.com), with Japan, the United Kingdom, and Germany each with over $1 million. The biggest web advertising outlet in the U.S., Netscape Communications (http://www.netscape.com), had a second quarter revenue of $7.75 million in 1996.

Table 6.1   Advertising Expenditures in 1995

Industry Segment	Expenditure in Billions of Dollars
Television	30.6
Cable and satellite TV	5.3
Radio	11.3
Newspaper	36.0
Magazine	14.6
Others	5.2
Total	103.0

Source: Veronis, Suhler and Associates (http://www.vsacomm.com/pr/prcif96.htm).

From 1995 to 1996, Internet advertising revenues have grown from under $50 million to about $200 million. Whether or not this trend will continue depends on the effectiveness of Internet advertising. Because it is recognized as an effective alternative to traditional media, the Internet's share in the total advertising expenditure may grow. Frost & Sullivan (http://www.frost.com), a market consulting firm, predicts that the share will be over 20 percent of the total (about $5.5 billion) within five years. Advertising on the Internet, however, is still in its infancy and its characteristics will change dramatically, making projections based on current behaviors highly unreliable. Revenues spent on the Internet may grow, but the real issue is how and where they are spent.

Table 6.1 shows how dependent the newspaper industry is on advertising revenues. A third of its advertising income is from classified advertising. Numerous "for sale" newsgroups are replacing traditional classified newspaper, magazine, and penny shoppers. With the possibility of losing revenues, newspapers confront the growing Internet advertising in two ways. First, newspapers establish an online channel for their service. Several leading daily newspapers operate an online classified advertising service. Career Path (http://www.careerpath.com), for example, lists "help wanted" advertising that allows consumers to search and categorize. Second, online newspapers themselves have become a substantial source of advertising income. According to the

Newspaper Association of America (http://www.naa.org), a trade association for newspaper publishers, a third of online newspapers made money in 1996. A similar trend is forecast for online versions of traditional media newspapers within four years. Over half of newspapers now have staff dedicated to online production and sales.

Advertising revenue figures are based on the conventional definition of advertising: the payment of sponsors whose ads are displayed to web browsers. Web pages are sprinkled with more and more tiny electronic billboards to grab the viewer's attention—just as printed advertisements and commercials work for newspapers and television. Although this type of "conventional" advertising is gaining a more ready audience in the World Wide Web universe, the Internet also offers other advertising mechanisms, including topical and for sale newsgroups, mailing lists, web links, and e-mails. Web storefronts also serve the same function as advertising. The expenses spent on these are not included in most ad revenue estimates, which might be even higher than the $200 to $300 million estimated for 1996. The other channels of online advertising include postings on related newsgroups and mailing lists, junk e-mails, and selling advertisements directly to consumers.

Types of Internet Advertising

A fundamental consideration in Internet advertising is finding ways to distribute information to consumers or inducing consumers to visit web sites. When firms solicit customers, however, such activities are regulated under various statues governing disclosure, liabilities, and truth in advertising. Therefore, what constitutes advertising on the Internet is an important issue to be settled in the near future.

The Federal Trade Commission's (FTC) Bureau of Consumer Protection, for example, recently forced Apple Computers, Inc. to offer $599 bargain upgrades to its customers who purchased entry-level Performa models; Apple's advertisements had given a false impression that the upgrade would be inexpensive and timely. The upgrade was so expensive that it equaled prices of a new computer. To protect consumers from such instances, the FTC monitors and evaluates advertising activities. Does product endorsement on newsgroups constitute advertising? Should the FTC scrutinize all types of newsgroup postings, web links, e-mails, and so on? The Federal Drug Administration has strict rules on how drugs are marketed. Should product information pages on a pharmaceutical firm's web page be treated as advertising? Can one of its employees mention its products on a chat line or post information on a mailing list?

The dilemma shows how diverse advertising channels are in the electronic marketplace. The conventional definition of advertising does not include the more subtle ways of soliciting business on the Internet, such as:

- Endorsing and reviewing products on newsgroups by firms and customers
- Soliciting listings from search services
- Soliciting and exchanging web links
- Providing product-oriented mailing lists and e-mail updates
- Web storefronts, which can be no more than a standing advertisement for a firm

Currently, the main channels of online advertising consist of banners on the World Wide Web and e-mailings. A more significant development in online advertising is selling advertisements to consumers directly and indirectly. The following sections review some of the issues regarding these main channels.

Banner Ads

There are two pressing issues regarding banner ads on the Internet. First, several studies are under way to clarify how effective banner ads are as a marketing mechanism. Banners are bandwidth hogs that delay downloading and frustrate web users. Some advertisers are reluctant to pay fees based on the number of consumers who see the ads (impressions), but insist on measuring "click-throughs" (that is, consumers must actually click the banner ad and visit the firm's web site). On the other hand, many consumers tolerate banner ads to avoid paying for contents; some studies argue that they are effective even without click-throughs. Section 6.4 discusses the question of advertising effectiveness.

The second issue relates to the lack of standards regarding size, placement, and fees for banners. Although there is no compelling need for standardization, some factors favor standardization. The Internet Advertising Bureau (IAB) and the Coalition for Advertising Supported Information and Entertainment (CASIE), a trade association for advertisers and advertising agencies, for example, argue that standardized banners will simplify production and placement of these ads, reducing costs and setting an industry-wide basis for calculating ad rates. Whether rates should depend on the size, layout, or technologies involved must be determined through dialogs among advertisers and ad carriers. The IAB/CASIE proposal has been endorsed in 1997 by the Newspaper Association of America (http://www.naa.org).

Because e-mailing has become the hottest use of the Internet, "junk e-mails" have been filling e-mailboxes. Junk e-mails are compared to phone solicitation and junk mails but with a fundamental difference: recipients of junk e-mails usually have to pay to receive them. Although recipients can delete e-mails they do not want, downloading e-mails requires connection and storage costs. Furthermore, junk e-mails may "bomb" one's mailbox, effectively disabling e-mail service. To the extent that junk e-mails hinder one's ability to use the service, they resemble sending advertisements via fax machines. Several states, including Nevada, California, Virginia, and Connecticut, are considering measures to make sending junk e-mails a misdemeanor. Considering that recipients are forced to pay for something they don't want, legislative response has been surprisingly slow. Rather, junk e-mails are countered by anti-junk e-mails and complaints made to account administrators.

Unlike Post Office mails, e-mail advertisers might never be able to pay the entire cost of sending an e-mail. An alternative is to pay recipients or to compensate them with other services. This approach seems to be gaining wide support in the online community.

Selling Advertising to Consumers

The conventional wisdom is that advertisements cannot be sold to consumers. To many, advertisements and commercials are eye sores and intrusive messages to be tolerated only for such reasons as lowered costs (of newspapers and TV programs). A new trend in electronic commerce, however, is converting advertisements into a commodity that can be traded at a price. The mass media acts as a brokering mechanism between advertisers and consumers, where the price of advertising is often difficult to measure. In contrast, the Internet has opened up a means to sell advertisements to consumers through either bartering or direct sales.

Indirect bartering is still a transitory way of selling advertisements. Consumers are offered free e-mail service or Internet access in return for revealing their preferences, which service providers use to assign and send advertisements. Because their revenues come from advertisers, these services are basically in the same league with search services with advertisements. There are, however, minor differences. Although search services use technologies to learn consumer preferences, sometimes surreptitiously, these services are based on voluntary revelation by consumers. Secondly, consumers enter into a contract with service providers, bartering the value of services offered with advertisements. In the process, consumers develop a clear notion about the value of advertisements. An added benefit for consumers is the permanency of their e-mail addresses, which ordinarily change as one switches service provider, school, or employer. Many e-mail services forward messages to a user-chosen e-mail account, allow users to choose unique domain addresses, and provide protection from junk e-mails and other services (see table 6.2). In comparison, can anyone expect to choose an individual telephone number, to carry the same number for life, and to be protected from pesky telemarketers? Using the same forwarding principle, these services can also direct web users to a permanent web URL.

Table 6.2   Advertiser-Supported E-Mail and Internet Service Providers

Service	URL	Comments
NetForward	www.netforward.com	Ads may be removed (for a fee)
EMAILS.COM	www.emails.com	Allows personalized names
iName	www.iname.com	Allows personalized names
PostOne	www.post1.com	Provides an e-mail forwarding service
Bigfoot	www.bigfoot.com	Protects against junk e-mail; offers non-English services
StarMail	www.starmail.com	Allows personalized names
pobox	pobox.com	Provides three months free service; uses aliases
RocketMail	www.rocketmail.com	Web-based
Friendly E-mail	mypad.com	Web-based
Hotmail	www.hotmail.com	Web-based
NetAddress	www.netadress.com	Ads may be removed (for a fee)
Juno	www.juno.com	Ads are displayed in a window
GeoCities	www.geocities.com	Offers free web home pages

Selling advertisements directly to consumers is only a small step from this process. Consumers need advertisements to find the products they want. With an interactive media such as the Internet, advertisers and consumers can negotiate directly without the help of intermediary markets, in which unrelated products—television programs, newspaper and magazine articles, search services, and e-mail services—are exchanged to convert the consumer's attention into advertising dollars. Instead, advertisers can offer consumers payments for viewing and responding to their ads. Thus, a new trend has emerged to convert advertising into commodities in electronic commerce. Cybergold (http://www.cybergold.com) offers direct payments to consumers who read advertising messages. Nissan plans to pay approximately $1 to visitors to its web pages. "Micropayments," digital coins and coupons, will make this process much easier in the future. Advertisers will have a better way to evaluate the reach and effectiveness of their marketing efforts; consumers will benefit from reduced search costs. Section 6.4 discusses in more detail the economic implications of selling advertisements.

Web Storefronts

Opening a web storefront establishes a company's presence on a new communications medium. Although most advertisers spend only a small amount of their advertising expenditure on the Internet, the costs of developing and maintaining web storefronts or company home pages should be considered as part of the advertising expenses.

A web store invariably includes information about products. By providing extensive information about products, a web store may have a better chance to succeed. GolfWeb (http://www.golfweb.com), for example, draws customers by giving a wide array of information related to golf (see fig. 6.1). Started in 1994, GolfWeb offers 35,000 pages of information, including a database on 19,000 golf courses, instructional tips, and discussion groups. These contents draw consumers because they appeal to the general interest rather than specific segments of consumers who might be looking to purchase a product. In a similar vein, a computer modem seller might provide extensive information about communications standards, network architecture, and so forth to appeal to a wide audience. Content-rich web pages lure visitors just as flashy advertisements induce consumers.

Figure 6.1 The GolfWeb home page.

By providing interaction with consumers, web pages also act as efficient sales assistants who not only provide product information but also help consumers to choose a product. Such a two-way interaction through sales assistance often improves the market efficiency by providing a better match between consumers and products (Wernerfelt, 1994). Therefore, a web store-front goes beyond simply being an alternative advertising channel, but becomes a tool for integrated marketing.

Offering sales assistance via web storefronts bypasses the problem of trust. Although knowledgeable sales assistants provide invaluable services, buyers often do not fully trust them. In physical markets, buyers are uncertain whether sales assistants are telling them all they need to know, whether they are saying different stories to different customers, and whether their assistance is trustworthy. Many people suspect a sales assistant will try to sway them to buy more expensive items than is necessary.

On the Internet, what the electronic sales assistant provides to customers is "printed on the wall" for everyone to see. Automated sales assistants cannot lie and thus are more credible than human assistants. To make web page assistants more like their human counterparts, a web store can customize its information and present it to predetermined, screened customers, increasing the possibility of telling different stories to different customers. Nevertheless, the prevalence of computer hackers and online pseudo-identities makes such targeted sales pitches (or lying) more difficult than in physical markets.

6.2.   The Economics of Advertising

The goal of advertising is to inform and/or influence consumer demand in a competitive market. The manner in which advertising informs consumers differs widely according to the type of product involved and the structure of the product's market. In some cases, advertising is essential for a market to function; in others, it creates unnecessary and unfounded differences in products costing the society in general. This section summarizes the economics of advertising by reviewing the roles advertising plays and evaluating its effects in terms of market variables such as prices, competition, and consumer welfare.

The Economic Roles of Advertising

Firms use advertising to achieve one or more of the following objectives:

- To inform consumers
- To increase demand
- To increase or decrease demand elasticity
- To discourage entry by potential competitors
- To differentiate the firm from existing competitors

In a perfectly competitive market, which assumes perfect information, there is no need for advertising because firms need only lower prices to attract more customers. In real markets, however, neither buyers nor sellers possess all the pertinent facts necessary to trade products and services efficiently. The acquisition of this knowledge is facilitated by informing consumers about the existence of a seller and a product, its price and other terms of sale, the retail location or ordering information, the product quality, and other physical conditions of the good or service in question. By informing consumers who were previously unaware of the product, those who knew of it but could not locate a seller, or those who were only familiar with a competitor's products, a firm can increase the demand for its product. At the same time, firms can reduce the price elasticity of demand and produce a steeper demand curve by convincing buyers that their products are better than competitors' or by simply differentiating themselves and establishing their own identity and reputation.

Figure 6.2 depicts how the demand schedule for a firm selling a product can change with advertising. The solid line, D, and its associated marginal revenue line, MR, represent the pre-advertising level of demand. The firm's demand is shown to be price-elastic, implying that the firm's product is differentiated or that the firm is a local monopoly. Given a constant marginal cost (MC), the pre-advertising price, P, is determined by the condition MC = MR.

At that price, the number of units sold is Q. Upon advertising, the demand schedule shifts to the right, implying that each consumer is willing to pay more because of the better product information. Consequently, at each given price there are more consumers who are willing to buy the product. With its new demand and marginal revenue schedules, both the price and the quantity sold increase to P' and Q', respectively. The firm's revenue increases because more units are sold at a higher per-unit price. The firm's net profit from advertising depends on the shape of the marginal cost and the cost of advertising. In the simplified scenario shown in figure 6.2, the maximum increase in profit is the shaded area {(P'–P)Q' + (P – MC)(Q'–Q)}.

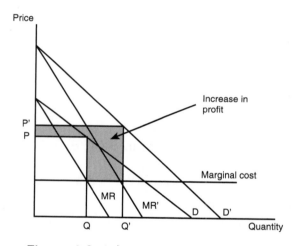

Figure 6.2 Advertising and demand.

The fact that advertising may change the elasticity of demand is depicted by a rotation of the demand schedule. In figure 6.2, the new line D' has a steeper slope than the old demand schedule D; thus the new consumer demand is less elastic to changes in price. When elasticity is low, a firm can raise a product's price without reduced sales. See figure 6.3 to compare changes in quantity demanded given a change in price. Here, price is increased from P to P'. The reduction in quantity demanded is smaller for inelastic demand (from Q to Qi) than for elastic demand (from Q to Qe). In other words, a product with an inelastic demand (that is, a low elasticity of demand) is more stable in terms of consumers substituting it with other products. If the product in question is a competitor's, the desired strategy is to increase its demand elasticity (a flatter demand curve) so that it is easier to encourage substitution. To put it another way, the firm can increase its market power (monopolistic control) or increase price and profit through advertising.

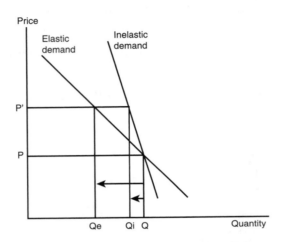

Figure 6.3 Elastic and inelastic demands.

Because advertising is not without cost, a critical decision a firm must make is where to set a profit-maximizing level of advertising. Consider a market with N number of consumers and multiple firms selling a similar (homogeneous) product. Initially, none of the N consumers know about the product (existence, price, seller's location, and so forth). The cost of advertising varies according to the method chosen—word-of-mouth, billboards, signs posted on shop windows, mass mailings, newspaper or television advertising. A cost curve can be drawn for each advertising method based on the number of consumers reached. Figure 6.4, for example, draws the total cost curves for television and newspaper advertising. In this example, newspaper advertising costs less than television advertising when the number of the target audience is small. It is shown to cost about twice as much as television advertising, however, when a large number of the audience is desired. The figure represents the common notion that newspapers are an effective advertising channel in small local markets, and television advertising is cost effective at the national scale.

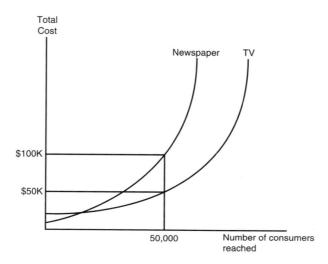

Figure 6.4 Advertising cost curves.

The shape of these curves is convex through the origin, implying the following:

- No cost is associated with no advertising
- The cost of reaching more consumers increases at a growing rate
- It is impossible (that is, the cost is infinite) to reach all consumers

This type of convex cost is only theoretical; alternative assumptions are possible. A concave cost function, for example, implies that the cost of reaching more consumers increases but at a decreasing rate. A straight line implies that the cost of reaching one more consumer is always the same: $10,000 to reach 5,000 people, $20,000 to reach 10,000 people, and so on. If two curves do not cross each other—other than at the origin—one advertising channel would be more cost effective at all levels of audience reach than the other.

The cost function can be represented by the following mathematical function:

$A(m, n)$

in which m = 1,..., m denotes a specific advertising method (or channel), and n means the number of consumers reached. For example, m = 1 may mean newspaper advertising; m = 2 may mean television advertising, and so forth.

For the television advertising shown in figure 6.4, this means that A(2, 50000) = $50,000. With *N* consumers in the market, the preceding three implications can be represented mathematically as follows:

$A(m, 0) = 0$, $A_n(m, n) > 0$, and $A(m, N) =$

for all advertising methods m, where a subscript denotes a partial derivative. Using these assumptions about advertising costs, economic models of advertising examine a firm's strategies in selecting the optimal number of consumers to be informed by each advertising method and the resulting levels of prices.

The profit for a firm with advertising is total revenue minus total costs. First, the firm chooses the number of products to produce, the methods of advertising, and how much to spend for each advertising method. The cost function for advertising indicates how much it costs to reach a certain number of consumers. The cost function can also be represented so that it tells how many consumers can be reached given some amount of advertising expense. Let that function be n(A, m), which is an inverted function of A(m, n). The function n(A, m) tells us that if one spends $50,000 for television advertising, for example, 50,000 customers will be reached by that advertising campaign.

When a firm uses multiple methods of advertising, it can divide its sales into separate markets based on advertising method and sum up revenues and costs over all market segments. To simplify, let the number of consumers reached by a method, n(A), be dependent on the advertising expenditure. Then, represent the total revenue of the firm as R[Q, n(A)]. Costs consist of the production cost, including materials and labor, and the advertising costs for all of the methods chosen. The firm's profit, given the number of sales and advertising expenditure, is as follows:

$$\text{Profit} = R[Q, n(A)] - C(Q) - \sum_m A(m, n)$$

The firm's strategy is to maximize its profit, deciding the level of production (Q) and the expenditure for each advertising method (m). The strategy can be summarized by the following two first-order conditions:

$$R_Q = C'$$

and

$$R_n = A'(n) \text{ for each m}$$

in which subscripts denote partial derivatives, C' is the marginal cost of production, and $A'(n)$ is the marginal cost of reaching one more consumer with a given advertising method. The first equation simply restates the condition that the marginal cost of production be equal to the marginal revenue. The second equation states that the optimal level of advertising occurs when the marginal increase in revenue due to advertising is equal to the marginal cost of reaching that marginal consumer. Given a convex advertising cost curve, the number of consumers informed will never be N, because the marginal revenue associated with advertising (R_n) will not be infinite. If, however, one assumes that the advertising costs are constant—or at least concave—the optimal number of advertising may very well be N.

The shape of the advertising cost function, therefore, is a matter of considerable interest in electronic commerce. If the marginal cost of advertising, that is, $A'(n)$, is zero on the Internet, firms should reach out for all consumers in the marketplace. Such a market with fully informed consumers is not feasible in physical markets due to the increasing cost of advertising at the margin. On the other hand, Internet advertising may substantially improve the market efficiency through lowering advertising costs. Nevertheless, not all consumers read or view advertisements. Therefore, although the cost function for Internet advertising might be lower than that of traditional media, it will not be zero or flat (constant) as one attempts to reach more consumers.

Business and marketing professionals would like to learn more about the shape of the cost function $A(m, n)$. An efficient advertising strategy displays lower total advertising cost at any level of n (its cost function lies below the others as in figure 6.4). Because empirical studies are not yet available, one cannot speculate how efficient the Internet-based advertising is compared to other media. Nevertheless, one of the main attractions of the Internet as an advertising channel is its relative cost compared to traditional mass media.

Also, the pull model of advertising implies that consumers choose to visit a firm's web site, thereby incurring some of costs traditionally paid for by sellers (mailing costs, for example). As a result, more consumers will be informed about products in electronic commerce than in physical markets unless having more informed consumers negatively affects the firm's revenue.

Although the preceding discussion focuses on increasing demand, the other two purposes of advertising—to discourage entry and to differentiate from competitors—relate to advertising's effect on competition. Advertising raises the entry barrier because new entrants must advertise as much as the incumbent to inform consumers. Thus, advertising costs are considered to be "sunk costs." When sunk costs are high, the market is said to have a high entry barrier (Bain, 1956). At the same time, incumbent firms sell differentiated products that may be of different quality or that may only differ in brand and image aided by advertising. The proliferation of differentiated products is well-documented in the case of the breakfast cereal market, in which a small number of sellers "cover the product space," sometimes with an excessive number of brands and advertising, not allowing a sufficient number of competitors to enter the market (Grossman and Shapiro, 1984).

A competitive market is one with a low entry barrier and a low exit cost so that potential competitors can enter and exit when there is an opportunity to make a profit. Most markets, however, have a certain degree of barriers to entry. A patent, for example, is a legal barrier to a market. Technological superiority or a firm's lower cost structure also act as barriers to entry. In some industries, such as the utility industry, an artificial barrier is erected in the form of a regulated monopoly to maximize the scale of economy and reduce wasteful duplication in production. In a similar manner, advertising raises the entry barrier. To the extent that advertising costs less in electronic commerce, the market will become more competitive. The form and content of advertising on the Internet, however, differs significantly from those of the physical product markets, which may change its character as well as its cost structure.

The Informational Content of Advertising

The economic affects of advertising lead to a better understanding of why to advertise but give less direction on the question of what kind of advertising to employ. The content of advertising messages shifts dramatically depending on whether their function is to inform consumers about price, product quality, and product uses (as in informative advertising), or whether it is designed to shift consumer tastes (as in persuasive advertising). Informative advertising can include a description or a picture of the product, whereas persuasive advertising tries to portray the act of using a product as popular and desirable based on factors unrelated to the product itself. The distinction between informative and persuasive advertising, however, is somewhat arbitrary, because a persuasive advertisement about a product—"using a multimedia computer is cool!," for example—may be informative to those searching for a "cool" computer.

Advertising content also varies with the type of product. For goods whose quality can be learned before consuming (search goods), advertising tends to be informative. A picture or a description of a product tells buyers the necessary information. Other products must be consumed before their quality is known (experience goods), such as automobiles, household appliances, and computer programs. Some products are simply too complicated for consumers to understand and evaluate the quality. For these products, even detailed product information is not enough to resolve the uncertainty about the product. For this reason, advertising for experience goods tends to be more persuasive than informative. Although both informative and persuasive advertising can be provided for experience goods, it is often better to use other promotional methods than advertising, such as free trials, warranties, and so forth.

Information about Information Products

If the purpose of advertising is to reveal the quality of a product, digital products have a unique problem in that the product information must not reveal the product itself. Compare the ways to describe an automobile and an information product. To say that an automobile has 300 horsepower, 8 cylinders, and a sun roof does not interfere with selling or consuming the product, because the product information is not the physical automobile itself. On the other hand, describing a news story or a book often reveals the product itself. A good summary of an article may be sufficient for many consumers who will forgo buying and reading the actual article. This section describes the nature of this problem with an example, and discusses a possible application of a cryptographic algorithm—known as zero-knowledge proofing—to convey product information.

Suppose that Alice has found an effective way of solving scheduling conflicts of video conferencing in a virtual firm whose offices are located in different time zones. As CEO of a virtual firm, Bob wants to hire Alice as a consultant but is not sure whether such a scheduling mechanism can be found. If Alice publishes her scheduling algorithm on her web page, Bob does not have to pay for it once he reads the information. If Alice charges Bob to read her web pages, Bob has to be convinced about the algorithm prior to buying it. Therefore, Alice's problem is to convince Bob that she can actually provide such a service without revealing her algorithm.

Such a situation is very common for all types of information products, because it is difficult to verify the truthfulness (or the quality) of information unless the information is revealed. As an information vendor, however, you do not want to reveal the information prior to getting paid. Similarly, suppose that you have found a winning strategy in picking stocks. To maximize your profit, you want to persuade several investors that your strategy really works without revealing what that strategy is.

Some types of signals are used in such situations where the information cannot be revealed. Publishing the previous results of stock picking is such a signal. The education level of prospective employees is often used as a signal for productivity. Such signals, however, are often incomplete and are not definite proofs of the information one wants. Similarly, if one wants to advertise the quality of one's digital product, customers can be convinced only if the full information is provided. Nevertheless, a certain mechanism may be found to give a complete proof of quality without revealing the product. In the preceding example, if Alice can show Bob that she indeed knows how to schedule a virtual video conference without letting Bob know of the secret algorithm, such a procedure is called a "zero-knowledge proof" of the product.

A zero-knowledge proof is a signal that provides complete and perfect information about the quality without revealing the information (Goldreich et al., 1986 and Blum, 1986). Using the simple example by Quisquater and Guillou (1990), suppose that there is a cave with a hidden path between the points B and C (see fig. 6.5). Alice tries to convince Bob that she knows the secret passage, which no one else knows. An interactive zero-knowledge proof protocol proceeds as follows:

1. Bob stands outside the cave entrance where he cannot see point A so that he does not know whether Alice goes to the right or left once she enters the cave.

2. Alice enters the cave and goes to either point B or C.

3. Bob enters the cave and stands at point A.

4. Bob asks Alice to come out either from right (B) or left (C).

5. Alice complies, using the secret passage if she has to.

6. Alice and Bob repeat steps 1–5 several times.

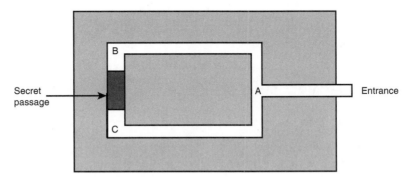

Figure 6.5 A cave with a secret passage.

If Alice was lucky at first trial in choosing B or C, which Bob subsequently calls out, Alice may be able to convince Bob about her capability to find the secret passage without knowing the passage. This possibility decreases, however, as they repeat this game. After three games, the probability that Alice is guessing or being lucky goes down to 1/8. In such a protocol, Alice can show Bob convincingly that she does know about the secret passage, and Bob does not learn anything about the passage.

Consequently, such proofs can be used on web pages to advertise a product whose quality can be proven through interactive protocols. It is uncertain, however, whether such proofing protocols can be found for all problems. To use the previous example, Alice selling the scheduling program may generate examples of hard-to-do scheduling and publish solutions to these problems, but there is no way to prove that the problems are not rigged in the first place. An alternative is to use an example given by a potential client, Bob. Instead of using Bob's example, Alice may generate a similar but sufficiently different problem and then show a solution; this proves the capability of her algorithm but Bob cannot use the result. If Bob needs Alice's service repeatedly, an alternate way to prove her ability is either to give Bob a trial period or to give him a demo version that expires at a certain time. Still another option is for Alice and Bob to enter into a contract that spells out the performance. Nevertheless, the zero-knowledge protocol has many important applications in electronic commerce where the privacy of individual identity, private encryption keys, or the serial numbers of digital coins is to be preserved but at the same time the information (or the quality) must be verifiable without revealing the information.

The Effect of Advertising on Price

Although the prime focus so far has been on the effect of advertising on demand, a practical concern is on price. Because advertising costs need to be reflected in the final price consumers pay, it seems obvious that firms who advertise heavily might have to raise their prices. There is also a countering force, however, that tends to reduce prices when firms advertise.

The various effects of advertising on price can be analyzed in terms of absolute prices and price dispersion. As benchmark cases, imagine two markets: one is populated by perfectly informed consumers, and the other by consumers who have no information about products and prices. Suppose also that product information is conveyed only by advertising.

In the market with perfectly informed consumers, there can only be one price for an identical product. Otherwise, firms charging a higher price would lose all customers. In the market with uninformed consumers, however, firms can charge any price they want as long as consumers do not search for price information. After some consumers start to visit other stores and compare prices, the market will consist of informed and uninformed consumers. Most real markets are this type of partially informed markets in which either consumer search or advertising provides information about prices to some but not all consumers. It is generally not possible or economically efficient to inform all consumers because of the costs involved or because some consumers will not receive information willingly or miss it by accident.

Among informed consumers, advertising may raise or lower the level of absolute prices depending on the strategy. When advertising highlights relative price information, prices tend to go down as low-price firms become known and it becomes easier for consumers to compare prices. When advertising is persuasive rather than informative, however, the goal of advertisers is to manipulate demand for their products and to increase their market power. As a result, persuasive advertising helps firms to raise prices. For this reason, persuasive advertising that emphasizes brand recognition and the image of a product is much more common than informative advertising. For some professional groups, such as physicians and lawyers, informative advertising with relative price information is often prohibited to maintain high prices, although the basis for such prohibition is often to ensure quality.

The question at hand is whether persuasive information for digital products is effective in the electronic marketplace. Considering that an author's point of view is an important aspect in selling literary works, news, data, and other information products, persuasive advertising may actually end up being the mainstay in advertising digital products. Furthermore, because the information about a product is often the product itself, persuasive advertising may be preferred to detailed product description.

Sellers may have to take into account, however, the fact that some consumers will start to comparison shop despite the efforts of persuasive advertising. In a situation in which consumers are partially informed, many prices can coexist for a product. Those who cater to informed customers will charge a uniformly low price. On the other hand, uninformed consumers can be charged different prices. Consider informed consumers to be natives and uninformed consumers to be tourists. The price for natives is lower than that for tourists because natives are more familiar with the market. As more consumers are informed (become natives), the two prices become closer and the degree of price dispersion is reduced. Because advertising and searches by consumers are costly, however, there will always be some non-advertisers charging higher prices, which can be lowered only if all consumers become natives (informed consumers).

Who corresponds to natives and tourists on the Internet? Natives are those who are fully informed about sellers, products, and prices, whereas tourists are not informed for any number of reasons. In a geographical model, tourists may be unfamiliar with local merchants and stores. In other words, tourists must pay higher costs to find out prices. On the Internet, the difference between natives and tourists may lie in their ability to search and navigate the electronic marketplace. In this respect, an easy user interface such as the web technology has reduced the technological barrier for some to enter the marketplace and has turned many tourists into natives. Nevertheless, as long as the technologies are cumbersome, difficult to master, and expensive, the electronic marketplace will not be so efficient as to avoid dispersed prices altogether. Also, dividing consumers into separate groups by limiting their access based on their classification naturally enables sellers to separate them into natives and tourists. In this sense, proprietary networks favored by some sellers create artificially separated markets with the potential to increase prices.

A corollary to advertising's effect on product prices is the efficiency effect of advertising. By providing consumers with product information, advertising improves market efficiency by lessening the search costs and facilitating seller-buyer matching. When the price or product information is not provided by sellers, for example, consumers have to incur the search costs by reading newspapers or visiting stores. Thus, when firms provide advertising, the total price paid by a buyer is lowered by the amount of the consumer search costs. The overall efficiency of a market with advertising is higher if the firm's advertising expense is lower than the sum of all consumers' individual search costs, which is more than likely in most cases. Thus, when advertising is informative, its economic effects are unambiguously beneficial. Advertising can be wasteful, however, if it is purely of a persuasive nature, creating non-existent differences in products. As a preemptive strategy, advertising in its extreme may erect barriers to entry, lowering the level of competition and raising prices.

Advertising and Product Differentiation

Informative advertising is most desirable when products are differentiated and consumers find it difficult to select the ones that best fit their preferences. Chapter 8 discusses product differentiation in more detail. This chapter summarizes only the effects of advertising on product differentiation. Products are said to be "vertically differentiated" if all consumers agree on which product is better. If two products differ in terms of quality, for example, all consumers will want a higher quality product if the two products are priced the same. If two products have the same quality but differ only in color, however, some consumers will prefer red whereas others will prefer blue even when the prices are the same. The latter is a case of "horizontal product differentiation."

For horizontally differentiated products, informative advertising enables a consumer to find a product that best matches his or her preference. A consumer's preferences can be graphed as locations in a spatial market or city. The distance between the locations of a firm and a consumer represents the difference between a product and the consumer's preference. Therefore, an advertisement about a product's location (that is, specification) helps the consumer find out which product is closer to one's location (or taste).

The obvious incentives for firms to convey product information to consumers are the increase in sales and the reduced demand elasticity due to consumers' knowledge that competing products do not offer a better match.

After consumers find their match, advertising builds brand loyalty and increases the firm's market power. Also, a firm's advertising is bound to inform some consumers that its product does not match their tastes. In a simplified market with two firms, one firm's advertising is beneficial to its competitor—a type of public good (Meurer and Stahl, 1994). Eaton and Grossman (1986) have also shown that informative advertising actually reduces price competition among firms; thus consumer welfare is lowered despite a better preference-product matching. The loss to consumers is due to a higher price; as a result, there is an incentive for firms to provide excessive informative advertising (Grossman and Shapiro, 1984).

Does advertising affect product differentiation itself? In some cases, advertising can result in spurious product differentiation by which consumers are persuaded to think, albeit mistakenly, that there are differences in competing products. Many over-the-counter drugs and household chemicals have essentially the same ingredients but consumers perceive them to be different largely because of advertising.

When products are vertically differentiated (for example, by quality), truthful advertising may solve the lemons problem discussed in Chapter 4 by signaling quality. If all buyers are informed about product quality, a high-quality good should command a higher price than a low-quality good. If advertising is truthful and credible, higher price means higher quality.

Prices, however, are an imperfect indicator of quality. If buyers are unable to assess the quality of a product, either price or advertising can supply some information. Will a product that is either priced high or advertised heavily really be a high quality product? As an empirical case study, Caves and Greene (1996) calculated the rank correlation between product quality ratings, prices, and advertising outlays for approximately 200 products. They found a weak correlation between prices and quality and no significant relationship between advertising and quality. In other words, advertising is not a reliable signal for quality. They also report that the price-quality correlation is most notable for convenience products such as frequently purchased consumption goods. For these products, firms have an incentive to maintain a high-quality corresponding to a high price in order to ensure repeat purchases. But the overall weak relationship between advertising and quality is consistent with the observation that advertising is mostly persuasive. For experience goods whose quality must be learned, advertising cannot supply any information about the product quality but must instead persuade consumers to try out a product. For digital products, being experience goods, advertising will be more persuasive than informative, which further diminishes the value of advertising as a signal for quality.

6.3.   Other Strategies to Convey Product Information

Providing product information through advertising and other direct means to verify product quality is effective for search goods. For experience goods, however, no amount of advertising can settle the question of quality. A conventional method to counter the quality uncertainty is to provide a guarantee for quality or a refund. Another important mechanism is to build a brand name and seller-specific reputation. This section reviews these "non-advertising" means to convey product information and evaluates how the nature of digital products affects their effectiveness in the electronic marketplace.

Repeat Purchases and Reputation

Reputation is strategically important when a firm is a long-run player or if a product is purchased repeatedly. A recognizable brand name is built over a period of time if a consumer's expectation for quality is consistently fulfilled. For products that are used only once, the reputation is built for the firm rather than the product, so that firm-specific reputation becomes the "brand name" by which the firm may transfer a consumer's trust from product to product. When both products and firms are short-lived, neither the brand name nor the firm's reputation resolves the quality uncertainty.

Reputation Building in Electronic Commerce

Short-run players invest little in reputation. A shop selling mainly to tourists, for example, has little incentive to maintain its reputation of selling a certain quality consistently. Reputation pays off when consumers and firms intend to stay in the market for the long haul. Internet commerce is relatively new and there is no clear long-run profit incentives to induce heavy investment in reputation. Some Internet services, however, are already recognized as essential for the success of electronic commerce. In those areas of service, the clear winners are the ones who have built some reputation. The success of Yahoo! (http://www.yahoo.com) as the leader in search services, for example, depends largely on its reputation as a pioneer. In certification and security services, RSA Data Security, Inc. (http://www.rsa.com) is the front-runner due to its reputation in cryptography technologies (see fig. 6.6). Visitors at RSA Data Security, Inc. are informed that the firm's product is the world's brand name for cryptography, is implemented in many familiar products, and is the de facto standard on the Internet. The firm's selling point is its reputation.

Figure 6.6 The home page of RSA Data Security, Inc.

Although these Internet-native firms have built their reputation based on new products, firms with an established reputation in physical markets may be able to transfer their firm-specific reputation to the electronic marketplace. Microsoft (http://www.microsoft.com) and IBM (http://www.ibm.com) try to use their reputations and brand names in physical markets as an entry strategy to Internet commerce. This may give them an advantage over new Internet-native firms and, if successful, signal a possible dominance by existing firms in the new marketplace. Such transferred reputation, however, needs to be reinforced by continued approval by consumers in terms of products and services in the new market. Thus, in electronic commerce, the value of transferred reputation may be short-lived if product quality is not met consistently.

Renting a Reputation

A *firm-specific reputation* is an example in which the reputation built by one quality product is transferred to other products sold by the same seller. A seller without a reputation can use such reputation spill-over to rent the reputation of others. Suppose, for example, that Alice is a retailer of computer software with a reputation for high quality. Bob enters the software market with a new product. Having no reputation of his own, Bob must induce buyers to try his products, perhaps with promotional low prices or by offering free demo versions. An alternate strategy for Bob is to sell his software through Alice (Chu and Chu, 1994). Similarly, many foreign car manufacturers sell their automobiles under American brands. Thus, renting a reputation can be used as an entry strategy when products are experience goods and the sellers do not have a reputation.

In electronic commerce, renting a reputation can be used more widely because sellers of digital products are more diverse and short-lived than in physical markets. Suppose, for example, that you want to sell an article you have written. As a short-term player or a micro-product seller, you have little incentive to invest in reputation building. A viable strategy is to sell your articles through a reputable intermediary, for example CNN (http://www.cnn.com) or *The New York Times* (http://www.nytimes.com). As long-run players, these intermediaries have an incentive to maintain their reputation.

The buyers of an article are thus ensured of its quality, knowing that the intermediaries check the content of the article.

Shareware and Wasted Investments

The nature of digital products explains the prevalence of shareware and freeware on the Internet. As an experience good, the quality of a digital product such as computer software is learned from use. But consumers are reluctant to try a product of unknown quality. Thus, the objective in distributing shareware and freeware is to allow consumers to experience or try out the product. A reputation is built with those consumers who are convinced about the usefulness or the quality after the initial trial.

Shareware is not freeware because users are legally required to pay for it after a certain trial period. Rather, what characterizes shareware is its distributional nature in which consumers are allowed to try out the product first, and pay for it if they find it useful. This point is emphasized by the Association of Shareware Professionals (http://www.asp-shareware.org), which defines shareware as:

> (Shareware is) a marketing method, not a type of software. Unlike software marketed through normal retail channels, where you are forced to pay for the product before you've even seen it, the shareware marketing method lets you try a program for a period of time before you buy it. Since you've tried a shareware program, you know whether it will meet your needs before you pay for it. Shareware programs are just like programs you find in major stores, catalogs, and other places where people purchase software—except you get to use them, on your own computer, before paying for them.

As the ASP contends, the profitability of shareware depends on consumers recognizing its quality. Furthermore, a distribution system, like shareware, would be beneficial to consumers, because the sellers have an incentive to produce and maintain high quality.

How different is shareware from freeware? Shareware seldom has a mechanism to enforce payments. A program might expire after a trial period, but users can simply download another copy. Some customers might pay for printed manuals, customer service, or technical support. Although the data on how many shareware users actually pay the authors is insufficient, there is scant difference between shareware and freeware in terms of both payments and distribution. They are freely distributed products.

Providing free products, however, serves the critical function of signaling quality. In this sense, free product distribution is similar to advertising in which the cost is sunk but is recovered from future sales. Successful shareware programs also earn revenue from later sales. Once popular among users, for example, many shareware programs are licensed to larger companies who incorporate them into computer operating systems and commercial programs. Examples include encryption and compression software and anti-virus programs that started as shareware but later were purchased to be included in the Macintosh or Windows operating systems.

Free products are provided to overcome the problem of quality uncertainty and, ultimately, to generate profits. A different motive exists for free products, however, where the cost of freely distributing products is not recovered. Instead, such free distribution, advertising, or other costly promotions may be undertaken to raise the entry barrier or to discourage competition. To compete effectively, a new entrant has to match the level of advertising spent by its competitor. Thus, the cost of such advertising often raises the minimum capital requirement for an entrant. This capital investment is "wasted" in the sense that it cannot be recovered, but serves to protect the market for an incumbent firm.

Quality Guarantees for Digital Products

An easy way to resolve the uncertainty about quality is to provide a guarantee or a full refund for dissatisfied customers. A return policy enables consumers to try out the product. Such a policy, however, might not be feasible for digital products for several reasons.

First, many digital products such as information are fully consumed when the information is viewed by consumers. After they are consumed, therefore, returning the products has little meaning. Suppose that Alice sells a map of the most scenic route from Los Angeles to New York. Although Bob may search for such a route himself, the cost of doing so justifies buying the map from Alice, who provides a full money-back guarantee. Bob finds the map useful and does not ask for a refund. But Charlie, a habitual returner of everything he buys, asks for a refund even though he also finds the route exceptional. For Charlie, the map is no longer useful or needed; that is, he doesn't intend to travel the route again or he is sure that he remembers the route. In any case, Alice cannot ask Charlie to forget about the route or to prove that he did not make a copy of the map. Unlike physical products, returning a digital product seldom prevents the consumer from using the product in the future.

Second, returning a product or refunding a purchase price may be impractical due to transaction costs. A microproduct—a small digital product costing a few cents or less—for example, may cost more to transport twice over the network, or the cost for refund may exceed the price. Microproducts supported by micropayments, therefore, may not be sold with any quality guarantee or a refund. Rather, transactions for such products require an intermediary with whom consumers have an account that may be settled periodically when the amount becomes substantial.

6.4. Marketing Strategies for the Internet

As a marketing medium, the Internet presents many advantages over traditional media. With the Internet's capability to target customers, advertising is more efficient; with its flexibility in interacting with customers, web storefronts combine many functions of marketing in a seamless, organizationally superior process. Advertising and other forms of conveying product information, however, are only part of the overall process of selling a product in the electronic marketplace. Consumers themselves invest in searching for products, which is discussed in the following chapter. Producers also interact with consumers to develop and customize their products to match consumer tastes, varying prices in the process. Therefore, product customization and pricing may occur prior to marketing a product or concurrently, which is elaborated in Chapter 8. This section, however, focuses on the narrow definition of Internet marketing—providing product information in the hope of increasing sales— and evaluates the various strategies currently used or advocated. We first review popular myths and wisdom regarding Internet marketing, and analyze in-depth several popular notions, such as targeted advertising, push versus pull models, and active marketing. We end by summarizing some empirical studies on the effectiveness of these methods.

Myths and Popular Wisdom about Online Advertising

Advertising, like television programming, is driven by instinct as much as by theory. Experience, however, has evolved into a certain set of rules to which most advertising professionals adhere. These rules are by no means hard and fast theories. One advertising executive, for example, argues that no advertising can turn a niche product into a mass-appeal product. To others, on the other hand, the objective of advertising seems to be just that: to make a product appeal to a wider market. Even allowing this difference of opinion among advertising professionals, however, there are some commonly accepted tenets, or commandments, of advertising in mass media, which naturally translate into online strategies. These include the following:

- **Advertisements should be visually appealing.** In mass media, advertisements are colorful, often sex-oriented, and designed to catch the reader's attention. On the Internet, this principle translates into lively, interactive web content that grabs the visitor's attention and draws repeated visits.

- **Advertisements must be targeted to specific consumers.** Ads are customized and speak on a personal level.

- **The content should be valuable to consumers.** Web pages should provide valuable information, not useless and large files that slow downloading time.

- **Advertisements must emphasize brands and a firm's image.** Ads emphasize how a firm is different from other firms on the Internet.

- **Advertisements should be persuasive.** Ads do not force consumers to visit web pages, but through interesting and valuable content they should persuade consumers to visit again and again.

- **Advertisements must be part of an overall marketing strategy.** Firms should actively participate in all types of Internet activities, such as newsgroups, mailing lists, and bulletin boards.

From these observations, three popular principles of Internet advertising and marketing can be extracted:

- Internet advertising must be targeted.
- Internet advertising must be based on a pull, not push, model of advertising.
- Internet marketing is active, not passive.

Broadcast versus Targeted Advertising

In general, sellers want to send advertisements only to potential buyers. For products that most consumers purchase on a regular basis, such as toothpaste, soap, and so forth, there is little concern about waste in using mass market advertising. Although the broadcast media is well-suited for such consumption goods, a seller of a product with limited buyer appeal needs to focus its advertising more narrowly, using special interest magazines, for example.

Advertisers have honed a wide array of techniques to focus their advertising most efficiently. Advertisers, for example, have refined their techniques for focusing by using demographics data and readership profiles. Because the Internet is capable of supporting very small special interest groups, which cannot be efficiently supported through magazines, and so forth, the Internet offers even more focused venues for targeted advertising. Furthermore, advertisers can latch on to keywords supplied by consumers to present a focused advertisement (see figs. 6.7 and 6.8). When a user searches for something about books, an advertisement for a bookstore appears on the web page; when the search is related to music, the search service presents an advertisement for a music store. The more advertisers there are, the more precise the match between the keywords and the advertisement will become.

Figure 6.7 The search result presented by Lycos (http://lycos.cs.cmu.edu) when the search keywords were "novel book historical FAQ." A banner ad for an Internet bookstore appears.

Figure 6.8 The search result presented by Lycos (http://lycos.cs.cmu.edu) when the search keywords were "Patsy Cline song." A banner ad for an Internet music store appears.

Targeting advertisements in this way is assumed to increase effectiveness. In one way or another, marketing professionals are trying to learn and incorporate consumer preferences in their product development and marketing plans. Once marketers learn who wants what products through market surveys, focus groups, and test marketing, they target the consumer groups who match the demographics. On the Internet, consumers often reveal their preferences by visiting a specific web site. Someone who visits GolfWeb (http://www. golfweb.com) will more likely be a golfer; a visitor to an automobile review site may be thinking about buying a car. Because of the presumed effectiveness of targeted advertisements, web pages command a high price for advertisements. GolfWeb, for example, earns between $30 to $40 per 1,000 impressions (that is, 1,000 times an ad is viewed). Some popular computer-related sites command twice that much for the same number of impressions.

The difference between audience targeting in the broadcast media and on the Internet is clearly a matter of degree. Although the Internet allows a more precise targeting than the broadcast media, its advantage over traditional broadcasting media is still only incremental. Although it is often termed as "narrow-casting," the Internet advertising being promoted today as a winning strategy is still based on a model of broadcasting.

However well-targeted, this type of advertising is still intrusive to consumers who prefer to be left alone. The underlying principle in this type of advertising is one-way communication from sellers to buyers, as in physical markets. In contrast, the Internet is a two-way communication medium where consumers actively seek out information about products. Therefore, in the case of the electronic marketplace, the objective of advertising should change from sending product information to buyers to an interactive conversation between sellers and buyers to match the consumption needs with the products. Internet advertising is, in fact, "needs-based advertising;" consumers request an advertisement when it is needed. Even if a reader remembers a particular ad in a newspaper, she may have difficulty recalling or finding the ad when she really needs it. On the Internet, when you want to buy a product, you can search for the ads on the fly.

Active and intrusive advertising, such as mass e-mailings, is also redundant and wasteful; it sends out messages that are of no value to many receivers and are therefore wasted. Although over-the-air broadcasting also generates this waste, messages floating in the air do not have as significant an effect as those flowing through wired communications networks. Compared to mass media advertising, then, reducing such wastes seems to be one area in which Internet advertising can improve market efficiency substantially. For those who are familiar with mass-media, "pushed" messages often appear to be more efficient than "pulled" messages.

Push versus Pull Advertising

Although some people believe that conventional advertising is not effective on the Internet, web pages now carry an increasing amount of advertisements through banners. E-mail solicitations continue even though they are denounced as an unacceptable use of the medium. Banner ads and e-mail solicitations are electronic versions of traditional advertising. Sellers "push" product information to consumers whether or not they are interested. On the Internet, however, such advertising is highly customized and targeted. With such refinements, some people believe that the push model of advertising can work on the Internet.

Software that pushes products and information to consumers uses the Internet as a broadcast medium. Push software is gaining popularity especially in the area of an intranet (the Internet used within a corporation) because it reduces the amount of traffic and delivers timely and useful information. Employees at an electric utility firm, for example, need to be informed about rapidly changing weather. When employees search for weather information, many problems can arise: some employees might not find the information, or others might forget to search for it. Instead of relying on information being pulled by employees, push software delivers the information to those who need to be informed in a timely and efficient manner. Wayfarer Communications' Incisa (http://www.incisa.com) is a leading intranet Webcasting software that broadcasts information to "alert" employees. In an environment in which

control over information is not an issue, this push model may prove important. On the Internet, PointCast (http://www.pointcast.com) and BackWeb
Technologies (http://www.backweb.com) are the main players in delivering
products to consumers.

In a market situation, on the other hand, consumers take a more active role
in determining what information is needed and search for that information.
Unlike on corporate intranets, no one on the Internet can decide for others
what information is useful. Consumers search the Internet with a purpose. As
an advertiser, an Internet merchant must stand ready to provide visitors all the
information they need to make a purchase. Therefore, consumers are "pulled"
by the content of the web storefronts and advertisements—in short, consumers
come to the sellers. Therefore, the pull model is a desirable method of Internet
advertising.

Many factors make Internet marketers skeptical of the pull model of
advertising. Sellers are finding that the euphoria of a horde of customers
knocking on the door is never fulfilled. A critical factor is the inadequacy of
search facilities. In the fast-growing and ever-changing world of the web,
electronic catalogs and directories are far from sufficient to guide consumers to
appropriate places. Internet traffic tends to gather in a few web sites and often
redirects itself. Coupled with the lack of content and suitable payment methods, consumers as well as sellers are not piqued at the Internet's commercial
potential. The result is that sellers use the Internet as what they always considered it to be: an efficient and inexpensive communications medium. Push
advertising on the Internet is increasing. Like television broadcasters, Internet
search service providers rely on advertiser support. In the process, the transmission becomes slower due to the multimedia content of advertisements, and the
search database itself is organized to promote certain web sites based on revenues and profits.

It is important to note, however, that what is called a "push" technology is
only a hybrid of push and pull methods of delivering products online. Sending
e-mail to an unsuspecting consumer is undoubtedly pushy. Pointcast and
BackWeb, however, deliver products based on what their customers have
requested in the first place. Without continued interaction with the customers

regarding their preferences, customer interest will wane after a while; customers might consider what is being delivered to be worthless and intrusive. The viability of this so-called push technology ultimately depends on how successfully it accounts for the need and the desire to pull information among consumers.

Advertisements as Commodities

Two trends might discourage push advertising. One trend is the effort to sell advertisements as products. CyberGold (http://www.cybergold.com) has the novel concept of marketing personalized advertisements to interested consumers who voluntarily read the ads in exchange for direct payments from the advertisers. Consumers fill out data on personal interests, and CyberGold distributes targeted advertisements based on the personal profile. Each banner is denoted with the amount of payment (see fig. 6.9). If interested, the reader clicks the banner to read it and, passing some tests on its content, is paid for the effort. Readers can sort and choose what they read, and the advertisers can vary payments to reflect the frequency and desirability of readers. Advertisers on mass media pay based on inadequate measures of audience. In contrast, CyberGold's model is a sophisticated and direct means of advertisement.

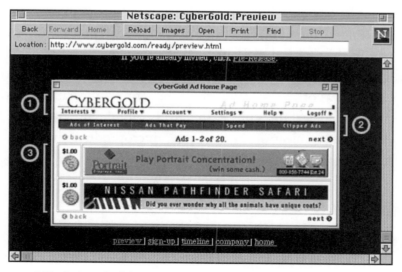

Figure 6.9 CyberGold's proposed personalized advertising page.

The second trend against the use of push advertising is the emerging payment methods for electronic commerce. The television industry, for example, relies on advertisers because it lacks a suitable way of charging its audience. Thus, television networks are ultimately in the business of selling the audience, not the programming, which is simply a means to achieve their ultimate goal. Likewise, Internet search service providers contend that their business is selling consumers or consumer information to advertisers, rather than the search database they provide. To be an information seller, there must be a suitable way to charge consumers for searches. Therefore, the use of advertising banners by search sites is a temporary solution until there is a suitable payment mechanism. Instead of paying for search services, some consumers might prefer to tolerate electronic banners. Internet advertisers, however, insist on paying based on click-throughs instead of on the number of banners displayed. Consumers must click the ad and connect to the advertising site before the advertiser pays the search engine provider. In that case, CyberGold's innovative model will be more appropriate for the consumer, and the direct payment from the advertisers may exceed the payment required to do searches.

Among the various payment mechanisms proposed for electronic commerce, micropayments will play an important role in implementing the preceding scenario. Search services may operate on a subscription basis that may not require micropayments. The subscription model, however, duplicates what is prevalent in the physical markets such as newspapers and cable television service. In both cases, some consumers—occasional readers or viewers—are not served whereas others—heavy users—benefit from such subscription schemes. Technological difficulties, in part, justify the use of subscriptions in traditional media. In electronic commerce, microproducts and micropayments will certainly improve the efficiency.

Passive versus Active Marketing

In physical markets, consumers often prefer passive marketing. Automobile dealers, for example, have successively used no-hassle pricing to attract more customers. Similarly, the pull model of web merchandising implies passive marketing.

This impression, however, is only superficial. Web-based marketers need to be active, not in the sense of pushing products, but in interacting with customers. Instead of passively displaying product and purchase information on their web pages, marketers need to receive and process input from customers to assist in their purchase decision and to customize products based on consumer preferences. This interactivity does not require a real-time application. Rather, consumer-seller interactions occur on the web because web storefronts incorporate many functions of a physical store. Sales assistants in physical markets, for example, help consumers pick out products; web pages must also act as a sales assistant, guiding customers in their purchasing decision. Web stores also perform the functions of production, delivery, and customer service. An active web store takes advantage in organizing such diverse functions in a dynamic process. A passive web store is static and only offers a take-it-or-leave-it option.

Electronic Malls and Intermediaries

Developers of electronic shopping malls are preoccupied in perfecting a visually attractive and operationally efficient—in terms of directing traffic—user interface on the Internet. An electronic shopping mall generally contains a list of sellers assembled in one electronic domain, either physically or through links. The concept of a mall as a space is faithfully duplicated; the proximity works for the tenants in generating traffic. The stores in the virtual marketplace need not be located side by side on a list, but should be linked with a purpose. A web store selling collectable coins, for example, might have a reference page that discusses the history of money. Bookstores can be logically linked on that page rather than on a separate "links" page. In other words, web store proximity is based on the closeness in subject, material, or consumption behaviors of the visitors.

As discussed in Chapter 4, online intermediaries are more like *The New York Times* and CNN, who mediate information markets between producers and consumers—unlike a mall where different types of shops are located centrally to maximize the benefits of spatial convenience. A centralized marketplace in electronic commerce will be an intermediary, which may be essential for the reason discussed to resolve quality uncertainty. New entrants and small-scale producers of digital products can rent the reputation of a marketplace or an intermediary who, because of its scale, length of operation, and reputation, is trusted by consumers. Chapter 4 describes how intermediaries can build and maintain customer trust.

Is Online Advertising Effective?

Despite many rosy projections regarding the size of Internet advertising, skeptics still abound. The skepticism is sometimes based on verifiable facts, but in most cases is a matter of opinion. A report at Web Advertising '96 (Tchong, 1996) discusses six major myths regarding web advertising:

- **There is no adequate tool to measure consumer response to web advertising.**

  The fact is that the World Wide Web is more sophisticated in measuring consumer response to advertisements than traditional media. The abundance and detail of data enables researchers to probe deep into the reasons why consumers click through banner ads. Such a detailed study is impossible for mass media advertisements.

- **Consumers are either annoyed by banner ads or ignore them completely.**

  Surveys conducted by *Advertising Age* (http://www.adage.com) and *BYTE* found that over half of consumers surveyed look at banner ads and think banner ads are effective. Whether this translates into sales is a different matter. It is equally difficult, however, to make a connection between television program ratings, the effectiveness of the commercials shown, and their impact on actual sales. Nevertheless, measures such as hit rates are used to measure consumer response just as the number of eyeballs is used for television advertisements and the certified number of circulation for newspapers and magazines.

- **Nobody shops on the Internet.**

  Because the size and demographics of Internet users change rapidly, any study on this subject is inescapably outdated. If Internet sales figure are limited to actual online ordering, they will not discern how online advertising induces consumers to purchase offline. Although the lack of payment methods limits online purchases, digital currency, micro-payments, and more secure online credit card payment mechanisms will certainly have a great impact in the near future.

- **Consumers do not respond after repeated exposure to banner ads.**

  Recent studies on click-through rates show that consumers respond better to repeated exposure for banner ads than for print ads. (See Donatello, 1997 for an analysis of Infoseek's study on the subject; see Cyberatlas, 1996 for an analysis of I/PRO and DoubleClick's study.)

- **Web advertising forecasts are bogus.**

  All forecasts are based on the growth rates of the past period. Therefore, web advertising revenue forecasts may be biased because advertising revenues grew phenomenally in the past two years because the industry is still young. Two reasons may explain why web advertising revenues will continue to grow rapidly. First, the Internet may become an alternative channel for the direct mail business, which had an estimated revenue of over $30 billion in 1996. Even the television-based Home Shopping Network may conduct its business online. Second, expenditures on web storefronts and other forms of advertising and marketing have been ignored in calculating the size of the online advertising market. Considering such expenditure, today's estimates seem too small.

- **Advertisers are still committed to traditional media.**

  The trend toward an integrated marketing effort implies that firms realize the Internet is an alternative marketing channel that they cannot ignore. More importantly, digital products are emerging as native commodities of the Internet; online marketing for digital products is a necessity. An effective advertising strategy must consider not only the character of the communicating medium but also the characteristics of the products being sold and the manner in which products are sold.

Providing Consumer Information

Another economic issue in the efficiency of signaling quality and product information is whether firms have an incentive to provide complete information to consumers. Lewis and Sappington (1994) argue that either a firm will supply the best possible information or none at all.

Suppose there are two types of consumers: high and low. The seller sells only one product; the high-type consumers derive $100 worth of enjoyment from the product, and the low-type consumers derive only $50. Consumers cannot tell whether they will be a high type or a low type, but know the chance is even. Without any information about the product, a consumer is willing to pay $75 (the expected value) on average for the product. If the cost of the product is $30, the seller's profit margin is $45 for each unit sold with no product information. If the consumers are given product information to find out what value they would derive from consumption, half the consumers (the low types) will not buy the product at $75 but will pay only $50, meaning a profit margin of $20. The high-type consumers, on the other hand, will pay $100, meaning a profit margin of $70. If the seller can charge separate prices with no consumer arbitrage, the seller is indifferent between providing the full product information and no information. If, however, there is consumer arbitrage such that only one price can be sustained, the maximum price is $50, and the seller will not provide any information.

If the product's cost is $60, the seller can maximize profit by fully informing buyers and selling the product for $100 only to high-type consumers—equating to a $40 profit margin compared to $30 for no information and selling to both types. This is an example of a high-cost, high-value product for which product information is always provided. When the cost of a product is low, the seller often has no incentive to provide information unless it can discriminate buyers.

Finally, on a technological level, the Internet poses a unique problem because, unlike in mass media, technologies are rapidly developing to counter electronic advertising and to give consumers control over messages. PrivNet (http://www.privnet.com) has developed software that blocks memory-grabbing features of a web page, such as graphics, blinking texts, and ads, and disables web cookies, which record what a browser viewed in a web site. The same technology that offers online advertisers a sophisticated tool also affords consumers a means to combat intrusive messages. Filtering technologies are necessary to solve information overload and to limit intrusive uses of the Internet such as junk e-mails. These technologies have the potential to limit further the effectiveness of online advertising.

6.5.   Summary

When consumers have little or no information about product quality, the market generally fails or the quality of the product deteriorates. One market mechanism that prevents such market inefficiency is for the seller to provide product information directly to consumers through advertising or to send certain signals to convince consumers about the quality. This chapter reviewed such seller-initiated information methods. An important aspect of online advertising and marketing is that the medium facilitates integrating various selling processes. Web storefronts, therefore, are a focal point in combining product development, advertising, and ordering as well as customer service in a seamless process of marketing. An equally possible alternative to seller-provided information is for consumers to search for information, which is the focus of the next chapter.

References

Bain, J.S. *Barriers to New Competition: Their Character and Consequences in Manufacturing Industries.* Cambridge: Harvard University Press, 1956.

Blum, M. "How to Prove a Theorem So No One Else Can Claim It." Proceedings of the International Congress of Mathematicians, Berkeley, CA, 1986.

Caves, R.E., and D.P. Greene. "Brands' Quality Levels, Prices, and Advertising Outlays: Empirical Evidence on Signals and Information Costs." *International Journal of Industrial Organization.* 14: 29–52. 1996.

Chu, W., and W. Chu. "Signaling Quality by Selling through a Reputable Retailer: an Example of Renting the Reputation of another Agent." *Marketing Science.* 13(2) (1994): 177–189.

Cyberatlas, 1996. "What Makes People Click?" Available at http://ww.cyberatlas.com/wip2.html.

Donatello, M., 1997. "How Do I Click Thee? Let Me Count the Ways..." Available at http://www.naa.org/edge/eresearch.html.

Eaton, J., and G.M. Grossman. "The Provision of Information as Marketing Strategy." *Oxford Economic Papers*, 38 (1986): 166–183.

Goldreich, O., S. Micali, and A. Wigderson. "Proofs that Yield Nothing but their Validity and a Methodology of Cryptographic Protocol Design." Proceedings of the 27th IEEE Symposium on the Foundations of Computer Science. 1986.

Grossman, G.M., and C. Shapiro. "Informative Advertising with Differentiated Products." *Review of Economic Studies*, 51 (1984): 63–81.

Lewis, T.R., and D.E. Sappington. "Supplying Information to Facilitate Price Discrimination." *International Economic Review*, 35(2)(1994): 309-327.

Meurer, M., and D.O. Stahl. "Informative Advertising and Product Match." *International Journal of Industrial Organization*, 12 (1994): 1–19.

Quisquater, J.J., and S. Guillou. "How to Explain Zero-Knowledge Protocols to Your Children." Advances in Cryptography—CRYPTO '89 Proceedings. Berlin: Springer-Verlag.

Shapiro, C. "Consumer Information, Product Quality, and Seller Reputation." *Bell Journal of Economics* 13, (1992): 20–35.

Tchong, M., 1996. "Debunking Common Web Advertising Myths." Web Advertising '96 Report. Available at http://www.cyberatlas.com/wa96_tchong.htm.

Wernerfelt, B. "On the Function of Sales Assistance." *Marketing Science*, 13(1) (1994): 68–82.

Suggested Readings and Notes

Advertising and Competition

Good summary treatments of advertising in terms of market competition can be found in the following:

Bain (1956) provides a classic discussion of barriers to entry.

Butters, G. "Equilibrium Distributions of Sales and Advertising Prices." *Review of Economic Studies,* 44(3) (1977): 465–491.

This paper studies a case where advertisements contain price information. Advertisements in Grossman and Shapiro (1984), on the other hand, contain product specifications.

Comanor, W.S., and T.A. Wilson. "Advertising and Competition: A Survey." *Journal of Economic Literature,* 17 (1979): 453–76.

Ekelund, R.B., and D.S. Saurman. *Advertising and the Market Process.* San Francisco: Pacific Research Institute for Public Policy. 1988.

Schmalensee, R. *The Economics of Advertising.* New York: Humanities Press, 1973.

Signaling

Cho, I. K., and Kreps, D.M. "Signaling Games and Stable Equilibria." *Quarterly Journal of Economics,* 95 (1987): 1–24.

Spence, A.M. *Market Signaling: Information Transfer in Hiring and Related Processes.* Cambridge: Harvard University Press, 1973.

Internet Resources

Web Directory for Advertising

Advertising World Directory, Department of Advertising, the University of Texas at Austin (http://www.utexas.edu/coc/adv/world/) has an extensive list of Internet resources (see fig. 6.10).

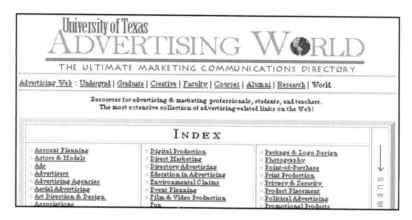

Figure 6.10 Advertising World web page.

Popular Wisdom on Internet Marketing

"The Eleven Commandments of Internet Marketing," by the Marketing Consortium:

http://deck.com/mrkt_consortium/commandments.html

"The Ten Commandments of Successful Business Advertising," by Temkin & Temkin Advertising:

http://www.temkin.com/10comman.htm

"The 10 Commandments for Successful Marketing Communications" on the Web by Werbal Advertising Agency:

http://www.spectraweb.ch/~verbal/english/10commandments.html

Shareware Resources

The Association of Shareware Producers' FAQ is available at http://www.asp-shareware.org/sharewar.html.

The newsgroup, alt.comp.shareware, has a FAQ available at http://mini.net/pub/acs-faq.txt.

The following are some popular web sites that offer shareware:

- Arizona Mac Users Group: http://cdrom.amug.org
- BestZips: http://www.bestzips.com
- CNET's Shareware site: http://www.shareware.com
- Educational Software Cooperative: http://members.aol.com/edsoftcoop
- FTP search by program name: http://ftpsearch.ntnu.no/ftpsearch
- Shareware Trade Association: http://www.shareware.org
- Ziff-Davis Interactive: http://www.zdnet.com/zdi/software

CHAPTER 7

Consumers' Search for Information

Any discussion of the economic implications of the means by which sellers provide information to consumers needs to consider the means by which consumers search for product information in a digital world. In physical markets, consumer search activities include reading advertisements, calling vendors, and visiting stores. In a virtual marketplace, all these activities converge into web searches and web browsing. Not surprisingly, search services were the first market infrastructure to be built in the electronic marketplace. The focus of this chapter is to investigate the nature of existing search mechanisms as information channels. It also evaluates the effectiveness of search services and information intermediaries in terms of the economic efficiency that the digital information market may achieve through the proliferation of these search channels.

7.1. Consumer Searches and Economic Efficiency

A market is considered to be economically efficient when a product is sold at the lowest possible price or at the marginal cost of production for a given level of quality. For a standard product that can be produced by many firms using a common technology, an efficient price is unique. In real markets, however, a uniform price is seldom observed because sellers and buyers have different information about the price and quality of a product. Bargain hunters must visit many stores to gather information on different prices and product specifications, and compare their records before deciding which offers the best deal. This search process clearly has costs associated with it. To obtain full information about prices and product qualities, consumers must incur unnecessarily high search expenses and duplicate the efforts of other consumers. An efficient solution strikes a balance between the benefits of an efficient marginal price and the costs required to inform all market participants about price and product quality.

In general, firms know more about their products than do the consumers. This informational advantage gives firms some degree of market power, which is usually manifested in the form of a product price greater than the competitive price. If consumers were to receive advertising about price and product quality from all sellers in the market, their purchase decision would be based on who offered the lowest price or the best price for the desired quality. However, consumers do not tend to receive all the relevant market information, because some sellers may not advertise or some advertisements may not reach all the intended audience. This lack of consumer knowledge creates inefficiencies in the form of sellers charging higher prices than the marginal costs of production, or the existence of multiple prices that discriminate against some consumers. In an extreme case, quality uncertainty may result in the complete failure of a market, as in the lemons market problem discussed in Chapter 4. For all these reasons, an efficient market for product information is necessary for the existence of an efficient product market.

Search Costs

The cost of a search is any amount of money, time, or effort that buyers may incur in obtaining price and quality information for products. Examples of costly information gathering are visits to stores (which involve transportation and time costs), telephone calls, buying newspapers, and so on. In physical markets, searches usually happen sequentially—that is, consumers visit one store, gather information, decide whether or not to purchase, and visit the next store if the product is not bought (see fig. 7.1).

Suppose that Alice goes to the store #1, and finds the offer price is $10. Suppose also that it costs $1 to visit each store, and that, for simplicity, this cost is the same for all visits. Including the search cost, she faces the total price of $11 at the first store she visits. She must decide whether to accept or reject the offer. Her purchasing process may be either "take-it-or-leave-it" (accepting the posted price), or "bargaining." If she goes to a second store, she incurs another $1 for her search. If the second store offers the same product at $9.50, Alice would have been better off buying it at the first store, because the total price at the second store is $11.50 ($9.50 + $1 + $1). Suppose that $9.50 is the competitive price and every consumer knows that fact. However, despite consumers' knowledge, prices higher than the competitive price are still observed in the market because of the search cost. If all sellers follow this reasoning, there can only be one stable equilibrium price, which is at the monopoly price. Even when the search cost is reduced to an arbitrarily small amount, the logic of this result remains valid unless the search cost actually becomes zero. In summary, this scenario demonstrates that prices will be monopolistic—or arbitrarily high—even when there are many competing sellers, as long as consumers are not informed and must incur search costs.

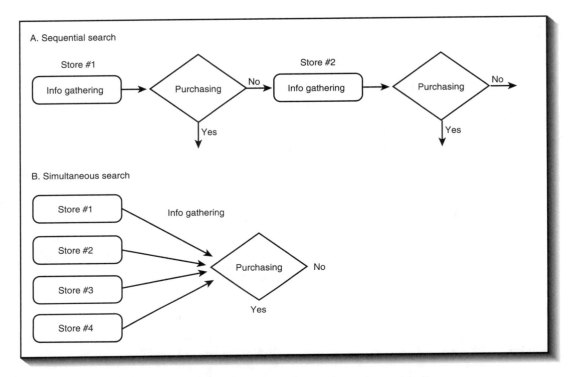

Figure 7.1 Sequential and simultaneous searches.

The search cost scenario changes significantly in the case of repeat purchases. When consumers buy the same products repeatedly over a long period of time, they become familiar with the prices charged by each seller in the market. Except for the case in which everyone shops at the same store, some sellers may actually lower prices to attract more customers. In a sense, buyers accumulate price information and make their purchasing decisions based on this simultaneously (refer to fig. 7.1). For those who have pricing information, prices become efficient, approaching the competitive level if stores compete fiercely in price. Consumers who prefer to shop at the same store are not informed, and some stores continue to charge higher prices than the competitive price, depending upon uninformed consumers. Repeat purchasers are somewhat like "natives," who have information about prices charged by local merchants, while those without information are "tourists." In this version of the native-and-tourist model, a range of prices can be observed that discriminate against uninformed consumers.

Consumer Searches and Electronic Commerce

Similar to searches in physical markets, online searches can also be carried out either sequentially or simultaneously. Surfing through different web stores is a *sequential search*; a price search based on a price database is an example of a *simultaneous search*. In either case, an online search offers a tremendous advantage over a physical search. Besides the lowered costs for time and transportation, a computer-based search allows consumers to remember and compare information gathered from many stores. Furthermore, online searches enable consumers to process a wide range of information other than price, such as location and name of vendors, terms of sales, quality and performance variables, brand names, sizes and other product characteristics, and so forth. Comparing prices alone strains the capacity to process information in physical markets, especially if shopping involves many products. Online search technologies automate this process and allow consumers to engage in more sophisticated and efficient searches.

The search and information transmission mechanisms used in the electronic marketplace are too new for researchers to have determined their efficiency. In fact, there are contradicting predictions about what will happen. One view is that with computer technologies such as search engines and intelligent software agents, consumers may be able to search the whole information space at no cost. For example, suppose you want to buy a product. Using a computer program, you initiate a search mechanism that searches all the web pages on the Internet for a product that matches your needs. The search generates a table of names of sellers, prices, locations, and product specifications, as well as other relevant information such as seller reputation, past sales records, and so forth. You then choose a seller among the candidates, and initiate a purchase order. Although this scenario is close to one with no search costs, which produces an efficient market, there are many reasons why the electronic marketplace may not actually be so efficient. In the first place, sellers may not provide relevant information. Secondly, search algorithms or techniques may not be sufficient to gather all the relevant information. This may be because of access difficulties (because some web sites do not allow access), or because all searches inevitably select and process information based on prescribed criteria that may have non-technical problems. Lastly, economic analyses indicate that a non-zero search cost, however small it may be, results in noncompetitive pricing. Using electronic media may reduce search costs to an arbitrarily small amount, but the cost is still non-zero. In mathematical models, a reduction in search costs is quite different from an elimination of search costs. In this regard, it may be reasonable to assume that the problems associated with information will persist in electronic commerce as they do in physical markets.

As section 7.4 discusses in more detail, some authors argue that increasing advertising (such as information provided by sellers) tends to be a better means of producing an efficient market than is efficient consumer searching. The argument is that competition through advertising tends to lower prices, whereas consumers do not usually search for all information because of the search costs involved or the difficulty of processing information. The resulting lack of full information on the part of consumers often gives some firms an incentive to raise their prices. It is still not certain that advertising will be a better information channel than a consumer search in electronic commerce. Broadcast-based advertising has many obvious drawbacks, the most glaring of which is that mass advertising is strongly resisted and discouraged on the Internet, because Internet users must pay for connection and downloading time to receive ads. Also, by its nature, advertising is necessarily duplicative and wasteful (as discussed in Chapter 6), not to speak of its side effect of cluttering precious bandwidth. At the same time, Internet consumers seem to prefer to access product information actively. The conclusion is that searches initiated by consumers based on their identified needs will surely be more efficient (in terms of costs and effectiveness) in reaching the intended audience than duplicative broadcast advertising will be.

Finally, consumers may behave differently in the electronic marketplace than in physical markets where search costs are usually positive. This positive—however small—search cost results in higher than competitive prices. This phenomenon is popularly known as the "Diamond paradox" (Diamond, 1971). Are search costs always positive? Admittedly, some shoppers realize an enjoyment benefit to shopping rather than a cost. On the Internet, "surfers" often resemble those shoppers who happily visit stores to simply look at the merchandise. Armed with powerful archiving programs, online surfers are able to gather information while enjoying themselves. When they process this information to make a purchasing decision, the net cost of search may indeed be zero—or certainly not positive—debunking the paradoxical result of monopoly price equilibrium under positive search costs (Stahl, 1996).

Digital Products and Consumer Searches

The effectiveness of consumer searches depends not only on the consumer's willingness to incur the cost (and time) involved, but also on the type of product and the type of search. A simple search may consist primarily of obtaining price quotes from sellers, assuming that the consumer already knows about product quality. And indeed, for a product whose quality can be judged by simple inspection of a picture, often called a *search good*, its price is the most relevant unknown variable. However, when a product is an *"experience good,"* it is quite a different matter to assess its quality prior to actual consumption, as discussed in Chapter 4. The best a consumer can do with an experience good is to collect all the information about product specifications to evaluate the product. Because most information products are experience goods, a search involves a much more complex process of information selection and access than merely getting price quotes. Furthermore, the efficiency of the search depends on how much product information is provided by sellers, and how truthful and reliable the provided information is. The challenge here is that the product information for certain products is the product itself, as is the case for much computer software. In that case, the search may involve actually trying out the product in the form of demo or shareware versions or free initial trials.

Given the importance and difficulties, it is little wonder that a large segment of the electronic market is devoted to search activities. Search services on the Internet are visited most frequently by web browsers, according to the 100 Hot sites list (http://www.100hot.com) in September, 1996. In fact, almost half of the top 15 sites are actually search services, including the most popular, Yahoo! (http://www.yahoo.com), as well as other search sites such as WebCrawler (http://www.webcrawler.com), PathFinder (http://www.pathfinder.com), Excite (http://www.excite.com), Magellan (http://www.mckinley.com), AltaVista (http://www.altavista.digital.com), and Lycos (http://www.lycos.com) (see fig. 7.2). For the purpose of analyzing this significant sector in a broad context of the electronic market, the search market is defined as all aspects of search activities including content provision, location, and retrieving, all of which of course include intermediaries providing search services.

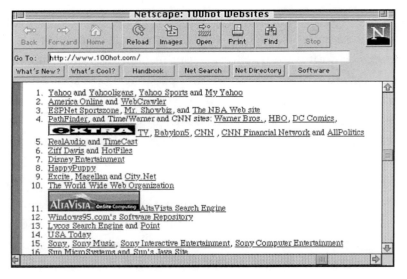

Figure 7.2 100 Hot sites.

7.2.   The Search Market and Intermediaries

The Internet search market, similar to all markets, finds its roots in identifying its customers' needs. Quite simply, to complete a search process, consumers must know what they are looking for. After the need for information is identified, the search is completed by locating and selecting the source of information, then by accessing and retrieving it. The *search market* is the space in which all these processes are conducted, whereas a *search service* is one intermediary that facilitates the process of selection. The efficiency of the search market may be analyzed according to three criteria: market efficiency, network efficiency, and information efficiency. Market efficiency is concerned with whether useful information is present and whether adequate access to the information is supported by the market. Network efficiency, on the other hand, deals with the organizational aspects of various search patterns. Finally, informational efficiency examines the quality and value of search results.

Search Market Efficiency

A search market consists of three components: content providers, selection process, and access. Before discussing how the three components work together, however, it is important to understand each one separately.

- **Content Providers**   The content provided by sellers largely defines the informational space a search can occupy. Understandably, some product information may not yet be available in digital format. Information that does already exist includes primary sources such as company web pages and secondary sources such as bot-generated indexes and evaluation databases. Secondary sources often filter and reduce the amount of information but add the expertise of the information brokers.

- **Selection**   The process of electronic selection involves various forms of information query based on keywords or subjects. Interactive queries result in individualized sorts. A non-interactive selection process uses classified ads, directories, or other types of information brokers, in which entries are organized by some preselected criteria. Internet searches on Lycos or Yahoo! use this selection process.

- **Access**   Through selection, consumers acquire lists of information sites that fit their search criteria. But, to actually view these documents, selected information must be downloaded or accessed by visiting the web sites. The access occurs in two stages: the connecting and retrieving processes.

The search market in this formulation extends beyond electronic searches to include many forms of advertising. Advertising through mass mailing, for example, consists of content providers and access, but the selection process is entirely determined by the senders. In other words, it lacks the consumers' selective initiative. Classified ads offer contents and selection, where contents are the ads and the selection is provided by classification schemes, but consumers must rely on different media to actually access the information, for example, contact a store or a person offering the information. Directories may provide contents if their classifications are useful in distinguishing entries. On the other hand, directories like the white pages of the telephone book often provide only selection because they do not have description and because consumers need to place the call themselves. Internet search services such as Yahoo! (http:// www.yahoo.com) and AltaVista (http:// www.altavista.digital.com) combine all three components, offering contents, some selection mechanisms, and hyperlinks to access the contents; but the search services differ in their scope of content and their selection mechanisms.

Although Internet search services focus on selection and access processes, the relevant contents must be exhaustive for a search to be efficient. The contents need to include not only price and location of the sellers but also related product information and the terms of sales. As content providers, web pages should be configured to act as a sales person providing information such as product specification, differences from other products, recommendations, and so on. For example, to buy a shirt, a consumer may want to know the fabric, type of care required, appropriate style consideration, size and fit, and so forth. Consumers may also want to know third-party evaluations and safety records. In short, web pages are expected to offer the knowledge and expertise that a trained sales staff is expected to provide in a physical market.

An ideal search market, therefore, allows consumers to take their searches through a series of filtering processes by which they may reduce the universe of available information to a manageable and meaningful size. An efficient Internet search market can be depicted, as in figure 7.3, as the content space available on the Internet containing the set of selected information, which also contains accessed information space. In this case, even though some product information is only available offline, the online search market is efficient because all contents that are relevant (the area of the pentagon) exist online (the rounded rectangle). In other words, one is a proper subset of the other in the order of contents, selection, and access. If any or some of them are not a proper subset, the search market is not efficient. For example, if some contents, which are needed in the selection process, are not available online, the search process cannot be efficient. In figure 7.4, (a) shows a case where some information, although relevant, is not available online. As a result, only the contents accessible online are retrieved.

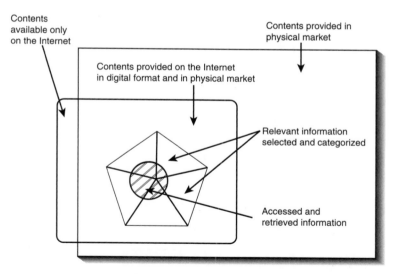

Figure 7.3 An efficient Internet search market.

Even when contents are available online, the search market may fail if these contents are not accessible due, for example, to access restriction or congestion (see (b) and (c) in fig. 7.4). Finally, consumers may have to rely on both online and offline information channels to complete a search (see (d) in fig. 7.4), as is the case with today's market. The obvious implication is that the information available in the physical market must also be available online to prevent search problems such as (a) and (d) in figure 7.4.

(a) Some information relevant to selection is not available online.

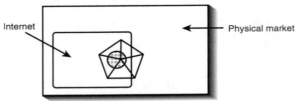

(b) Access problem, where relevant information is not accessible.

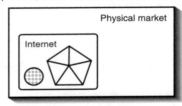

(c) Access problem, where only some relevant information is accessible.

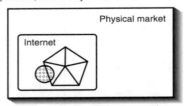

(d) Traditional information access, where both online and offline methods have to be used.

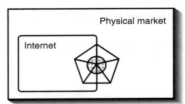

Figure 7.4 Examples of an inefficient search market.

As contents are converted into digital forms, and new types of information are provided online, almost all contents may be available both online and offline. As contents become larger and more complicated, the efficiency of the selection process becomes a critical factor in consumer searches. The most efficient selection process is achieved when all accessed information is indeed relevant to a purchasing decision. In other words, the result of a search using the AltaVista search engine produces only useful information rather than the thousands of documents today's search services tend to generate. To increase selection efficiency, Internet search engines offer different ways to conduct a search. The simplest search consists of typing in some keywords. This process often produces many irrelevant documents and links, but it enables searchers full access to the complete database. On the other hand, search services need to exercise some value judgment in compiling directories. Although directories are familiar to consumers and easy to use, classifying an entry can be arbitrary when a document belongs to different categories. Evaluated and recommended lists of sites and documents (for example, "What's New" or "What's Hot" lists) can be even more arbitrary as consumers have a minimal amount of input in selecting them. This type of service is not really a search service but rather more of an advertisement.

Despite their limitations, search services play an important role by aiding consumers in the selection process. Search engines are in fact intermediaries who broker product information between sellers and buyers. According to the theory of disintermediation, electronic commerce represents a market where intermediaries disappear because consumers can interact directly with producers. In such a market, consumers do not need search intermediaries because, for example, consumers are able to use powerful search programs of their own. Today's search engines in fact send out intelligent programs or automated robots to gather information about web documents. Consumers, in theory, can employ their own agents that roam cyberspace with a predetermined mission and report back to their owners. On the other hand, search intermediaries may continue to serve in the electronic marketplace for several reasons, which are discussed in the following sections.

Search Efficiency in Intermediaries

In terms of network traffic, individual agent-based searches generate much duplication in both accessing and downloading information, because each consumer must send its own query over the network. This duplicative traffic can be minimized by using intermediaries who collect, process, and store the information.

The efficiency in intermediating potentially duplicative and wasteful efforts to access information on the Internet resembles that of wholesaling and retailing in physical markets. By handling products in bulk, wholesalers and retailers in physical markets minimize transportation costs involved in distributing these products to geographically dispersed end users. For digital products, however, a producer needs only to send one copy to a wholesaler or a retailer, and therefore has no reason to be concerned with minimizing distribution costs. And because no online retailer is closer to consumers than their suppliers, distributive efficiency is not an issue. Nevertheless, an online intermediary minimizes distribution costs in its own way by reducing costs associated with network traffic. As shown in figure 7.5, the similarity between intermediated and disintermediated markets is striking.

The stylized diagram, figure 7.5, shows how consumers access product information. In (a), each buyer sends a query to all sellers to get product information, whereas in (b), buyers can get information from the intermediary who receives information packages from all these sellers. In a similar delivery scheme in physical markets, such an intermediated structure may not be efficient if some sellers are located closer to buyers than is the intermediary. A significant inefficiency can occur in the hub-and-spoke system used by airlines if some passengers (buyers) are forced to go through the hub (intermediary) regardless of the extra distance involved. In the virtual environment of the electronic marketplace, however, an intermediated search market dramatically reduces duplicated traffic and enhances network efficiency.

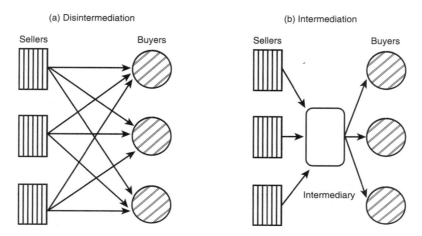

Figure 7.5 Information access with and without an intermediary.

This network efficiency has little to do with the intermediary's role in assisting consumers' selection processes; the efficiency results simply from the existence of a centralized outlet for all sellers. But this centralization need not require that the same contents be stored in both the producers' and the intermediary's web sites—a wasteful duplication. Instead, the product information at the intermediary's web site has only the information necessary for buyers to make purchase decisions. In a way, the intermediary also acts as an information filtering agent, which is the second type of efficiency in intermediation. Beyond intermediaries, consumers have many tools to filter information.

In an extreme case, for proper selection and evaluation of a product a consumer may require the full information contained in the seller's web site rather than a summary provided by an intermediary. In that case, face-to-face information exchanges can actually be more efficient than intermediation because of the latter's unnecessary duplication. But this is more of an exception than the rule in electronic commerce, because the quality of a digital product is difficult to evaluate even with full information or the product itself. More importantly, intermediaries also resolve the quality uncertainty problem, which was discussed in Chapter 4. If buyers contact sellers directly, the accessed information may not be reliable unless the content providers are known to be trustworthy. As discussed in Chapter 4, a simple contract can make intermediaries become trusted third parties in electronic commerce even without verifying all products they broker.

Search Efficiency in Informational Content

The primary way to search for products and price information in physical markets is to visit stores. In the electronic marketplace, physical limitation is replaced with a problem: locating and processing the relevant information is difficult not because of the lack of such information but because of the very abundance of it.

The prevalence of electronic catalogs, directories, and search services on the Internet signals a new age of information overload. Although the incredible amount of information provided on the Internet helps consumers to find products matching their preferences, managing this information becomes a new task for consumers who want to maximize the informational benefit of this new communication medium. In the electronic marketplace, where geographical residence has little meaning, the "natives" in the native-and-tourist model of price dispersion are those who can use computer programs comfortably, who know where to find relevant information, and who have the correct type of software agents and brokers to help them in processing the information. Those who have the ability to navigate the sea of information have a clear economic advantage over electronic "tourists" in finding the right products at the right prices.

In electronic commerce, however, most consumers may enjoy the benefit of being a native because information processing—or navigating the sea of information—can be automated to be run by computer programs (also called *intelligent agents*) or relegated to information intermediaries who sell their expertise in organizing information. Both of these tools help consumers to search, locate, retrieve, filter, and process information without incurring as high a cost as they do in physical markets.

Intelligent or software agents, or *bots*, are computer programs that carry out a specific task as programmed by a user. (A more detailed discussion is included in section 7.3). For example, they can screen incoming e-mail messages, evaluate them, and sort them out according to prescribed priorities, often generating automatic replies when required. Some agents can be sent over the network to search for information and report the results back to the owner. In a similar manner, most web page databases of Internet search services are generated by sending intelligent agents or bots, which can be highly individualized to match users' preferences. Using artificial intelligence, these agents can be trained over a period of time to refine their processing power. With future developments in intelligent agents, the gain in closer preference matching may even be more substantial than the gains in network efficiency that have been achieved through the use of intermediaries.

However, in a non-intermediated search market, the problem of information uncertainty still exists. Simply put, consumers must trust what the sellers say about their products. Often sellers may not provide enough information for consumers to fully evaluate their products, or the information received may be inadequate for consumers to judge whether the sellers are reputable companies or fly-by-night operators. Without some guarantee about the information and remedies available in the event that there is a dispute over payment, delivery, or post-sale service, face-to-face sales must be carried out on the basis of the seller's reputation. In light of this, an intermediary's role in a search market extends beyond being an information depository and distribution center. An information intermediary processes the information gathered by selecting, classifying, and evaluating it. With an added function as an information retailer, an information intermediary can also act as a third party that manages quality and service disputes between the buyer and the seller. Nevertheless, the primary advantage of using an information intermediary lies in the resulting increases in informational efficiency, both in quality and content.

Information is considered to be efficient if it is precise and correct. Suppose there is an uncertain state of the world, such as tomorrow's temperature in Austin, Texas. The actual temperature can be any number. After tomorrow, you will know the temperature—a certainty by then. The usefulness of information is in guiding us from the uncertain state to the certain state of the world. In forecasting tomorrow's temperature, certain information is useful, such as the location of the place, the season, previous temperatures, and so forth. Some information may only help us to narrow the temperature down into possible ranges, perhaps between 90 and 100. The more precise the information is, the more valuable. Although a forecast of a temperature may be correct in that it predicts the actual range, it may still be imprecise. The degree of precision required depends on one's needs.

The primary function—and added value—of an information intermediary is in enhancing the precision and "correctness" or accuracy of the information collected. As such, users can access precise and correct information with minimal effort by sending a query to a search service rather than embarking on their own worldwide searches of the World Wide Web. But how can intermediaries enhance the value of information? The answer lies in their expertise: information brokers are equipped with more experience and greater technical ability to process information. Secondly, they are better able to evaluate the information and can offer a greater reliability to consumers as one advantage of using their service rather than searching themselves. Initially, the success of an intermediary depends upon the reputation and reliability of its service, which is an added incentive for service providers to maintain better information. Information efficiency is therefore an added value obtained by a search market organized around intermediaries.

7.3.   Search Engines on the Internet

This section and the two that follow examine various search engines on the Internet in terms of the search market and the information efficiencies discussed in the preceding sections. They also compare the network efficiency of information search channels and discuss some of the implications for market organization and advertising.

Search or Surf?

Searching on the Internet starts with a need or a motive to find something, in stark contradiction to the popular Internet surfing, which implies a random, aimless hopping through hyperlinks for fun. Less than five years ago, "surfing the net" was the main activity for many Internet users. Today, online users begin by visiting their bookmarked sites or by searching for specific sites. The growth in search activity on the Internet represents a new phase in the development of the virtual space. What used to be something equivalent to taking a stroll has become more of an organized mission focused upon compiling a list of links, bookmarks, and recommended sites, and ultimately an organized personal directory. Such a directory is extremely useful in mapping out the virtual space. A directory should be complete, accurate, meaningful and objective. Current search services are lacking in these aspects.

Inadequacies of Search Engines

A complete listing of web sites and their documents currently does not exist. Instead, consumers need to visit different search sites or relevant web sites that might have useful links. This lack of a complete directory is not in itself a new problem. In physical markets, a telephone directory only lists local businesses, and there are a number of specialized directories for different industries and markets. However, there is no reason why all information housed in a library's reference section cannot be combined into one database, especially on the Internet. Combining different Internet search databases can further alleviate the hassle of having to use several search engines and the duplicative costs of having many users collecting the same information. To recover the cost of compiling an Internet database, more and more search engines are preoccupied with soliciting advertisers rather than improving data integrity and search efficiency. Search engines may be one of a few Internet services that are truly essential in enhancing the usability and usefulness of the Internet for commerce. An incomplete search engine is as useful as a partial phone directory.

Internet search databases are also inaccurate and outdated because web sites are constantly changing. They often give consumers links that no longer exist.

In such an environment, updating may require as much effort as compiling the initial database. An alternative may be to accept—or require—submissions by site owners about changes. Another inaccuracy stems from web sites misrepresenting and pretending to be something that they are not. That possibility compels data compilers to verify each site manually, further increasing the costs of maintaining an accurate database. A more coordinated system of feedback among content providers, users, and search engines are needed.

A third inadequacy of current search engines are the irrelevancy of some sites matching search keywords. One problem stems from the lack of sophisticated and complex search mechanisms to weed out irrelevant information. Equally lacking is a proper description for each web site and its materials upon which to base a search. As a result, a simple search often produces tens of thousands of meaningless links. Digital document metadata standards need to be established and accepted by content providers and become part of content creation.

Finally, search results need to be objective. Results can be skewed if the database itself consists of information that is pre-selected based on arbitrary criteria. Some search engines do not include personal homepages or materials residing on university web sites. Others reject web sites that are considered offensive, indecent, or frivolous by their own standards. Also, with the increasing commercialization, some search engine providers may give preference to paying advertisers. Although all these are reasonable behaviors for private enterprises, what would be the use of a phone directory that omitted all "Smiths" or those living in an area with a particular zip code? An Internet search engine is no longer just a springboard for Internet surfing. Rather, as an essential infrastructure, its database needs to be complete and accurate to foster an efficient information exchange.

7.4.   Market Efficiency in Various Information Sources

Information takes many forms and is scattered around in various subspaces on the Internet. The most recognizable information source by far is the World

Wide Web, with the largest and the fastest-growing servers today. Nevertheless, the web is only one of a large number of digital information resources. Despite the growing trend to move files from non-web servers to web servers, some files may be better served through traditional information channels such as anonymous FTP. One example is the downloading of free software, which is far easier and is customizable with an anonymous FTP program than with the World Wide Web. In addition, one of the advantages of the World Wide Web is its capability to handle different data servers, including FTP, Gopher, electronic mail, and others. Precisely for this reason, FTP and Gopher files need not be moved into the web (HTTP) server, which will prolong the life of many non-web information servers.

Numerous introductory books have been written with step-by-step user instructions that inventory all types of resources and services available on the Internet (see, for example Hahn, 1996). The following review of Internet services is not meant to provide an exhaustive description, but rather to highlight the characteristics of the information provided and each service's efficiency in facilitating information searches. For the purposes of this discussion, the wide range of Internet information sources can be divided into three broad groups:

- Services based on file transfers: World Wide Web, Gopher, FTP and Telnet
- Services used for broadcasting and exchanging information: UseNet, mailing lists, and electronic messaging
- Services that involve real-time interactions: talk, Internet Relay Chat, and Multiple User Dungeons (MUDs)

Although these services are not an altogether practical way of storing and searching information for real-time services, they are discussed here.

The World Wide Web

The World Wide Web is a system of servers interconnected throughout the world that is capable of providing all types of data including text, graphics, videos, and audio, through viewing programs called *browsers*. Anyone using a web browser becomes a client and can connect to any web server that provides content. The two overwhelming advantages of the web over other information channels are (1) its multimedia capability, and (2) its capability to interface with web servers as well as to e-mail, gopher, UseNet, and so on. These advantages are so overpowering that the web is well on its way to superceding all other information access methods in the future. Other advantages of the web include the capability to jump from place to place via hypertext links, and an easy and familiar graphical user interface, although these features are not necessarily the ones that are driving the popularity of the web in the long run. In fact, navigating through too many jumps and links can often result in an unmanageable work session.

As the web becomes the dominant means of accessing information on the Internet, information based on non-web technologies is moving to web servers. Previously, one needed to search different types of information space. In the end, all information searches will be done within the web environment as FTP and Gopher files are also cataloged and accessible through web servers. Although it is fast becoming a necessary evil, transforming contents into HTML files for the web is more time-consuming than for FTP or Gopher servers, which essentially use text files without the additional command insertions that are required for HTML files. Although programs are available that facilitate file conversions to HTML, shifting a large number of files from non-web servers to web servers is still a laborious process. Concurrently, as the web space explodes, managing indexes and devising more efficient search methods is becoming increasingly complicated, because web documents are more diverse than those residing in non-web servers.

Web Searches

The challenge for web search servers and consumers is how to filter, organize, and process search information, which is essentially information (indexes) about information (web contents). The following sections first focus on non-web information sources and provide a brief description of the search methods of each. Section 7.5 focuses on the informational efficiency of web search services in more detail.

Gopher

The gopher system is quite similar to the web in most of its methods of accessing and distributing information. Since its development in April, 1991 at the University of Minnesota, it has seen phenomenal growth in the number of servers and files offered, but then a precipitous decline due to the popularity of the web. Gopher is essentially a system of Gopher servers containing files that can be connected and accessed by others using Gopher client programs. In its architecture, the Gopher is not much different from the web. However, Gopher was developed as a cheap and easy way to share information resources in a wide area network called *Gopherspace*. It presents a simple text-based menu of files and directories of other gopher servers. It can also handle non-text formats such as graphic and sound files. To view these, Gopher uses helper applications, just as web browsers do, to process images and sounds. In this respect, however, the web server is more versatile and can process multimedia files seamlessly. Also, the graphic-rich user interface of the web and the ability of web users to publish and present their content online have made the web the overwhelming choice for Internet information interchange.

Despite the decline of the Gopher system, however, it remains an easy-to-use, fast source of text-based information. An immense amount of information, saved as simple text files, is available under gopher servers. Public, governmental, and educational institutions in particular maintain a large database of information on their Gopher servers. Many of these files await conversion to web resources, but many will remain as Gopher files that can be accessed by web browsers.

Gopher Search

Gopherspace increased, and in 1992 a method of keeping track of all menus and files on local Gopher servers was developed. The system, called Veronica, periodically sends requests to all gopher servers for a copy of all menus, which itself becomes a searchable database. A Veronica query consists of keywords a user specifies; results are presented in a menu of found items. Veronica servers are set up by major organizations around the world as a public service. Because of their comprehensiveness and limited number, Veronica servers are often busy, but the search databases cover the Gopherspace more completely than web search indexes currently can for web pages.

Anonymous FTP and Telnet

The web and Gopher are both, in essence, automated file transfer programs. Computer networks were first built to exchange files among different computers using a set File Transfer Protocol (FTP) to ensure interoperability. The development of various Internet services has been the result of technological progress in making this file transfer process easier and broadening it to enable all types of files to be transferred and viewed. The web is merely the latest stage of this development.

FTP, on the other hand, was the first interactive service between computers that required users to have a user ID and password to log in. Even in this age of web browsing, file transfers between two machines or computer accounts are accomplished via FTP. *Anonymous FTP* refers to an FTP server that is configured to accept anonymous logins so that even users who do not have an account with the host computer can log in, view, and download files, although uploading is often limited to authorized persons.

The importance of anonymous FTP service lies in the immense mountain of information that resides on these servers. Archives of most information channels are stored in anonymous FTP servers, but most importantly Internet software, both freeware and shareware, is distributed via anonymous FTP.

Telnet is similar in appearance to an FTP program in that users establish a connection to a host computer and log in using their user ID and password. However, Telnet allows users far wider control over the session. Users can "telnet" to a computer where they have an account and work remotely doing most operations as if they were directly logged on to the host computer.

Telnet is one piece of the enabling environment that makes the prospect of telecommuting over the Internet possible because users can be anywhere and still access their office computers. Similarly, you no longer need to go to a library to use its online catalog. Customers can remotely log in to the library Telnet system and browse and search for information, because most bulletin board systems are running on Telnet. In situations where an information service provider is centrally located with users scattered, as in many government services, Telnet is an efficient and cost-effective means to provide information. It is primarily used to access public information resources such as library catalogs, public bulletin board systems, and information kiosks where user inputs—such as choices of menu or form submission—are necessary. The World Wide Web can also process user inputs through script-based programs, but Telnet is more suitable for a remote working session.

FTP Search by Archie

Similar to Veronica servers for gopherspace, Archie servers routinely connect to all known anonymous FTP sites and download a listing of files. When a user makes a query using keywords, Archie searches its database and presents relevant file names and FTP site address. Archie servers are efficiently divided to cover certain geographical areas, which in turn share their databases with others.

UseNet

UseNet is a system of discussion groups, called *newsgroups*, which distributes messages worldwide. UseNet is essentially a global broadcast system where users can "tune in" by connecting to a newsgroup and selectively reading messages. All readers can also be originators of a broadcast message, creating a type of two-way broadcast system. However, there is actually no central UseNet site that administers message distribution. Instead, there are regional and local UseNet news servers that keep a copy of each message and enable their users to download. When a user sends a message to this local server, that server broadcasts the same message to all other servers. In effect, UseNet is an elaborate system that connects numerous local broadcasters. Newsgroups can be created and used locally, or they can be carried by thousands of news servers around the world.

Because UseNet discussions are generally focused on a given topic, UseNet messages contain a wide range of information pertinent to that topic. In this sense, UseNet archives would resemble a depository of humanity's knowledge and experience in any one area. At present, however, messages are not archived because there is no single news server that controls all the messages posted to a newsgroup. If someone archives these messages, there is a good chance that others are doing the same duplicative archiving. More importantly, a great portion of UseNet messages are considered to be repetitive, personal, flaming, and sometimes irrelevant. Nevertheless, given the vast number of participants, if you have a question, chances are good that there is someone on a newsgroup with the answer. The type of query and information obtained is determined by the culture of UseNet discussion. Because of the ephemeral nature of broadcast messages, the information usually concerns very specific and current information. But many have also used the UseNet as a publishing forum, posting their papers, essays, lists, compiled information, and so forth. Because all messages are purged frequently from each news server, these resources disappear. With the exception of FAQs (Frequently Asked Questions), which are archived (for example, at the anonymous FTP site rtfm.mit.edu), there is no way to search through past information other than by requesting a repost.

UseNet discussions adhere to an etiquette all their own. UseNet readers frequently complain about messages that are too long or unrelated to the newsgroup's topic. Advertising and *spamming* (sending multiple posts to often unrelated newsgroups) are generally condemned by vigorous protest from readers, prompting local UseNet administrators and e-mail servers to take actions against the perpetrators. Beyond the problem it poses in terms of information overload, the fierce reaction to superfluous messages is due both to the bandwidth bottleneck and the inadequate pricing method. Long and irrelevant messages exacerbate the waiting time for downloading all the messages in a newsgroup. As a typical Internet user pays for downloading time, the advertising costs are borne by consumers. Even when Internet services devise a payment scheme to distinguish between access charges and content charges, there is no way for a reader to tell the content of a downloaded message prior to downloading. The problems related to information pricing are discussed in more detail in Chapter 8. But the lack of control over messages is one of the reasons why a more controlled broadcast environment is needed. One way of achieving this goal is to make a newsgroup moderated by someone who approves all posted messages before forwarding them to newsgroups. To minimize a moderator's work load, intelligence agents may be used to screen messages, which is called *bot moderation*. Bot moderation is another application for information filtering technologies and is discussed in more detail in section 7.6. Another way to maintain control over messages is to use mailing lists.

Mailing Lists

Mailing lists broadcast messages similar to UseNet newsgroups (in fact, many mailing lists are available for reading under bit.listserv newsgroup hierarchy) but they restrict posting to subscribers only. The significant difference between mailing lists and UseNet is that the subject of discussion is even further specialized and the messages are often archived for mailing lists. Also, unlike UseNet, which does not have a central administrator, mailing lists are run by managers of mail servers and by the owners of the list, who control all aspects of information exchange and subscription. Consequently, many mailing lists are run by commercial interests. The nature of focused and controlled broadcasting through a mailing list has made it a favored marketing tool for sellers, who can mass-distribute ads and other messages to subscribers (see fig. 7.6). It seems an ideal environment, where consumers voluntarily request product information and still retain control over the channel because they can unsubscribe at any time.

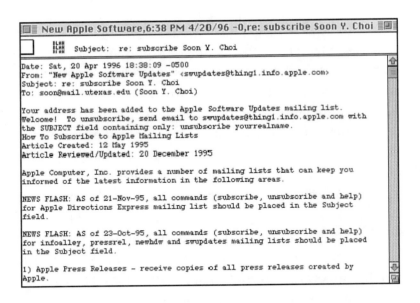

Figure 7.6 Apple Computer Software Update mailing list.

If a UseNet newsgroup is not carried by a local news server, users who have access to that news server cannot read messages posted on that newsgroup. In contrast, users can subscribe to any mailing list as long as they have e-mail accounts. However, the mailing list itself may be restricted unless it is open to subscription by all Internet users. For example, Historical Fiction Writers Group mailing list is open to all subscriptions (see fig. 7.7), meaning anyone can subscribe. But because it allows the owners to remove any subscriber, its membership can be controlled. Mailing list owners can also hide their lists from any data query, and if a list only appears on its local list server outsiders have difficulty in discovering the list and sending unwanted messages. But choosing this option makes it difficult to compile a complete database of mailing lists.

Electronic Messaging

Electronic messaging—or mail—refers to e-mailing, which is by far the most popular use of the Internet. Mailing lists are one of the uses of electronic messaging, but it has other uses that may play an important role in the future.

Besides the actual e-mail text message being exchanged, e-mail is frequently used to transfer files. Although e-mail can handle only text files, non-text formats such as graphics, audio and video files as well as binary files (for example, Microsoft Word files) can be sent as attachments when the mail servers at both ends support Multi-purpose Internet Mail Extensions (MIME). In addition, HTML documents can be sent via e-mail (because they are basically text files) and viewed on a simplified web browser or even an e-mail program with helper applications.

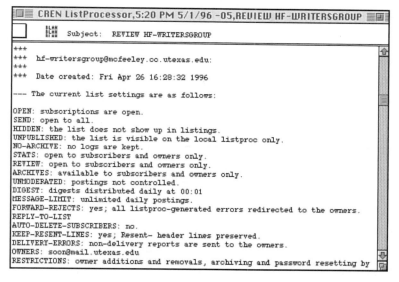

Figure 7.7 A typical setting for a mailing list (example of "Historical Fiction Writers Group" mailing list).

As a messaging system, electronic mail lacks many of the standards for services, such as receipt acknowledgment, registered mail, and insurance, which are available with postal services. The lack of such services makes it a poor medium to conduct commercial and legal transactions. However, e-mails are delivered at all times, and users can distribute files to multiple recipients as well as screen incoming messages. Its instant, universal, and reliable messaging should make it a better medium to conduct business than posts or faxes after basic standards are in place.

E-mail Address Search

Because of e-mail's private nature, there is no archive for messages, and they will never be fully cataloged on the Internet. However, e-mail addresses can be searched using directories based on X.500 standards if the addresses are known. As in most EDI standards, X.500 standards only allow limited data fields such as names and addresses (see fig. 7.8), but these fields can be generated efficiently. If the address is unknown, worldwide searches can be done by logging into NetFind or Finger, which contain X.500 databases. To search for an e-mail address, the searcher specifies a combination of domain names and user names. For example, if someone knows only the last name of an individual and the name of the school he attends, he can use these items as a search string, and NetFind or Finger searches all X.500 directories in the school's known computer domains, and produces a list of e-mail addresses that contain the last name specified.

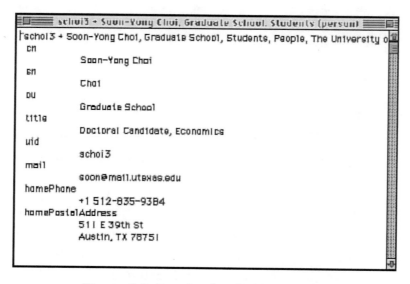

Figure 7.8   Result of an X.500 search.

Consumer Learning and Search

Newsgroups and mailing lists become online communities where like-minded consumers congregate and exchange information. Although messages may not be archived for accessing and searching, information is transmitted to group members who may individually store that information. Because of the homogeneity of each group, these online communities are where consumers learn about new products and trust the information, such as reviews and endorsements. These groups, as a result, become an important means to search for and disseminate product information as well as to advertise. A physical market equivalent is word-of-mouth advertising. But unlike in physical markets, these word-of-mouth circles are real and approachable through electronic messaging. Consequently, commercial, informational, and economic uses of these communities seem boundless.

For example, market surveys and focus groups are often conducted on samples that are at best incomplete. To estimate the demand for a new product, a random sample is drawn, and even when the sample universe is carefully chosen, the sample is far less desirable than a newsgroup composed of those consumers who buy similar products. These online groups can also be used to introduce new products. If there is a generally favorable review of a product, it is more than likely that others in the same group will favor that product. By providing advertising, sellers can also connect their marketing efforts with consumers' search and learning activities, which are the basis of online messaging. In this regard, a healthy growth in UseNet and mailing lists activities can be beneficial for consumers and sellers as well as researchers who constantly have to improve market estimation techniques against odds. Dismissing UseNet activities as frivolous, or harming them by spamming indiscriminate advertisements, is extremely detrimental to the future of electronic commerce.

Real-time applications on the Internet admittedly have little do with consumer searches for information, because contents of these services are not archived. Rather, they signal future uses of truly interactive services via the Internet and are growing rapidly. Talk, for example, is a real-time simple message exchange method between two logged-on users of Unix system computers; each conversation is presented simultaneously on a divided screen. When users talk to an audience of multiple users, the system is called *chat*, as in America Online's chat rooms, where dozens of people carry on simultaneous conversations. A general chat program for the Internet uses the Internet Relay Chat (IRC) program, which connects computers temporarily to create an IRC network. Each IRC user becomes a client connected to an IRC server, usually provided locally, which in turn is connected to a major IRC network such as EFNet and Undernet. Similar to UseNet, chat groups are divided into channels, each with its own topic of conversation. Web browsers can also be used to connect to a talk server, but due to the technical limitations of the web, sending and receiving messages is not as smooth or as real-time. By sending audio and video rather than texts, Internetters can use it as an alternative to telephone service or video conferencing.

In a chat or IRC environment, each person is represented by a line of text following a prompt that contains the person's name. As people talk, a screen scrolls continuously with new lines, that is, pieces of conversation. But imagine a graphical environment—for example, a room, a park, or a medieval castle—which is presented to all participants. There may be some human characters there as well (called *avatars*), which represent the participants. When someone talks, then, the avatar speaks online, and the message is relayed to the person to whom the avatar is speaking. Objects in this graphical environment can be programmed to interact with avatars. For example, an avatar can lift a lamp and break it, or can play a piano. Such a three-dimensional environment in which users interact in real-time is called a *MUD*, which stands for Multi-User Dungeon among interactive game players or Multi-User Domain for more generic uses. MUDs and other virtual reality worlds on the Internet offer a realistic way to represent the physical world. As such, they may become valuable tools to present future web pages and to interact with visitors.

7.5.   Information Efficiency in Web Search Engines

Numerous web search services exist on the Internet, some with access to information on tens of millions of web pages. According to an estimate by

International Data Corporation (http://www.idcresearch.com), the Internet had about 37 million users and 107 million web pages in March, 1997. This number is growing at about 2 percent every month. As the web becomes the dominant information channel, it is important to focus on how web search services are organized and to evaluate their efficiency in providing relevant information to users.

Many personal web pages can actually be considered to be the result of a personalized search service in its simplest form. In many cases the pages contain nothing more than links to other web pages that the page creator collected and organized under his or her interest areas, such as "My Favorite Internet Bookstores" or "Audrey Hepburn's Unofficial Homepage." In a fundamental way, these links represent a process of filtering of information, that is, choosing information based on a relevancy criterion, evaluated by the author, and presented to the public. Web search engines go through a similar process, although they cover a wider area of web space and may use more sophisticated selection criteria, the main topic of this section.

Adequate search facilities are an integral prerequisite to informational use of the web. Surprisingly, however, the initial popularity of the web was due to its recreational, not informational, use. The distinctive feature of the web is the capability it gives users to jump from one place to another by clicking on hypertext links. In fact, the web authoring language is named HyperText Markup Language (HTML) and the addresses of web pages are designated by HTTP (HyperText Transfer Protocol), all of which emphasize the hypertext links and jumps. Therefore, it is not strange that the web users were said to be "surfing the net," which signifies a random clicking and jumping between places and an assumption that users were not searching for specific information but spending time reading whatever web pages they happened to encounter. Even today, some search engines offer visitors an option to surf through randomly chosen web sites.

Surfing the net in this way is still the only way some web pages can be found, because not all pages are indexed or cataloged. Users of search engines are essentially limited to the web space that their search intermediaries have mapped out. Although this may be a limitation, relying on search engines are still the easiest way to find specific information. Because the search space is limited by the will of the service providers, gains in efficiency must be weighed against the losses involved in foregoing some information not included in the search database. The extent of the loss or gain depends on how the search intermediaries filter information when preparing their databases.

Information filtering is done by search intermediaries in two stages: (1) selection and (2) presentation. In each stage, some arbitrary value judgment is imposed that may or may not affect the information efficiency for the consumers. In terms of selection, search services quote how many unique web addresses (URLs) their databases cover. The numbers range from tens of millions to several hundred thousands. Some URLs are not visited, and bot-resistant sites may be omitted. Some URLs are not added if they are deemed to be of minor interest. The criteria used are, for example, informational content, graphical presentation, and other interesting features. Knowing how each search database is compiled helps users select a search provider. For example, some search databases give high marks for jazzy graphical contents and technological sophistication. For content-oriented users, these sites, albeit valued highly by database compilers, may appear as a poor source for information. Selection criteria are often discussed in the "About and FAQ pages" of search engines.

After databases of this information are made, search intermediaries can use different methods of accessing them for consumers. In one polar case, the database may be presented as is so that when consumers search by keywords, the results are displayed based on some relevancy criteria only. *Relevancy criteria* are such measures as how many words in the document match the search words, or whether the search word appears in the title or the URL, which results in a higher relevancy score. Keyword strings can be enclosed in quotes, as in "historical fiction," which narrows the search to select only those documents that contain the phrase. Even with this and other improvements in querying, the result of a search is often overwhelming. For example, 6,000

documents are shown as a result of AltaVista search (http://
www.altavista.digital.com) using "historical fiction" and FAQ as keywords (see
fig. 7.9), but presented in the order of how many words are matched. In this
case, the information filtering by the intermediary (who simply presents all
matching entries) is minimal. On the other end of the extreme, intermediaries
may present sites evaluated and recommended by their staff, such as the
"What's New" and "What's Hot" lists.

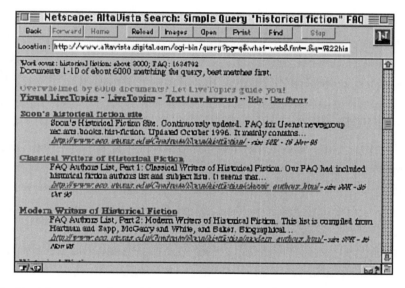

Figure 7.9 AltaVista search result using "historical fiction" and FAQ as keywords.

Rather than using relevancy tests such as keyword matching, some intermediaries organize their databases by categories; Yahoo!'s subject listings are a
good example. Keyword searches may end up presenting irrelevant information that uses the search word in a totally different context; subject listings or
directories, however, present more reliable information on a given subject. It is
sometimes difficult to characterize a web page by one subject, though, and
intermediaries must exercise certain value judgments in deciding under what
subject a web page should be classified. This arbitrary decision introduces
errors as significant as those borne by keyword searches.

In another extreme case, search intermediaries present predetermined lists
of web sites to searchers. These sites have promotional materials or are paying

advertisers. There is no way of knowing what criteria are used to select the recommended or suggested web pages. By mixing data with plain advertising links, the objectivity of the third-party intermediary is seriously compromised.

Information Acquisition and Efficiency

The process of information filtering has more facets than you may imagine. Search intermediaries represent an example of information filtering occurring in the middle of the information acquisition process. Although controlling and filtering information at the source may be the result of censorship, firms may also voluntarily restrict consumers' access to product information by not providing certain information over the network. Another example of extreme information filtering is broadcast television, where consumers have no control over which programs are broadcast.

To increase consumer choices for information acquisition and consumption, information filtering must occur in the later stages of the acquisition process. Information filtering can be delayed until all information reaches the consumers. Filtering agents, which can be programmed to sort out incoming messages and to manage files, have become popular because of the increase in information overload. Artificial intelligence-based summarizers can scan all incoming information and present summaries according to a prescribed format or filtering profile. Through the application of artificial intelligence, filtering agents can be trained according to user tastes, reducing the margin of error. Also, consumers can send out intelligent agents to search for information just as search intermediaries have used their agents, such as bots, spiders, and so forth, to compile their database. In this case, the role of search intermediary is replaced by intelligent software agents, and information filtering is done by the consumers themselves.

Information filtering is based on a simple procedure that places a filtering program between a user and the content server (see fig. 7.10). The filtering agent carries out selection processes based on user-determined filtering criteria known as *scripts* or *profiles*, which are continuously updated via feedback. In a collaborative filtering scheme, scripts and profiles are exchanged among different users. An increasingly popular use of filtering agents among parents and educators is to block certain web sites that contain inappropriate or indecent materials. Some examples are: Cyberpatrol (http://www.cyberpatrol.com), Cybersitter (http://www.solidoak.com), and NetNanny (http://www.netnanny.com). Although these examples are software programs that can be downloaded or installed by individual users, N2H2 (http://www.n2h2.com) provides server-based solutions, where filtering is implemented for all users connected to the server. The same filtering scheme is used to remove only the unwanted portion of a web document. In the WebFilter implementation developed by Axel Boldt (http://www.math.ucsb.edu/~boldt/), the filter is a proxy server that retrieves a document and removes prescribed features such as advertising banners or large graphics before presenting it to a user.

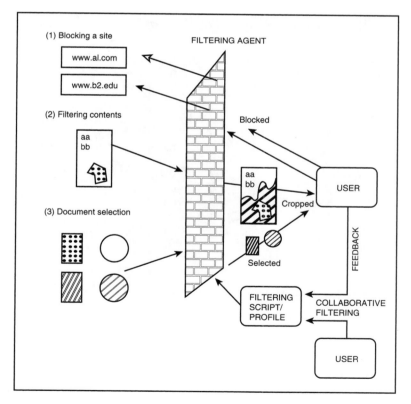

Figure 7.10 Various functions of a filtering agent.

Finally, the filter can be used as an agent that selects (that is, filters) documents from all incoming messages. This use of information filtering is gaining popularity because of the tremendous growth in junk e-mails and spamming on UseNet newsgroups. For example, suppose that you have received 50 e-mail messages. Rather than opening and reading them one by one, you can use a filtering program, which assigns a value to each message based on your selection profile. A message from a known advertiser will get a zero score; and a message dealing with your favorite subject gets a higher score. The result is then displayed on your screen so that you can decide which one to read and whether you want to respond. InfoScan (http://www.machinasapiens.qc.ca/infoscanang.html), a filtering program, displays the result on a radar screen (see fig. 7.11), where only five out of 50 messages are selected as relevant, the ones closest to the center of the radar screen have the highest scores.

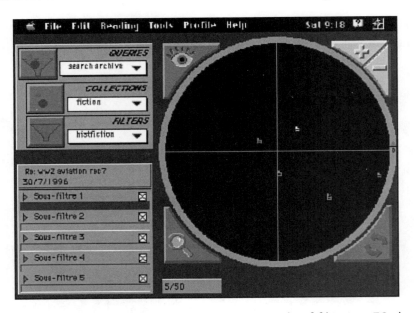

Figure 7.11 InfoScan's radar screen presents its result of filtering 50 documents.

An interesting application of this filtering agent is gaining support to counter spamming on the UseNet. A UseNet newsgroup can be either moderated or unmoderated. A moderated group has one or more moderators who screen all messages before forwarding them to the UseNet. The majority of newsgroups are unmoderated for several reasons: UseNet users prefer unfettered, equal participation; unpaid moderators have to spend time and effort to screen messages; and messages may be delayed unnecessarily. However, due to the increasing level of abuse in many newsgroups, some type of moderation will be needed for most newsgroups in the near future. A hybrid solution is to use an intelligent software agent. This "bot moderation" or "robomoderation" screens messages, rejecting those with "MAKE EASY MONEY" or those cross-posted in many newsgroups. Also, the robomoderator handles notification, acceptance, and forwarding automatically, reducing the workload of human moderators. For example, Secure Team-based UseNet Moderation Program (STUMP), a freely available program (see "Online Resources" at the end of this chapter), can save time needed for moderation but also allows messages to be archived as web pages.

Although user-oriented filtering agents are acquiring more diverse uses, in terms of network efficiency, a middle ground may entail using intermediaries, which filter information in the middle of the acquisition process. If a large number of such intermediaries exists, consumers can also be guaranteed a choice. One thing to note, however, is that intermediaries are increasingly using advertising, which may unfortunately cause consumers to doubt the objectivity of their search results. In some economic activities, independent third-party status is clearly important, and information search is one of these activities. An element of trust and neutrality is necessary so that filtering is not seen to be a result of censorship or blatant advertising. Therefore, rather than advertising, search intermediaries may benefit from the adoption of micropayment methods by which consumers pay a small amount, say a penny, for each search, and intermediaries guarantee full and unbiased access to their databases.

An efficient search mechanism is critical in guaranteeing seller competitiveness and consumer welfare. To make searches efficient, sellers must be willing to offer the maximum amount of information about their products, selection process should be based on clearly defined and objective criteria, and consumers must be allowed full access to this information. Online contents are growing and information filtering programs are beginning to address the problem of information overload, pointing to a more efficient market for searches. But a technical problem remains in setting a standard to describe a digital document, which can facilitate the task of summarizing and compiling search databases. Also, search services, being the first significant commercial projects on the Internet, increasingly depend on advertising revenues to provide a service that is essential for the electronic marketplace to be efficient. This section examines these issues, and also briefly compares consumer searches with advertising (two topics discussed in this and the last chapters) to examine whether one or the other channel of information may be more desirable for electronic commerce.

Cataloging millions of web documents is significantly different from compiling a phone directory or an economic database because of the diversity of web documents. They are in general in multimedia format. That is, a document contains not only texts, for which summarizing consists of abstracting a few keywords, but also graphics, sound files, and animated images. A suitable standard to describe such complex files is a prerequisite to building an efficient search database.

Geographic information systems managers are familiar with metadata standards, by which all geographic data is summarized and described. Metadata is data about data, and accompanies all distributed geographic data to simplify importing and exporting them. Metainformation, in the same manner, is defined as information about information. Metainformation describes an information product, its variables, size, quality, author, and other characteristics. Metainformation itself can be an information product. In fact, in search markets what is exchanged is not information products but metainformation. To illustrate the concept of metainformation, take the case of data and metadata. Suppose you have census data for the city of Austin, Texas. The data contains the number of households in each census tract, sorted by age groups, income groups, home ownership status, and marital status. The data set is a spread sheet with columns of variables and rows of census tracts. The column headings are written as AGE01, AGE02, and so on for, say, 10 age groups; and INC01, INC02, and so on for, say, 20 income groups, and so on. Census tracts are written on the rows as 1.01, 1.02, 2.01, 2.02, and so forth.

The table itself contains data, but no metadata. To help users, you can provide an additional description of the data. For example, AGE01 means the number of persons 1-year-old or under on September, 1989. INC01 refers to the number of households with $5,000 or less in annual income in the year 1988. You can also provide street names that bound each census tract to help plot the data on a map. Other information is also necessary to be able to interpret the data fully, such as error correction procedures, weighting methods, missing value treatments, and information about census survey methods.

All this data does not describe the actual households that are the subject of the census. Instead, it describes, or refers to, the collected data, and in this sense, it is called metadata—data about data. Metadata standards are being developed for many types of information: digital catalog standards are being prepared by digital library associations, metadata standards are under development by the Federal Geographic Data Committee, and most pertinent to the topic of the Internet, private efforts are under way to establish header information for digital files and software.

What is called metadata for databases is called metainformation for information. Digital catalog standards attempt to establish a certain number of variables that describe a digital file. Variables include the name of the author and copyright holders, publication date, size of the file, type of file, system requirement for viewing the file, and others. In a unified digital environment, catalogs, headers, and codebooks have to be merged into one standardized document called metainformation. Unlike library catalog cards or database codebooks, digital headers, catalogs, and metainformation will be attached to the document itself, and will become an integral tool in using and accessing the document. For microproducts and microbundles, standardized metainformation can be viewed rather than actual products, facilitating transactions and minimizing concerns for copyright infringement.

Although search service providers and market analysts tend to focus on the technical aspects of search engines and algorithms, or the commercial aspect of a search service as an advertising conduit, in fact the greatest asset of the Yahoo! directory is said to be its database of consumer preferences gathered from monitoring access. The objective of managing Yahoo!'s directory information is changing from providing a more efficient search mechanism to maximizing advertising revenues. Advertising can be justified on search engines in that it allows the service to be offered free to consumers, who otherwise would need to pay a small fee.

An advertising-based search service brings to mind broadcast television. Just as TV programming decisions are influenced by sponsors, search services may also give preference to advertisers by presenting their URLs first. Also, advertiser-supported TV programs target the broadest possible audience by catering to the lowest common denominators of the viewers. Such inefficiencies may appear in advertiser-supported search services as well. For example, there may end up being a lack of specialized search services, or search databases may ignore highly specialized web pages. On the other hand, various search services may catalog mainly popular web sites so that more people will visit them. Having a huge database of seldom-visited web sites does not bring in as high a hit rate as does one with popular sites. Because maintaining an up-to-date search database becomes more complex and expensive, numerous advertiser-supported search services—competing for the same customers—will hardly justify maintaining a complete, accurate and ever-expanding database.

An alternative is to consolidate search services, not necessarily by supporting only one provider but by linking databases. If advertising is to continue, there may be a revenue sharing agreement to support linked databases. Another way to avoid the pitfalls of broadcast business models is to implement micropayments, perhaps in conjunction with distributing small payments or coupons for reading advertisements online. When a commodity (such as searches) is not arbitrarily tied with external goods (such as advertising) the market becomes more efficient in the type of goods produced and in allocating resources.

Advertising versus Consumer Searching

Internet advertising is currently a curious mixture of passive and active information queries. Although Internet broadcasting of advertising is discouraged, electronic billboards are springing up in various places, and search engines are actively seeking sponsors whose advertising is presented based on consumer queries. If someone searches for a specific country music artist, for example, an advertising banner for a country music shop is presented. This is similar to targeted advertising in special interest magazines and journals, in which readers that share a common preference can be exploited by a certain type of business. Because Internet consumer profiles can be far more detailed than subscription databases for magazines, the potential of Internet advertising is great. Eventually, this vast pool of consumer information will enable sellers to send highly individualized advertising. If advertisers have precise and detailed data about consumer preferences, their advertising messages might be as good as what consumers try to obtain through searches. There may be no difference between advertising (seller-initiated information transfer) and searches (buyer-initiated information transfer) in such a market.

First, consider whether advertising and consumer searches are true alternatives, that is, whether they have the same economic implications. When advertising is costless, competing firms advertise for lower prices, and this price competition (known as Bertrand competition) leads to competitive prices as consumers are fully informed. When search cost is zero, consumers again obtain full information by visiting all stores, and prices are competitive. Therefore, the two channels of information seem to be equivalent in the limit case where costs are absolutely zero. In intermediate cases, positive costs of advertising and search lead to above-marginal-cost prices because there are always some consumers who are not fully informed, which gives firms an incentive to raise prices.

However, consider a more realistic case in which firms advertise and consumers search. Suppose that either advertising cost or search cost is lowered toward zero by some technological developments but does not reach exactly zero. If the cost of advertising and consumer search are equivalent, it is reasonable to expect the same result whether the cost reduction is in advertising or in consumer searches. However, Robert and Stahl (1993) show that the effect of reducing advertising cost is very much different from that of lowering search cost. When advertising cost is lowered, firms tend to send more advertisements and prices approach the marginal cost. On the other hand, if the advantage is with consumers whose search costs decline, Robert and Stahl show that firms reduce advertising drastically. Because there are uninformed consumers as long as search costs are not exactly zero, prices tend to rise above the marginal cost. In short, cost changes in advertising and searches do have different market implications.

As long as there are non-zero, positive costs for advertising and search, then, this surprising result implies that reductions in advertising costs do a better job of bringing about lower prices than does improving search processes. This does not mean that it is appropriate to ignore efficiency issues in the search market; advertising alone does not bring about lower prices unless its cost becomes zero. Rather, this result cautions against the notion that efficient searches in electronic commerce will necessarily result in fully informed consumers and competitive prices. A few observations are in order. Section 7.1, earlier in this chapter, discussed the possibility that search costs may indeed be zero or even negative (for consumers who actually enjoy searching). In that case, an efficient search market may produce competitive prices even without advertising. Also, as in most economic models of advertising, consumers are treated as potential customers so that any advertisement sent to a consumer is read. In reality, unwanted advertisements cause resentment among consumers and waste resources. In electronic commerce, however, technological developments will reduce wasteful advertising as well as enable more efficient searches. In fact, advertising and searches will be indistinguishable in the electronic marketplace, as the following sections explain.

Marketing professionals are familiar with consumer advertising in the world of one-way broadcasting media. However, in two-way communication, consumer queries become far more important. Imagine that a consumer wants to buy a product and can send a request for quotes to various sellers of that product. This process is often used to contract out high-value projects in which the cost to sellers of preparing and processing bid information can be justified. In electronic commerce, consumer searches resemble this process. Rather than sending indiscriminate advertising to all consumers, sellers can maintain their web pages with elaborate product and price information, which is then accessed by potential customers. Consumers may have to pay the costs of access (for example, the costs of connection fees or search services), if not for the product information itself. With a micropayment system, at least some consumers will prefer this need-based search-advertising method over broadcasting-based advertising. In the electronic marketplace, therefore, consumer searches and advertising are part of an integrated process of price discovery. Targeted advertising together with efficient search mechanisms will push down prices to a competitive level for many products.

7.6. Summary

Advertising and search processes complement each other in electronic commerce and are essential in reducing the uncertainty about product quality and in preventing a possible market failure. Although search services on the Internet are very popular, consumers often have to access different search engines that cover different sources. Some search engines emphasize evaluation and categorizing while others simply try to catalog as many web pages as possible, but the sheer volume of Internet information often makes it impossible to compile an adequate level of information from all resources that exist on the Internet. Additionally, the rapid changes on the Internet often make the information and links outdated.

Despite these drawbacks, search engines are an essential tool in navigating the virtual marketplace. This chapter has discussed the importance of Internet search engines in terms of consumer search theory in economics. It is possible in the future that consumers themselves may send out bots or other automated intelligent agents to search the web space according to the owner's specification. Rather than clogging the bandwidth with advertising, such bots or agents could be charged a minute amount of money to be allowed to access certain metainformation of a web page.

Finally, the efficiency gained from consumer searches and advertising is necessary for two more compelling reasons in electronic commerce. First, digital products are highly customized, and will have numerous producers. In such a market with fragmented products and multiple vendors, all types of information channels need to be efficient. Secondly, product differentiation results in market segmentation, which increases sellers' market power. Therefore, even with numerous sellers in the market, prices will tend to rise more than in a market with homogeneous products. Efficient searches and advertising are two elements that may counter potentially high prices in electronic commerce. The next chapter discusses product customization and pricing issues.

References

Diamond, P.A., 1971. "A Model of Price Adjustment." *Journal of Economic Theory* 3: 156–168.

Hahn, H., 1996. *The Internet: Complete Reference.* Second edition. Berkeley: Osborne McGraw-Hill.

Robert, R. and D.O. Stahl, 1993. "Informative Price Advertising In a Sequential Search Model." *Econometrica* 61 (3): 657–686.

Stahl, D.O., 1996. "Oligopolistic Pricing with Heterogeneous Consumer Search." *International Journal of Industrial Organization,* 14:242–268.

Suggested Readings and Notes

Consumer Search

Stigler, J., 1961. "The Economics of Information." *Journal of Political Economy,* 69: 213–225. This paper investigates the effects of costly information acquisition by consumers, one of which is price dispersion rather than a competitive market price under full information. For an earlier survey, see Rothschild, M., 1973, "Models of Market Organization with Imperfect Information: A Survey." *Journal of Political Economy,* 81: 1283–1308.

Diamond, P.A. (1971) demonstrates the paradoxical result that the equilibrium price is monopolistic when consumers have strictly positive search costs. For a more recent work of Diamond, see his *A Search-Equilibrium Approach to the Micro Foundation of Macroeconomics,* 1984. Cambridge, Mass.: MIT Press.

Robert and Stahl (1993) compare economic efficiencies of advertising and search channels.

Search and negotiation process is common in the labor market, where "visiting the next store" has much more significant implications than in commodity transactions. For an empirical study on job search and unemployment, see: Kiefer, N. and G. Neumann, 1979, "An Empirical Job Search Model with a Test of the Constant Reservation Wage Hypothesis." *Journal of Political Economy*, 87: 69–82. For a survey of labor search theory, see Mortensen, D., 1984, "Job Search and Labor Market Analysis," in *Handbook of Labour Economics*, R. Layard and O. Ashenfelter, eds. Amsterdam: North-Holland.

Negotiation is part of the search process. For a model that specifies the negotiation process more explicitly, see Rubinstein, A. and A. Wolinsky, 1985, "Equilibrium In a Market with Sequential Bargaining," *Econometrica*, 53: 1133–50.

Internet Resources

Search Engines

To browse all types of search engines, see:

Internet Directories and Searching Services at http://www.sil.org/internet/guides.html; and

Babbage at http://www.bbcnc.org.uk/babbage/iap.html.

Software Agents and Filtering

Software agents are an application of artificial intelligence. A great number of materials can be found at MIT Media lab (http://www.media.edu).

For articles on intelligent agents, see a special issue of *The Communications of the ACM*, July, 1994 (vol. 37, no. 7). See also special issue on new horizons of commercial and industrial artificial intelligence, *The Communications of the ACM*, November, 1995 (vol. 38, no. 11). CACM's web address is http://www.acm.org/.

For collaborative filtering, see an archive at http://www.sims.berleley.edu/resources/collab.

Robomoderation

For information about STUMP, see http://www.algebra.com/~ichudov/usenet/scrm/robomod/robomod.html.

STUMP is freely available at ftp://ftp.algebra.com/users/ichudov/pub/stump/stump.tar.gz.

CHAPTER 8

Product Choices and Discriminatory Pricing

Historical battles show that a policy of competition based only on price is often ineffective because profits for all competitors are sacrificed as prices are lowered in each round of struggle for market share. This is known to economists as a Bertrand price competition result. Well aware of this, sellers are constantly seeking out non-price forms of competition. This chapter focuses on one form of non-price competition—product differentiation. The economics of product differentiation are first reviewed to help explain why sellers differentiate products. Although product differentiation is observed in physical markets, it will be more widely practiced in electronic commerce because the transmutability of digital products makes them highly customizable (see Chapter 2). Furthermore, detailed data on consumer preferences are more abundant in computerized market environments. As a result, consumers obtain a higher degree of satisfaction from customized products than average-quality products, and prices can efficiently reflect costs and consumer preferences. Efficient pricing strategies, such as multi-part tariffs and discriminatory pricing, are improved by the combination of detailed consumer information and customized products. The objective of this chapter is to present an overview of product selection and pricing strategies for digital products, emphasizing the significance of consumer information and privacy in transactions.

Next, this chapter investigates the sellers' product choices and the customization of digital products. Customization is an extreme example of product differentiation in which products are manufactured to match the specific demand of a small group of consumers or even one individual. Using examples currently found on the Internet, the effects of customization on prices and consumer welfare are evaluated. For example, a high degree of customization discourages satisfied consumers from reselling or sharing their products. This is especially advantageous for products that can be reproduced easily and allows sellers to set prices based on the consumers' willingness to pay.

To effectively customize products and charge individualized prices, producers desired detailed knowledge of consumer preferences. In section 8.3, the issue of privacy in transaction and the use of consumer information in terms of product differentiation and price discrimination are examined. Although the legal aspects of privacy and anonymity have received considerable attention in the press and among professionals in the nascent field of electronic commerce, this chapter focuses on the economic impact of the use of personal information. This includes not only such obvious information as names, addresses, and phone numbers but more importantly information about consumers' tastes. Disclosure of personal preferences provides consumers with custom-built products, but they may have to pay higher prices for them.

Finally, various pricing methods for digital products are evaluated. When products are differentiated, pricing strategies become extremely complex because both product specifications and prices can vary according to differences in consumer tastes and usage patterns. Product differentiation and consumer information enable various sales mechanisms—subscription, licensing, renting, leasing, and bundling—that exploit differences in consumer preferences to control the usage of a product. While current pricing practices are dominated by licensing (for computer software) and subscription (for digital information products), other methods including unbundling, customization, and need-based software distribution become possible as new technologies such as applets and micropayments are perfected and more widely accepted. The pricing and marketing of digital products indicates the competitiveness and profitability of electronic commerce. Consequently, this has generated many preliminary works in digital product pricing. Most of these, however, do not consider the characteristics of digital products and the electronic marketplace. This chapter extends these works by considering the problem of quality uncertainty and its effect on the market.

8.1. Product Differentiation and Pricing in Economics

In a standard economics price competition model, products sold by competitors are assumed to be the same and homogeneous so that only prices matter to consumers. If products are differentiated, however, each seller has some degree of market power over those consumers who prefer their product. As a result, sellers do not necessarily lose all sales even when prices for differentiated products differ. This section reviews the economics of product differentiation and examines how product differentiation relates to product selection and pricing for digital products.

What Is Product Differentiation?

Differentiated products are classified in the same product group, yet they are not identical. The various brands of breakfast cereal are an example of product differentiation. Microsoft Word and WordPerfect are differentiated products in the product group of word processing programs. Notice that Word and WordPerfect are termed "differentiated" but not "different;" WordPerfect and a breakfast cereal are "different" products (that is they belong to different product groups). Another term that is often used with product differentiation is product variety, which refers to the number of products (or brands) in a product market. Note, product differentiation relates to the degree of dissimilarity. Thus, product differentiation may increase if two products become more dissimilar, while product variety remains the same.

Products are perceived to have a bundle of characteristics such as weight, size, volume, color, and other qualitative measures such as performance and easiness to use. Products in a group share the same characteristics, but each has a varying degree of these characteristics. While products can be differentiated in many ways if the characteristics dimension is complex, a useful distinction commonly made is between horizontal and vertical product differentiation.

Horizontal Differentiation

Products are considered to be differentiated horizontally if the difference is based on appearance or consumer preference. If consumers have different tastes (for example, some prefer the color blue while others prefer red) each differentiated product has a market share even when horizontally differentiated products are equally priced. Imagine a product space where a location represents the product's characteristics. Such a location model was first introduced by Hotelling (1929). In figure 8.1, notice that firm A sells a product which is bluer than that of the firm B, whose product is more red than blue. The price of each product is represented by the vertical line. Consumers are distributed along the same product space according to their tastes for color. The location of Alice along with the continuum of consumer tastes indicates that she tends to prefer a bluer product than Bob. However, neither Alice nor Bob gets a product that exactly matches her or his preference because the products are some distance away from their locations. The resulting dissatisfaction is represented by the increasing slope of the total price line, which is added to the product price. The cost of dissatisfaction, which is analogous to transportation costs in spatial terms, increases as the distance from the firm (that is factory specification) increases. Given the two products, consumers choose either firm A or firm B based on the total price, which is the sum of the constant factory price and the increasing dissatisfaction cost. Anyone whose taste lies to the left of the market boundary, including Alice, buys from firm A. When firm A raises its price slightly, its market share shrinks as the market boundary moves to the left.

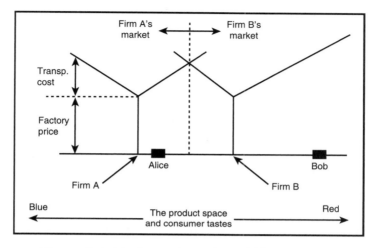

Figure 8.1 Horizontal product differentiation.

Vertical Differentiation

Products are considered to be vertically differentiated if all consumers prefer a product among equally priced products. For example, products are differentiated vertically if their qualities are different. Suppose that a firm sells personal computers with two types of microprocessor—one with 100 MHz clock speed and the other with 133 MHz—at the same price. Although other characteristics of a microprocessor besides clock speed are also usually considered, suppose all other variables are equal. In this case, because all consumers would naturally choose the 133 MHz microprocessor, the products are vertically differentiated. Of course, products may be differentiated both horizontally and vertically. For example, consider two horizontally differentiated banks that offer similar services. If one begins to offer remote access or online banking services, it will become vertically differentiated from the other firm. By offering online banking, therefore, a bank may be capable of enhancing its advantage with horizontal differentiation—that is offering branch offices closer to customers (Degryse, 1996).

Vertically differentiated products are often sold at different prices, and it is of considerable interest to economists to evaluate how price differences correspond to quality differences. Products of higher quality typically command higher prices than low-quality products, and, in a competitive market, the difference in prices are comparable to the difference in variable costs such as materials and labor inputs. Prices that reflect cost differences are *non-discriminatory*. On the other hand, discriminatory prices are observed when they include a quality premium or a quality discount. For example, suppose a basic subscription for database access is sold at $10 a month. If an expanded subscription is offered at $20 a month but the cost of offering such a service is only $5 more than the basic subscription, then the expanded subscription commands a quality premium, and the price of $20 is discriminatory in terms of quality. A quality discount is also possible if the expanded subscription service is priced at $12.50, where a part of the cost is absorbed by the seller. While quantity discounts are common, quality discounts are rarely observed. Rather, quality premium are prevalent because those who want better quality products are usually willing to pay more for quality. Note that a quantity discount is not necessarily a discriminatory price if the reduced price for a bundle reflects the reduced cost of production, packaging, and delivery.

The Incentive to Differentiate

The primary incentive for sellers to differentiate is the reduced substitutability between products as differentiated products become imperfect substitutes for each other. For example, consider two spreadsheet programs with a similar appearance and performance such that the two products are perfectly substitutable. If one of the two companies changes the look and feel of its program, the two products are differentiated and some consumers may choose a program because of the new difference. Therefore, the two products are no longer perfect substitutes. With reduced substitutability between products, retaliatory price-cutting does not result in a complete loss of one's market share. Product differentiation thus gives a firm a certain power within its own market. Such a market is called a *monopolistically competitive* market.

Chamberlinian Monopolistic Competition

The model of a monopolistically competitive market (Chamberlin, 1933) characterizes each firm as having a distinct product with some measure of market power. Therefore, unlike a firm in a competitive market which must charge the prevailing price, a monopolistically competitive firm can choose a profit maximizing price level instead of merely accepting the market price. Because consumers view the product of a monopolistically competitive firm differently from its competition, the firm faces a downward-sloping (residual) demand curve. This means that some consumers will continue to buy the product at different prices. Nevertheless, the firm does not make a positive profit in the long run. If so, another firm will enter the market offering a slightly different product to exploit the profit opportunity. As long as there is no substantial barrier to entry, this process results in zero-profit for all monopolistically competitive firms.

Figure 8.2a shows the demand curve of a monopolistically competitive firm at its long run equilibrium. At the equilibrium price and quantity (P, Q), the firm makes zero profit, but it does not operate at the most efficient (lowest average cost) level. The slope of the demand curve indicates how elastic the demand is with respect to price changes. In figure 8.2b, given a price increase, customers in a flatter demand curve will defect more readily than those in a steeper demand curve. A fully competitive firm (figure 8.2c) faces a flat demand curve; if the firm raises its price slightly, no customers will support it.

A monopolistically competitive firm makes zero profit—charging the average cost to break even—despite its market power because if other firms are able to freely enter the market, there will no longer remain any profit opportunity. With free entry, all firms operate at an inefficient level of production (to the left of the lowest average cost as seen in figure 8.2). For this reason, a single, undifferentiated firm may be able to operate more efficiently in terms of scale economy and if the benefit to consumers from product variety is ignored.

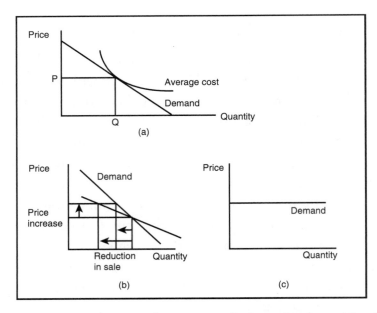

Figure 8.2 Demand curves for monopolistic and competitive firms.

Price Discrimination

The monopolistic competition model was originally developed for single-product firms, however, a firm may decide to differentiate its own product. A reason for this is the desire to cover the market by introducing different brands. For example, a firm may introduce different cereal brands or soft drinks with different flavor or caloric content. Still, the firm's incentive to differentiate is the same—to reduce substitutability between its products and their markets. Under product differentiation, discriminatory prices are possible because the firm can sell differentiated products at different net prices.

Discriminatory prices do not reflect the difference in production or transaction costs. This means that different consumers are charged different prices for the same product. An efficient and competitive market supports one uniform price for all consumers regardless of their private valuations for the product. However, discriminatory prices are introduced to take advantage of differences in consumer valuations. For example, a consumer with a high income or with an urgent need may be willing to pay a higher price for the same product than another consumer with a lower income or no immediate need. If sellers can distinguish between these consumers, they can charge a higher price for the former and establish a lower price for the latter. Group discounts or senior discounts are based on this principle which is an example of third-degree price discrimination.

Discriminatory pricing based on identification is called third-degree price discrimination. In the absence of a means to identify consumers, sellers have to rely on the incentives of each group to select an intended variety. This condition is called the self selection or incentive compatibility requirement (see section 8.4, "Pricing Digital Products," for more detail). This means that given optimal product choices, consumers will sort themselves out according to product characteristics and a price schedule that reveals their preferences. This scheme based on consumers' voluntary choices is called second-degree price discrimination. First-degree or perfect—price discrimination refers to charging individual prices for each buyer, which are usually determined by the consumer's maximum willingness to pay.

Discriminatory pricing should be used whenever possible because it is always more profitable than uniform pricing (Phlips, 1983, p. 18). Not surprisingly, price discrimination is a common practice. However, these are usually second-degree price discriminations based on incentive schemes, or third-degree price discriminations based on consumer groups. First-degree, or perfect-price discrimination requires detailed consumer information, and the ability to charge different prices for different consumers. Therefore, prices are individualized to extract all individual consumer surplus and reselling among consumers must be prevented. This possibility was once considered to be only of academic interest, but the increasing availability of detailed consumer profiles based on electronic transactions information greatly reduces information uncertainty—a major impediment to practicing perfect price discrimination. Sellers are increasingly able to introduce individualized prices through online price negotiation and auctions.

In electronic commerce, the combination of three factors raises the possibility of perfect-price discrimination. First, sellers gain detailed information about consumer tastes. Second, products can be customized without much added cost. And third, consumers can be billed independently. In each of these aspects, physical markets are highly constrained by transaction costs consisting of information costs, product variation costs, and costs for elaborate billing.

Variations in Consumption Values: A Simple Case of Price Discrimination

Discriminatory pricing does not necessarily accompany product differentiation; it can be used independently as well. One requirement for price discrimination is the seller's ability to differentiate customers and charge them individually by using, for example, identification cards or personalized billing accounts. A demand schedule for a hypothetical product is shown in figure 8.3. The demand schedule, curve ACB, is drawn by positioning all consumers by their willingness to pay, starting from the highest point on the left to the lowest point on the right of the quantity axis.

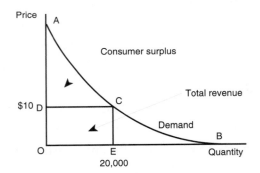

Figure 8.3 Consumer surplus and revenue.

The demand curve shows that, at a price D ($10), for example, the demand is at E, 20,000 units. If 20,000 units are sold at $10, the total revenue is the area ODCE, which equals $200,000. While the 20,000th customer, the marginal consumer, pays exactly the amount he is willing to pay, all others, the inframarginal consumers, pay less than what they are prepared to pay. The area ADC is the sum of the benefits consumers retain from this market. If the seller has information about each consumer's valuation and is able to negotiate the price with each, he can charge each consumer what they are prepared to pay. For example, Alice who has the highest valuation at, say, $100, is asked to pay $100. Otherwise, the seller refuses to sell while preventing all others from reselling or sharing theirs with Alice. Also knowing that Bob has the next highest valuation at $80, the seller demands $80 for Bob, and so on. In this case, the area ADC is the potential gain for the seller who engages in discriminatory pricing instead of using $10 posted price for all its customers. Ordinarily the negotiation process and information gathering requirement would be more costly than the extra revenue. But when the transaction costs decrease significantly, discriminatory prices can be justified. Electronic commerce appears to be one market where this is the case.

Product Matching

Whenever possible, sellers charge different prices for the same product. Discounts for groups, children, students, and senior citizens are used to increase demand without lowering the price for other groups. In this case, discriminatory prices actually help serve more consumers and increase economic efficiency and social welfare. But in most cases, products are differentiated for specific consumer groups. If these differentiated products have different prices due to cost differences, these prices are not discriminatory. However, price differentials may not correspond to differences in costs. For educational markets, for example, software vendors may intentionally disable certain functions and capabilities of a program to distinguish these products from those for non-educational markets. Despite the added cost of disabling the program, products for educational markets are lower than their commercial versions (Deneckere and McAfee, 1996). Dividing audience seats by sections in a theater achieves a similar effect.

In physical markets, the key to effectively segment the market with differentiated products is knowing what one feature each group of consumers wants that is not wanted by other groups. To prevent high-valuation customers on the left side of the demand schedule from masquerading as low-valuation customers on the right side of the demand schedule, sellers must be able to distinguish buyers through some means of identification. In both third- and second-degree price discriminations, the power of the sellers is limited and incomplete because they still cannot discriminate consumers within each group.

In electronic commerce, sellers may finally have the means to practice first-degree price discrimination by which each individual buyer pays the maximum price they are willing to pay. In order to achieve a complete price discrimination, sellers must have control over four factors of transactions: preference profile, product differentiation, personalized billing, and consumer arbitrage. Product differentiation is not a fundamental requirement, but it does reduce the resistance of consumers and regulators to discriminatory prices, and it also prevents or minimizes consumer arbitrage.

The control over preference profile means that sellers must know what each customer wants. To date, market research and surveys have been important aspects in product development and successful retailing. As society moves from anonymous cash transactions to card-based payments and electronic payment systems, sellers find it easier to collect information about consumers' purchasing behaviors. In electronic commerce, this possibility is magnified exponentially. But the possibility of gathering extensive personalized information is not guaranteed in the future. Anonymous transactions lessen the sellers' discriminatory power over consumers. To complete the sellers' market control, the payment system must be non-anonymous to prevent one consumer masquerading as another. Because consumers are becoming increasingly aware and resistant to releasing private information, it is difficult to predict what kinds of pricing regime will be prevalent in future electronic commerce. But with the trend toward selling personalized products via subscription, there will be in all certainty a heightened debate regarding consumer privacy and anonymity in transactions and payments. At present, the debate revolves around the privacy right, free speech, and other legal points of view. Instead, this chapter focuses on the economic links between privacy and product selection as well as price discrimination.

8.2.   Product Customization

Digital product markets will differ significantly from physical markets both in terms of production and marketing. For online marketing, the emphasis is on the interaction between the seller and its customers. This increased interaction is important in production as well. This section examines why product differentiation becomes the most important aspect of digital goods production and evaluates the economic benefits and costs of varying product specification to the extent of customization.

The distinction between product differentiation and customization may be considered by the economic literature to be a simple matter of degree. A finely differentiated product can indeed be considered to be customized. However, product customization goes far beyond producing a limited number of brands or qualities of a product, and it raises completely different economic issues. The number of differentiated products in a market has been an important issue in the economics of product differentiation where efficiency in production is often achieved by a standardized product. However, cost-reducing mass production technology is no longer a major concern for digital products, where the cost of reproduction becomes minimal. The economic efficiencies that this section is concerned with are not those of economies of scale but rather those that relate to product matching and reduced uncertainties in market demand. Apart from this, product customization is an important strategy which addresses the problem of unauthorized reproduction and distribution of digital products by consumers. Finally, because customization is predicated upon detailed information about consumer preferences, it is intrinsically related to issues such as digital copyrights and privacy.

Sellers' Use of Transmutability

As we discussed in Chapter 7, "Consumers' Search for Information," in relation to searches, information filtering becomes increasingly critical as consumers are faced with an overload of information. To process and select only relevant information, consumers use filtering agents or programs that not only weed out irrelevant information but also organize and present relevant information in a format useful to them. Filtering agents, to be reliable, must be trained by the user, who specifies the appropriate selection criteria. However, this filtering process may be undertaken by the seller rather than the consumer: if a producer modifies the product according to the user's criteria, the product becomes customized. In this regard, product customization is simply an example of filtering accomplished by the seller.

A seller uses product attributes to differentiate products. There may be many factors that determine the quality of a product. In the case of an information service, this could be timeliness, detail, response time, and so on. Let a vector S_i, where i = 1,..., k, represent these quality attributes. For example, S_1 may be timeliness, S_2 may be whether it accommodates graphics, S_3 may be the size of the file, and so on, up to k different variables. By mixing these variables, the seller practices product differentiation.

For a simple case of product differentiation, let's consider when consumer valuations change with respect to timeliness of information. Suppose that a seller sends information to buyers according to a prearranged delivery schedule. Each buyer's value is a simple function of the order in which they receive the information. Thus the value continues to decline as the delay increases but this does not affect the values to the earlier buyers. If the seller announces different prices for different delivery times, for example $10 for instant delivery, $8 for a five-minute delay, and so on, his product is differentiated because delayed information has a lower value than up-to-the-minute information. In this case, discriminatory prices are implemented conventionally by pricing the product as a function of time—buyers reveal their preferences by deciding how urgent their needs are, and by paying their reservation prices. Priority-based prices of this type are a result of product differentiation where the product content is preserved but the access privileges are varied.

A slightly different procedure of this principle involves selling multiple versions of a product while charging different subscription fees for each class of information even when they are delivered at the same time. In paper-based information industries, products typically contain superfluous information not desired by some consumers. Instead of printing several versions, newspapers, for example, contain many sections in an unmanageable volume, which often makes finding the right information difficult and creates waste. Special interest magazines and newsletters have developed from the need for more focused information delivery. Specialization also implies more in-depth and thereby useful information.

With digitization, newspaper publishers are now focusing on customizing their products. For example, *Personal Journal* (http://bis.dowjones.com/pj.html) offered by Dow Jones & Company, Inc., publisher of *The Wall Street Journal*, allows subscribers to create their own portfolio of companies and stock information. Any relevant news or articles involving these companies and stocks are delivered to the subscriber. It is aptly advertised as not requiring consumers to surf or search to obtain the relevant information. Instead, the filtering or customization of information is performed by the seller.

Similarly, the PointCast Network (http://www.pointcast.com) delivers customized news based on personal news profiles. It is supported by advertising and anyone can download the software for PointCast Network to receive personalized news for free, which is presented on its version of a screen saver called SmartScreen. Current news is downloaded when the user's computer is inactive and is organized in channels ranging from headline news, company profiles, weather, sports, industries, and so on.

Both these examples of customization are based on horizontal product differentiation, where products differ in choices but not in quality. With horizontally differentiated products, prices are often uniform because the cost of allowing choices typically does not justify charging different prices. For example, each subscriber of *Personal Journal* may follow a different set of 25 companies, but the number of firms is the same for all subscribers (see figure 8.4). However, products are vertically differentiated if the difference lies in the number of companies that one can select. For example, one customer may be allowed to select 50 firms instead of 25, where the number represents one dimension of product quality. Prices will also vary according to the number of firms selected. A simple price schedule may be linear based on a fixed amount for each company selected, for example $0.25 per company. A more complex pricing strategy involves quantity discount or discounts based on tiers. Such relationships between product differentiation and pricing are discussed in more detail in section 8.4.

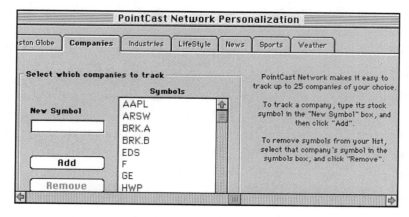

Figure 8.4 An example of customization.

Gains and Losses from Customization

The primary economic benefits of product customization stem from the fact that products match consumers' needs better than undifferentiated products which correspond to the taste of the average consumer. For sellers, better product matching means a reduced opportunity for consumer arbitrage. For consumers and society, customized products reduce wastes but may cause higher prices.

Consumer Arbitrage

By customizing their products, digital product sellers can discourage consumers from unauthorized reproduction and distribution. In the example of customized news services, the product delivered to one person may not be valuable to another if they are interested in different sets of companies. Because digital products are prone to copyright violations by users, personalized products have an obvious advantage if unauthorized distribution (consumer arbitrage) is limited. Limiting consumer arbitrage is the most important requirement for successful discriminatory pricing. For example, if a seller tries to charge different prices to different buyers in a situation where buyers are able to exchange products, buyers who pay the lowest price will try to resell to others. Therefore, the seller is not able to charge any price higher than the lowest price.

Reduced Waste

Industrial goods manufactured with mass production technologies have made many convenience goods more affordable to more consumers than ever before, but these products are often made for the average or representative consumer. For physical products such as toothbrushes, one or a few differentiated models may suffice to satisfy the needs of the majority of consumers. Digital products, however, are more individualized. For example, people read a newspaper for various reasons—today's headline news, sports scores, weather, want ads, entertainment, and so on. To accommodate these needs, a newspaper carries all types of information, but many sections are never read. However, a digital newspaper does not need to be constrained by printing technologies that have shaped the way newspapers are produced and distributed in the physical world. Instead of simply producing an electronic edition of a newspaper consisting of the same material as the paper version, a digital newspaper can be customized to deliver only the information needed by readers, who are no longer faced with the disposing of unwanted portions of the newspaper.

Price Discrimination

Reduced personal arbitrage also supports discriminatory prices, which means that sellers can charge the maximum amount that consumers are willing to pay. With no possibility to arbitrage, the price can be monopolistically determined.

The most important aspect of discriminatory pricing is that prices are based on user valuation, not on production costs. In a competitive market where sellers do not have market power, prices tend to equal marginal costs regardless of the level of user valuation. Consumers retain any surplus, which is the difference between what they are prepared to pay—the so-called reservation prices—and the prevailing market price. In non-competitive markets, prices tend to approach the monopoly level at which consumers are made to pay the highest price. When consumers differ in their valuation, firms with market power try to individualize prices to further discriminate customers by using such measures as multi-part tariffs. Customization is an extreme example of the individualization of products and prices.

In electronic commerce, a pricing strategy based on user valuation is more prominent because of product customization. Due to the product's reproducibility, the marginal production cost of digital products is negligible, so marginal prices have little significance in determining efficient prices. When copyright payments are considered as variable costs of production, competitive prices may amount to these payments. More likely, an efficient and competitive electronic market may have prices based on average costs of production where each firm is at its break-even level of production. A detailed examination of costs and prices is postponed until the last section of this chapter, but it is emphasized here that the standard economic argument that the market price is equated with the marginal cost (price = marginal revenue = marginal cost) has little relevancy in the digital marketplace. Copyright payments, as variable costs, also may not be uniform but variable for every instance of sale, moving further from today's practice that distinguishes payments according to major sales channels. Rather, the transmutability of digital products together with readily accessible consumer information in electronic transactions help authors or firms to focus on discriminatory pricing. Under this type of market condition, consumers are forced to choose between buying products that match their tastes and paying their reservation prices, the highest level of prices. To determine which choice results in greater consumer welfare requires a full specification about the value of having products that match consumer tastes. But generally, discriminatory pricing may involve a transfer of income from buyers to sellers. In a case when previously unserved consumers buy products because new brands are offered, the market becomes more efficient with product differentiation.

8.3. Use of Consumer Information

The ability to effectively customize a product depends on the producer's knowledge of what a buyer wants. If consumer tastes vary greatly—as is evident for knowledge-based products—products tend to be more differentiated, but if tastes are similar, firms are required to produce fairly similar products. A wide distribution of taste means that consumers are scattered throughout the product's characteristics space; if consumers' preferences are alike, they are bunched in a smaller area. Therefore, it is important to know where consumers are located. Market surveys are one way to gain such information, but surveys only measure relative shapes of the distribution. In contrast, consumer information collected on the Internet not only reveals the shape of the preference distribution but also identifies which consumers want certain products. This section examines what type of consumer information is collected and how it is currently used in electronic commerce. Future methods of information collection are discussed in Chapter 12 (see section 12.5, "The Virtual Economy in Action"). Depending on how the information is used or traded among sellers, it may be used to erect entry barriers and reduce competition in digital product markets.

Primary and Secondary Consumer Information

Identifiable consumer information was an integral part of marketing strategy even before the advent of electronic commerce. To obtain a customized product, a prospective buyer needs to reveal its preferences to the seller. Buyers today are required to fill out personal information in most economic transactions or use non-cash payment methods that leave a trail of information. As a result, when a consumer visits a gas station to change oil for his car, he will not only get a reminder for another oil change in a few months but will also receive advertisements from tire stores, automotive supply stores, and so on. In turn, this personal information is often sold to a third party, who dissects and analyzes the information by cross referencing and matching it with other data.

The raw data collected in transactions is considered primary information, while the cross-matched processed data is secondary information. The real power of compiling a consumer profile lies in the processed information. For example, suppose that an airline tries to promote its new East-to-West Coast flights. To send mass-mail advertisements, it needs to select a target audience—this may include people who have rented cars in New York and Los Angeles and who frequently make coast-to-coast long distance calls, and so on. Given the willingness of those who have primary information to provide the data, this type of targeted advertising has become a lucrative revenue source for telephone companies, credit card services, and Internet search services. Visa (http://www.visa.com), for example, has introduced a service which allows banks to analyze the consumption habits of its cardholders, giving banks another source of revenue in the tight bank card business. By cross-referencing this with other information such as telephone call records, hotel reservations, and so on, any seller can establish a detailed profile for virtually anyone.

A proposed Minnesota bill (H.B. 2816, available at http://www.epic.org/privacy/internet/MinnHB2816.html) defines identifiable consumer information as information that

- Identifies a person by physical or electronic address or telephone numbers
- Identifies a person as having requested or obtained specific materials or services
- Identifies Internet sites visited by a person
- Identifies any of the contents of a person's data storage device

The first item above is the conventional definition of identifiable information, while the remaining three arise in electronic commerce because of the nature of communication on the Internet. The public has access to a great deal of personal information. According to a disclosure by Equifax (http://www.equifax.com), a credit reporting agency, a credit report typically contains the following:

- Identity information: name, current and previous addresses, date of birth, marital status, and social security number

- Employment data: present position, length of employment, and previous jobs

- Credit history: credit experiences with specific credit grantors

- Public record information: civil suits and judgments, tax liens, bankruptcy records, and other legal proceedings recorded by a court involving a monetary obligation

- Credit inquiry information: a listing of all credit grantors who have requested a copy of the person's credit life within the last two years. (From Equifax FAQs) (http://www.equifax.com/consumer/faqs/answer7.html)

Even universities routinely sell their lists of student names and addresses to outside merchants who want to use them for marketing purposes. Controlling this information does not pose a significant legal challenge. What is at issue in terms of economics is the use of consumer profiles that describe a person's consumption behaviors and preferences collected on the Internet through subtle methods such as menus given to web browsers. Unlike information such as names, addresses, and social security numbers to which laws governing consumer protection and disclosure may already apply, there is no basic agreement on how to treat consumer information gained by processing communications data.

Because data gathering activities are based on monitoring Internet usage, a leading legal question is the degree of monitoring allowable in electronic transactions. Currently, web servers record the domain name or IP address of a visitor, the time accessed, the action such as downloading (GET commands in figure 8.5), and the document accessed. By accessing the preference setting that users specify in their browsers, servers can also record the person's name, affiliation, address, and so on. Cookie technology allows servers far more sophisticated operations, which not only record access activities but also interact and control these activities (see the sidebar, "Cookies and Consumer

Information"). Excessive monitoring is also a concern at workplaces where employers can monitor computer usage by employees for use in evaluating work performance. Workplace computers are routinely used for auditing, tracking, and process accounting, but there is always room for abuse.

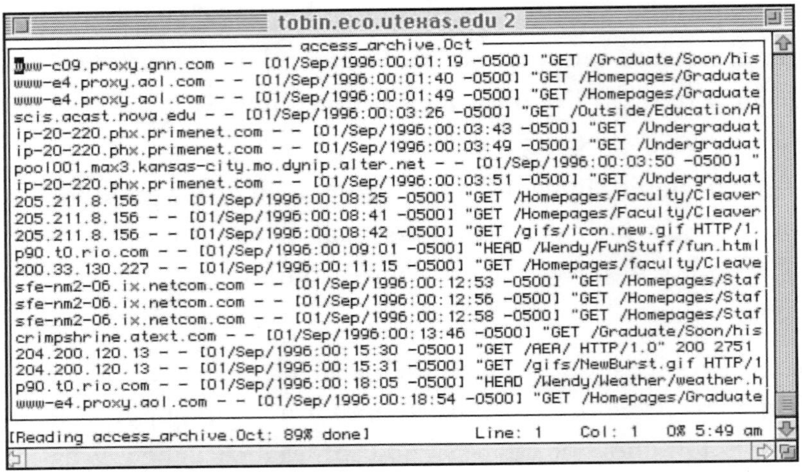

Figure 8.5 An example web access log.

Cookies and Consumer Information

What Is a Cookie? Cookies are text files stored at the client's (that is, visitor's) hard drive (usually in the Preferences folder). When a web browser requests a document using Netscape Navigator or Internet Explorer, the web server generates a piece of data which is sent to the browser and stored at the browser's (client's) computer. Later, when the browser requests another document, the cookie is sent along with the request. The piece of information given by the web server is called a cookie and may contain various types of data that can be defined by the server.

Why Do We Need Cookies? A cookie on the Internet is much like the caller ID provided by telephone companies by which a telemarketer can bring up all relevant customer information—name, address, previous purchase payment records, and so on—by the time a sales representative answers a call. A web site consists of many files stored in various subdirectories, and, when a client accesses a particular page or document, a separate web connection is made and the previous connection is lost. Suppose that a web grocer divides all its merchandise in subdirectories such as produce, meat, and drinks.

When a customer moves from the produce section (that is, page) to the meat section, the customer is actually making a separate call, to use the telephone analogy. To provide a continuous service so that the customer can browse different pages, select items, and pay for all items at once, a continuous database (or connection) of the customer is needed. The cookie technology is therefore necessary in the web environment to overcome the lack of continuity in connection. Such an environment without a persistent connection is called "stateless." In this sense, a cookie is often referred to as persistent client state information.

What's in a Cookie? Currently, a cookie contains the following five information fields: data string, expiration date, domain, path, and security preference. A detailed specification for cookies is available at http://www.netscape.com/newsref/std/cookie_spec.html.

(1) The most common field of information (and the only required field) in a cookie file is the data string in the form of **name=VALUE**. **Name** can be any variable name followed by any VALUE assigned by the server. For example, strings such as

> Customer_Name=Alice_Arthur
>
> Taste=Historical_Fiction
>
> Item_Number=Part0012
>
> Payment_Preferred=Ecash

can store information about the customer's name, preference or taste, the item purchased, or the payment method used. The remaining four fields of information are optional.

(2) The **expires=DATE** attribute sets the valid lifetime of a cookie.

(3) The **domain=DOMAIN_NAME** field specifies the host name of the server which generated the cookie. A client searches its cookie file to find all matching cookies so that they may be sent to a server when requesting a document.

(4) The **path=PATH** attribute specifies the subset of web pages (URLs) for which the cookie is valid. The most general path is "path=/" which indicates that the cookie is valid (or should be sent to the server) for all pages. If the **path** is not specified, the default path is the current page when the cookie is sent by the server.

(5) Finally, a cookie may be specified to be sent only when the communication channel is secure by including the **secure** command. If **secure** is not specified, a cookie is sent without regard to security.

continues

continued

Clickstream. The **path** attribute is the second most important piece of information stored in a cookie by which a server can keep a log of the pages that a client visits. For example, suppose that Bob is an online bookseller specializing in mysteries and historical fiction. All entries of mystery books are stored in "/mysteries" subdirectory, while historical novels are in "/historical_fiction" subdirectory. All other books are in the root directory ("/"). When Alice connects to Bob's home page, Bob sends a cookie to Alice with the following information:

Customer_Name=Alice; path=/; expires=Friday, 31-Dec-99 23:59:59 GMT

This cookie is valid until the end of 1999 for all Bob's pages including all subdirectories. Thus, Alice sends the information Customer_Name=Alice whenever she accesses Bob's site. When Alice accesses a mysteries page (/mysteries/mystery_list.html), Bob sends Alice another cookie with the information:

Taste=Mysteries; path=/mysteries; expires=Friday, 31-Dec-99 23:59:59 GMT

which is valid for the all pages in the "/mysteries" subdirectory (and all subdirectories below that directory). Therefore, when Alice visits Bob's web site the next time, her browser checks all its cookies (by the domain name) and selects all cookies that match Bob's domain name. Then, her browser sends all cookies valid for the specific path. For example, if Alice wants to look at the file "/mysteries/mystery_list_update.html", she should send both cookies containing the information Customer_Name=Alice and Taste=Mysteries.

Other Uses of Cookies. The information provided by cookies can be used to customize web pages and sales. When caller ID is augmented by a computer database, a sales representative has all the information it needs to assist the customer or to target the customer for specific sales. Similarly, a web server may present a different web page to each customer based on the information provided by cookies. Customers are not required to enter user name, passwords, or other registration information repeatedly. Also, cookie-generated web pages can adapt to the needs of dynamic interactive communications without much hassle. With such tools, web customers are made to talk to "personalized" sales representatives who can best assist them.

Another potentially interesting use of cookies is to distribute customer-specific coupons as cookies. For example, suppose that a customer has visited a certain page (perhaps one that provides an advertisement), and the merchant sends a coupon-cookie to the customer. When the customer accesses a different page (where a sale product is displayed), she sends the cookie which counts as a discount coupon to the purchase of that item.

The clickstream information is extremely valuable to a web administrator in improving the efficiency in web access. For example, a log file of all accesses during a month may reveal that a particular page (or an item) is most popular, but its location requires many clicks through subdirectories. Such pages may be rearranged based on user access patterns, resulting in an easy and convenient usage.

Privacy and Anonymity

The debate about privacy of Internet transactions focuses on the right of consumers to control the use of data about themselves. Not surprisingly, consumer information collected by monitoring the World Wide Web has become a contentious issue. Consumer information is inevitably revealed in ordinary business transactions, and when products are customized, the most valuable commodity is the information about consumers' preferences. The impact of firms' using this consumer information can be quite significant. Targeted junk mail based on previous purchase records may be the least worrisome aspect of this abuse. More seriously, a person may be denied medical insurance or a loan from a bank, or may be fired from work because of information that may not be voluntarily available. In terms of economics, the use of consumer information can lead to price discrimination, which often involves monopoly prices.

Anonymity as a Myth

We have seen that information contained in a credit report is quite extensive. However, we tend to think that such information is difficult to collect and disseminate on the Internet because of the anonymity. Anonymity, the absence of identity, is pervasive in Usenet discussion groups where participants find it useful to assume an "online identity" to engage in sensitive or inflammatory discourse. Anonymity can encourage political speech, reducing the risk of punishment, and it is useful when requesting sensitive, personal, and potentially embarrassing information and services. But at the same time, this advantage may elicit criminal, unlawful, or libelous conduct. How anonymous is

Internet communication? Although the Internet affords a far greater degree of anonymity than physical markets, many cases of anonymous messages can actually be "traced" back to the original sender, which is often necessary if one desires a reply. Untraceable anonymity requires either an unscrupulous remailer—or a proxy server—who forwards messages without attaching information about the original sender, or a remailer who destroys its log information. To optimize anonymity, one can route one's message through several remailers, all of whom must cooperate to divulge the identity. Nevertheless, the fact of the matter is that the majority of Internet messages are traceable and identifiable, and consumers are unaware of being identified.

A popular myth was declared, "On the Internet, nobody knows you're a dog" (*The New Yorker*, May 7, 1993, p. 61) (see figure 8.6). In reality, the server computer knows a lot about its client. You can test how much a server knows about yourself by logging into the Anonymizer.com server (see figure 8.7). The sample data shows your affiliation, location, the type of computer and browser that you use, the mode of connection, and the pages you have visited at the server. The use of Java-based applets and cookies further necessitate establishing traceable identity on the Internet. And applets often establish a concurrent, third-party connection, as seen with advertising banners which send and receive information from a different site than the document they are shown. Therefore, even when personal information is offered voluntarily, there is a danger that that information may be collected by a third party, who disguises itself as a legitimate server. This is called *spoofing* (see "Internet Resources" at the end of this chapter). But, there are at least two other ways besides anonymity to maintain consumer privacy.

Figure 8.6 The Internet dog.

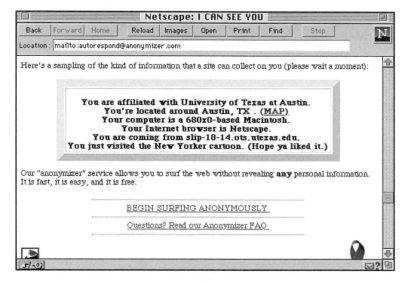

Figure 8.7 Information collected by Anonymizer.com server.

Legal Efforts to Protect Privacy

Techniques to preserve privacy do not necessarily conceal the identity of the sender or the receiver, instead they protects the content and integrity of a message or a transmission by keeping it secret and private. Encryption technologies address the need to keep contents, but not identity, private. Anonymity, however, bypasses the privacy issue by concealing identifiable consumer information and makes secondary information useless as it cannot be cross-referenced. Besides relying on anonymity, however, consumers may be protected from illicit gathering and use of their identifiable information either by legal and regulatory efforts or through trading personal information in an open market.

Various privacy laws restrict the distribution of identifiable consumer information. While the issue of anonymity is involved with free speech, the First Amendment, as well as libel law and copyrights, the focus of this discussion is on the control over the use of consumer information. The legal basis of consumers' control of personal information is found in the Fourth Amendment right to privacy, which protects persons against illegal searches. Just like homes, personal information may be considered to be in private domain. For example, personal information may be given to another for the purpose of a transaction but with a specific restriction. Suppose Alice buys a document called "How Not to Take a Bath for a Week" from Bob, he does not have an explicit right to inform everybody that Alice indeed purchased that product, therefore insinuating that Alice is a filthy person. To protect his business, Bob probably will not willingly divulge such information, but additional revenues from such a sale have proven to be an effective lure for many sellers.

The legal approach toward privacy is to clarify the restrictions for appropriate conducts among transacting parties. For transactional purposes, Bob can clearly have a right to obtain and verify Alice's identity. Even in cash transactions, laws require vendors to verify personal information, for example with alcohol, tobacco, or prescription drug sales. Legal guidelines, however, are clearly lacking as to what Bob can do with his customer information. Because much of this information is publicly available, consumer rights are often limited to correcting errors and updating one's data, while information and direct marketing industries operate under a largely self-regulatory policy toward privacy, under which consumers can request that their names be removed from their database. Relying on self-regulation does not afford consumers any legal recourse to address what they regard as a blatant misuse of their information. Juno Online Services (http://www.juno.com), a free e-mail service company, used to display their promise not to sell or distribute its subscribers' information, but its actual agreement reserved their right to do so. Upon confrontation by the New York attorney general's office, Juno's president affirmed its policy not to distribute personal information, saying: "We didn't anticipate doing it, didn't intend to do it and didn't do it." (*Newsday*, December 11, 1996, A51, as quoted in *Edupage*, a mailing list distributed by listproc@educom.unc.edu).

Instead of relying on the grace and trustworthiness of each seller, efforts are under way to elucidate the rights and obligations of transacting parties. The Minnesota bill aims at regulating the use and distribution of personal information by information service providers, by requiring sellers to obtain explicit consent from their customers to disseminate their personal information. Consent is obtained in a written agreement where consumers specify whether they do or do not object to the release of their personal information. Going a step further, however, related legal and regulatory hassles can be avoided by establishing consent with contracts or agreements to sell in the market.

Market-Based Solution to Protect Personal Information

Although some sellers are indeed surreptitiously collecting consumer information, others offer some type of service in exchange for voluntarily revealed information. For example, a free Internet e-mail service provider, Juno Online Services (http://www.juno.com), offers its free service because they make their profits from advertising. CyberGold (http://www.cybergold.com) also offers similar service where clients are paid for reading advertisements. Whether the payment is in the form of free service or money, both Juno and CyberGold leverage identifiable consumer information through market mechanisms.

Juno's clients first answer about 20 questions for their Member Profile. Then Juno selects and sends targeted advertisements that are displayed as a banner on their e-mail reader program (see figure 8.8) or as a separate web page. Based on consumer-revealed information, Juno brokers between consumers and advertisers, where consumers have merchandised their private information for service or money. Similarly to CyberGold, Millennium Interactive Technologies Corp. (http://www.mitnet.com) proposes to forward e-mail advertising to its subscribers who get credits. Firefly (http://www.ffly.com) offers various Internet services such as newsgroups, discussion groups, and chat rooms where like customers exchange product reviews and word-of-mouth information. Firefly in turn offers a specialized interaction group as a niche market to advertisers.

When one can obtain free service or monetary compensation based on one's personal information, how would anyone be allowed to freely collect and process such information? Should the collection of personal information using cookies (see the sidebar in section 8.3 for cookies) and similar technologies be prohibited? If there is a market price for consumer information, that product is to be "exchanged" rather than "surrendered" when accessing a web site. In such a case, what would be the equitable price for the goods being exchanged, that is the product sought by the consumer and the information sought by the seller? Prices for information that used to be freely or publicly available have not been researched properly by economists, but they will demand more attention in the future. One problem in determining a proper price for consumer information is the truthfulness of voluntarily revealed information. Firms such as Juno may have to rely on an incentive compatible mechanism to induce consumers to truthfully reveal personal information. (See section 8.4, "Pricing Digital Products," for incentive compatible mechanisms.) A fundamental incentive is the cost in reading uninteresting advertisements, which discourages someone to lie.

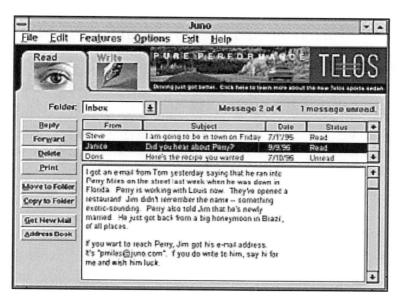

Figure 8.8 Juno's advertisement is placed as a banner while a user reads or writes an e-mail.

Finally, note that the issue of privacy goes beyond devising legal or market protection for personal information. As stated earlier, complete anonymity depends on the trustworthiness of the third party who mediates a message transfer or a transaction. Intermediaries, therefore, can introduce proper measures to ensure consumer privacy. Secondly, privacy in transaction is an important issue in electronic payment systems. Separate from the security issue of protecting credit card numbers and the like, an added concern is preserving the privacy of buying habits and other consumption-related information when transactions are conducted using digital credit cards and digital currency. Payment-related issues are examined in Chapter 10, "Electronic Payment Systems."

Consumer Information and Discriminatory Pricing

The effect of sellers' use of information about market behavior on consumer welfare is important to consider. Sellers of information argue that it reduces prices and enables consumers to buy better products because sellers gain efficiency in production and marketing. These benefits are possible, but so are other scenarios. Prices might actually increase, sellers may even refuse to sell to certain "identified" customers, and only profitable types of products may be marketed. The economic arguments against information revelation are numerous, but the possibility of first-degree price discrimination based on consumer information has largely been ignored.

For some products, consumers voluntarily reveal their needs and preferences. For others, reluctant consumers have raised the issues of anonymity and privacy in transactions. Faced with informational uncertainty, the sellers want to know consumer's private information as much as the buyers want to know the quality of the product. But, a seller with consumer information may set prices according to an individual consumer's marginal valuation rather than the marginal cost of the product. If the firm does not restrict the quantity, there is no loss in social welfare (the sum of the seller's and buyer's surpluses). Indeed, unlike monopoly prices, discriminatory prices generally increase market efficiency by expanding the market and allocating resources according to consumers' marginal willingness to pay.

From a distributional point of view, the gain to consumers may be lower than the benefit to the sellers. Under perfect price discrimination, a seller sells his product by charging the maximum price each consumer is willing to pay. This may be socially efficient but consumers are seldom willing to pay the highest price without complaint. Moreover, the firm may prefer to restrict quantity or refuse to deal with some consumers based on their profiles. In a sense, consumers lose their bargaining power by revealing personal information to the firm.

If a buyer's identity is not revealed, the pricing strategy will usually be conventional. For example, suppose Charlie sells an online magazine in a market where there are only two consumers: Alice and Bob. Charlie knows that one of them will value his magazine at $10, and the other at $5, so the seller has only a general knowledge about the distribution of consumer preferences and values. Also, suppose that consumers likewise are not sure whether the magazine will be worth $10 or $5 prior to purchase. When consumer identity is not known to Charlie, he can only price his magazine at $7.50, the average price. Because that price is the average, both Alice and Bob are likely to buy it at that price. However, one of them will be disappointed after finding out that the magazine was worth only $5. This conventional pricing and sale works if

1. The sale occurs only once

2. Consumers do not know their valuation of the product prior to purchase

3. The seller cannot distinguish between its customers

If sales are based on repeat purchases, consumers learn product quality, and either Alice or Bob will drop out of the market after the first bitter experience. Then, Charlie can price its magazine at $10 and sell only to the remaining customer. This higher price is only possible after consumers learn about the product's quality or about their valuations of the product. Otherwise, if the product is offered at $10 in the first period, no one will buy it because the price exceeds the average valuation—the amount both Alice and Bob expect to get at the maximum.

What is the benefit to the buyer if the buyer reveals private information? Suppose Alice is the one with high valuation and Bob has the low valuation. Then, it may be beneficial to Bob if Charlie is willing to charge a lower price of $5—assuming that this price is still higher than the cost. On the other hand, Alice will not reveal her preference and pretend to be Bob, because she enjoys a positive surplus at $7.50 or at $5. Therefore, revealing private information is beneficial to consumers with low valuation. Those with high valuation must be given sufficient incentives to reveal their preference.

An ideal pricing scheme calls for charging Alice $10 and Bob $5. To implement prices based on consumer valuations, Charlie needs to know the identity of the buyer, and have a means to prevent Bob from buying two copies and selling a copy to Alice at a price lower than $10 (this is consumer arbitrage). The latter can be prevented if he sells only one copy to each customer, but this requires the ability to identify and distinguish his customers. In the absence of identifiable information, Charlie can only sell his magazine at $7.50 for one-time customers, or at $10 and forgo part of the market (again assuming that consumers know the product quality). The result is that Bob is either disappointed (or enraged by a "rip-off") or not served.

In sum, by revealing their information, more consumers may be served and products will be at their valuation. Similarly, discriminatory (or differential) prices allow sellers to serve a larger market, increasing market efficiency. But, as mentioned earlier, charging different prices involves some consumers paying a higher price than in a market with incomplete information. Therefore, sellers need some mechanisms to satisfy consumers who are charged differently. One is differentiating products to persuade them, rightly or not, that they are buying different products. If products are differentiated in a way to segment the market, Alice will not pretend to be Bob in order to pay a lower price. The next section continues this discussion and other strategic considerations involving product choice and pricing.

It suffices to note here that although the prospect of complete price discrimination is great in electronic commerce due to the availability of identifiable consumer information, many arguments can be made in favor of allowing sellers access to such information. The previous example identified two such arguments: consumers with different valuations can be served, and products can be tailored to match differences in consumer tastes. Furthermore, information on the market and consumers has a value of its own. If not, there would be no incentive for market research. The value of market information derives from its use in reducing uncertainty in the quantity and quality demanded for a product. The reduced uncertainty helps formulate more effective competitive strategies as well as regulatory policies. With an uncertain demand, a firm's fixed investments may result in waste from idle production capacity, misjudgment of consumer tastes, an so on. An informed firm can increase its profit by reducing this waste as well as by finding markets that uninformed firms may not serve. More precise demand information and production creates increased satisfaction for consumers, who are no longer uncertain about the quantity and product specification.

In fact, Ponssard (1979) has demonstrated that consumer welfare increases when firms have better information on market demand. However, his model also shows that the increase in profit and the value of the information diminishes as more firms acquire this information. Ponssard refers to information about the market in general, not about individual preferences. As long as the better information is about the market but not about identifiable information, resolving market and demand uncertainties does not pose a direct threat to consumer welfare. For example, better economic planning can benefit all sectors of society and, even when consumer information is used to customize products, consumers do not suffer losses if the new products are sold to indistinguishable customers. It's only when consumer information is linked to payment and thereby to discriminatory pricing that we are presented with both the gain in total welfare through efficiency and the loss in consumer surplus due to higher prices. In electronic commerce, both the availability of identifiable consumer information and the use of product differentiation greatly facilitates discriminatory prices, alternatively known as differential, nonlinear, or non-uniform prices.

8.4.   Pricing Digital Products

Basic economic research shows that in a competitive market prices are determined by the level of demand and the cost of supply, or production. In other words, the market-determined price is efficient in terms of production and consumption, and the firm operates efficiently at the lowest average cost, while no consumers who are willing to consume the product are denied. However, digital products fall into a gray area where such standard economic reasoning fails to give an insightful answer to business professionals looking to know how to price their products. The foremost difficulty stems from the cost structure of digital products, which is unlike that of most physical products. Furthermore, most digital products are customized and consist of numerous component products. As a result, neither the seller nor the market can be expected to operate with one price for all differentiated products and for all consumers. Rather, pricing strategies become as complex as the products themselves and their applications. This section reviews the economic factors that influence digital product pricing and examines various strategies of multi-product nonlinear pricing, which operates under atypical market conditions.

Cost Curves

Introductory economics and management classes teach that the total cost of production consists of fixed cost and variable costs. The fixed cost is the initial investment needed to produce the first unit, such as the factory, machines, and research and development. Once production begins, the fixed cost does not vary whether the firm produces one unit or one thousand units, and thus it is also known as "sunk cost." The variable cost, on the other hand, is the sum of the material and labor costs that are needed to produce each unit. Consequently, the variable cost of producing ten units may be ten times the cost of producing one unit.

Standard U-Shaped Average Cost Curve

Figure 8.9 shows typical shapes of fixed and variable costs. Graphs A and C are total fixed and total variable costs shown in terms of the number of the output (Q). In this case, the total fixed cost is constant over a range of output because it is "sunk" at the beginning and does not increase as the output is raised. The total variable cost increases proportionately to the number of output, but later increases at a faster rate due to congestion, which is one example of diseconomies of scale. As more employees are put to work to increase the output beyond an optimal level of operation, the per-unit variable cost increases faster and productivity decreases. The total cost of production—the sum of total fixed and total variable costs—understandably increases as output is increased. However, the per-unit cost of production, or the average cost, behaves quite differently. For example, the average cost may decline until the maximum level of operation and increase afterward. The decreasing average cost is first due to wider sharing of the fixed costs. Graph B in figure 8.9 shows the average fixed cost, which declines as an increasing number of units of output "share" the initial cost. Graph D is the average variable cost that is constant up to a level and then increases. The sum of B and D is the aveage (total) costs of production shown in graph E. Because of the declining average fixed cost, the average cost first declines but increases later when the effect of the increasing average variable cost takes effect. The result is a well-known U-shaped average cost curve. In terms of per-unit production cost, a production process with a U-shaped average cost curve achieves an efficient level of production when the average cost is at its lowest.

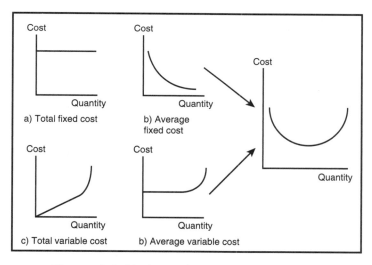

Figure 8.9 U-shaped average cost curve.

Average Cost Curve of a Digital Product

In stark contrast with the standard example above, the bulk of the production cost of a digital product consists of fixed cost. Once the first unit is produced, the additional variable costs are negligible regardless of the output level.

Although some assume that the variable reproduction cost will be zero, the author believes that it will be a substantial, albeit constant, amount due to the per-copy copyright payment. Regardless of the assumption on variable costs, the declining average fixed cost coupled with zero or constant variable costs implies that the (total) average cost of a digital product will be similar to graph B in figure 8.9.

Other industry comparisons may be helpful in determining the economic implications of a declining average cost (AC). Declining average cost is common in the utility and communications industries due to the extreme size of the initial investment in infrastructure. As the per-unit cost of one firm declines, it makes little sense to allow a competitor, which would result in two firms operating at non-optimal levels of production. In these often highly regulated industries, one firm will be more efficient in exhausting the economies of scale manifested in the declining AC. However, the one firm, as a monopolist, may engage in inefficient market behavior such as heightened prices and output restriction. There is a large body of economic literature that studies pricing practices under declining average costs, especially on how to apply marginal cost pricing to guarantee that a natural monopolist breaks even and still maximize social welfare (see the "Suggested Readings and Notes" list at the end of this chapter).

The fundamental difference between a monopolist, or firms with some market power, and a competitive firm is that a monopolist can raise prices and increase profits without suffering a complete loss of customers. In a competitive market, a firm loses all its customers if it raises prices above the prevailing market level. Graphically, the difference is whether the firm's market demand is flat or declining: a firm with market power faces a declining demand schedule while a competitive firm faces a flat demand curve. However, no competitive firm will survive if they have declining AC curves. In figure 8.10, graph A shows a firm in a competitive market where only one price (p) prevails initially for some reason. But competition implies that a competitor will try to undercut its price, which will become zero after a round of price cuts. At a price of zero, no firm will survive. For digital products such as databases, many competitors would not survive if they sell similar products.

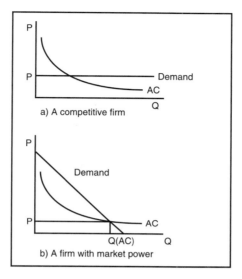

Figure 8.10 Demand and declining average cost in competitive and monopolistic markets.

When products are differentiated, they are targeted at different segments of a market. Due to the reluctance to switch between products, because of low substitutability, each seller or a differentiated product has some market power, which produces a declining demand curve as in graph B of figure 8.10. The price (p) and quantity (Q(AC)), determined by the AC curve crossing the demand curve, is the break-even market solution. This price is the lowest price possible in the market, but it is not the most economically efficient. The most efficient solution is determined by the marginal cost. The marginal cost (MC) curve is below the AC curve because MC must be smaller than AC at each output level if the AC curve is to continue declining. As a result, the MC curve crosses the demand curve at a larger output level than Q(AC). In this case, the standard marginal cost-based pricing (that is MC = demand) results in a larger output at a lower price than shown in graph B. Nevertheless, such a price-quantity combination is not produced because the price and the total revenue is insufficient to recover the total costs of production. The price-quantity solution shown in the graph is second-best even though the firm only breaks even.

Because the firm has some market power, however, it may raise the price still further. This restricts the output but increases the profit as the price is above the per-unit average cost. Because of this profit motive, digital product prices tend to be monopolistic: they will be higher than the marginal cost with restricted output. The fundamental reason for this is seen in the shape of the average cost curve. Although some argue that digital products should be made freely available because they cost nothing to reproduce, any market price must be sufficient for the seller to recover its fixed cost. Even with zero reproduction costs, the break-even price is not zero, especially if the level of demand is at the low output level where the average cost is still substantial. Nevertheless, the valid concern remains that the seller will tend to raise prices and restrict the number of consumers who can buy the product.

Strategic Factors in Pricing

As discussed earlier, the level of fixed cost determines the price and quantity of the digital products produced. Here, a model that describes different choices in fixed investments is presented. This model also incorporates the critical issue of product differentiation, a decision that needs to be made at the initial stage of production. Because of the transmutability of digital products, the electronic marketplace is characterized by similar but different products. An economic motive for differentiation is the desire to minimize the effect of competition among identical products, which destroys the market due to the declining average cost of digital products. Thus, this model emphasizes the nature of multi-product production in electronic commerce. Pricing becomes more complex when a seller is faced with many similar but different products targeted at different segments of consumers. Our objective is to present some fundamental principles of multi-product pricing.

Quality Choices

Conventional supply and demand models describe the relationship between the price and quantity produced with average and marginal costs calculated in terms of output. For physical products, such a model may be adequate because the primary economic concern is determining the quantity of products to produce and their price. Most observers of the digital market realize that the choices in terms of product quality and variety supersede concerns of output levels in electronic commerce. The question of output level is still important because it determines how many consumers may have access to products, but this is an issue of price, not a question of whether material and labor inputs can be allocated more efficiently as output increases. The resource allocation problem for digital products occurs when the first unit of a product is produced.

Application of the price-quantity model often results in erroneous conclusions in the case of digital products. In general, when the price of a product equals its marginal cost (MC) of production, the resources are allocated efficiently. But what is the marginal cost of production for a digital product? In terms of output, the MC is the added cost of producing an additional copy, which is mistakenly believed to be almost zero in electronic commerce. If this were true, an efficient price for a digital product would be close to zero, allowing virtually free dissemination. This does not work for two reasons. At the very least, the MC consists of the per-copy copyright payment. So an appropriate price for any product is the amount due to the creator, which is most certainly a non-zero figure. In addition, the marginal cost to consider is production, not distribution, costs.

To derive the marginal cost of production, first consider the total cost function for a digital product. A digital product may have many characteristics such as size, the number of multimedia components, accuracy of the data, and so on. We denote those characteristics as S_1, S_2, ... , S_n, having a number of n characteristics. A digital product is thus completely described by a series of numbers, or a vector, $(S_1, S_2, ... ,S_n)$. Suppose that S_1 corresponds to the accuracy of a database, taking a value ranging from 0 (completely inaccurate) to 1 (completely accurate). Figure 8.12 shows the total cost needed to achieve a certain level of accuracy. The graph shows a high cost for a totally inaccurate database because it takes time and effort to manually "disguise" the data. The lowest point in the curve may represent the initial state of a database: it costs more either to intentionally make the database worse or to verify each data entry. The optimal level of accuracy depends on the willingness of consumers to pay for this, as represented by the line. For example, the slope of the line indicates that consumers are willing to pay one additional dollar for every improvement of .1 in accuracy. At S_1^*, the marginal cost of improving the database's accuracy equals that marginal willingness to pay. Above S_1^*, the producer must spend more than $1 to achieve an improvement of .1, which cannot be recovered from the consumers. The producer's optimal choice is clearly S*. Note that because the marginal willingness to pay has a positive slope, no producers will actually attempt to corrupt the database. For this reason, we may consider a simplified cost curve that increases for all values of S_1.

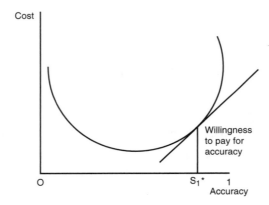

Figure 8.11 The cost curve for accurateness of a database.

A digital product producer decides on the levels of all the product characteristics in the same way. These levels are determined efficiently if the marginal willingness to pay is equal to the marginal cost for all characteristics. Let S represent the aggregated characteristics of a digital product. The cost function of this product can be specified as C(S), and its marginal cost as the derivative of C(S), or C'(S). Given that the consumers' willingness to pay for a level of S is W, resources are allocated efficiently if C'(S) = W = P. In other words, the relevant price for a digital product is determined by the marginal cost of producing a certain quality that is desired by consumers. The marginal cost of reproduction or distribution has little relevancy.

Product Differentiation

A basic opportunity (and challenge) for all businesses is that consumers have different preferences and price sensitivities. For example, suppose that some consumers are willing to pay $2 for an improvement of .1 in accuracy—a steeper line than the one in figure 8.11. Equating the marginal cost of accuracy improvement to this group's higher willingness to pay will result in a higher accuracy $S_1^{**} > S_1^*$. However, the price will also be higher so that those with a lower willingness to pay may not purchase the improved product. To capture both types of consumer, the producer may sell two versions of the product: basic and improved.

In this way, product differentiation is born! This situation is depicted in figure 8.12, where the aggregated quality, S, is considered rather that the accuracy. The subscript H (L) represents consumers with high (low) willingness to pay.

In figure 8.12, both high-type and low-type consumers get an efficient level of quality when their willingness to pay equals the marginal cost of producing the assigned quality. The market for each variety is separated by different prices and qualities. The lines corresponding to consumer types can be interpreted as indifference curves (or lines) of prices at each level of quality. Any price-quality combination lying under the line will be a better deal because the consumer pays less for the same quality. In this interpretation, each type of consumer prefers what is targeted for them, as the alternative always lies above their indifference curves. Implementing product choice and pricing strategies of this type requires the seller to know the consumers, or the market demand. In fact, analysis of market segmentation and collection and processing of consumer demand information form the foundation of product differentiation.

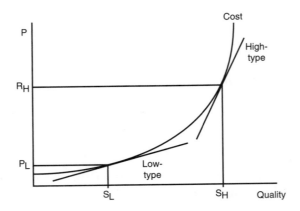

Figure 8.12 Selling differentiated products to two consumer groups.

Incentive Compatible Prices

Assuming that the digital product producer does not face direct competition, there are ways to increase profit. In figure 8.12, P_H and P_L are equal to the marginal cost of production. In terms of output, they are equal to the average prices for breaking even. When raising prices, the firm needs to consider the interaction between the two groups of consumers. At some price-quality combinations, high-type consumers may prefer to buy the low-quality product, and low-type consumers may purchase the high-quality product. To maintain targeted marketing, the firm has two alternatives.

One method of customer targeting is to negotiate with each consumer—that is, to give a "take-it-or-leave-it" deal. A strategy of this type works only if the firm knows its consumers well. With increasingly detailed consumer profiling, this type of information may be available in the electronic commerce world. In addition, the firm should also be able to prevent consumers' reselling among themselves, as some might find it profitable to exchange products among themselves.

The second alternative is to craft the offer (prices and qualities) in such a way that high-type consumers have no incentive to purchase the product intended for low-type consumers, and vice versa. In this scheme, both types of consumers benefit from buying what is intended for them, or at least they will be indifferent. This strategy is called an incentive compatible (IC) solution.

The resulting profit level is lower than the first alternative because there is some cost necessary to maintain incentive compatibility. Nevertheless, an IC solution does not require the seller to have detailed information about consumers, who sort themselves out according to their type.

The cost in maintaining the IC solution stems from the fact that at least one type of consumer, or a segment of a market, has a choice. For example, if both types have no ability to switch products, the firm is free to charge whatever it wishes, just like individual negotiations. However, if both types can switch, the market is not at all separated. To illustrate the cost of the IC condition graphically, see figure 8.13. In this modified version of figure 8.12, the firm decides to raise the price of the high-quality product whose intended customers have a higher willingness to pay. The initial price-quality combinations are A (P_H, S_H) and D (P_L, S_L). As the firm increases the price for its high-quality product, high-type consumers move from A to B and then to C. Choice C is the maximum price the firm can charge because it intersects the origin where both price and quality are zero, signifying no purchases. If the firm raises the price beyond C, high-type consumers simply do not buy. However, high-type consumers may simply switch to D because it lies below the curve going through C, and thus it represents a better deal which is in fact better than not buying any product. Because high-type consumers have alternatives, the maximum price that the firm can charge is B, at which point high-type consumers are indifferent between the high-quality product and the low-quality product.

Low-type consumers, meanwhile, do not have an incentive to switch to the high-quality product as all combinations of A, B, and C are above their indifference curves and represent a worse deal. In sum, the firm would like to charge C, but is constrained to charge a lower price, B, because it cannot force high-type consumers to stick to the high-quality product. This consideration is known as the incentive compatibility constraint, and it limits the firm's profit maximization. Regardless of the limitation, because B is above the original price, A, the firm makes positive profits. An astute firm first raises the price for the low-quality product, maximizing the profit from low-type consumers, and only then it should raise the price of the high-quality product to the IC level.

In this way, low-type consumers are charged their maximum price while high-type consumers in general pay a price somewhat lower than their maximum, B, rather than C.

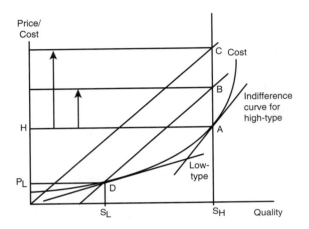

Figure 8.13 Incentive compatible product choices.

The incentive compatibility condition exists whenever products are differentiated and the seller can enforce product choices by intended consumer groups only through market mechanisms. This type of pricing practice is known as second-degree price discrimination. A common example of this is the quantity discount where, as one purchases more units of a product, the per-unit price is lowered. Considering different bundles as differentiated products, high-type consumers buying a bigger bundle are charged a lower price per unit than low-type consumers.

Another instance where the IC condition applies is when prices are divided into access and usage charges—for example, an entrance fee to an amusement park where each ride cost extra, or a long distance calling plan that charges a fixed monthly fee plus per-minute usage charges. Similar non-uniform prices and multi-part tariffs are intended to separate consumers by their preferences, and in general high-type consumers receive a relatively better deal due to the IC condition.

The complexity in pricing digital products stems from the need to differentiate products and devise pricing strategies that separate consumers according

to their willingness to pay. Our discussion of incentive compatibility is meaningless if the market consists of consumers with identical tastes. In this case,
one price for one product suffices and is determined by the market demand.
Many have observed that such simplified pricing strategies work well for
information products in physical markets. For example, newspapers charge a
uniform subscription price; cable operators charge one price for a bundle of
basic channels. However, prices for a newspaper differ between delivery and
vending, and discount prices are available for student and delivery plans. Even
cable service is increasingly divided into many tiers to reflect the diversity in
consumer tastes. The physical and technological constraints that have largely
influenced the way newspapers and cable services are sold will no longer be
paramount for digital products. Nevertheless, some pricing strategies used in
physical markets may be used in electronic commerce: for example, leasing
options, subscription-based pricing, and bundling techniques may be employed.

Selling versus Renting Digital Products

A basic truth of marketing is that if the value of a product is much less than
the cost or price of the product, not a single consumer will be willing to
purchase it. Even in this case, sales are possible. In such a situation, a group of
consumers may form a club if each individual's share of the price and the
accompanying transaction costs, such as waiting time for one's turn, are still
lower than the price of the product. A club good is classified between a pure
public good and a pure private good (Buchanan, 1965). A pure public good is
one whose optimum number of users is all consumers in the market, while this
number for a pure private good is one—here, individual consumption is
preferred. The optimum number of users in club goods is determined by the
marginal condition that the benefit of adding a marginal member must be
equal to the associated cost. When forming a club to share a product, several
factors must be considered: the group's benefit may increase by adding a
member (association benefits), the user cost may increase (congestion effects),
or the production cost (purchasing price) may be lowered (economies of scale).

Association benefits are common in social clubs but not in private good clubs, although a similar benefit is observed in pure private goods such as computer software, which is called a network effect. Congestion effects are evident in the example of library books, where more members create more waiting for a turn to borrow. The economy of scale effect is simply the reduced per-member cost to purchase a book. Taking the price as fixed cost, this is quite similar to the case of declining average cost, which is not surprising because natural monopolies in utility industries are forms of clubs.

When a product has a cost structure of this type or is prone to a sharing arrangement, a viable club can be formed (see Sorenson et al., 1978), but the seller may find it more profitable to arrange a sharing scheme himself instead of selling directly to the consumers. A product sharing scheme initiated by the seller, who maintains ownership of the product, is known as renting or leasing. The objective is to discourage arbitrage by consumers and to avoid the restrictions imposed by the first sale doctrine.

A library is an example of a sharing mechanism by which consumers who are not willing to pay for a book may still use it. Suppose that Peter is trying to sell a book titled *The History of Libraries* priced at $20. If Alice thinks that reading the book is worth more than $20, she will prefer to buy it. However, Peter cannot sell it to anyone whose value for the book is less than $20. Still, if there are 10 people who each considers the book to be worth $5, their total valuation sums to $50. Suppose that the cost of sharing, in this case waiting to borrow, is $1. The maximum price that can be charged for the group of 10 is $4. Peter can either sell two copies of his book at $20 each, or one copy at $40 if he is able to separate the library from the retail market.

Sharing arrangements are common when a product is used only once and the quality of the product is not degraded. However, if a product is used more than once, consumers may prefer to buy it outright, especially if the sharing cost is high enough to justify the sale price because the total cost of an alternative to buying includes transaction costs. For instance, for casual reading, many depend on borrowing from a library, but they prefer to have their own copy if they plan to read a book more than once. Because the cost of borrowing from a library includes waiting time and the fact that one can only use the book for a limited time, the sum totals of these transactions costs and the sale price determine whether the consumer buys or shares. For digital libraries, both of these transaction costs may be negligible unless artificial restrictions for check-out and returns are imposed.

Sharing or renting is often preferred by the seller even for those whose valuation of the product exceeds the sale price. The reason for this has less to do with the desire to exploit the residual market; controlling consumer arbitrage is a important goal of the seller. After consumers buy a product, the first sale doctrine allows them to do whatever they want with it. The first sale doctrine means that a buyer may resell, rent, lease, or dispose of a product at will after the purchase. Copyright protection only applies to copying or reproducing the content of the book, and does not apply to selling the original copy. In contrast, renting or leasing does not change the ownership of the book, and here the first sale doctrine does not apply. In this case, the owner of the book (the seller) may establish certain rules regarding its use. A very elaborate form of such contractual restrictions is implemented by software licensing, which not only controls how many persons can use a program but also how often it is used in a given time period with the help of use-measurement software.

For functional products such as software, licensing may be an adequate method of maintaining ownership. However, as the complexity of networks and computer usage increases, a more flexible licensing regime is required. Although the number of licensed sites or users is relatively easy to manage, there is no adequate method of monitoring access and time of usage. Licensing terms are becoming increasingly complex—an increasing number of large corporations rely on third-party asset management firms to keep track of software purchases, updates, and usage.

Subscription and Bundling

Bundling of computer programs is one of several factors that complicates software licensing. Software vendors find it profitable to bundle products, some of which are used only on a limited basis, because buyers are often willing to pay for these products on a sharing basis. For these products, however, use-based distribution may be more efficient. Applets, for example, are needed on special occasions and are subsequently discarded after use. This strategy would not only be more efficient but is also consistent with the desire to minimize the effects of easy reproduction.

First, let's differentiate the concept of bundling from similar practices. The practice of *bundling* refers to packaging two or more products and selling the bundle in fixed proportions. In other words, if you buy 10 bundles, you get 10 units of each component of the bundle. Components of a bundle sold individually as well as in bundles is called a *mixed bundling* strategy. Microsoft, for example, uses a mixed bundling strategy in selling its various programs (including Word, Excel, PowerPoint, and Outlook) individually or as a bundle in a Microsoft Office suite. Narrowly defined, bundling always refers to a group of different products. When the bundle consists of the same product, this is called *quantity-dependent pricing*. For example, computer diskettes are sold in packages of 10 where the price is often lower than the sum of 10 individual diskettes sold separately. Also, bundling is different from tie-ins, where a buyer of one product is also required to buy another product. But unlike bundling, a buyer may consume different numbers of each component. Thus, if Word and Excel programs were tie-ins, one can buy only one Word program and be able (or, in some cases, the consumer is forced) to buy 10 or 20 units of Excel.

Adams and Yellen (1976) first showed that bundling is a useful price discrimination method, especially when valuations are negatively related. For example, suppose there are three consumers (Alice, Bob, and Charlie) and two computer programs (*Learn a Language*, and *Learn to Paint*). The valuations of three consumers for the two products are as shown in figure 8.15. Valuation for *Learn a Language* is $40, $50, and $60 for Alice, Bob, and Charlie, respectively, while valuation for *Learn to Paint* is the same as above but in the reverse order of Charlie, Bob, and Alice. Suppose that both products cost $40 to produce. If sold separately for $50, *Learn a Language* will be sold to Bob and Charlie, with a total profit of $20. *Learn to Paint* will fetch the same profit but will be sold to Alice and Bob. If the price is increased to $60, only one unit of each product will be sold—*Learn a Language* to Charlie and *Learn to Paint* to

Alice—which results in the same $20 profit for each product. However, if they are bundled and sold at $100, all three will buy the bundle, and the total profit is increased to $60. Although the increased profit from bundling may appear to be due to the negative relationship in the demand for *Learn a Language* and *Learn to Paint*, studies have shown that the negative correlation is not necessary for bundling to be more profitable than unbundling (Spence, 1980, under quantity-dependent pricing; Schmalensee, 1984, because of bunching consumers; and Salinger, 1995, for the reason of reduced cost). A positive relationship may be depicted as both demand curves have negative slopes or positive slopes compared to figure 8.14. McAfee et al. (1989) also show that, in most cases, a mixed bundling strategy almost always increases the seller's profit when compared to pure bundling or non-bundling.

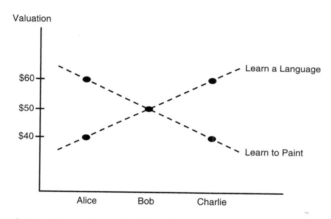

Figure 8.14 Negative relationship in valuations for a bundle.

Although the advantage of using mixed bundling is well known, most Internet services are sold by subscription without offering an usage based payment option. Because of this, some argue that microproducts and micropayments will become irrelevant in electronic commerce (Odlyzko, 1996) as digital product sellers are increasingly bundling their products and selling them as a package. Even downloadable applets, they contend, will be sold on a subscription, not on a per-use, basis.

Subscriptions are also favored in other communications media such as cable television, telephone services, and magazines. Subscription-based services are often priced at a flat fee, and provide no control over consumer usage. For example, America Online (http://www.aol.com) recently introduced a flat-fee subscription schedule which greatly increased the Internet connection by its members and aggravated congestion problems. If congestion is a potential problem, subscription fees can be differentiated either by using two-part tariffs of access and usage charges or by introducing a series of subscription tiers.

One reason why consumers favor fixed monthly fees based on a subscription plan is to balance expected fluctuations in consumption. Consider the example of telephone services. Even though telephone companies offer a lowest-price service with a minimum monthly charge but with a limited number of phone calls allowed, most consumers opt to pay a higher monthly charge with unlimited local calls even when they seldom make that many calls in a month. One explanation is that consumers may anticipate an increased use of calls in an emergency, and with the limited call plan, each call over the limit will cost a premium. Thus, subscribing to the higher-priced service is a better option for risk-averse consumers. Similarly, cable customers find a bundled service to be more desirable than separately paying for each channel or pay per view.

However, this conclusion, based on non-digital markets, may not be valid in electronic commerce. In physical markets, options presented to consumers are often incomplete. For example, a cable service has never been offered to consumers where one can truly select any number of channels. Most likely, the lack of this option is due to technological reasons, but if it were feasible, cable operators might have introduced such an option simply because it allows finer segmentation of the market. The effort to segment the market is seen in mushrooming cable service tiers. Typically, these tiers are vertically differentiated by quality in such a way that a standard basic tier (a low-quality product) is included in an expanded basic tier (a high-quality product). Such product pricing schemes are aimed at differentiating those who are willing to pay more for better quality from those who are not. This type of pricing is one example of second-degree price discrimination as discussed in section 8.1, "Product Differentiation and Pricing in Economics."

The Case for Microbundles and Micropayments

If there is a cost-effective way to provide a service that offers consumers to choose any combination of channels or programs, prices will reflect the cost and some consumers will benefit from unbundling and unsubscription as well. The lack of consumer choice is somewhat responsible for the low, overall cable subscription rate that remains between 60 percent and 70 percent of the homes passed by cable. Today's cable subscription scheme resembles the licensing and bundling of software where the seller exploits the residual demand. Selling only a bundled service forces some consumers to pay for unnecessary items unless an option to buy an unbundled product is available. In electronic commerce, currently employed technologies offer more choices, and accordingly traditional pricing models observed in physical markets do not reflect the dynamics of the electronic marketplace.

Most information products are sold as bundles. Newspapers, databases, and magazines all contain various items of news, data, and articles. Although individual items in these examples may be sold separately, the demand in the market often does not justify individual sales. The primary reason is that the price of offering an individual piece of news or data often far exceeds what an interested buyer is willing to pay. For example, a newspaper containing about 50 pages of news and information cost about 50 cents. Suppose that the value of each page ranges from one cent to 10 cents. The distribution of this value differs according to each reader's preferences among a variety of interests, such as world or local news, lifestyle, entertainment news, sports, business news, and classified advertisements. Nonetheless, the sum of the consumer's values on individual items must exceed 50 cents to justify buying the newspaper. At the least, cost savings from bundling allows the seller to offer a price low enough to attract customers.

A cost-saving strategy has its own costs, however. Many pages of a newspaper are wasted to those who do not value those pages. And secondly, some consumers are denied the sale of a newspaper when their total valuation is below 50 cents. For example, if someone only wants weather information, a bundled newspaper does not serve his need for information. Both of these inefficiencies can be eliminated if the publisher is able to offer individual articles or sections as well as the newspaper as a bundle—using a strategy of mixed bundling.

To unbundle and sell an individual item at such a low price, cost-effective technologies for production, distribution, and payment are essential. For newspapers, electronic commerce offers such technologies and an opportunity to gain market efficiencies. Even though electronic newspapers are sold by subscription, some forms of micro-subscription will offer all the advantages of an unbundled service. Subscribers to a digital newspaper paying a fixed fee for identical reproductions receive a product similar to a paper newspaper. However, if the digital newspaper is customized, and consumers are able to select only those items that interest them, the subscription service differs from newspaper or magazine subscription in physical markets. Importantly, this eliminates waste and provides service to more segments of the market. Already, digital news items can be produced and delivered as an individual product or as a microbundle. A mechanism for micropayments remains to be implemented to support mixed bundling in electronic commerce.

This section cautions against the notion that digital product pricing will closely resemble physical product pricing regimes where bundled products are sold at a flat-fee, ignoring qualitative differences in production, delivery, and consumption process in electronic commerce. Indiscriminate bundling and subscriptions based on flat fees cause congestion, inefficient resource allocation, and other problems. Because technological constraints in physical markets do not exist in electronic commerce, the ability to select and buy an individual item needs to be expanded. Another critical advantage of mixed bundling and microbundles is that they help resolve uncertainties about quality. Unbundling digital products, by either selling individual items or by allowing customization, encourages consumers to sample quality by accessing a portion of the product. An option for micropurchases gives valuable information to consumers to learn about the quality of the product. Micropayments and digital currency involve critical technologies to implement unbundling and micropurchases which are further discussed in Chapter 10.

8.5.   Summary

Our discussion in this chapter focused on three related issues: product differentiation, price discrimination, and the use of consumer information. Because of their transmutability, digital products are extremely customizable. When individual preferences are known, the seller has an incentive to price customized products according to the consumer's valuation. However, the very nature of digital products raise the issue of control. Sellers are concerned with how consumers use the product, and most importantly with rampant unauthorized reproduction and distribution. One means for sellers to discriminate its customers, that is to charge different prices, while preventing consumer arbitrage, is an incentive compatible pricing strategy.

The electronic marketplace may be the most advanced in terms of communications and transactional efficiencies. But, from an economics point of view, the practices of product differentiation and non-uniform pricing complicates the task of determining the competitiveness and efficiency of the overall market. Non-sale methods, such as licensing, leasing, bundling, and subscriptions, are prevalent in electronic commerce because of the concern for copyright infringement and the influence of physical markets. These pricing strategies are relatively simpler to analyze and implement, thus they are eagerly implemented compared to mixed bundling and non-linear pricing strategies. Electronic commerce offers fresh ground for research in the areas of quality choices and multi-product pricing, giving economists an incentive to explore such areas, with a wide ranging empirical applicability. Simultaneously, market processes of production, delivery, payment, and consumption for digital products will be quite different from those for physical products. As pricing strategies cannot be evaluated without considering all market processes, it is unwise to treat digital products as we do their physical counterparts or to carelessly convince digital product sellers that existing economic models can simply be reinterpreted for electronic commerce.

References

Adams, W.J., and J.L. Yellen, 1976. "Commodity Bundling and the Burden of Monopoly." *Quarterly Journal of Economics*, 90: 475–498.

Buchanan, J.M., 1965. "An Economic Theory of Clubs." *Econometrica*, 32: 1–14.

Chamberlin, E.H., 1933. *The Theory of Monopolistic Competition*. Cambridge, Mass.: Harvard University Press.

Degryse, H., 1996. "On the Interaction Between Vertical and Horizontal Product Differentiation: An application to banking." *The Journal of Industrial Economics*, 44(2): 169–186.

Deneckere, R., and R.P. McAfee, 1996. "Damaged Goods." *Journal of Economics and Management Strategy*, 5(2): 149–174.

Hotelling, H., 1929. "Stability in Competition." *Economic Journal*, 39: 41–57.

McAfee, R.P., J. McMillan, and M.D. Whinston, 1989. "Multiproduct Monopoly, Commodity Bundling, and Correlation of values." *Quarterly Journal of Economics*, 93: 371–383.

Odlyzko, A., 1996. "The Bumpy Road of Electronic Commerce." Presented at the *WebNet '96* conference, October 16–19, 1996. An electronic version is available at http://aace.virginia.edu/aace/conf/webnet.html.

Salinger, M.A., 1995. "A Graphical Analysis of Bundling." *Journal of Business*, 68(1): 85–98.

Schmalensee, R., 1984. "Gaussian Demand and Commodity Bundling." *Journal of Business*, 57: S211–30.

Sorenson, J.R., J.T. Tschirhart and A.B. Whinston, 1978. "Private Good Clubs and the Core." *Journal of Public Economics*, 10: 77–95.

Spence, A.M., 1980. "Multiproduct Quantity-Dependent Prices and Profitability Constraints." *Review of Economic Studies*, 47: 821–42.

Suggested Readings and Notes

Nonlinear Pricing

Nonlinear pricing is used in a wide variety of situations when there is incomplete information, and its application is seen in utility pricing, block tariffs, bundling and bunching, and incentive compatible solutions in taxation and quality choices.

For a good introduction to pricing strategies under decreasing average cost, see Train, K.E., 1991, *Optimal Regulation: The Economic Theory of Natural Monopoly*, Cambridge, Mass.: The MIT Press.

For incentive compatibility, see Myerson, R.B., 1985, "Bayesian Equilibrium and Incentive Compatibility: An Introduction," *Social Goals and Social Organization: Essays in Memory of Elisha Pazner*, L. Hurwicz, D. Schmeidler and H. Sonnenschein, eds., Cambridge: Cambridge University Press.

For block tariffs and nonlinear prices, see Schmalensee, R., 1981, "Monopolistic Two-part Pricing arrangements," *The Bell Journal of Economics*, 12: 445–466; Goldman, M.B., H.E. Leland and D.S. Sibley, 1984, "Optimal Nonuniform Prices," *Review of Economic Studies*, 51: 305–319; Maskin, E. and J. Riley, 1984, "Monopoly with Incomplete Information," *The Rand Journal of Economics*, 15(2): 171–196; and Armstrong, M., 1996, "Multiproduct Nonlinear Pricing," *Econometrica*, 64(1): 51–75.

For quality choices and nonlinear pricing, see the seminal paper on the subject by Mussa, M. and S. Rosen, 1978, "Monopoly and Product Quality," *Journal of Economic Theory*, 18: 301–317.

The problem of stability in tariff-like pricing is discussed in Sorenson, J.R., J.T. Tschirhart and A.B. Whinston, 1978, "A Theory of Pricing under Decreasing Costs," *American Economic Review*, 68(4): 614–624.

Product Differentiation

Horizontal product differentiation was first discussed in Hotelling, H., 1929, "Stability in Competition," *Economic Journal* 39:41-57.

A linear city used by Hotelling assumes that two individuals located at each end are quite different. That might be reasonable in geographical differentiation, although the earth is round. Product characteristics space may be better represented by a circular city model where every consumer finds a similar taste in each direction. For this latter specification, see Perloff, J.M and S.C. Salop, 1985, "Equilibrium with Product Differentiation," *Review of Economic Studies* 52: 107–20.

Hart, O.D., 1979, "Monopolistic Competition in a Large Economy with Differentiated Commodities," *Review of Economic Studies* 46: 1–30, discusses the Chamberlinian model of monopolistic competition.

Price Discrimination

A general introduction of the topic with industry practices is by L. Phlips, 1983, *The Economics of Price Discrimination*, Cambridge: Cambridge University Press.

Lewis, T. and D. Sappington, 1994, "Supplying Information to Facilitate Price Discrimination," *International Economic Review* 35(2): 309–327, examines whether a firm has an incentive to allow consumers to try out its product.

Internet Resources

Customized Internet Products

Personalized news by PointCast Network: http://www.pointcast.com.

Personal Journal (a newspaper) by *The Wall Street Journal*: http://bis.dowjones.com/pj.html.

Personalized, remote shopping by Personal Shoppers: http://www.yourcommand.com.

Privacy on the Internet

Privacy & Anonymity FAQ: Available through anonymous FTP to pit-manager@mit.edu, in the directory /pub/usenet/news.answers/net-privacy/.

Internet Privacy Coalition: http://www.privacy.org/ipc/, whose mission "is to promote privacy and security on the Internet through widespread public availability of strong encryption and the relaxation of export controls on cryptography."

Electronic Privacy Information Center (EPIC): http://epic.org, which is "a public interest research center in Washington, D.C. It was established in 1994 to focus public attention on emerging civil liberties issues and to protect privacy, the First Amendment, and constitutional values."

Electronic Frontier Foundation (EFF): http://www.eff.org, maintains an extensive database of materials related to the privacy issue on the Internet including texts of proposed legislation. These files may be obtained through its web page or via anonymous FTP to ftp.eff.org in the /pub directory.

A 1996 Georgia Tech survey found that many web users are against disclosing their personal information. The survey result is available at http://www.cc.gatech.edu/gvu/user_surveys.

Cookies

For technical specification, see http://www.netscape.com/newsref/std/cookie_spec.html.

JavaScript Tip of the Week: Everything You Ever Wanted to Know about Cookies available at http://webreference.com/javascript/961125/index.html.

"Are Web-Based Cookies a Treat or a Recipe for Trouble?", *PC Week* article, June 26, 1996. Available at http://www.pcweek.com/reviews/0624/24cook.html.

For cookies related sites, visit *Malcom's Guide to Persistent Cookies* resources at http://www.emf.net/~mal/cookiesinfo.html.

Spoofing on the Internet

Princeton research report on spoofing is at http://www.cs.princeton.edu/sip/pub/spoofing.html.

CHAPTER 9

Financial Intermediaries and Electronic Commerce

Playing the devil's advocate, you can ask whether using the Internet to transact financial business will bring about a fundamental change in financial markets and institutions that are already at the forefront of electronic transactions. Banks, for example, already clear their accounts via domestic and international electronic funds transfers (EFTs). Today's security markets also use highly automated account-clearing systems and automated exchanges. The New York Stock Exchange (NYSE, http://www.nyse.com), for instance, has allowed after-hours electronic trading without specialists since 1991, while stock or commodity traders have access to around-the-clock electronic markets through Reuters Holdings' Instinet (http://www.instinet.com) or Jeffries Group's Posit. Although clearly advanced, these technologies are generally limited to business-to-business transactions. Using the Instinet for financial transactions will affect not only the already sophisticated financial institutions but individual consumers and businesses. By expanding the use of electronic technologies to consumers and non-financial institutions, the Internet not only economizes costs but also provides opportunities to reinvent business processes and to develop radically new products and services.

The advent of electronic payment systems and electronic commerce un-doubtedly signal the next stage in the evolution of financial institutions and markets. Technology has changed the banking business and financial-service sector many times in the past by transforming the way people pay for goods and services and the way financial markets are organized and operated. With each new introduction— the telegraph, wire transfers, EFTs, credit cards, and automatic teller machines—financial markets have become more convenient and efficient. It is still too early to predict how electronic commerce will change the financial market's organization and institutional structure. But this chapter provides an analytical framework for evaluating such a question by identifying the roles of financial intermediaries in traditional capital markets, and then examining which aspects of the new technologies of electronic commerce will affect these roles.

Many financial products and services can be digitized and analyzed as digital products. Digital cash—already considered the next "killer application" for electronic commerce—is a digital product whose viability will be determined by market supply and demand. Virtual banks, such as Mark Twain Bank (http://www.marktwain.com), and certification authorities (CAs), such as Verisign (http://www.verisign.com), deal with digital currency and digital certificates, which are poised to compete with traditional financial intermediaries for business. Furthermore, a number of firms are trying to capitalize on the Internet by using the Internet and the web for initial public offerings of their stocks, which are then traded in automated 24-hour stock-trading markets on the net. The Internet is well-suited for this because stocks and other forms of financial claims are excellent examples of products that can be digitized. In sum, although their role is clearly one of a vehicle of change for other businesses entering the electronic market, financial institutions will undergo a transformation as well. This chapter focuses on the effects of this transformation on financial intermediary markets for security and asset brokerage, asset transformation and financial information trading. Chapter 10 follows up by discussing another important function of financial intermediaries: payment-related services.

9.1.   Types of Financial Intermediaries

Chapter 4 introduced in detail the role of the intermediary in the context of quality uncertainty and market efficiency. Financial intermediaries are just one example of intermediaries for digital products, in this case for digital financial and payment services. In many ways, their function is similar to that of other intermediaries outside electronic commerce.

Cable News Network (http://www.cnn.com), for example, serves as an information intermediary, collecting, combining, and selling information products—leveraging the needs of information producers and consumers. More importantly, CNN also acts as a quality guarantor, whereby information buyers are assured by CNN's reputation for the quality of their news. Likewise, firms trading on the NYSE are credible as an investment opportunity, as a news report broadcast on CNN is credible as a source of information. NYSE's member firms are also subject to the exchange's rules and regulations, which engenders confidence among investors in the trading environment and the firms.

Despite the significant role the financial sector plays in our economy (see sidebar, "The Financial Sector"), there is a dire lack of studies dealing with banks, insurance companies, or brokers at the institutional level. To understand how electronic commerce will affect the future of these institutions, you must first investigate their functions and, second, analyze how these functions will change given new technologies and market conditions.

An intermediary is a middleman who facilitates transactions between potential traders. Intermediaries conduct the following activities:

- Match buyers with sellers (broker, see section 9.2, "Transactional Efficiencies")

- Buy goods from sellers and then sell the goods to buyers (retailer, see section 9.2)

- Buy goods and sell them after modifications (transformation, see section 9.3, "Transformation Functions")
- Sell only transaction-related information (information brokerage, see section 9.4, "Information Brokerage")

The first case describes a simple brokerage connecting a buyer with a seller. The more buyers and sellers the more marketable a commodity becomes because the probability of finding a match increases. A corollary to this, however, is the increased difficulty in matching bid and ask prices to complete the trade. For example, it may take longer to contact, inquire and negotiate a deal due to the sheer size of the market. The need for better communication between sellers and buyers prompted the organization of exchange markets at a central location, such as commodity trading markets or stock exchanges. In this brokerage function, the commission paid to a broker reflects the cost of the intermediary's search.

Commercial banks and a large group of financial institutions handling payment clearing services are the primary players in capital markets, although we usually distinguish them from securities exchange market players. Payment service intermediaries go between a payer and a payee and act as account settlers, which can be characterized as the first type of intermediaries. In this sense, deposit-taking banks, payment clearing houses, and credit card services are broker-type intermediaries.

In the second case, the intermediary becomes an owner-seller instead of a simple matchmaker. Although a consignment store is a broker of the first type, most retail stores fall under this second category. Take the historical example of a Venetian trader, whose ship load of Eastern goods would be a loss to him, not to Asian sellers, if his ship were to sink. Compared to a brokerage situation in which sellers need to interact with buyers to negotiate a sale or contract (albeit via an intermediary), in the retail scenario, the intermediary needs to be most concerned with the ultimate buyers of the goods because the intermediary's profits originate from the spread between the bid (of the buyers) and ask (of the sellers) prices in the market. This spread is often made possible by the intermediary's economies of scale in information gathering, processing and monitoring or from the law of large numbers—the ability to pool and spread risks. This second case is more akin to *dealers* than *brokers*. Traditionally, stock brokers are distinguished from stock dealers in that brokers only match sellers with buyers whereas dealers purchase stocks from sellers and sell them to buyers. However, both share a primary function: to smooth out search and transaction processes among traders.

You can consider the third example of an intermediary a *value-added retailer* who goes beyond simple brokeraging or distributing goods. A mutual-fund manager who sells a share of a fund of combined products from different producers is an intermediary of the third type because what buyers buy is different from what sellers sell to the fund manager. This intermediary's function involves some type of transformation in the characteristics of the product. For example, a bank receives deposits from savers and makes loans to borrowers. Thus, a bank is not only a dealer but also changes the nature of the purchased product—deposits—into a different kind of financial product—a loan.

Finally, intermediaries can function as market information service providers. Their collection of company performance data, macroeconomic indicators, stock quotes, and so on, facilitates financial transactions. Stock brokers, on top of their brokerage functions, often make buy and sell recommendations to their customers based on their own information and analysis. In this case, they are performing two different functions of an intermediary. Publishers of financial newspapers and newsletters, financial cable networks, and online business information services are specialized information sellers and do not deal directly with financial assets. In the electronic market as well, the information function of collecting, evaluating and monitoring agents may or may not be tied to trading of digital financial instruments.

The remaining sections revisit each of the functions of financial intermediaries to show more clearly how the introduction of Internet-based commerce affects each intermediary function.

The Financial Sector

Financial markets play a key role in an economy by channeling necessary funds from savers to borrowers who are looking to invest in productive activities. Not surprisingly, the market and operational efficiencies of financial markets have long-term effects that determine the levels of future production and consumption. In fact, the financial intermediation sector alone accounts for over 15 percent of the gross national production in the United States. Table 9.1 shows the amount of national income generated by industry in 1996. The amount contributed by the financial sector is greater than that of the wholesale and retail trades combined and it is second only to the service industry in sectoral importance to the national economy.

Table 9.1 National Income by Industry

Industry	Billions of Dollars
Agriculture, forestry, and fishing	121.8
Mining	45.2
Construction	284.0
Manufacturing—durable goods	637.0
Manufacturing—non-durable goods	444.4
Transportation and public utilities	477.6
Wholesale trade	351.4
Retail trade	510.7
Finance, insurance and real estate	1,047.5
Services	1,458.3
Government	846.8
Total domestic	6,224.7

Source: Survey of Current Business, February 1997, Table 6.1C. Figures are for the third quarter, 1996, adjusted at annual rates.

9.2. Transactional Efficiencies

The spread of automated financial transactions conducted over the Internet will change the technologically less efficient traditional brokerage functions of financial intermediation. It is no coincidence that Charles Schwab & Co., for example, is pushing for online ordering and payment for stocks and mutual funds. Already, 20 percent of its business is conducted online and this figure is projected to grow steadily over the next few years. However, electronic markets imply more than mere automated ordering systems. A market not only provides a meeting place for sellers and buyers but also performs other economic roles, such as price setting, payment and delivery. Electronic commerce offers the potential for efficiency gains in each of these transactional phases.

Phases of Transaction

The transaction of matching buyers and sellers, which financial intermediaries facilitate, can be broken down into the following market interaction processes:

- Search
- Negotiation
- Settlement

These processes are much like the processes of visiting a store, negotiating for a price and purchasing an item. As in consumer searches, these processes may proceed sequentially until a transaction is settled or may be conducted simultaneously through a bidding or auction mechanism.

Efficiency in Search Process

As the first step in the brokerage function, potential traders need to search for and identify trading partners in the initial search phase. After potential partners express interest, a negotiation phase follows between sellers and buyers regarding prices and product specifications. If they reach agreement, traders enter into the third stage—settlement—which includes contracting, payment settlement, and delivery.

Of these three phases, the search and settlement processes can be automated without much difficulty. The negotiation process, on the other hand, may require some intermediary intervention or a sophisticated automated program to execute. Because of this, fewer examples of increased market efficiency are seen in this phase.

In the search phase of intermediation, market efficiency increases if the time it takes to find someone with matching goods and needs is decreased. In physical markets, an intermediary achieves this by transporting goods from one place to another so that geographically distant sellers and buyers are matched. A financial intermediary—a middleman, in essence—collects selling and buying information (that is, bid and ask prices) and proceeds to find a match. When the size of the market is large, as it is in electronic commerce, it becomes increasingly time-consuming for a seller to meet all potential buyers or vice versa. The trading floors in stock exchange markets, for example, are fundamentally central locations where all interested traders gather to minimize search costs.

Within the large body of economic literature focusing on search costs (see discussions in Chapters 4 and 7), Rubinstein and Wolinsky (1987) offer a useful comparison between a broker and a dealer, even though their model is not set up for financial markets. Their economic model is based on an intermediary as a time-saving institution. The transaction cost incurred by potential traders in their model is the waiting time needed to find a trader with matching needs or products. A middleman in such a market may act either as a dealer or a broker, that is, he may either buy a good from a seller and offer it to another buyer or he may simply obtain the product on consignment, paying the seller only upon completing the sale.

The extent to which a middleman improves search efficiency for buyers and sellers depends on how quickly a buyer and a seller find each other. Rubinstein and Wolinsky's research determined interesting differential effects of brokers and dealers on the gains of sellers versus buyers. They found that when the middleman is a broker, that is, a consignment intermediary, the gains to sellers and buyers are symmetric. In other words, the broker does not worry about the seller's profit from the final sale price, but focuses on finding a match. But if the middleman is a dealer, the buyer gains more from the trade than does the seller because the middleman's bargaining position is worsened by his incentive to unload the product. The dealer has a sunk cost (the purchase price), which becomes a factor in negotiating with potential buyers. A simple brokerage method results in less distortion as a market clearing system than a dealer's market does.

One example of an efficient trading mechanism in which the electronic network acts as a broker is an automated electronic bulletin board. Regardless of the difference between a broker and a dealer, the middleman's profit comes from his ability to shorten the time and cost in finding a match. In an electronic bulletin board, sellers and buyers still have to read or search all offers listed, incurring considerable costs. But an intelligent software program may be used to search and find interesting offers. Similarly, middlemen are involved in trading places for cattle, produce, commodities, stocks, and various products, where the marketplace or the trading floor may be considered as a middleman for middlemen (see fig. 9.1). While middlemen representing sellers and buyers are engaged in searches, the meeting place provides a forum for negotiation and settlement.

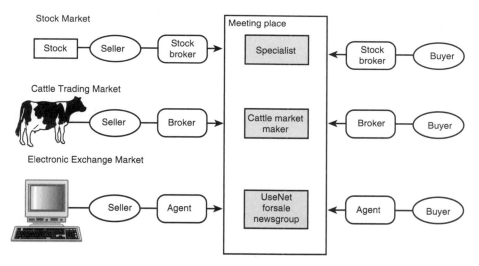

Figure 9.1 Brokered markets.

Negotiation and Settlement Processes

The meeting place, or market, is where prices are discovered and sales are made through negotiation. At one extreme, trades may be based on take-it-or-leave-it offers with posted prices. Shopping at retail stores usually involves posted prices. At the other extreme, prices may be settled after exhaustive bargaining.

Most price-discovery processes incorporate both methods: an item is offered for a price or *best offer*.

Stock markets also utilize a structured bargaining process in which negotiation proceeds with posted prices that are raised or lowered depending on supply and demand. Ascending and descending price auctions are similarly structured so as to adjust posted prices. This structured bargaining process lends itself to easy automation. Computerized exchange markets in electronic commerce can therefore integrate search and brokerage functions with the price discovery process, and settle accounts through electronic messaging and payment systems.

Although the electronic market offers clear opportunities for more efficient search and settlement processes, automating the negotiation process poses more difficulties. To incorporate the negotiation process into automated trading mechanisms, each offer or bid has to contain extended specifications, such as predefined price limits, volume and time, and the market has to provide coordination and clearing mechanisms. Automated negotiation often necessitates an elaborate process, such as an electronic auction, which requires the continuous participation of all parties at the same time. Although technically feasible, the difficulties involved hamper its more widespread use.

Financial Intermediaries: Electronic Market Case Studies

The following sections present two examples of using the Internet in lieu of existing financial markets: initial public offerings (IPOs) on the Internet and computerized exchange markets. These examples demonstrate how easy it is to convert transactional aspects of capital markets into electronic markets. These developments will not have a significant impact on existing financial markets in the short run. But they are significant in pointing out the role of investment firms, underwriters and stock brokers as artificial gatekeepers to the exchange markets, from which they derive their income. As transaction costs decrease via automated trading, simple brokerage (that is, executing buy or sell orders on behalf of customers) will no longer provide a significant source of income.

Internet Initial Public Offerings

Financial service firms channel funds from savers to borrowers by selling financial instruments, also known as securities. These instruments consist of primary securities issued by borrowers, often in large denominations, and secondary securities issued by intermediaries such as commercial banks, savings banks, savings and loans, insurance companies, mutual funds, and so on, in more accessible smaller denominations. Stocks and bonds are primary securities when issued for the first time in initial public offerings (IPOs), considered a primary market. These securities can then be traded in the secondary market, where stocks may be sold and bought. In this way, IPOs are like new products whereas the stocks traded on stock exchanges are like used goods.

Companies offer IPOs to raise capital for their business projects. Traditionally, an underwriter, such as an investment bank, determines share prices, handles the printing and distribution of prospectuses, and arranges the sale of stocks to large institutional investors and brokerage firms. They, in turn, sell the stocks to individual investors.

Recently, using the Internet for capitalization has become not only viable but fashionable. In 1995, Spring Street Brewing Company, a microbrewery in New York, offered the first Internet IPO, raising $1.6 million from 3,500 shareholders without using Wall Street underwriters. Its offerings were open to all potential buyers without the need to rely on brokers or to pay commissions. By bypassing underwriters and brokers, the firm and individual investors can trade capital assets at a lower cost. Since its first Internet IPO, Spring Street Brewery has formed an online investment and brokerage firm, Wit Capital Corporation (see fig. 9.2; http://www.witcap.com), to promote Internet IPOs and subsequent public trading of stocks in secondary markets. A growing list of Internet IPO firms includes Internet Capital Exchange (http://www.inetcapital.com) and Web IPO—Capital Formation Group (http://www.webipo.com).

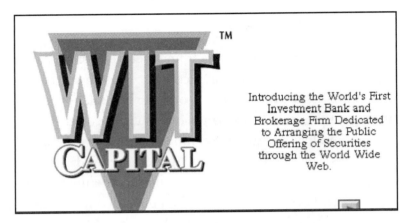

Figure 9.2 Wit Capital home page.

Internet IPOs' main selling point has been cost reduction. Wit Capital, for example, claims to eliminate layers of intermediaries who increase transaction costs through commissions and inefficient operation costs. Ultimately, however, qualitative efficiency gains will be more important to the success of Internet financial-service firms.

Traditionally, financial brokers' access to investment information makes them better equipped than their clients to analyze the value of IPOs, thereby reducing the buyer's quality uncertainty. In the Internet environment, as well, investors need to be convinced that their access to financial information is complete and that the information is accurate. Although it is easy to convince investors of the Internet's transactional efficiency, it is a different matter to convince them of the quality of service, risk evaluation, and the ultimate performance of their investment, or profits.

Although the need for information efficiency and quality uncertainty may make many investors cautious, this does not imply that Internet capital firms will have no substantial advantage over traditional underwriters and brokerage firms. Consumers who have access to complete and up-to-date information about investment projects may be more willing to forego brokerage services and turn to Internet markets. Furthermore, as access increases informational content and computational programs to evaluate the content, consumers will need to rely less on brokers.

The long-term effects on financial service intermediaries of open electronic markets are not clear. However, in terms of the transactional functions of financial intermediaries, using the World Wide Web to search for information may become a model for seeking investment opportunities and potential investors—eliminating any qualitative difference between the NYSE and electronic markets on the Internet. Online brokerage firms are fighting to lower processing costs and commission rates, but, ultimately, their functions will be replaced by more efficient computer programs and electronic markets. Nevertheless, stock brokers will survive by unbundling other service activities, which are discussed in sections 9.3 and 9.4.

Digital Exchange Markets

Internet IPOs, as discussed, are an example of primary markets for securities where borrowers (companies) sell claims to their assets directly to buyers. Secondary markets for securities then develop where all non-IPO securities or bond issues are traded without the involvement of the original seller or the issuer. A major incentive to open secondary markets, such as NYSE, is to provide liquidity to asset holders. Securities represent frozen money holdings and need to be converted into money, that is, sold, if one needs access to ready cash. Holders of an equity or a financial instrument that is not traded suffer from a liquidity problem. Therefore, Internet financial-service firms tend to offer both Internet IPOs and subsequent trading in secondary exchange markets to accommodate consumers' need for liquidity. Wit Capital Corporation and Internet Capital Exchange, for example, operate web-based digital exchange markets.

Online sale of securities has existed for many years, but Internet exchange markets differ considerably from computerized exchange systems. Internet exchange markets offer an opportunity to organize new capital markets from the ground up, whereas online brokerage services offer outlets of computerized trading systems owned and operated by such exchanges as NYSE or the National Association of Securities Dealers Average Quotient (NASDAQ; http://www.nasdaq.com).

Using screen terminals connected worldwide, investors' online access has steadily increased over the years. Instinet (http://www.instinet.com) has conducted real-time stock trading since 1969. Similarly, NYSE uses its SuperDOT system to clear members' sell and buy orders electronically before it opens for trading each day. Since 1991, the Big Board also has phased in for its members an after-hours, fully electronic trading period between 4:15 and 5 p.m. And, in 1993, the New York Mercantile Exchange (NYMEX) and AT&T introduced NYMEX ACCESS, an electronic after-hours options and futures trading system. Despite these improvements, access to these automated exchange systems remains limited to professionals and brokers. Access to Instinet, for example, is limited to such security professionals as institutional fund managers, brokers, dealers, and exchange specialists who, in turn, take orders from individual investors.

Individual investors can buy and sell without a broker through private online trading houses, such as Datek Securities Corp., which provides access to NASDAQ's computerized Small Order Execution System or NYSE's SuperDOT system. Nevertheless, these systems still rely on brokers' terminals being linked to the computerized exchange systems of NYSE or NASDAQ, and investors must pay commissions. Many Internet brokerages, such as e.Schwab of Charles Schwab (http://www.schwab.com) or E*Trade online brokerage of E*Trade Group (http://www.etrade.com), further extend access to such computerized trading systems by allowing investors to use the web instead of dedicated terminals owned by brokers. But the commissions paid to the online trading houses remain substantial, ranging from $20 to $40 per trade. More importantly, no significant change occurs in the structure of the exchange markets, which are essentially broker-organized marketplaces that centralize the trading and settlements of payments.

In comparison, a computerized exchange market on the Internet has the potential to change capital markets in a fundamental way. First, because exchange markets and brokerage firms traditionally act as coordinating mechanisms for market clearing, their role must change when a computer exchange takes over coordinating buyers and sellers. Second, as capital markets expand to include a wide range of investors and borrowers, new types of financial instruments and capital markets may evolve that combine equities, various financial derivatives, and bond and commodity trading markets in one seamless capital market.

Market clearing is mediated by brokers and dealers instead of relying on prices that reflect the demand and supply of financial assets. The possibility of influencing prices in a brokered market often means higher profits for brokers. For example, brokers and dealers artificially intervene as market makers and specialists, often widening the spread between bid and ask prices irrespective of market conditions (Morgenson, 1996). The Securities and Exchange Commission reprimanded NASDAQ in August, 1996 for failing to police its brokerage firms, which used secret trading agreements to suppress competitive effects on stock prices. An Internet-based exchange market will not only automate ordering and settlement clearing procedures, as traditional exchange markets have done, but will also rely on technologies to automate the price discovery process, in which all market participants observe true prices.

Internet-based exchange markets for capital assets are a long way from becoming a full-fledged alternative to existing capital markets. In terms of technology, it is often said that the real-life market process is hard to program even with a super-computer and that electronic commerce may be unable to perform the intricate tasks of brokers observed on the floor of exchanges. However, the behavior of brokers often adds noise to the market clearing process instead of facilitating it. For example, price movements based on broker-initiated spreads do not reflect a true market condition. In an ideal market, demand and supply alone should determine prices. Automating transactions eliminates this noise. Such an automated auction market sells computers and software on the Internet; Onsale.com (http://www.onsale.com) holds auctions to sell the computers online. Usually, multiple units of each item are available for sale and the auction floor—the web screen (see fig. 9.3)—shows all bidders with their bids. Despite technologies being tested and improved, however, it is still argued that investors, because of institutional inertia, will stay with established markets such as the NYSE; this, in turn, will reinforce the advantage of size in the entrenched market, offering traders the greatest liquidity for their assets. Although this may be true, if Internet capital markets become accepted by traders, the liquidity of the electronic market will increase correspondingly.

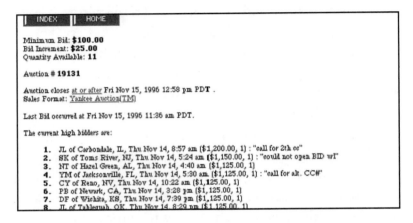

Figure 9.3 Onsale.com auction page.

9.3. Transformation Functions

Brokerage is not the only intermediation a financial intermediary can adopt to increase market efficiency. Just as finding a suitable trader imposes costs, products that do not match the needs of buyers and sellers become a source of market friction and failure. An intermediary then may transform assets purchased from sellers to better accommodate the needs of buyers. This, obviously, involves more than buying a product from a seller and selling it to a buyer as a dealer would do, as discussed earlier. Financial intermediaries perform these transformations of assets in two ways: in terms of maturity and volume.

Maturity Transformation

Holders of financial assets have differing degrees of liquidity preference. Some savers may anticipate expenses in six months or a year and hold cash balances or keep their money in short-term instruments. Those saving for retirement, on the other hand, have a longer investment horizon, allowing banks or fund managers to invest in long-term bonds or investment projects. Borrowers often have a longer time-horizon than do lenders.

Without the use of an intermediary, borrowers would have to deal with many short-term lenders to finance a project. In this case, the firm would incur higher transaction costs or may have to pay higher interest rates to obtain longer-term lending. Financial intermediaries who accept short-term deposits and make loans on a long-term basis can thus accommodate lenders and borrowers with different maturity preferences.

As of now, automated transaction systems cannot perform transformational intermediation. However, electronic markets will economize transactional efficiency of financial intermediation and also will highlight where the advantages of traditional institutions lie.

Volume Transformation

Similar to maturity transformation, financial intermediaries match the different needs of lenders and borrowers in terms of volume. For example, banks collect funds from small-scale depositors and combine them to lend larger sums. Otherwise, the borrower would again have to locate and negotiate with individual lenders to acquire the necessary amount of capital. Furthermore, matching a number of lenders with a single borrower would involve more than a brokerage function because individual lenders have different preferences for liquidity. Thus, an intermediary smoothes out the differences in volume and maturity of available funds.

Electronic Commerce Effects

Although transforming the maturity and volume of available funds is an important aspect of financial intermediation, scant literature exists on which to base an analysis regarding the future of financial institutions. Nevertheless, a basic conclusion is that transformation functions are one of the strengths of traditional deposit-taking banks, whose electronic commerce strategy may be to augment this advantage. The entry into home-banking by software producers such as Intuit (http://www.intuit.com) or Microsoft (http://www.microsoft.com) will have a significant effect in diverting the customer base of traditional banks. However, while the entry represents an erosion in the banks' power as gatekeepers to financial products, it also challenges banks to be more creative and flexible in developing and providing new financial services to accommodate the diverse needs of consumers and investors.

9.4.   Information Brokerage

The information function of financial intermediaries refers to the sale of information to prospective traders of financial assets. Capital markets are information driven and, accordingly, the economic literature on financial markets and institutions emphasizes information asymmetry between lenders and borrowers as the primary factor necessitating an intermediary. Often lenders have no adequate means to monitor or verify the investment activities of borrowers. Thus, risk-averse lenders may be unwilling to participate in capital markets. An intermediary offers a way to share or reduce the risks inherent to individual lenders by monitoring borrowers.

Information Uncertainty and Risk

Intermediaries are typically more efficient at monitoring borrowers because they can access more information and process the information more efficiently, and because they can reduce monitoring costs by exploiting the scale of operation. For example, to be well informed, a trader may subscribe to various newspapers, newsletters and databases. Subscription costs do not increase with the amount of funds a trader handles. Therefore, the per-transaction cost of information decreases as the scale of operation increases. Furthermore, the efficiency in processing this information may increase over time as the trader accumulates knowledge and expertise.

Even more importantly, an intermediary may spread the risk inherent in uncertain projects by diversifying its portfolio. Diamond (1984) studies such a case in which lenders contract with a risk-neutral intermediary. The fundamental reason for increased efficiency through an intermediary in this case is the law of large numbers. As the number of uncertain investment projects, that is, borrowers, increases, a form of portfolio diversification occurs. In contrast, individual investors risk a total loss when a one-project portfolio folds. Similarly, in Boyd and Prescott (1986) and Williamson (1987), financial intermediaries arise to economize the costs of acquiring information through an intermediary.

This situation is completely reversed in open electronic markets. In automated trading systems, traders bypass risk-sharing intermediaries. Thus, instead of relying on the law of large numbers, traders must resolve the uncertainty by acquiring more and better information. For this reason, you can anticipate seeing more active participation from specialized information sellers in electronic commerce.

Information Trading

Information can be key to financial intermediaries in more ways than one. Some financial intermediaries restrict their operations to selling investment information in the form of newsletters. Brokers and other intermediaries are opening new business units to utilize their advantage in information access and processing. For example, Merrill Lynch & Co. plans to organize its online business as an information and financial service provider by offering online investment information as well as related services, such as stock quotes and online statements. Numerous other news organizations and information dealers have already staked out their web storefronts, reflecting the perception that the Internet is truly a marketplace for information.

In choosing which method to use, a seller of information must consider the effects of externality: the more people know about the information, the more diminished its value. Admati and Pfleiderer (1986, 1990) distinguish between direct and indirect methods of selling financial information under externality. Direct sale refers to the unconditional selling of information to buyers. For example, subscribers to newsletters purchase unrestricted use of the information for any investment purpose. An indirect sale of financial information refers to a case in which a stock dealer presents buyers with a choice of stocks to buy. Buyers do not observe the information, but only the stocks chosen on the basis of the information.

In the case of direct sale, buyers use the information to maximize their gains from trading; the information is revealed in the market price or price movement. Admati and Pfleiderer (1986) show that a direct seller of information can increase profits or restrict the use of information by adding noise, that is, selling slightly less precise information. In the case of severe externality, an even more effective method to control information usage is through an indirect sale rather than through a direct sale with added noise or restricted subscribership because these inevitably still transmit some information to those who observe market prices (Admati and Pfleiderer, 1990).

An indirect sale of information couples the sale of information with the sale of securities, which has traditionally been practiced by brokers and dealers. If the coupling of information with securities is not possible, specialized information sellers have to rely on other methods to control the use of information by their clients. In the past, financial intermediaries have produced, collected, and disseminated the largest amount of information. However, their control over information is waning as fast as the Internet is growing. Soon, individual investors will have the same access to up-to-date and complete information as only brokers used to have. An example is the online availability of the Securities Exchange Commission's Electronic Data Gathering, Analysis, and Retrieval (EDGAR).

The Securities and Exchange Commission (http://www.sec.gov) requires public companies to file information that it must make available to the public. The SEC defines EDGAR (http://www.sec.gov/edgarhp.htm), shown in figure 9.4, as a system that performs automated collection, validation, indexing, acceptance, and forwarding of submissions by companies. Its purpose is to increase the efficiency and to ensure the fairness of the securities market by making time-sensitive corporate information available to investors. The type of information found on EDGAR includes annual reports (Form 10K), quarterly reports (Form 10Q), proxy statements (annual reports to shareholders) and other reports voluntarily filed by companies. Since the SEC has phased in electronic filing of required forms, retrieval and search by individuals has become immediate, convenient, and cost-effective.

A question immediately arises: how can information sellers make profits when investors have convenient access to primary sources of information? One way is to focus on processing the information; that is, the information sellers filter available information and present it in a form customers find useful. In the age of information overload, the amount of information is no longer as important as the effective filtering and selection of relevant information (see section 7.5 for information filtering).

The problem of externality remains, however. In general, the information seller has to limit subscribership. Even with limited subscribership, the window of opportunity for an information seller may be small because market prices tend to reflect the information investors have and others who simply observe prices can deduce the content of the information. In short, information trading does not add much value when the information infrastructure and market is as efficient as in electronic commerce. To control the use of information and to extract the most surplus from consumers requires bundling information services with other financial services, as shown in Chapter 8.

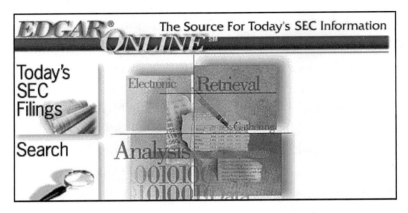

Figure 9.4 EDGAR Online home page.

Certification and Assurance

Although information is clearly disseminated more efficiently in electronic commerce, this efficiency does not increase the reliability of the information. Unreliable information about borrowers and investment projects, even when obtained efficiently, is still unreliable. The problem is compounded because of the nature of digital communication, in which no established means of online verification is available. Information provided on a web page may be as reliable and authentic as it is bogus. Even establishing the identity of a seller or a buyer requires an elaborate procedure. In the future, e-mail addresses may become as easily identifiable as a postal address or a phone number, or online transactions may be conducted via video phones with digitized driver's licenses. Until then, temporary solutions are offered by new types of financial intermediaries, called certification authorities, which are appearing to address the verification problems peculiar to electronic commerce.

A *certification authority* (CA) is a public or private entity that issues digital certificates to be used by sellers and buyers to authenticate identities and messages, or to attest that a deed has occurred. In physical markets, checking an ID or a signature is usually enough to establish identity and trust among traders. However, in an electronic market, where face-to-face interactions are replaced by electronic messages, even the identity of an e-mail sender cannot be easily verified. A CA, therefore, acts as a trusted third party who issues digital IDs and other certificates that use strong encryption technologies to prevent tampering (see the following sidebar, "Types of Digital Certificates").

Types of Digital Certificates

Froomkin (1997) identifies the following four types of certificates likely to be issued by CAs:

Identifying Certificates Identifying certificates, or digital IDs, attest to the identity of a person. A leading provider of digital IDs is VeriSign, Inc. (http://www.verisign.com), a spin-off of the encryption technology firm RSA Data Security, Inc. (http://www.rsa.com). VeriSign offers different levels of digital IDs, ranging from Class 1 identifying certificates, which verify only the uniqueness of a name or e-mail address without contacting the person, to Class 4 indentifying certificates, which are issued after VeriSign investigates the person thoroughly and personally.

Authorizing Certificates Whereas an identifying certificate connects a person with a name, authorizing certificates verify attributes of a person other than the identity. Such attributes may include the age of a person, whether the person is a citizen of the U.S. or belongs to a certain membership group, or whether the person owns a car or other products. An example of using authorizing certificates is when adult-only materials are sold to those who present "over-18" certificates. Although the same goal might be achieved via an identifying certificate, authorizing certificates maintain the anonymity of the buyer.

Transactional Certificates Transactional certificates attest that a certain fact or incident has occurred and been witnessed by the attester. For example, when an e-mail is to be certified, a CA may attached a digital signature verifying that the e-mail was indeed sent by the person. This is most akin to the certification provided by public notary services.

Time-Stamping Services If it is important to show not only that something took place but also when, a time stamp can be added to a document based on its hash value (see sidebar, "Cryptography and Electronic Commerce"). By linking the unique hash value of a document with a published hash value (for example, in *The New York Times*), it can be verified not only whether the document was modified but also when.

The reliability of digital certificates depends heavily on the strength of the cryptographic technologies employed, which is why VeriSign is a natural extension of RSA Data Security's cryptographic business. In general, public key encryption and digest function (see sidebar, "Cryptography and Electronic Commerce") are two important technologies that enable digital signatures and time stamping.

As far as identification is concerned, commercial certification services may have a disadvantage compared to established businesses and government agencies that are already engaged in some type of identification function—issuing and assigning for Social Security, sales tax permits, driver's licenses, postal addresses, phone numbers, and so on. After various ID systems are digitized in a way to give these entities some advantage, private certification services may focus on non-identification functions such as transactional certificates and time stamping.

Cryptography and Electronic Commerce

An *encrypted* message is a plain-text document that is scrambled to keep its contents secret. An *encryption scheme* scrambles the text; a *decryption scheme* unscrambles an encrypted text. Encryption schemes are typically based on mathematical algorithms and keys. For example, suppose you replace every letter in a document with the letter that comes three places after it in the alphabet; for example, replace "A" with "D," "B" with "E," and so on. "Replacing with another letter" is your *encryption algorithm* and the number "three" is your *encryption key*. Julius Caesar reportedly first used this algorithm and key more than 2,000 years ago. The same encryption algorithm may have different keys, for example, the key of "four" means that you replace "A" with "E" instead of "D."

Encryption schemes can be divided into two classes: secret key and public key. *Secret key* schemes depend on securing the secrecy of the key used to encrypt and decrypt a message. There are many problems with this scheme, the main one being if the key is discovered. In this case, there is a key exchange problem because new keys must be relayed securely every time keys are changed. *Public key* schemes, on the other hand, use one key to encrypt (a public key), which is published or given out freely, and another to decrypt (a private key), which is kept secret. These two keys are mathematically related to an encryption algorithm, and a message encrypted by a public key must be decrypted by its associated private key, and vice versa.

The public key system is quite simple to implement. Suppose Alice and Bob want to communicate securely. Both publish their public keys, keeping their private keys secret. When Alice wants to send a secret message to Bob, she uses Bob's public key to encrypt, which only he can decrypt with his private key. To prove that the message did indeed come from Alice, she can reverse the process by encrypting her message using her private key. Bob can then decrypt Alice's message using her public key and he knows that it could have come from Alice and no one else. This latter example captures the essence of how public key encryption can be used as a digital signature.

Digital signatures can be used not only to identify the sender but also to authenticate the content of a document when used with digest functions. A digest function, also known as a one-way *hash value*, is an arithmetic number that describes a document. Suppose Alice adds up all the 1s in her digital document that consists of 1s and 0s, and generates a certain value. Mathematically, you can manipulate this number so as to make it impossible to alter a document and come up with the same hash value. Alice can then encrypt the hash value with her private key, attach it to the document and send it to Bob. Bob can verify whether the document was altered in transit by re-computing the hash value of the document and comparing it with the encrypted hash value. Encrypted hash values are used when it is time-consuming and expensive to encrypt the whole message. Instead, the encrypted hash value and signature can be transmitted for verification purposes.

To authenticate not only the content of a document but the time it was created, Alice may send the message via a trusted third party, say Charlie, who adds a unique and essentially unforgettable time stamp and digitally signs the document. The time stamp is based on a number Charlie generates using several documents sent to him for time stamping. For example, by adding the hash values of two previous messages sent to him by people unknown to Alice, all documents sent via Charlie have a unique time stamp that can be verified by looking at Charlie's log of entries. To alter the time stamp, you would first have to find the two previous messages.

Whether CAs provide reliable services will depend on how willingly their certificates are accepted in the marketplace, because the information provided by a certificate is as valid as the trustworthiness of the issuing CA. It is understood that, prior to issuing a certificate, the CA investigates the subject in question. But what happens when a person with a certificate issued by a CA turns out to not be the person he claims to be? This question of CAs' or certificate carriers' liability in such cases is just one of a number of legal issues being researched and developed. As Froomkin (1997) argues, a certificate can be considered either as representing an investigative service or simply a document—a good—or both. Depending on the interpretation, different sets of commercial liability laws apply.

Two basic systems can be developed to implement the requisite network of trust needed for certification schemes: a hierarchical structure of certifying authorities, and a market-oriented trust infrastructure. In the hierarchical model, one CA is certified by another CA, and so on. This system may ultimately be backed by trusted government agencies or public corporations. One drawback is that its structure can be unnecessarily complex without a clear delineation of responsibility, not to mention redundancy (see Rivest and Lampson, 1996 for decentralized scheme). In a market-oriented trust infrastructure, on the other hand, the acceptability of a CA depends on its market reputation among consumers. Already, a healthy competition among established industry players is beginning to emerge. In addition to VeriSign, the U.S. Postal Service plans to begin stamping e-mail, digitally signing it and delivering it on the Internet at a cost of 22 cents for a document of 50 KB or less. They also will offer a wide variety of authentication and verification functions for e-mail that are currently standards for conventional mail service.

In comparison to certification authorities, assurance services are concerned with not only the information's authenticity but also its relevancy. Information technology has brought a seemingly unlimited amount of information to consumers—as the popular press describes it, the age of "information overload." As a consequence, the burden of processing information shifts from the seller to the buyer, who must analyze and select the information relevant to his decision making. Therefore, improving the quality of information means not only searching and retrieving relevant information but also processing and selecting this information based on information profiles or a user's predetermined needs. Such tasks this can be achieved through the use of intelligent software agents or human intermediaries (see section 7.5 for software agents). An intermediary or a business that deals with processing information is called an *assurance service provider*.

One example of assurance service geared toward analyzing and improving the quality of information is the effort by the American Institute of Certified Public Accountants (AICPA). AICPA defines its new area of assurance services as:

"CPA services that improve the quality of information or its context for decision-makers through the application of independent professional judgment."

This may entail the development of intelligent agents or computer programs using existing decision-making algorithms or engaging in contractual and consulting services to design and train software agents, assess the quality of information, and interpret and summarize information for clients. In both cases, the subject is no longer the amount of accessible information but the quality and the level of usefulness of increasingly overloaded information. Whether human-oriented assurance services or computer-based intelligent agents will dominate information-processing markets is anybody's guess. But the complexity of analyzing data may favor specialized and flexible human intermediaries.

9.5. Summary

Of all the functions financial intermediaries perform—transactional, transformational, and informational—transactional functions relating to market-making activities will be affected most by the emerging computerized markets. This will occur as increasingly more efficient processes of finding opportunities to trade and matching buyers and sellers are demanded. On the other hand, transformational functions will be the least affected by the increasing use of the Internet for trading capital assets. The need for product transformation will persist separate from the revolutionary changes in how transactions are organized. As such, existing financial institutions have a tremendous advantage in terms of experience and expertise over newer entries in electronic commerce. However, it is not clear how existing intermediaries will adapt their services and products to maximize this advantage.

As transactional functions undergo substantial changes with the advent of automated exchange markets, financial intermediaries may specialize in informational functions to maximize their comparative advantage in information acquisition and analysis. Examples of information intermediaries who deal only with the qualitative aspects of information are financial certification authorities and assurance services. These Internet-native intermediaries pose a new threat to existing financial institutions by specializing in certain aspects of the market. Nevertheless, an information seller still needs to combine his expertise in information with transactional aspects of the market. Otherwise, the value accruing to the intermediary will decrease as the information market becomes more efficient and the profit-making margin shrinks. Selling capital market information, therefore, is often optimized when the information is combined with the assets (for example, a stock portfolio), whereby the information is sold only indirectly. In a way, this indirect sale of information affords intermediaries more market power, and discourages them from specializing in only one type of service in financial services.

One economic function of a financial intermediary—its allocative efficiency—has not received much attention. An intermediary as a market institution is traditionally evaluated in terms of transaction costs. In that sense, the predominant concern in "virtual" financial services has been that of controlling and reducing operating costs. Allocative efficiency, on the other hand, deals with whether available financial assets are distributed or allocated adequately based on the risk and financial potential of borrowers' projects. When the market is inefficient, credit rationing, that is, allocating funds without regard to the profitability of each project, is observed (Stiglitz and Weiss, 1981). While the effect of network technology on operational efficiency is an important factor in assessing the profitability of online financial services, it is still unknown how online financial intermediaries will affect the way financial resources are allocated. This may well be a future direction of economic studies.

References

Admati, A.R., and P. Pfleiderer, 1986. "A Monopolistic Market for Information." *Journal of Economic Theory*, 39: 400–438.

"Direct and Indirect Sale of Information." 1990. *Econometrica*, 58(4): 901–928.

AICPA, 1995. Report by AICPA Special Committee on Assurance Services.

Boyd, J.H., and E.C. Prescott, 1986. "Financial Intermediary-Coalitions." *Journal of Economic Theory*, 38: 211–232.

Diamond, D., 1984. "Financial Intermediation and Delegated Monitoring." *Review of Economic Studies*, 51: 393–414.

Froomkin, A.M., 1997. "The Essential Role of Trusted Third Parties in Electronic Commerce." In Kalakota, R., and A. Whinston, eds., *Readings in Electronic Commerce*. Reading, Mass.: Addison-Wesley.

Kalakota, R., and A. Whinston, 1997. *Electronic Commerce: A Manager's Guide*. Reading, Mass.: Addison-Wesley.

Morgenson, G. 1996. *One Day Soon the Music's Going to Stop*. Available at http:// www.inetcapital.com/ music2.htm.

Rivest, R.L., and B. Lampson, 1996. *SDSI—A Simple Distributed Security Infrastructure*. Available at http://theory.lcs.mit.edu/~rivest/sdsi10.html.

Rubinstein, A., and A. Wolinsky, 1987. "Middlemen." *Quarterly Journal of Economics*, 102: 581–593.

Stiglitz, J., and A. Weiss, 1981. "Credit Rationing in Markets with Imperfect Information." *American Economic Review*, 70: 393–410.

Williamson, S.D., 1987. "Recent Developments in Modeling Financial Intermediation." Federal Reserve Bank of Minneapolis, *Quarterly Review*, Summer 1987.

Suggested Readings and Notes

Financial Intermediation and Credit Rationing

In addition to Boyd and Prescott, 1986, and Williamson, S.D., 1987:

Blinder, A., and J. Stiglitz, 1983. "Money, Credit Constraints, and Economic Activity." *American Economic Review*, May.

Campbell, T., and W. Kracaw, 1980. "Information Production, Market Signalling and the Theory of Financial Intermediation." *Journal of Finance*, 35: 863–881.

Jaffe, D., and R. Russell, 1966. "Imperfect Information, Uncertainty and Credit Rationing." *Quarterly Journal of Economics*, 90: 651–666.

Williamson, S.D. 1986. "Costly Monitoring, Financial Intermediation, and Equilibrium Credit Rationing." *Journal of Monetary Economics*, 18: 159–179. This paper shows that credit rationing may result even with a model that is primarily geared to explain why intermediaries arise. In Boyd and Prescott, credit is not rationed.

Internet Resources

Electronic Banking Resource Center

http://www.cob.ohio-state.edu/~richards

Encryption Technologies

David G. Post, 1994. "Encryption—It's Not Just for Spies Anymore." *American Lawyer*, December 1994. Available at http://www.eff.org/pub/ Publications/ David_Post/ crypto_not_just_spies_post.article.

Tatu Ylonen. "Introduction to Cryptography." Available at http:// www.cs.hut.fi/ssh/crypto/ intro.html.

Cryptography FAQ posted to sci.crypt and talk.politics.crypto newsgroups can be found at http://www.cis.ohio-state.edu/hypertext/faq/usenet/ cryptography-faq.

Cypherpunks is a mailing list discussing cryptography and its implementation on the Internet. To subscribe, send e-mail to: majordomo@toad.com with one line of text that reads: subscribe cypherpunks your_email_address.

ACM's cryptography page is at http://www.acm.org/usacm/crypto.html.

Pretty Good Privacy by Phil Zimmerman at http://www.pgp.com

MIT's PGP version 2.6 FAQ at http://web.mit.edu/afs/net/mit/jis/www/ pgpfaq.html

Internet Privacy Coalition's crypto resources page: http://www.privacy.org/ ipc/#Resources.

White House's white paper on key escrow policy calling for international key escrow systems is archived at EPIC, available at http://www.epic.org/crypto/key_escrow/white_paper.html.

Financial Services on the Internet

A good place to start is Yahoo!'s subject listing:

http:// www.yahoo.com/Business_and_Economy/ Companies/ Financial_Services.

Financial Services Technology Consortium (FSTC; http://www.fstc.org) is a non-profit consortium of financial service companies and research organizations.

Online trading services in addition to e.schwab and E*Trade mentioned in the text:

- eBroker (http://www.ebroker.com)
- Lombard Institutional Brokerage (http://www.lombard.com)
- National Discount Brokers (http://pawwws.secapl.com/Broker/Ndb)
- Net Investor (http://pawwws.com/tni)
- K. Aufhauser & Company (http://www.aufhauser.com)

Digital Signature and Certification Services

Legislations dealing with certification authorities and digital signature:

- Georgia Digital Signature Act, 1997, draft, at http://www.efga.org/digsig/lawdraft.htm
- Florida's Digital Signature Advisory Committee report regarding amendments to the Electronic Signature Act of 1996 at http://www.dos.state.fl.us/digsig/finalreport.html

- California Digital Signature Act, 1995, at http://www.gcwf.com/articles\digsig.htm

- Utah Digital Signature Act, 1995, http://www.jmls.edu/cyber/statutes/udsa.html. For analysis, see Bender, N.S., 1995, *Digital Commerce and the Utah Digital Signature Act*, available at http://www.library.law.miami.edu/~bender/internt.html

- The American Bar Association's Digital Signature Guidelines, 1995, is available at http://www.law.vill.edu/vls/student_home/courses/computer-law/abaguid.htm or contact ABA's site at http://www.abanet.org/scitech/ec/home.html

- An analysis of the Digital Signature Standards, developed by the National Institute of Standards and Technology in 1994 and adopted as the federal standards for authenticating digital documents, is available at http://www.epic.org/crypto/dss/new_nist_nsa_revelations.html

Carl Ellision, 1996, *Establishing Identity Without Certification Authorities.* Available at http://www.clark.net/pub/cme/usenix.html

CHAPTER 10

Electronic Payment Systems

For electronic commerce to have a chance to meet the soaring expectations set in the press with regards to the Internet, efficient and effective payment services need to be established and accepted by businesses and consumers alike. Recognizing this, virtually all interested parties in academia, governments, and financial services are exploring various types of payment services and the issues surrounding electronic payment systems and digital currency. Some proposed electronic payment systems are simply electronic versions of existing payment systems, such as checks and credit cards, whereas others are based on digital currency technology and have the potential for definitive impact on today's financial and monetary systems. While the popular press and developers of payment systems predict fundamental changes in the financial sector because of innovations in electronic payment, Alan Greenspan, chairman of the board of governors of the Federal Reserve System, recently reiterated the general sentiment among monetary officials, that "electronic money is likely to spread only gradually and play a much smaller role in our economy than private currency did historically" (Greenspan, 1996).

This chapter reviews and categorizes major types of electronic payment systems, investigates the economic and financial roles these innovations play, and finally, examines their impact on existing financial and monetary systems. After the overview, section 10.2 discusses payment clearing services based on an intermediary, followed by section 10.3 on notational funds transfers such as digital checks and credit cards. Of particular importance and interest are digital currency products. These, in effect, are digital products that can be sold and bought in the marketplace, which determines their value, usefulness and profitability. As tradable products, they will also be subject to product differentiation and the problem of quality uncertainty, as discussed in previous chapters. Sections 10.4 and 10.5 examine digital currency products in detail. This chapter concludes by evaluating the effects of online payment systems on the financial service sector, the economy, the monetary system and government policies.

10.1. Electronic Payment Systems: An Overview

Electronic payment systems can be considered merely the next—albeit significant—step in a long line of changes in payment clearing systems. The electronic settling of accounts, for example, has long been an integral part of payment systems using credit cards, debit cards, automatic teller machines, and prepaid cards. What enables any payment mechanism to be processed electronically is the fact that unlike currency, bills, or coins that carry monetary values, non-cash mechanisms are promises or contracts of payments. Based on the information transmitted following a transaction, the appropriate accounts representing notational money are adjusted between banks and financial institutions. Checks are a primary example in which an intrinsically worthless piece of paper, which nonetheless conveys important information, is exchanged for settlement.

Payment Patterns

Today, electronic payment systems account for a very small number of payments made in the United States. According to the Federal Reserve Bank of St. Louis (1995), about 80 percent of all retail purchases are paid for by cash in the U.S. And 96 percent of all business-to-business transactions are completed using paper checks. Despite these impressive numbers, in terms of total value, payments via cash and checks account for only a small portion of total financial transactions. Although no hard data on cash transactions exists, table 10.1 shows a summary in terms of total volume (number of transactions) and total value (dollar amount) of other payment methods used in 1995 by businesses. Although electronic payment systems were used in less than 5 percent of the transactions, they covered almost 88 percent of the total transactional value.

Of the non-check electronic payment methods, Fedwire of the Federal Reserve and Clearing House Interbank Payments System (CHIPS) of the New York Clearing House are primarily used for large-value transactions. Banks use Fedwire to clear end-of-the-day accounts, whereas businesses use CHIPS transfers to settle large domestic payments and foreign exchange transactions. Transfers based on the Automated Clearing House (ACH) are conducted via value-added private networks (VPNs) without the involvement of the Federal Reserve. ACHs are set up to automate payments for goods and services between corporations and their suppliers. Accordingly, ACH payments are relatively high-volume but low-value transactions compared to Fedwire or CHIPS.

Table 10.1 Non-Cash Payments in the U.S. (1995)

Type of Payment	Volume (%) in Millions of Transactions	Value (%) in Trillions of Dollars
Checks	59,400.0 (96.3%)	68.3 (12.5%)
Fedwire	69.7 (.1%)	207.6 (37.9%)
CHIPS	42.4 (.1%)	262.3 (47.9%)
ACH	2,200.0 (3.5%)	9.3 (1.7%)
Total	61,712.1	547.5

Source: Knudson, et al. (1994).

Even after decades of using electronic payment systems such as ACH, the frequency with which paper checks are still used for payment in the U.S. is surprising: 200 million checks a day! Checks continue to reign supreme not only because of entrenched habits. Another reason is that individuals and businesses can generate interest while checks are being cleared, which normally takes several days. This delay in check-clearing is called *float*, and is an important factor in business financial calculations. For example, General Motors Corporation persuaded its suppliers to accept a three-day delay in their electronic payments, even though payments can be made instantly, because it normally took 3.6 days for checks to clear. This example strongly suggests that a choice of payment method is influenced by factors other than simple convenience or lower transaction costs.

Types of Electronic Payment Systems

Electronic commerce, especially that involving consumers and digital products, places stringent demands on a payment system. Electronic commerce payment systems must be convenient for web purchasing, transportable over the network, strong enough to thwart electronic interference, and cost-effective for extremely low-value transactions. Despite this impressive set of requirements, more than two dozen Internet payment standards or protocols have been proposed. These range from Anonymous Internet Mercantile Protocols by AT&T Bell Labs (http://www.bell-labscom) to Conditional Access for Europe (CAFE) for the European community, to Secure Electronic Transaction (SET) promoted by MasterCard (http://www.mastercard.com) and Visa (http://www.visa.com). Many software and hardware products based on these open standards are being offered, including CyberCash, DigiCash, Mondex, NetBill and NetCheque. The diversity of these products indicates a healthy competition, but confuses ordinary Internet users and merchants trying to choose an appropriate payment mechanism. To structure the following discussion of types, this chapter broadly classifies all electronic payment systems into three groups: payment through an intermediary, payment based on Electronic Funds Transfer (EFT) and payment based on electronic currency.

Conventional Payment Process

A conventional process of payment and settlement involves a buyer-to-seller transfer of cash or payment information (for example, credit card or check). The settlement of payment takes place in the financial processing network. A cash payment requires a buyer's withdrawal from his bank account, a transfer of cash to the seller, and the seller's deposit of the payment to his account. Non-cash payment mechanisms are settled by adjusting, that is, crediting and debiting, the appropriate accounts between banks based on payment information conveyed via check or credit card.

Figure 10.1 is a simplified diagram for both cash and non-cash transactions. Cash moves from the buyer's bank to the seller's bank through face-to-face exchanges in the market. If a buyer uses a non-cash method of payment, payment information instead of cash flows from the buyer to the seller, and ultimately payments are settled between affected banks who notationally adjust accounts based on the payment information. In real markets, this clearing process involves intermediaries, such as credit card services or check clearing companies. Schematically, then, most payment systems are based on similar processes. The information conveyed to settle payments can be one of the following:

- Information about the identities of the seller and the buyer, and some instruction to settle payments without revealing financial information (payment clearing systems, discussed in section 10.2, "Payment Clearing Services")

- Financial information, such as credit card or bank account numbers (including checks and debit cards) (notational funds transfer, discussed in section 10.3, "Notational Funds Transfer")

- Actual values represented by digital currency (digital currency payment systems, discussed in sections 10.4, "Digital Currency Payment Systems," and 10.5, "Properties and Specifications of Digital Currencies")

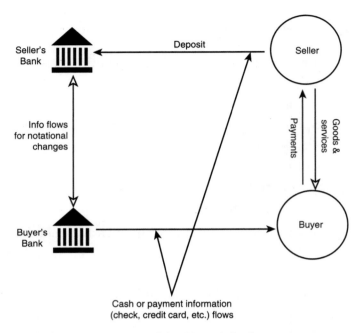

Figure 10.1 A simplified model of transaction.

When face-to-face purchase is replaced with online commerce, many aspects of a transaction occur instantly, under which various processes of a normal business interaction are subsumed. For example, a typical purchase involves stages of locating a seller, selecting a product, asking a price quote, making an offer, agreeing over payment means, checking the identity and validity of the payment mechanism, and transferring goods and receipts. To be used as a substitute for face-to-face payments, online payment systems must incorporate all or some of these stages within their payment functions.

The lack of face-to-face interaction also leads to the development of more secure methods of payment for electronic commerce, to deal with the security problems for sensitive information and uncertainty about identity. Consequently, electronic commerce transactions require intermediaries to provide security, identification, and authentication, as well as payment support.

Figure 10.2 shows a stylized transaction for online commerce using an intermediary. In this model, the intermediary not only settles payments, but also takes care of such needs as confirming seller and buyer identities, authenticating and verifying ordering and payment information, and other transactional requirements lacking in virtual interactions. In the figure, two boxes delineate online purchasing and secure or offline payment clearing processes. Payment settlement in this figure follows the example of the traditional EFT model, which uses secured private value-added networks. The intermediary contributes to market efficiency by resolving uncertainties about security and identity and relieving vendors of the need to set up duplicative hardware and software to handle the online payment clearing process.

Payment information transmitted by the buyer may be one of three types. First, it may contain only customer order information, such as the identity of the buyer and seller, name of the product, amount of payment, and other sale conditions—but no payment information, such as credit card numbers or checking account numbers. In this case, the intermediary acts as a centralized commerce enabler, maintaining membership and payment information for sellers and buyers. A buyer need only send the seller his identification number assigned by the intermediary. Upon receiving the purchase order, the intermediary verifies it with the buyer and seller and handles all sensitive payment information on behalf of both. This is the electronic commerce model followed by First Virtual Holdings, Inc. (http://www.fv.com).

The key benefit of this payment clearing system is that it separates sensitive and non-sensitive information, and only non-sensitive information is exchanged online. This alleviates security concerns often seen as a serious barrier to online commerce. First Virtual does not even rely on encryption for messages between buyers and sellers. A critical requisite for this system to work is the users' trust in the intermediaries.

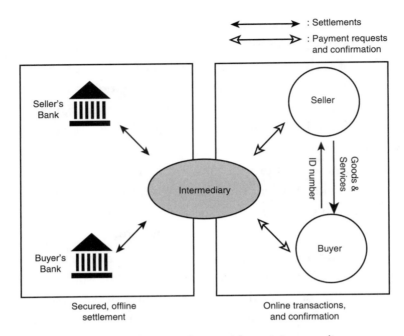

Figure 10.2 Transactions with an intermediary.

The second type of payment system does not depend on a central processing intermediary. Instead, sensitive payment information (such as a credit card or bank account number) is transmitted along with orders. This is, in effect, an open Internet implementation of financial electronic data interchange (EDI) (see fig. 10.3). An electronic funds transfer (EFT) is a financial application of EDI, which sends credit card numbers or electronic checks via secured private networks between banks and major corporations. To use EFTs to clear payments and settle accounts, an online payment service will need to add capabilities to process orders, accounts and receipts. In its simplest form, payment system may use digital checks—simply images of checks—and rely on existing payment clearing networks. The Secure Electronic Transaction (SET) protocol—a credit card-based system supported by Visa and MasterCard—uses digital certificates, which are digital credit cards. This type of payment system is called a notational funds transfer system because it resembles traditional electronic fund transfers and wire transfers, which settle notational accounts of buyers and sellers.

Notational funds transfer systems differ from payment-clearing services in that the payment information transferred online contains sensitive financial information. Thus, if a third party intercepts the sensitive information, it may be abused like stolen credit cards or debit cards. A majority of proposed electronic payment systems fall into this second type of payment system. The objective of these systems is to extend the benefit and convenience of EFT to consumers and small businesses. However, unlike EFTs, the Internet is open and not as secure as private value-added networks (VANs). The challenge to these systems is how to secure the integrity of the payment messages being transmitted and to ensure the interoperability between different sets of payment protocols.

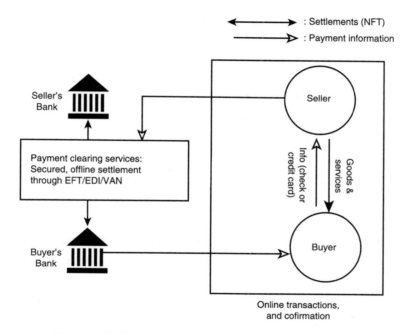

Figure 10.3 Notational Funds Transfer system.

The third type of payment system does not transmit payment information but a digital product representing values: electronic currency. The nature of digital currency mirrors that of paper money as a means of payment. As such, digital currency payment systems have the same advantages as paper currency payment, namely anonymity and convenience. As in other electronic payment systems, security during transmission and storage is a concern, although from a different perspective. For digital currency systems, double-spending, counter-feiting, and storage become critical issues, whereas for notational funds transfers, eavesdropping and liability (when charges are made without authori-zation) are important concerns. Figure 10.4 shows a digital currency payment scheme.

The only difference from the figure is that the intermediary in figure 10.4 acts as an electronic bank that converts outside money (for example, U.S. currency) into inside money (for example, tokens or Ecash), which is circu-lated within online markets. However, as a private monetary system, digital currency will have a wide-ranging impact on money and monetary systems with implications extending far beyond mere transactional efficiency. Digital currency already has spawned many types of new businesses: software vendors for currency server systems; hardware vendors for smart-card readers and other interface devices; technology firms for security, encryption and authentication; and new banking services interfacing accounts in digital currency and conven-tional currency, for example, Mark Twain Bank (http://www.marktwain.com). Many of these new players navigate through areas uncharted by researchers and government policymakers. Old maps used to inscribe unknown territories with "Here Be Dragons," a cartographic term for uncertainty. What kinds of dangerous, as well as fascinating, "dragons" we will encounter in this new world of electronic payments is the subject of the remaining sections.

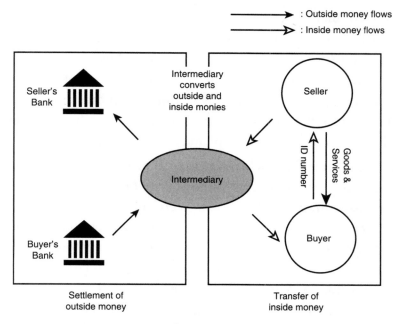

Figure 10.4 Digital currency payment system.

10.2.   Payment Clearing Services

Payment clearing services (PCSs), as discussed earlier, handle only instructions to settle payments and are organized around a trusted third party (TTP). Sellers and buyers open an account with a TTP, which issues identification numbers to account holders. A TTP may either simply establish an online payment clearing relationship with members' chosen banks or may require members to transfer money into TTP accounts. In both cases, the financial information needed to establish membership is transmitted and verified via secured channels, such as offline, or by encrypted messages. After the accounts are established, members only need to exchange identification numbers and purchase details such as product specifications, prices, and other sales terms, omitting all sensitive financial information. Actual payment clearing is done by the TTP, which intermediates members' accounts in one or more banks through secured, private channels. By setting up a proper protocol, a TTP can incorporate in its service not only ordering but also marketing, sales negotiation, delivery, inventory, and receipt and account management.

Because sensitive financial information is never transmitted online in a payment clearing service system, the insecurity of the Internet is not a concern. The critical issue in using a PCS as an electronic commerce payment method is the trustworthiness of a TTP. A TTP acts like a firewall that maintains the integrity of the payment and sometimes the whole commerce system. Thus, if the firewall breaks down, the whole system's security is compromised. The concern in this case is if financial information, as well as consumer purchasing information, is collected by this centralized entity which may breach the confidential nature of business transactions if not handled with restraint.

The advantage of a PCS, especially for small vendors and consumers, is that it offers a secure commerce environment without heavy investment in security technologies and hardware. Transactions can be as open as possible, which fits the Internet culture.

First Virtual Holdings (http://www.fv.com), shown in figure 10.5, is an example of a TTP that does not even use encryption for its messages. First Virtual instead relies on an architecture that separates sensitive information, such as members' bank and credit card numbers, from everyday commercial transactions. First Virtual created its Internet Payment System based on three working assumptions. First, it only deals with information products, that is, digital products that can be delivered via the network. One characteristic of digital products is reproducibility, which eliminates the need for warehousing multiple copies. Therefore, instead of being a distributor, First Virtual acts as a market maker. Also, unlike physical products, unwanted digital products can be destroyed at a minimum material cost to a vendor. Second, First Virtual offers consumers an opportunity to browse or try out digital products prior to purchase. Payments are made only if consumers deem the products worthwhile. Again, this is soundly based on the characteristics of digital products, especially the difficulty to convey or verify quality, as discussed in Chapter 4. Third, First Virtual offers an inexpensive way to handle a costly payment network (see sidebar, "How the First Virtual Payment System Works"). By eliminating the need for costly software and hardware to secure online transactions, this model substantially reduces costs and enables any firm or consumer to engage in electronic commerce today instead of tomorrow.

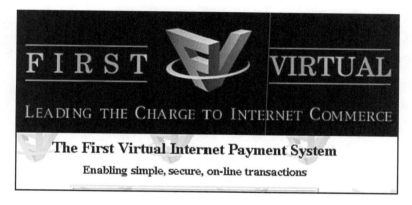

Figure 10.5 First Virtual home page.

A similar payment architecture is proposed by NetBill (http:// www.ini.cmu.edu:80/ netbill), which was developed as part of Carnegie Mellon's graduate program in Information Networking. As in the First Virtual model, buyers and sellers open NetBill accounts with a server that maintains all sensitive information and clears payments with merchants' and customers' banks.

How the First Virtual Payment System Works

Using the First Virtual (FV) payment systems consists of the following steps (shown in figure 10.6):

(1) Alice acquires an account number by filling out a registration form, which gives FV a customer profile and establishes an account backed by a traditional financial instrument, such as her credit card. Bob, the merchant, also goes through the same process.

(2) To purchase an article, product, or other information offered by Bob (who displays the FV logo at his web store), Alice requests the item from Bob, sending her FV account number. The purchase can be automated by authorizing Bob to access her FV account and bill her via browser settings, or she can type in her account information.

(3) Bob sends the requested file directly to Alice.

(4) After sending the product, Bob contacts the FV payment server to verify Alice's account number and request for payment.

(5) The FV payment server verifies Alice's account number for the vendor and checks for sufficient funds.

(6) The FV payment server sends an electronic message to Alice. This message could be an automatic World Wide Web form, or a simple e-mail.

(7) Alice responds to the form or e-mail in one of three ways: Yes, I agree to pay; No, I will not pay; or Fraud, I never asked for this. A "No" response can be used by FV's members if the downloaded file is not what they expected.

(8) If the FV payment server receives a "Yes" from Alice, Bob's account is credited by FV, and Alice's account is debited. If the answer is "No," no further action is taken.

(9) If FV receives no response from Alice, it tries to contact her again. But, after a certain number of tries, FV may cancel her account because FV requires members to check e-mail regularly. If a member always responds "No," FV also may discontinue the account.

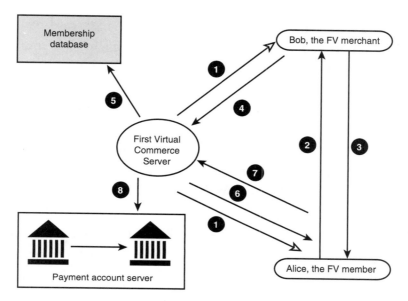

Figure 10.6 First Virtual payment clearing process.

10.3. Notational Funds Transfer

Although payment clearing services have decided advantages for registered members, these advantages cannot be transferred to non-members. To transact with non-members, online shoppers and merchants may have to rely on traditional payment methods, such as checks and credit cards, which are accepted as payment by almost all vendors. Using one of these payment methods requires buyers to send their account or credit card information to sellers, who forward it to an intermediary or a currency server, which verifies the information and relays it to the affected financial institutions. The banks, in turn, adjust the users' notational accounts. Thus, you call this system a notational funds transfer system (NFT).

Any Internet payment system that is check- or credit card-based is an example of an NFT. The Interbank Check Imaging (ICI) system (http://www.fstc.org/projects/imaging), developed by the Financial Services Technology Consortium [FSTC (http://www.fstc.org)], is a direct application of imaging and network technologies to a financial payment system. Whether an image of a check is transmitted or credit card numbers are merely exchanged, NFT systems are the most prevalent payment mechanisms for Internet commerce simply because they represent a natural extension of the existing electronic funds transfer (EFT) system.

As in payment clearing systems, an NFT system still involves an intermediary. The intermediary's role in this case is limited to serving as a conduit of messages between the open Internet and closed financial networks. For example, CyberCash's payment system (http://www.cybercash.com), another implementation of an NFT, uses CyberCash servers to authorize transactions and forward payment information to banks and processing houses. At the shopper's computer, a software program called CyberCash Internet Wallet contains the shopper's credit card information (see fig. 10.7), which is forwarded to merchants and then to a CyberCash server that handles payment clearing with banks (see sidebar: How CyberCash Works). Online shoppers interact with the CyberCash server via a merchant CyberCash server, which transmits the information using public key encryption. Because credit card information is already encrypted at the shopper's computer, merchants can only verify its validity without discovering this sensitive information. In this model, more important than the trust issue, is the concern when security as private information is being transmitted. CyberCash relies on both public key and secret key encryption technologies to secure its messages (see section 9.4 for encryption technologies).

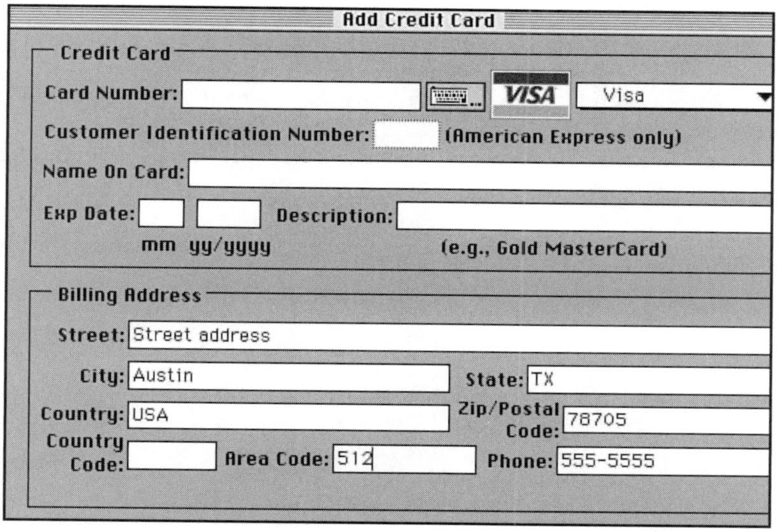

Figure 10.7 CyberCash Internet Wallet keeps user's credit card information.

How CyberCash Works

CyberCash transactions are completed through three software programs: one program resides on the consumer's PC (CyberCash Internet Wallet), one operates as part of the merchant server, and one operates within the CyberCash servers. Before shopping with CyberCash, consumers download the CyberCash Wallet program, which is available free from CyberCash (http://www.cybercash.com). Because CyberCash Wallet is a separate piece of software, consumers can use any type of credit card. A CyberCash payment process, depicted in figure 10.8, works in the following manner:

(1) The consumer selects items for purchase and fills out the merchant's order form, complete with necessary shipping information.

(2) When the shopper chooses to pay with CyberCash, the merchant server presents an invoice to the consumer and requests payment, sending a special message to the consumer's CyberCash Wallet. The consumer simply chooses which credit card to pay with and clicks it.

continues

continued

(3) CyberCash Wallet sends the credit card information to the merchant server.

(4) The merchant server verifies the validity and integrity of the received message, that is, checks whether it was tampered with, and sends the message to a CyberCash server.

(5) The CyberCash server is linked to a credit card payment network, through which accounts are settled by conventional processes.

(6) The payment settlement result is forwarded to the CyberCash server.

(7) The merchant server is notified of the transaction result.

(8) The merchant sends the ordered items with a receipt to the shopper.

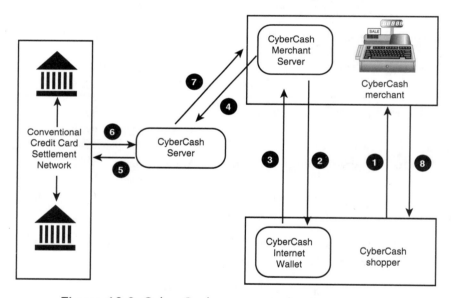

Figure 10.8 CyberCash payment clearing process.

As evident from the way CyberCash works, an NFT is an extension of traditional credit card-based transaction systems in which established players may have market advantages. To support the increasing use of credit card payments on the open Internet, Visa (http://www.visa.com) and MasterCard proposed in 1996 a protocol to ensure interoperability across different hardware platforms and web browsers. This protocol, named Secure Electronic Transaction (SET), is supported by Microsoft, Netscape, IBM, GTE, VeriSign and other major players in electronic commerce. Besides offering standard communication protocols and message formats for credit card-based transactions, SET provides confidentiality through encryption, message integrity using digital signatures, and authentication of consumer and merchant identities (see sidebar, "How SET is Set to Launch Credit Card Use in Cyberspace").

How SET is Set to Launch Credit Card Use in Cyberspace

Secure Electronic Transaction (SET) is an open specification developed jointly by Visa and MasterCard to secure credit card transactions over the Internet. SET relies on digital certificates issued to consumers; the certificates contain credit card information that is verified by credit card issuers through a certification authority. The document stating that a card is valid is secured by public key encryption and the issuing bank attaches its digital signature to the certificate. After consumers receive the certificates, they store them in their personal computers, and send them to merchants when making purchases on the Internet. Merchants also resister with their banks, who issue digital certificates to be displayed on their web pages.

During a transaction, consumers send the merchant their digital certificates for payment. In a sense, the digital certificate is a digital credit card, which merchants simply pass on to their banks for approval. The merchant certificate is equivalent to the logos of accepted cards displayed in store windows. For more information, see "Internet Resources" at the end of this chapter.

The dominant issue today in electronic commerce is security. The level of interest indicates that most merchants and other participants in Internet commerce are considering electronic payment systems based on traditional systems such as NFTs. This is despite the fact that First Virtual's payment system is much more secure, even without encryption technology, and does not require heavy investment or costs for merchants to participate. The fact that NFT payment systems simply extend the existing model of physical markets seems to suit vendors who sell physical products on the Internet, especially because consumers seem to prefer extended credit terms to cash payments. This said, even with greatly reduced transaction costs, credit card-based payments still are not suitable for small-value purchases. In these instances, digital currency payment systems have the advantage.

10.4. Digital Currency Payment Systems

Whereas electronic payment systems reviewed in the previous sections aim to adapt existing payment settlement processes to the open environment of the Internet, digital currency, also called electronic cash or electronic money, is a new development which has far-reaching commercial, monetary, and regulatory ramifications. One of the ways payment systems using digital currency differ from traditional electronic funds transfers is the transactional contents. In traditional EFT and many electronic payment systems proposed for Internet commerce, sensitive payment information (such as credit card numbers or bank account information) is transmitted over the network. For those transactions, the primary concern of businesses and consumers is security. When security is breached, this information may be used without authorization. But, swift counter-measures can remedy the situation. In the case of digital currency, the monetary value is being transferred instead of payment information. This is akin to sending a $20 bill in the mail. An intercepted digital currency transaction, therefore, is equivalent to outright theft, and the remedial measures needed are different from those addressing credit card fraud.

The primary motivation for digital currencies has been to preserve the privacy afforded by cash transactions. Privacy can be protected somewhat in non-cash payment systems by various encryption methods and trusted third parties. A more salient feature of digital cash as a payment system is the capability to make peer-to-peer transactions, either online or offline, in which two persons can exchange money without involving a third party. In this sense, digital currency is more than just an efficient electronic payment system; it is a monetary innovation that deserves closer economic analysis.

Money as a Medium of Exchange

Money has many origins and forms, but to be a viable medium of exchange, a monetary system must meet certain criteria. Primitive forms of money include virtually every type of goods with value, such as cash crops, cattle, and ornamental and precious objects. These objects are used to pay tributes, make peace offerings, compensate a bride's family, and fulfill other social customs. While these primitive forms of money could be used as a store of value and a means of payment, to act as a medium of exchange they need to be widely available and broadly accepted, as well as convenient. Monetary objects may have different uses, but an economic use of money as an exchange medium needs to simplify the cumbersome barter system of physical goods.

Coins or paper currency—also called fiat money—meet the criteria of acceptability, availability, and convenience as a medium of exchange. Precious metals, struck as coins, were commonly used as money until the 19th century. On the other hand, the origin of paper money goes back only to the late Middle Ages, when bank credits were transferred in the form of bills of credit, whose value depended on the issuer's credit worthiness. Until quite recently, paper money was issued by private banks as well as government agencies. In Canada, private banks were free to issue notes based on their assets until the beginning of this century. Even in the U.S., no national banking or currency system existed during the free-banking era prior to the Civil War. Although they were ultimately backed by government bonds, National Bank Notes had been issued by federally chartered national banks since 1863 under the National Bank Act. The National Bank Notes competed with Demand Notes (also known as the "greenbacks") and Legal Tender Notes (also known as United States Notes), both issued by the federal government. The Federal Reserve Act of 1913 phased out these privately issued notes and replaced them with Federal Reserve Notes by the late 1930s, but privately issued currency had been common in the history of U.S. money.

As the use of fiat money grew, it became possible to separate the role of exchange medium from the role of storing value. Paper currency does not have an intrinsic value other than the promise by the issuing bank or government to convert it into another form of stored value on demand. Ultimately, not even this convertibility is promised, and the value of paper money depends solely on the implicit trust among the public and between the public and the authority who issues the currency.

Inside Money and Outside Money

The amount of currency circulated today is quite small compared to the amount of money that exists in demand deposit and savings accounts. Even items of small value are purchased using debit cards and other electronic devices, further reducing the need to withdraw and carry bills and coins. Whereas coins and bills are exchanged physically to complete transactions, notational money in currency-denominated accounts is simply adjusted according to instructions given by affected parties. As the public's trust in financial institutions grows, the money that exists in notation can be converted into another form to address the needs of a market. When linked to a currency, called outside money, the new form of money is known as inside money because it is accepted within a certain market.

To be fully considered inside money, these instruments must be convertible into dollars, that is, redeemable for cash, accepted for various products, and transferable to other users for payment. Many forms of inside money already are in use: transit coupons and tokens, casino chips, stadium cards and prepaid telephone and copy cards. Inside money is circulated among those who trust and accept it, and the ultimate value of such a currency is in its capability to be converted to outside money.

The distinction between inside and outside monies is one of territory, in terms of transactional activities. Inside money is circulated within the territory of the money—that is, for the purposes specified by the money or for activities in which that money is recognized and accepted as payment—but cannot be used outside unless it is converted into outside money. Usually, outside money can be used for inside-money transactions, but for reasons such as convenience, inside money may be preferred. Inside money—for example, subway tokens, video game tokens, and paper money for amusement park rides—is created and used mainly for convenience, and as long as parity is maintained between inside and outside money, inside money remains as tokens. These tokens often don't circulate among users and have limited acceptability.

But certainly, any token may be transferred or traded among its holders and accepted by a large number of merchants. When these tokens are used for almost all payment and exchange needs, what is the difference from outside money? In other words, if one can use casino chips to buy clothes in a mall, to pay taxes, and to buy all kinds of products and services, has a new currency been created? Indeed, an extreme case of the inside money model would be private monies issued by malls and merchants. And an extreme case of this is the creation of digital currency for use in the world's largest mall—the Internet. If a digital currency gains the public's trust and is accepted by all merchants and consumers on the Internet, the distinction between that and outside money (that is, dollars or francs or pounds), will be arbitrary. In every sense of the word, digital currency is the same as cash.

When there is already a widely accepted and well-behaved national currency, why would anyone want a new currency? The following section enumerates some reasons digital currency is needed for online commercial transactions. These reasons are based on the difference between electronic commerce and physical markets.

However, there are arguments both for and against creating inside monies in physical markets. For example, Champ et al. (1996) examines Canadian and U.S. banking experiences during the late-19th century, and suggest that banking panics and failures are less severe when private monies or inside monies are available to alleviate liquidity constraints (that is, the lack of cash to meet cash demand). On the other hand, Williamson and Wright (1994) argue that private monies as a medium of exchange may fail to provide the reliability and ready acceptance of national outside monies. This may result in economic losses. For example, dollars facilitate transactions because everyone is willing to accept dollars to exchange commodities. In bartering, both parties must know the quality of each other's goods. With cash transactions, the uncertainty is less because at least the quality of the cash is certain. However, if that cash is private money, this type of transaction is no different from bartering.

Needs for Electronic Currency Payment Systems

In the physical world, despite the convenience of paying by check, credit card, or charge card, cash remains the most frequently used payment medium in terms of the number of transactions. Similarly, many factors in electronic commerce drive the need for a digital cash equivalent.

Anonymity in Transactions

The first basic need for digital cash harks back to the concern about consumer privacy discussed in Chapter 8. Non-cash payment systems also can implement anonymity, as encryption technologies separate payment information from buyer identification to conceal the buyer's identity from banks or sellers. In models using trusted third parties, the privacy of consumer information depends solely on this third party. While possible, none of these methods is as easy, complete, or efficient in preserving consumer privacy as digital currencies, in which only values are transferred without payer information. The bank issuing digital currency keeps track only of serial numbers to authenticate the value of a currency, and digital coins carry encrypted messages about the user, which can be revealed only by legal means.

Micropayments and the Internet

The second factor driving the use of digital currency is the economic need to minimize transaction costs. Non-cash payment systems, as discussed in earlier sections, require payees to verify and authenticate each payment, a highly inefficient method for small-value transactions. Developing a cost-effective payment mechanism to implement small-value transactions is a fundamental prerequisite in commercializing the Internet, where many information goods have values less than $1.

As the transaction costs of non-cash payment systems decrease, an increasing percentage of transactions may become cashless. However, despite increasingly sophisticated network financial technologies, paper- and electronic-based payment systems still incur significant costs for handling and authorization. Consequently, the use of cash has persisted. According to one estimate, cash is used in 85 percent of transactions although it accounts for only 0.5 percent of the value of transactions. Similar needs exist for electronic commerce. It is critical for digital currency to be fully developed and accepted if information trading is to take off on the Internet because neither a PCS nor an NFT payment method is adequate for micropayments. Although digital currency will not replace traditional payment methods for many products, it is certainly well-suited to pay for accessing web pages, for example, and for the commercialization of networked information.

The Transferability of Value

The third motivating factor behind digital cash is the need for transferability, by which two parties may exchange goods and services without an intervening third party. Non-cash payment systems are mediated by one or more third parties, such as check- or credit card-clearing services. A system involving a third party is a type of client-server in which the server (the third party) represents the authority who backs up the validity of transactions. In contrast, a transferable payment system supports peer-to-peer transactions in which the role of the third party is subsumed within the digital currency. Although transferability is not absolutely required to achieve payment and settlement between two parties, any non-transferable payment system unnecessarily increases the transaction costs and can delay the settlement process as an on-line third party is required for each transaction.

Despite clear incentives, initial proposals for digital cash are tempered by the fear of double spending and counterfeiting. For that reason Ecash by DigiCash (http://www.digicash.com), for example, requires payees to verify a coin's validity with a payment server or a bank. If valid, the coin is reissued under a new serial number. In an effort to make Ecash acceptable, an unnecessary third party and the associated transaction costs are involved. A truly transferable digital currency will be one that can be circulated peer-to-peer online and offline. The following section examines proposed digital currencies, including Ecash, in detail.

10.5.   Properties and Specifications of Digital Currencies

Digital currencies are digitally exchangeable cash. Therefore, digital currencies and payment systems must satisfy the monetary properties expected of cash and the requirements of the digital communication network. It is simple to extend the NFT model into a value transfer model in which monetary value is exchanged, similar to any type of currency, instead of account information. CyberCash, discussed as an NFT system in section 10.3, is implementing an extension of its system to enable peer-to-peer transactions that do not use a TTP for authentication.

Desirable Properties of Digital Currency

Developers of digital currency have a wide range of options for implementing strong safety requirements of transmitting values over the network. For example, a secure digital currency can be implemented by using strong encryption algorithms, by employing tamper-resistant hardware, or by securing the network communication. Although physical specifications of digital coins and tokens may vary, the following properties are fundamental to any digital currency payment system.

Monetary Value

To be used as a monetary unit, digital currency must have value that can be exchanged for other goods and services, be used to pay fiduciary obligations, or be transferred to another person. Because digital currency is essentially a file, it does not have an intrinsic value and must be linked to another system of value. The most common implementation is to base the value of digital currency on bank deposits, credits, or pre-payments using outside money. After a digital currency is convertible to dollars, the next step is for it to be accepted in the market as a monetary token. After becoming accepted and trusted, a digital currency can establish related properties, such as exchangeability and transferability.

Convenience

Convenience has been the biggest factor in the growth of notational currencies, such as checks, which are scalable and easy to transport. Similarly, digital currencies must be convenient to use, store, access, and transport. A digital file may allow remote access to money via telephone, modem, or Internet connection. Electronic storage and transfer devices or network capabilities will be needed. To gain wide acceptance, digital cash also must be convenient in terms of scalability and interoperability so that users need not carry multiple denominations or multiple versions for each operating system.

Security

To secure physical money and coins, one needs to store them in wallets, safes or other private places. If digital currencies are stored on hard drives connected to an open network, theoretically anybody can snoop and tamper with the money. Encryption protects digital currency against tampering. Some proposals using smart cards (for example, Mondex) store digital currency in tamper-resistant hardware that can be maintained offline. Ecash relies on the security of Ecash client software residing on users' computers.

At the same time, digital currencies must be resistant to accidents by owners. Dollar bills are printed on strong paper that withstands many adverse treatments, such as washing. To achieve similar security, adequate protection standards are needed in physical specifications of digital coins and in policy matters for legal and commercial liabilities.

Authentication

Money is authenticated by visually inspecting bills and coins. Although further tests could include weighing, chemical analysis, and contacting the authorities, authentication of physical currency is usually a simple matter. Digital currency, however, cannot be visually inspected, and it is difficult to distinguish the original from a counterfeit. Therefore, inspection of digital currency requires authenticating secondary information that accompanies the bills or coins, such as the digital signatures of banks or payers attached to the currency (serial number). A more rigid system will require contacting a third party each time a transaction is made. Although this system is more secure, the transaction costs may be too high for small-value purchases. A hardware-based system such as Mondex relies on software and hardware and does not require authentication for each transfer of values. Other systems will have to strengthen their client software or introduce hardware protection to allow peer-to-peer transactions.

Non-Refutability

Acknowledging payment and receipt is a basic property required of a payment system. In cash transactions, simple receipt is enough to establish non-refutability. A similar exchange of digital receipts can be used for digital transactions. An alternative is to append all transaction records into the digital currency. In this system, digital coins accumulate information about all parties involved in past transactions. These are called identified tokens, in contrast to anonymous tokens, which do not reveal information about users.

Accessibility and Reliability

One advantage of digital currency over cash is its capability to be transported over the network. Users can store digital money at home but access it remotely via telephone or modem, the same network used to clear payments. Because of this crucial role, digital payment systems must provide continuous, fast, and reliable connections.

Anonymity

Unlike checks and cards, cash transactions are anonymous. An anonymous payment system is needed to protect against revealing purchase patterns and other consumer information, although untraceable transactions are opposed by the government in view of possible criminal uses. Nevertheless, the need will persist, and anonymity is perhaps the single most important property of cash transactions.

Digital currency can be equipped with varying degrees of anonymity, masking the user identity to the bank, the payee, or both. Strong anonymity guarantees untraceability whereas a weaker version allows the user's identity to be traced when the need arises. The issue of anonymity may evokes debates about tax evasion, money laundering and other criminal uses of digital currency. But the economic rationale for simple, anonymous digital coins is that they reduce transaction costs by eliminating third parties and protect consumer information that could be used to price-discriminate among consumers.

Technical Specifications of Digital Currencies

Two types of digital currency have been developed, but the general trend appears to be toward a mixed system. Ecash, developed by DigiCash (http://www.digicash.com), is the forerunner of Internet payment systems based on online transactions. Mondex represents the other type of payment system, based on offline transactions. Unlike their online counterparts aimed at Internet users, offline payment systems grew out of existing EFT mechanisms using debit cards, such as telephone and copy cards. These cards hold prepaid account information and merchants who accept these cards are usually credited for the transaction amounts by the card issuer. By using computer chips embedded in these cards (hence the name smart cards) payment information and values can be transferred. As issuers develop network interface devices, smart cards can be used online as well, competing directly with online payment systems. Similarly, Ecash and other online payment systems are introducing electronic wallets similar to smart cards, enabling offline transactions. As the two become integrated, the distinction between online and offline systems is rapidly disappearing. More detailed discussions of Ecash and Mondex follow.

Ecash

Ecash is a digital currency protocol developed by DigiCash and tested extensively on the Internet. Ecash uses public key encryption technologies to maintain the integrity of digital coins. By varying the encryption, Ecash can have strong or weak anonymity. DigiCash licenses Ecash technologies to banks, which convert outside money into digital currency and serve as currency servers in authenticating, clearing and settling accounts. Mark Twain Bank of St. Louis (http://www.marktwain.com), shown in figure 10.9, is the first electronic bank to license the Ecash technology that serves interface functions between dollar-denominated accounts and Ecash accounts.

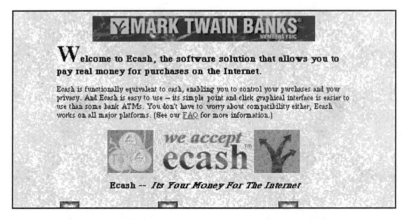

Figure 10.9 Mark Twain Bank's Ecash page.

In this version of Ecash, a user first establishes a WorldCurrency Access account with Mark Twain Bank by transferring money by check or wire. WorldCurrency Access accounts are denominated by outside money (dollars) and are regular bank accounts insured by the FDIC. The conversion from outside money into inside money occurs when the user requests a certain amount of money be put into the Ecash Mint, which manufactures electronic "coins." These coins are no longer insured by the FDIC—unless current law has changed. The customer uses Ecash software, downloaded from the bank and installed on his computer, to view and download these coins to his hard drive. Ecash Mint is where electronic currency is validated and certified. A user can move any amount of Ecash between his hard drive and Ecash Mint, as well as into WorldCurrency Access accounts (see fig. 10.10).

A user can then transfer a digital coin to a merchant who accepts Ecash and who also maintains an account with Mark Twain Bank. Upon receiving the coin, the merchant deposits it in his account. This implementation requires receivers of Ecash to present the Ecash to the bank or Ecash server for verification. Therefore, this is not really a peer-to-peer system in which no intermediaries are needed. But this requirement serves mainly to counter the security problem, and there is no reason why receivers cannot transfer it to a third person.

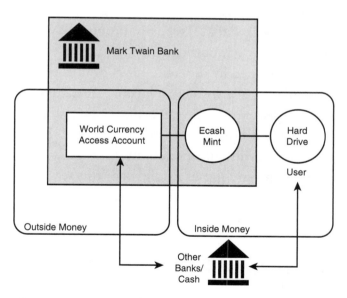

Figure 10.10 Ecash model of Mark Twain Bank.

In essence, a digital coin is merely an encrypted serial number. After money is transferred into Ecash Mint, coins are created when a user requests that Ecash Mint "mint" some money to be transferred to the user's hard drive.

The request is transmitted through Ecash software residing on the user's computer. According to DigiCash specification, a user's software generates a random number, which serves as a serial number or a note. The number is encrypted by the user's encryption keys and sent to the bank, which signs the note with its private signature to acknowledge that the note is backed by the user's account (which is at this point withdrawn from the outside money account), and returns the note to the user. The bank sees the coin again when it is deposited by the payee and records the number to check all later redemptions against it to detect double spending. Other information can also be attached to the coin. Revelation of this information depends on the encryption methods used. If the added information can be used to identify users, it is called an *identified coin*; coins without this information are called *anonymous coins*.

Many variations of digital cash exist that differ primarily in terms of how the coins are verified to prevent double spending. Whereas Ecash uses a central bank (such as Mark Twain Bank), NetCash, proposed by Information Science Institute of the University of Southern California, uses currency servers that may be owned and operated by different banks or non-bank organizations. Currently, NetBank (http://www.netbank.com/~netcash/) implements the NetCash protocol based on e-mail verification. NetCash is clearly aiming for a digital currency standard that can be widely accepted. However, to avoid double spending, a coin still must be submitted to a currency server which issues a new coin upon verifying its validity. For this reason, the system is difficult for implementing peer-to-peer transactions.

Millicent

An extreme opposite approach is Millicent, proposed by Digital Corporation (http://www.research.digital.com/SRC/millicent). The Millicent system, self-described as a pay-ahead coupon system, uses vendor-specific digital scrips, which are akin to merchant-issued coupons. Instead of using banks and other intermediaries to verify that a coin was not double spent, a scrip is presented to a merchant, who locally verifies its validity, that is, decrypts it. A scrip has a serial number with a particular value, an expiration date, and the name of the vendor who accepts the scrip. Because Millicent requires no currency servers and no intermediate steps to maintain its security and validity, it presents a viable medium for transactions of extremely low value, for example, one-tenth of a cent. Millicent is versatile enough to be used not only as microcurrency but also as tokens, coupons, and advertising rebates. To devise an effective sales promotion, a vendor has to target customers who need added incentives to purchase his product. By combining consumer information and the vendor-specific nature of a scrip, a seller can increase its market share while consumers gain from lowered prices (Bester and Petrakis, 1996).

Mondex

Mondex, developed by Mondex International (http://www.mondex.com/mondex), is a smart-card system that transfers stored balances. A smart card is a hardware platform with an integrated circuit inside that can be programmed to prevent double spending without resorting to online verification. Smart cards are different from debit cards, which do not require pre-withdrawal of cash. Similar to Ecash users, smart card users must withdraw money from a currency-denominated account to a digital currency account. Thus, a Mondex card is a portable hard drive with a built-in Ecash Mint. Both Ecash and Mondex are prepaid systems, unlike debit cards, which might be considered "just-in-time" pay cards.

The Mondex system contains a layer of market players. Mondex International holds worldwide ownership of its smart-card technology. In each country, it licenses the right to issue Mondex currency (for example, in Mondex dollar unit (M$) or Mondex pound unit ($£), and so on) to one issuer or a consortium of companies who, in a sense, mint Mondex currency and distribute it to financial intermediaries such as banks. Finally, multiple card sellers also sell smart cards directly to consumers, who may be individual banks or smart-card intermediaries.

Despite this complex layer of Mondex issuers and distributors, the Ecash model is organized in the same way, including Ecash patent holders, Mark

Twain Bank issuers and other intermediary Ecash distributors. The difference between Ecash and Mondex lies in their hardware organization. For one, a smart card is capable of offline transactions whereas Ecash needs to be online. For another, a smart card uses hardware to make the system tamper-resistant whereas Ecash relies on software encryption and a trusted third party or currency server. Despite the higher hardware costs, a smart card is a superior payment platform because of its security, its applicability to peer-to-peer transactions, and its versatility in handling multicurrency payments online or offline. This difference in hardware will soon disappear; Ecash can be sold in smart cards and Mondex cards will interface with computers and become part of the online electronic cash regime. The superiority or popularity of one system over the other will be determined in the marketplace, based on consumer acceptance and prices, which is discussed in the next section.

10.6. Evaluation and Policy Issues

The potential ramifications of widespread use of digital currency have spurred research and heated debate of key economic issues regarding electronic payment systems and intermediaries. Specific topic areas include the following:

- Information contents of transactions
- Transactional efficiency
- Monetary effects
- Organizational effects

Information Contents of Transactions

Discussion surrounding the information contents of transactions focuses on identifiable personal information of the buyer—such as name, physical or e-mail address, and telephone number— which can be matched with consumption or preference data. As discussed in Chapter 8, sellers could use consumer information to price-discriminate among buyers by personalizing their products and pricing them so as to charge the maximum amount each consumer is prepared to pay. The only protection consumers have to control information on their spending habits and preferences is through privacy in the transaction.

Payment systems based on trusted a third party rely on the intermediary to protect privacy. Sellers know the account or membership numbers of potential buyers, but sellers cannot link them with persons without the intermediary's help. If the account that a member keeps with the intermediary draws its balance directly from a source such as credit cards, purchase information may be completely shielded from credit card companies.

An NFT payment system such as CyberCash, however, is no different from conventional processes in which buyers give personal information to sellers. CyberCash does not allow merchants to read the payment information, which is encrypted, but merchants have a complete record of sales that may include the buyer's identity, depending on the way the payment system is implemented. At present, using a CyberCash ID number, CyberCash can inject a certain degree of anonymity. Buyers present only their CyberCash ID number to merchants, which is then verified by the merchant via a CyberCash server that confirms the validity of the number. Regardless of the way identification is implemented, however, credit card companies will have detailed information about consumer purchasing behaviors.

Digital currency, on the other hand, maintains the buyer's complete anonymity. In systems such as Mondex, peer-to-peer transfers are completely anonymous, and hence untraceable. In an Ecash implementation, digital coins may be completely anonymous or weakly anonymous. A completely anonymous system does not include any personal information in the coin other than a serial number, and allows indefinite circulation of the coin. A weakly anonymous coin may contain the name of the person who first purchased it, but the name is encrypted in such a way that it is revealed only if it is double-spent. Any proposed digital currency is capable of implementing strong and weak versions of anonymity.

Spending digital currency may generate more transaction data than a conventional cash transaction if a digital coin is required to be cleared each time it is spent. However, anonymity can still be maintained by *blinding* the digital coin. The process of creating a digital coin begins with a serial number generated by the user. A third party, such as a currency server, verifies this number. The serial number is the identifiable information that is linked to a user. However, after generating a serial number, the user may blind the number before sending it to be verified so that the intermediary cannot read it. This is done by multiplying the serial number with a random *blinding factor* that cannot be determined by the currency server. The user receives the coin (serial number) digitally signed by the server, and un-blinds it before spending it. Upon receiving the coin from a redeemer, the currency server verifies its digital signature and records the serial number on its list of spent numbers to prevent double spending. Note that in this blinding scheme, the server has no way of knowing who spent the coin.

Not surprisingly, the degree of anonymity afforded by electronic payment systems covers the same range of options offered by various conventional payment systems. As with conventional systems, the choice of a particular payment method in electronic commerce will be determined by the needs of each payment, based on such factors as convenience, anonymity, and costs.

Transactional Efficiency

Although anonymity has been the focal point in the debate on electronic payment proposals, the transaction cost will determine the future of any electronic payment system. For large-value transactions, existing payment methods using checks and credit cards can be adequately converted to the open Internet after security concerns are alleviated. More importantly, payment systems using the Internet can lower the cost of credit card-clearing services, for which expensive private closed networks are built. Using the Internet will eliminate a substantial portion of redundant infrastructure costs, and enable small merchants and individuals to offer check and credit card payment options for their customers.

In terms of reducing per-transaction cost, a PCS such as First Virtual appears to be in a position similar to NFT systems, as long as First Virtual uses credit cards or bank account transfers to settle payments. If First Virtual or a similar intermediary settles members' accounts only intermittently, it may offer a less costly way to handle repeated payment transactions, just as inter-bank payments are settled once a day via Fedwire or CHIPS. However, as proposed, First Virtual does not represent a significant reduction in transaction costs.

The cost of clearing a payment becomes critical for small-value transactions that might involve payment of a penny or less to view a web page. In the case of digital currency, the level of transactional efficiency depends on whether users need to interact with a third party to verify the currency's validity, which increases costs. After verification, the intermediary re-issues a new coin, making a digital coin in this scheme non-transferable. Bypassing this cumbersome and repetitive process may compromise the level of security against double spending or counterfeiting, or may require a secure hardware platform, as in Mondex. Because encryption technologies are adequate enough to support a high degree of security, systems such as Millicent may be viable for high-volume, low-value transactions at minimal transaction costs.

Monetary Effects

Digital currency payment systems have raised macroeconomic questions and concerns regarding their impact on the money supply and governments' control over monetary policy. In the U.S., research has shown, however, that the Federal Reserve system's control of the money supply can be adjusted to reflect the change in the money demand, and as such government officials consider the effect of digital currency on the monetary system to be minimal (Blinder, 1995). Nevertheless, proposed digital currency systems may affect the monetary system in two ways: they may influence the supply of money by changing the money multiplier, or they may change, in the long run, the velocity of money, affecting price levels and interest rates. The effect of digital currency on the money supply depends on how inside monies are created whereas its effect on the velocity of money is uncertain.

To address these issues, you must first review how the money supply is controlled by governments through central banks or, in the U.S., the Federal Reserve. The money stock (M1) consists of currency and checkable deposits held by the public. A larger definition of money stock (M2) includes time and savings deposits and money-market instruments in addition to the demand deposits included in M1. The public holds a portion of the currency as cash and the rest in banks as checkable deposits. The ratio of currency to deposits is called the currency-deposit ratio, which is about .4 in the U.S.—that is, $40 in cash is carried for every $100 deposit. Once deposited, the bank can lend the money to a third person, who in turn holds some of the money in cash and deposits the rest. The money supply is created through this process of deposits and lendings.

In the U.S., the Federal Reserve (the Fed) controls the money supply by changing the amount of currency in circulation and the bank's capability to lend. The Fed controls the amount of currency by selling and buying bonds through its open market operations. When the Fed sells (or buys) bonds, it reduces (or increases) the amount of currency circulating. The Fed also requires each bank to hold a portion of their money in cash or with the Federal Reserve banks to meet the cash demand of consumers. The resulting reserve-deposit ratio may be changed by the Fed, but is currently around 10 percent. This means that for every $10 of checkable deposits, a bank must have a cash reserve of $1.

The currency and the banks' deposits with the Fed are called the high-powered money or the monetary base. The effect of the Fed's monetary operations on the money stock involves the money multiplier, which is determined by the currency-deposit ratio and the reserve-deposit ratio. The money supply function can be expressed in the following equation:

Money Stock=(Money Multiplier)×(Monetary Base), where

$$\text{Money Multiplier}= \frac{(1+CD)}{(CD+RD)}$$

CD is the currency-deposit ratio, and RD is the reserve-deposit ratio. This means that the total stock of money in the economy is 2.8 times greater than the monetary base. The money multiplier and the stock of money can be graphed, as in figure 10.11, using the money multiplier.

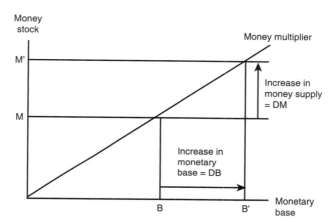

Figure 10.11 The monetary base and the money supply.

Figure 10.11 depicts a situation in which an increase in the monetary base, denoted as DB, increases the total money supply by DM. The exact monetary effect depends on the money multiplier, which is DM/DB in the graph. An increase in the money multiplier (a counter-clockwise rotation around the origin, that is, steeper, for the money multiplier line) implies that an increase in the monetary base causes a larger increase in the money supply.

Ecash, e-money, or CyberCash systems essentially create new currencies, but their effect on the money supply depends on whether they are backed by the national currency. If Ecash, for example, is backed by dollar-denominated currency accounts, inside (digital) money is exchanged with outside (fiat) money. For example, suppose Alice withdraws $100 from her conventional bank, deposits it with Mark Twain Bank's Ecash account, and converts it into $100 worth of Ecash coins. If Mark Twain Bank does not hold the $100 but deposits it with another bank, or lends the $100 under the same condition as any other bank, the supply of money does not change by Alice moving her money to the electronic bank.

However, say Alice withdraws $100 into cash to meet her need for cash transactions. Such cash holding by a consumer represents a reduction in demand deposits and the capacity to create money by lending institutions.

With Ecash instead of cash, Alice does not carry $100, which she would normally have held for cash transactions, and therefore more money is available for lending by banks. In other words, consumers will hold less cash and more deposits with the availability of digital currency, which decreases the currency-deposit ratio and increases the money multiplier (by reducing CD in the money supply equation). As a result, the overall money supply will increase if Mark Twain Bank, or any escrow intermediaries that hold backup outside money for digital currency, is allowed to operate as a lending institution. The effect on the money supply will be even greater if Mark Twain Bank is not subject to the Fed's normal reserve requirements and chooses to have a lower reserve ratio. On the other hand, if digital currency issuers are required to hold the dollar (outside money) in an escrow account and cannot lend the deposit to a third person, the same amount of cash balance is held, either in digital cash or fiat cash, with no effect on the money multiplier.

If, however, digital currency is not backed by dollars or any outside money, digital currency is then simply a product whose price is determined only by the supply and demand in the market, akin to holding foreign currency in lieu of the dollar for cash transactions. Imagine that U.S. residents are suddenly using Mexican pesos or German marks for everyday transactions. Its effects on the money supply and the dollar interest rates deserve a great deal of investigation. For example, suppose that residents in Texas adopt a digital currency, which is not linked to the dollar, for their cash transactions. Alternatively, suppose that members of the North American Free Trade Agreement (NAFTA) integrate their economies while their currencies are maintained separately, and Texas residents begin to use Mexican pesos instead of dollars for grocery shopping. The dollar demand for cash will be greatly reduced. To reduce the supply of dollars, the Fed may engage in open market operations, for example, selling government bonds to the public, thereby increasing its cash holding and taking cash out of circulation. U.S. monetary officials claim that changes in the money supply can be adequately met by the Federal Reserve System, through open market operations, whether or not digital currency is backed up by fiat money. Nevertheless, if the Fed wants to reduce the money supply as the demand for dollars decreases, it needs to raise the interest rate to sell bonds. At the same time, people want to dispose of their cash by buying bonds, so that the increased demand for bonds will lower interest rates. The net effect of the Fed's open market operations and the citizen's demand for bonds may very well offset each other to produce stable interest rates. However, if the Fed's operations are out of sync, temporary instability will have a significant effect on the economy—as evidenced by the stock market response to a quarter point increase in the interest rate.

It may be enlightening to contrast the workings of Mark Twain Bank and Visa International. The latter creates credit, but this is offset by the need for Visa's investors and owners to inject funds to cover the float between paying vendors and receiving payments from card users. Because the inflow, on average, equals the outflow, no net increase occurs in the money supply. Note that the borrowers do not deposit their unused credit with anyone. Credit is extended only when Visa incurs an obligation to the vendor, which is a debit for Visa covered by its investor-provided reserves. There is no multiplier effect like the bank deposit/loan phenomenon. The total credit enjoyed by card users is offset by the invested funds needed to cover the float.

Another long-term impact that some economists posit is the possibility of a change in money velocity due to the introduction of digital currency (Panurach, 1996). The *velocity of money* refers to the rate at which the money circulates. Suppose that each transaction is worth $10. If the total transactional size of an economy is $1,000, requiring 100 transactions, the money circulated may be $1,000, which means that each $10 bill is used only once. On the other hand, a fast circulating $10 bill may be used for all 100 transactions, resulting in a much higher velocity of money.

Changes in payment systems—for example, employee compensation, not payments for transactions—also affect the velocity of money, but these changes are usually institutional. For example, in recent years, the increasing use of electronic forms of wages has lowered average money balances. Suppose that a person gets paid $3,000 in cash at the beginning of each month and spends it by the end of a month. The average cash balance will be $1,500. But if he is paid $1,500 twice a month, the average balance is only $750. The economy will have to print $1,500 worth of money for the former, while it needs only $750 for the latter. If the size of the economy is the same, the latter meets the same transactional needs with less money; there is a higher velocity of money. Similarly, if people use more non-cash payment methods, the need for cash diminishes, and the economy will not need to have more cash. Given the cash holding, then, convenient forms of wage payment and transactions tend to increase the money velocity.

However, the change in transaction speed seldom affects the real economy. In the above example, the size of the economy remains the same regardless of the money velocity. On the other hand, the real economy will grow if transactional opportunities arise. More convenient money facilitates the way money circulates in an economy, but its real effect is in lowering transactions cost, which increases economic efficiency and the level of overall economy. Many proposed electronic payment systems may simply replace existing payment methods without any real economic effect, if they have little effect on transactions cost.

Another issue pertaining to having more convenient forms of money is the relationship between the velocity of money and inflation. The earliest monetary theory, the quantity theory of money equation, shows that inflation increases if the stock of money or the velocity of money increases. However, if the money stock adjusts to compensate the change in the velocity of money, the price level will not change. Furthermore, simply having more convenient money would not affect the real economy without fundamental changes. For example, it is true that whenever a $10 bill exchanges hands, a transaction value of $10 is created. If the same amount of money circulates twice as fast, twice as much value will be created. However, to have a real impact on the economy, these values have to represent changing levels of production in real goods. For example, the sum of weekly transactional values on the NYSE often exceeds that of the annual Gross Domestic Product (GDP) of the United States, but the figure is of transactional—financial nature. The simple fact that money changes hands more frequently does not mean it will have a real impact on the economy.

Finally, the Internet is global and may add significant instability to a nation's monetary system through mechanisms that are out of that government's control. For example, if offshore banks require no, or lower, cash reserves for deposits, this will effectively lower the reserve-deposit ratio. Also, if offshore banks offer higher interest rates, people will reduce their cash holding, depositing their cash at these banks—which lowers the currency-deposit ratio. As a result, the money multiplier increases. When the monetary base changes, the larger money multiplier will produce a more volatile money supply, and possibly changes in price levels and fluctuations in the nominal GDP. Furthermore, if most people prefer to hold international electronic currency, open market operations by a central bank or the Fed may not be effective in controlling the amount of currency or interest rates. Like a small country whose exchange rate floats with dominant foreign currencies, domestic monetary policies may be rendered ineffective by a worldwide digital currency.

Effects on Market Organization

A new form of payment settlement system creates a new type of financial intermediary. The changes will be especially significant not only because electronic payment systems duplicate payment systems used in physical markets but also because they incorporate market processes that are not traditionally part of the payment clearing process. For example, the identification, authentication, and certification functions needed to begin a transaction have largely remained separate from the payment clearing process. In a face-to-face purchase, these functions are performed by checking a driver's license or examining a signature. In contrast, electronic payment systems must support these pre-payment processes as well, integrating such diverse functions as payment, market infrastructure, certification, security, and insurance. This results in a new type of market institutions and value creation processes, affecting competition and facilitating vertical integration.

A payment clearing service such as First Virtual is more integrated than NFT methods because it basically forms a separate market in which First Virtual not only handles payments but also acts as a market maker, quality guarantor and security. As a result, First Virtual offers a cost-effective way to sell and buy products electronically. However, it lacks interoperability as its membership information is not shared with other similar services. Consumers have to register with each PCS that exists if the merchant membership does not overlap. Imagine having to be a member to shop at each mall, which has its own payment system!

As for NFT systems such as CyberCash and digital check or credit card services, the role of payment intermediary will continue to be that of expediting settlement. Just as you see Visa, MasterCard, and other credit card logos on a merchant's door, web pages will be strewn with electronic logos informing consumers of optional payment systems honored at their sites. Each consumer and merchant must open an account with CyberCash or other payment services offered in the market. Does this represent any improvement over physical markets? In this regard, digital credit cards using an industry standard such as SET may have an advantage over using numerous NFT intermediaries, each issuing their versions of electronic wallets. However, credit card-based systems simply extend existing payment networks to the Internet, which may be sufficient for old models of business. As electronic commerce demands new kinds of products and consumption behaviors, electronic payment systems must also reflect these changes. For example, a cost-effective micropayment system will be needed for microbundles and microsales of information products. Even for this purpose alone, digital currency and its related market infrastructure should be nurtured.

Left alone to markets, various forms of electronic payment systems will differentiate by price, convenience and quality. Price certainly will be determined by the difference between the cost of providing an electronic payment service and the cost of using a conventional system—or the consumer's willingness to pay given this opportunity cost. In terms of transaction costs, online transactions must be far more efficient to generate enough spread between the two options. Thus, efficiency gains are turned into profit opportunities. However, this ignores consumers' willingness to pay, which may very well increase because of convenience, anonymity and other factors that are not available offline. Greater willingness to pay will support electronic payment systems that may increase transaction costs. The major challenges of electronic payment systems are not in reducing transaction costs or perfecting security but in producing usage values to gain consumer acceptance and devising efficient pricing strategies for various payment intermediaries. For the Mondex system, (Clemons et al., 1997) identify various ways to charge consumers for its service: selling cards, renting cards, charging a fee for bank-to-card transfer, charging a fee for currency-to-Mondex exchange, or discounting when Mondex currencies are traded for outside monies. For digital currency, what is known as *seigniorage* can be a source of profit. Because this involves monetary policies, banking regulation and international currency exchanges, this chapter concludes by examining the role of governments in promoting digital currency.

10.7. Digital Currency and Governments

After being created, digital currency can be traded on the global Internet, meaning that digital currency is necessarily an international issue. It is not unimaginable that you will see the last of foreign currency trading due to global digital currency. Equally likely, however, is that digital currencies may add to the number of existing international units of money, further complicating foreign exchange rates and trading.

Despite these potentially serious impacts, the U.S. government's attitude toward digital currency is one of non-interference and sometimes one of promotion. The reasons for this policy can be summarized from recent remarks by the Federal Reserve chairman, Alan Greenspan (1996). First, in an environment without government intervention, private businesses are motivated to self-regulate. As firms compete for reputation and strive to inform consumers of their quality, they have ample incentive for self-regulation and industry-wide cooperation. Second, innovations mandated by governments often differ from market-driven solutions. The viability of any new product, such as a digital currency, must be proven in the marketplace by consumers and merchants rather than by policymaking bodies. Together, these rationales favor non-interference in the development of digital money.

This said, governments play an important role, by choice or by necessity, in several areas. The first issue demanding a closer examination is the possible reduction in government revenue due to private monies. Second, there are various regulatory issues involving consumer protection and law enforcement issues, such as money laundering, that demand government attention. Third, the legal and monetary ramifications of who can issue digital currency warrant closer attention by the government. Finally, a government action may have no impact on the Internet because an online operator can simply ship its operation to a server in another country, often involving no physical relocation.

Effects on Government Revenues

Money is exchanged with goods and services of equal value except when it is issued by the government, which gains from the difference between the cost of printing a dollar and the value of a dollar, known as the seigniorage. The government derives further revenue from dollar currency held by consumers, which amounts to interest-free lending to the government by the public—a privilege often abused by excessive printing. In 1994, most of the $20 billion generated by the Federal Reserve could be accounted for by the government's privilege to print money (Blinder, 1994). Thus, when private monies are issued, they take away some portion of the government's revenue related to seigniorage and other currency operations.

As long as a national government is the only currency issuer, its revenue related to seigniorage is the monopoly profit. If private firms are allowed to print money, the profit will be shared with these firms. The dollar is accepted by the public because of the public's confidence in the U.S. government. Likewise, the acceptance of private money will depend on the public's trust in the companies who issue the money. This does not mean that private companies will appropriate profits that previously were the government's revenues. Whether the profit is kept by them or is distributed to consumers will depend on the competitiveness in the currency industry. If, for example, online banks compete by paying interest on digital currency deposits, the interest paid to depositors is the seigniorage now being appropriated by governments. The competition among issuers may well drive the private profit to a level where a significant portion of the monopoly profit currently enjoyed by governments is instead given to consumers in the form of convenience, service, and quality.

Regulatory Issues

Governments play a role in a wide range of regulatory issues regarding the use of currency. Using the example of the U.S., this section discusses in detail how a current reading of relevant regulations and laws highlights the need for governments to resolve any uncertainty regarding the use of digital currency.

First, in terms of consumer protection, the Electronic Fund Transfer Act (EFTA) and its Federal Reserve implementation rules, known as Regulation E, determine the rights and responsibilities of consumers and financial institutions. EFTA and Regulation E establish the rights, liabilities, and responsibilities of parties in EFTs involving consumers. For example, under EFTA, consumers are liable only to a maximum of $500 for unauthorized use of a stolen or lost credit card. Further, this regulation establishes consumers' rights regarding account disputes, damages, and losses. However, these regulations are limited to EFTs and do not seem to cover, as written now, electronic currency because digital currency is not "transfer information" but rather money itself. Instead, if you lose a balance on your Mondex card, for example, the issuer must provide consumers with remedies. The terms of remedies will most likely need to be disclosed before consumers purchase digital currency. However, disclosure rules governed by EFTA and Regulation E also do not extend to digital currency. Unlike services based on dollar currency, digital currency intermediaries will have to assure consumers of their quality and reliability to succeed in the market. Through competition, it is likely that an assortment of digital currency will be offered to exploit various needs of transaction, with prices reflecting the degree of reliability and convenience.

Second, government agencies require banks to keep records and file reports on certain types of currency transactions to detect and counter money laundering and other criminal activities. The government's control over money laundering depends on its capability to follow the money trail. While the debate has been raging on whether to allow anonymous digital coins, a technical issue has not been resolved regarding who will provide routine data on money movements. The Bank Secrecy Act (BSA) requires banks and financial institutions to report certain transactions, for example, currency transactions exceeding $10,000. However, BSA definitions regarding financial institutions, currency, monetary instruments, and funds transfers may or may not apply to digital currency and currency servers. For example, financial institutions that are subject to the BSA regulation are entities licensed to transmit funds or an issuer, seller, or redeemer of traveler's checks. If digital currency is treated as a traveler's check, the BSA may apply to the issuer. But legal definitions must be cleared by legislators beforehand. Finally, the nature of digital currency may pose a problem for law enforcement. In general, digital currencies are expected to be used for extremely low-value transactions, which would be a poor medium for money laundering if regulatory agencies monitor the frequency of transactions as well as the amount. Existing control over dollar currency may be adequate to discourage criminal uses of digital currency.

Third, the advent of digital currency raises the need to reexamine existing state and federal laws, which regulate who can issue private monies and accept money as deposits. Until 1913, state-chartered private banks were allowed to issue currency in the United States subject to state regulations, and some states today have laws regulating the issuance of private monies. However, a federal law (18 U.S.C. 336), in addition to the U.S. Constitution's grant to Congress to coin money (Article 1, Section 8), appears to prohibit private businesses from issuing currency. 18 U.S.C. 336 codifies the 1862 Stamp Payments Act, which has a direct bearing on digital coins. It states that:

> "…whoever makes, issues, circulates, or pays out any note, check, memorandum, token, or other obligation for a sum of less than $1, intended to circulate as money or to be received or used in lieu of lawful money of the United States,"

is subject to a fine and six months' imprisonment. The Stamp Payments Act was enacted during the Civil War to counter inflationary effects of notes issued by merchants because of the disappearing U.S. coins (which were stockpiled because the coin's actual value was higher than its face value due to inflation). Although the Federal Reserve and other government agencies have maintained a laissez-faire attitude toward someone who can issue digital currency, this uncertainty needs to be addressed in a legal and concrete way.

An equally uncertain issue for digital currency issuers and servers is whether they are considered deposit takers. Under the Glass Steagall Act, Section 21, only banks can accept deposits, and deposit-taking institutions are prohibited from selling securities. Thus, only banks would be allowed to offer digital currency services if selling digital coins is considered to be accepting deposits. On the other hand, if digital currency is regarded as a digital commodity, any retailer could sell digital currency. Furthermore, if digital currency issuers are classified as banks, the Bank Holding Company Act (12 U.S.C. 1841) will prohibit any non-bank firm from owning a business that issues digital currency. The Federal Reserve closely controls deposit-taking banks through these regulations. However, if non-bank firms are allowed to issue digital currency, the Fed's control will be weakened, although Fed Reserve officials do not see a significant change in their ability to control the monetary policy. Nevertheless, Congress, the Federal Reserve, and the Justice Department should put forth their clear opinions regarding these issues if digital currency services are to be accepted for electronic commerce.

Issues in International Commerce

The nature of the Internet as an international network also raises the question of whether one governmental body can regulate banking and financial services that may operate overseas through offshore (Internet) banks and digital currency issuers. These overseas entities have the same local presence on the Internet while circumventing regulations imposed on local banks.

For example, offshore banks are usually not subject to income tax, reserve requirements, insurance premiums, and so on, which burden U.S. domestic banks. This lack of regulation means opportunities for banks and financial institutions. But, consumers also will benefit from the globalization of banking. Many offshore banks are already advertising on the Internet for their services, offering higher interest rates on deposits and better terms for loans. As they expand their ability to transfer money to offshore sites through cheaper communications media such as the Internet, ordinary consumers will gain access to more favorable offshore banking. To date, offshore banking has been available only to a few, whose large transactions justify offshore banking's high cost (White, 1996).

Offshore banks have these advantages because customers do not need foreign currency conversions. For example, Caribbean offshore banks allow dollar-denominated accounts to serve U.S. residents. If offshore banking involves foreign exchange, the benefit calculation will be more complex. Using the same currency, offshore depositors are able to exploit the differences in economic environment, such as banking regulations. However, if money is ubiquitous worldwide and physical location is no longer relevant, what would offshore banking mean? The increased use of worldwide digital currency may eliminate regulatory differences among governments, and with it, many advantages of offshore banking as well.

The prospect of a worldwide digital currency is at best puzzling as to its impacts on the parity of national currencies and economies. First, what would be the value of one, say, Digital Currency Unit (DCU$), if it is pegged to a dollar? Internet users in France may be paid in DCU$, but when they convert them into francs, they may have to use the dollar-to-franc exchange rate. The system of foreign exchange will resemble that of the physical market, where all currencies can be converted to a dollar. But the ever-changing exchange rates do cause inconvenience for non-U.S. countries. Will this mean that every country will issue digital currency denominated by its own currency unit? One thing is certain: digital currencies will reflect the real international economy as long as they remain as inside monies because their exchange values are determined by outside economies. Therefore, economic activities in the electronic marketplace will determine the characteristics of digital money, not vice versa.

10.8.   Summary

Although a plethora of disparate payment systems are offered for electronic commerce, many firms are reluctant to expand into online commerce because of a perceived lack of suitable payment mechanisms. Widely different technical specifications make it difficult to choose an appropriate payment method. This chapter, instead of focusing on the technical specifications of proposed electronic payment systems, distinguishes electronic payment methods based on what is transmitted over the network. Because consumers are familiar with credit card payment methods, they may accept electronic versions as the standard for electronic commerce.

Nevertheless, existing payment methods developed for relatively high-value transactions cannot adequately support web-based information trading. A cost-effective micropayment system is essential for transactions of extremely small value, just as cash remains the preferred payment method for these transactions. Anonymity is only one aspect of cash transaction, but it has received disproportionate, often sensational, attention in the press and by regulatory agencies while the economic need for a cash-like payment system in electronic commerce is largely ignored. Factors such as micropayments and peer-to-peer transfers in electronic commerce—especially for the information market—seem to indicate a healthy market for digital currency or small-value digital checks or credit cards.

In terms of the regulatory and monetary impact, private digital monies clearly present problems and opportunities. But, as with any digital product, the future of digital currency will be determined by the market demand and supply. Consequently, it is more than likely that each payment method reviewed in this chapter will find a niche market and consumers will selectively use an appropriate payment method depending on whether they prefer convenience, costs, privacy, or the advantage of credit extension. The usefulness of digital currency, however, has to be emphasized in terms of what a web-based information economy would mean for the future of electronic commerce and the Internet. With a suitable payment method, the age of information will manifest itself on the Internet, albeit in a commercial form.

References

Bester, H., and E. Petrakis, 1996. "Coupons and Oligopolistic Price Discrimination." *International Journal of Industrial Organization*, 14: 227–242.

Blinder, A.S., 1995. "Statements to the Congress." *Federal Reserve Bulletin*, 81(12): 1089–1093.

Champ, B., B.D. Smith and S.D. Williamson, 1996. "Currency Elasticity and Banking Panics: Theory and Evidence." *Canadian Journal of Economics*, 29(4): 828–864.

Clemons, E.K., D.C. Carson and B.W. Weber, 1997. "Reengineering Money: The Mondex Stored Value Card and Beyond." *International Journal of Electronic Commerce*, 1(2): 5–31.

Federal Reserve Bank of St. Louis, 1995. "A Payment Revolution in the Making." *1995 Annual Report.*

Greenspan, A., 1996. Remarks given to the U.S. Treasury Conference, "Toward Electronic Money and Banking: The Role of Government," September 19, 1996.

Kalakota, R., and A.B. Whinston, 1997. *Electronic Commerce: A Manager's Guide.* Reading, Mass.: Addison-Wesley.

Knudson, S.E., J.K. Walton, and F. M. Young, 1994. "Business-to-Business Payments and the Role of Financial Electronic Data Interchange." *Federal Reserve Bulletin*, 80(4): 269–278.

Panurach, P. 1996. "Money in Electronic Commerce: Digital Cash, Electronic Funds Transfer, and Ecash." *Communications of ACM*, 39(6): 45–50.

U.S. Department of the Treasury, 1996. "An Introduction to Electronic Money Issues." Prepared for the U.S. Department of the Treasury Conference *Toward Electronic Money and Banking: The Role of Government.*

White, L. 1996. *The Technology Revolution and Monetary Evolution.* Presented at the Cato Institute's 14th Annual Monetary Conference, May 23, 1996.

Williamson, S.,and R. Wright, 1994. "Barter and Monetary Exchange Under Private Information." *American Economic Review,* 84(1): 104–123.

Suggested Readings and Notes

Quantity Theory of Money

Dean, E., ed., 1965. *The Controversy over the Quantity Theory of Money.* Lexington, Mass.: Heath.

Judd, J.P., 1983. "The Recent Decline in Velocity: Instability in Money Demand or Inflation?" *Economic Review,* Federal Reserve Bank of San Francisco, Spring 1983, pp. 12–19.

Monetary Freedom

White, L., 1984. *Free Banking in Britain: Theory, Experience, Debate, 1800–1845.* Cambridge: Cambridge University Press.

Glasner, D., 1989. *Free Banking and Monetary Reform.* Cambridge Mass: Cambridge University Press.

Federal Reserve Bank of San Francisco. "A Brief History of Our Nation's Paper Money." *1995 Annual Report*, available at http://www.frbsf.org/frbsf/pubs/annualrpt/history.html.

Electronic Payment Systems

Micro Payment Transfer Protocol is a standard proposed in November, 1995 by the WWW Consortium (W3C) for micropayments on the Internet. Its draft is available at http://www.w3.org/hypertext/www/TR/WD-mptp.

For NetCash specification, see Medvinsky, G., and B.C. Neuman, 1993, "NetCash: A Design for Practical Electronic Currency on the Internet," in *Proceedings of the First ACM Conference on Computer and Communications Security*, November, 1993.

Flohr, U., 1996. "Electric Money." *Byte*, June, 1996, pp. 74–84.

The Economist. "Electronic Money: So Much for the Cashless Society." November 26, 1994, pp. 21–23.

Readers who are interested in traditional banking on the Internet, home banking, or web banking may consult Chapter 7 of Kalakota and Whinston (1997) mentioned above.

Internet Resources

Electronic Money Resources

Mondex FAQ is available at http://www.mondex.com/mondex/faq.htm.

For FSTC Check Imaging Information, see http://www.fstc.org/projects/ imaging.

Electronic Frontier Foundation's E-money and privacy archive is at http:// www.eff.org/pub/Privacy/Digital_money/.

Useful links to electronic money sites maintained by Roy Davies are found at http://www.ex.ac.uk/~RDavies/arian/emoney.html.

Electronic Banking Resource Center also has links to other sites and reading materials. See http://www2.cob.ohio-state.edu/~richards/bankpay.htm.

Standard Electronic Transactions (SET)

SET specification is available for review at either MasterCard or Visa home pages:

http://www.mastercard.com or http://www.visa.com.

The mailing list "set-discuss@commerce.net" is a discussion list maintained by CommerceNet consortium, a forum for comments and discussion about SET. To subscribe to the set-discuss mailing list, send e-mail to: majordomo@commerce.net with a message that reads "subscribe set-discuss."

CHAPTER 11

Business and Policy Implications of Electronic Commerce

Today, commerce on the Internet is frequently equated with the concept of doing business electronically and is often promoted as a means for businesses to lower their costs and improve their efficiency in various stages of business transactions. However, electronic commerce goes beyond the mere adoption of new Internet technology for conducting business according to traditional practices. Electronic commerce operates in a new electronic marketplace where the very players, products and processes are fundamentally changed. Drawing on insights from previous chapters, this chapter's goal is to summarize what previous chapters have advanced: the key to understanding and exploiting electronic commerce is to recognize it as a market mechanism in which all components of a market interact and must be analyzed collectively.

With this understanding, this chapter evaluates a number of factors that traditionally impact costs and efficiency. These include the size of the firm, product quality, reputation, consumer access to information and advertising. These and other business factors are intertwined with policy issues. The discussion expands to include the impact of electronic commerce on policies governing new market protection measures, such as digital copyrights, mass advertising on the Internet, and pricing strategies for digital products. The discussion of each topic highlights market aspects, which are consistently ignored in current debates, and raises issues that will require tackling in the future as electronic commerce continues to grow.

11.1.   Internet as the Great Equalizer

In physical markets, the size of a firm impacts its chances for success in a variety of ways. For example, large firms and corporations often have better access to the capital market than do small firms. Economies of scale often result in increased profits for large companies. And the widespread name recognition of large, established firms is a valuable asset in itself. Such advantages—for example, of General Motors over small-scale car manufacturers—translate into a dominance in physical markets.

The very different environment of electronic commerce has raised questions about whether size will have the same impact in this new marketplace. The virtual existence of companies on the Internet, for instance, makes it difficult to distinguish physical differences in their size. From this fact alone, a notion has developed that the electronic marketplace is the great equalizer, which accommodates big and small firms on equal terms.

The Virtual Equality

In a physical market, consumers easily recognize the difference between a posh department store and a discount store by their physical appearances. However, in the virtual world, physical appearance fails to convey information about the size and hence relative market position of the store. On the Internet, anyone with a web page can look as good as a large corporation and can in fact provide the same level of technical assistance and customer support through automated programs. Internet users do not know for certain with whom they are interacting. In fact, a popular cartoon about the net claims that "no one knows you are a dog on the Internet" (see fig. 8.6). Although there are means to learn about identities, the Internet provides a reasonable level of anonymity, and such anonymity can be useful in social communications, eliminating certain prejudices when gender-neutral aliases and pronouns are used. But will such an advantage translate into an economic benefit for companies?

The Reputational Transfer

Contrary to the popular vision of virtual equality that paints the future of electronic commerce as a market where the distinction between large and small becomes moot, there is ample evidence that large firms may dominate electronic commerce. First of all, a firm with an established reputation in physical markets may be able to transfer this reputation to the virtual market. To the extent that the company has established a reputation as a dominant and large firm in physical markets, this reputation transfer represents a form of size advantage in electronic commerce as well.

You can already see evidence of this in electronic commerce. During the first stage of market growth, small, entrepreneurial firms dominated the Internet scene. However, a reversal of fortune has become evident in many product markets. For example, Amazon.com (http://www.amazon.com), the largest and most successful online bookstore, faces stiff competition from established booksellers such as Barnes & Noble and Borders (http://www.borders.com). In another example, Netscape was the early entrant to the web-browser market, holding almost 90 percent of the market until the giant in the physical world entered. Microsoft's Internet Explorer has reduced Netscape Navigator's market share by 20 percent in just one year since its introduction. The question of quality—for example, downloading speed, ease of use, and features—often becomes secondary to Microsoft's reputation as the leader in physical markets. In addition, Microsoft can bundle its browser with its operating system software so that new users inadvertently become its customers. (For a comprehensive browser comparison, see C-Net's information page at http://www.cnet.com/Content/Reviews/Compare/Browsers/index.html.)

Other firms native to the Internet will soon face challenges from physically large firms as well. For example, VeriSign (http://www.verisign.com) has been the pioneer in certification services. But, the U.S. Postal Service (http://www.usps.gov) intends to enter the certification business, which requires verification technologies and the public's trust in a third party. Similarly, many Internet payment services companies will have to compete with large firms, such as national banks and Visa and MasterCard. Although Internet-native firms have been small, innovative enterprises, their competitive edge is being rapidly eroded as large firms with reputation, and the capital, in physical markets enter the arena. Transferred reputation is clearly one factor that makes size matter in electronic commerce.

Declining Average Costs and the Advantage of Size

Another reason why size will continue to matter in the electronic marketplace stems from an economic observation of the process of competition in digital products. A simplified competition process may take the following form. Given that a digital product requires a large initial investment to produce the first unit, the per-unit cost decreases as the number of units sold increases. In other words, a digital product producer has an increasing economy of scale—declining average costs—with respect to the number of sales. Understandably, each firm tries to maximize its market share. For a set quality, producers can determine the minimum number of sales needed to break even. In the case of competition among same-quality producers, this break-even price will be the same for all. Any price below that will increase market share, but the firm will not break even. If the firm is large enough, and possesses enough capital, a high-quality producer can cut its price and gain market share, despite losses, as a temporary strategy to drive out competitors. And as the firm's market size grows, it can further reduce its price as its average cost declines. Contrary to the common belief that the Internet is an equalizer of small and large firms, only firms with sizeable capital may survive a heated competition.

Because a sizeable market share is necessary to cover the initial fixed cost of production, the Internet as the "great equalizer" might well be a myth. A larger firm that can invest more in quality will command a higher share of the market. If products have the same price, a firm with higher quality will dominate the market because consumers learn about quality and repeat purchases.

Product Differentiation and Size

Economies of scale operate where products are homogeneous or if consumers regard different products as essentially the same. In some cases, products are homogenized especially to take advantage of the economies of scale. For example, Ford's Model T in the 1920s maintained a low price because the automobile manufacturer relied on mass production of only one model. As the market for automobiles grew, different models were offered that still benefited from the economies of scale afforded by increased sales—up to a certain ceiling. A specific car model may cost more if it is produced beyond, say, 300,000 units, because of the physical limitations of its manufacturing facilities.

This ceiling on economies of scale may not apply to digital products, which may not exhaust the economies of scale regardless of the market size. In this case, where the average cost would continue to decline ad infinitum, it would be better business sense to have one version of a product.

Some economists, observing the reproducibility of digital products, seem to feel that this infinitely declining average cost implies that companies will steer away from incurring the high cost of investing in new products. According to them, digital products are affected by economies of scale, interoperability, and standardization, all of which favor a dominant product instead of many competing products. As a result, in their view, consumers will be forced to accept a Model T of any digital product because it is most efficient.

In our view, consumer tastes differ, and products will be differentiated to match consumers' preferences regardless of the efficiency. Just as mass production technology—whose main objective is to minimize production costs—was the essence of earlier industrial development, recent computer-assisted manufacturing technologies have introduced the capability for customized production of physical products, say, automobiles, at a far smaller number with extreme model variations. Digital products, due to their transmutability, represent a further departure from mass production of a single average product. In addition, differentiated and niche market products can be marketed more efficiently on the Internet through targeted e-mailing, newsgroups, and discussion lists, as well as through direct consumer participation in product development. As a result, the conventional economic model, in which firms with declining average costs compete by lowering prices, will apply only when products are substantially homogeneous or substitutable.

When products are highly differentiated, producers possess a degree of market power over their market segment. To secure such market segments, smaller firms and individuals can rely on qualities that have little to do with the size of a firm or initial investment. For example, the value of point of view and authority in commentaries and intellectual works cannot be adequately represented by conventional economic modeling about costs. Having a point of view that is valued by consumers is not a simple function of fixed costs, such as years of education or experience. Given these other considerations, the dominance and the reputation of a firm in electronic commerce may not depend solely on the size or the initial investment, and producers of niche market products may taunt the prevailing economies of scale in the electronic marketplace.

11.2. Search Service and Its Market Implications

As mentioned earlier, the Internet is often touted as a means for firms large and small to improve their efficiency. However, efficiency in the electronic marketplace is critically dependent on efficiency in search activities. In physical markets, consumers learn about products and locate sellers through a variety of methods ranging from advertisements, word of mouth, directories and references, and pure chance. In contrast, the vastness of the virtual marketplace works to isolate consumers because of the lack of *immediate space*. Consumers cannot simply pass and remember stores while commuting to work. In the absence of this, search engines and online advertisements are key to helping consumers navigate the virtual marketplace.

Chapter 7 discussed several inadequacies of Internet search services in terms of completeness, accuracy, relevancy, and objectivity of information. For example, no complete listing of all Internet resources exists, and search information is often out-dated because the World Wide Web is changing constantly. However, the heated debate about the role of search services revolves around two other aspects: the use of consumer information and the commercialization of search services. Section 11.5, "Digital Products and Pricing," discusses in more detail the policy aspects of the availability of consumer information versus consumer privacy. This section explores the critical role of search services in market efficiency.

First, to be efficient, search services or their databases need to remain objective and public. Although commercial services can provide objective information at the lowest possible price by including advertisements, proper attention should be given to the possibility of introducing unnecessary inefficiencies under this advertiser-supported model of business. To understand this better, you can review examples found in mass media and advertising.

Advertising in Broadcast Media

Television and newspapers rely on paid advertisements because it is difficult to charge customers based on their usage and valuation. Because media companies cannot distinguish frequent TV watchers or newspaper readers from the occasional audience, there can only be one price for all consumers. In the case of television, broadcasters cannot even locate their customers to bill them individually. As a result, television programs are often considered similar to public goods for which adequate pricing mechanisms are hard to find. To solve the problem of billing, television broadcasters are in the business of selling to advertisers; the (paying) customers of TV broadcasters are not the audience but the advertisers; and their products are TV-watching *consumers*, not TV programs. In this way, two separate markets—TV programs and advertising markets—are combined via the intermediary role of broadcasters (see a.) in fig. 11.1). This peculiar business arrangement is not due to the characteristics of television programming or program consumption, but rather to the way television signals are carried over the air. Today, cable television gives broadcasters the capability to control their signals and monitor usage. In this case, as depicted in b.) of figure 11.1, the two markets can be separated. Nevertheless, the practice of advertiser-supported programming continues, even when consumers pay for subscription.

a.) TV program and advertising in one market with networks as intermediaries

b.) TV program market and advertising market

Figure 11.1 TV broadcasting and advertising.

One primary argument in favor of advertising in all broadcast media is the lower resulting price. Newspapers with advertisements would cost more, if they were able to exist at all, which might prevent many readers from subscribing. The quality of television might suffer if broadcasters could not rely on advertising revenues, again if they were able to exist at all. But, the argument that consumers get high-quality free products because of advertisements is weak on two accounts. First, these products are not free because consumers pay in the form of watching commercials or reading advertisements, for which no adequate compensation is paid. Second, television programs are manufactured to maximize audience—the number of eyeballs sold to advertisers—not to satisfy consumers' preferences. As a result, TV programs usually cater to the lowest common denominator—sex and violence—to maximize audience size. Program line-ups also reflect the need to maximize audience flow from program to program, and the need to dominate the ratings game when advertiser-sponsored audience measurements occur during the sweeps period.

When unrelated product markets are artificially linked, optimization cannot be expected to prevail. The objectives in the television programming market will only occasionally match the objectives of the advertising market. In the advertising-supported TV market, the type and quality of programs are determined not by consumer preferences but by the incentive to maximize profits from advertising. As a result, TV executives choose programs with little consideration for consumer demand. Similar inefficiencies will be observed in advertiser-supported search services.

Search Engines and Advertising

Search engine providers that use advertising are intermediaries, just like TV networks, that sell access to consumers or consumer information to advertisers. Their search databases are like television programs that attract an audience. However, why would a narrow-cast medium like the Internet need a business model that evolved to address the peculiar problem of selling over-the-air entertainment? Unlike in mass media markets, Internet markets for content and advertisements can be separated. In the advertisement market, sellers (advertisers) can sell their products directly to consumers. Consumers will be paid for reading advertisements. In the search market, consumers will pay service providers directly for the information. In either market, product selection and prices will be based on preferences and costs relevant to either advertisements or search information.

Some consumers prefer not to pay for search services and are willing to tolerate advertising banners that are presented with search results. Others are frustrated by the delay caused by graphic banners, which often maintain surreptitious connections with advertising servers. Even as bandwidth becomes cheaper, congestion will remain due to the ever-increasing size of content. In addition to the congestion problem, essential problems remain regarding advertiser-supported search services.

First, as in broadcasting, advertisers cannot be sure of the effectiveness of advertising. Second, while an advertiser-based free service (like TV) or a flat-fee billing system (like newspapers) may seem to be a cost-effective and equitable way of providing services, this is not the case. Some consumers are discouraged from using the service because of the distortion introduced by advertising. Others use the service beyond an efficient level, resulting in the abuse or waste of the resource because it is free or cheap to use.

The commercialization of search services best exemplifies how broadcast-based business models are commonly applied to electronic commerce without serious consideration of the implications. This section's discussion is not intended to press for a usage-based fee structure for search services, nor to advocate publicly supporting search services. The discussion does, however, demonstrate that the Internet's technological differences warrant a reexamination of business models based on mass communications media.

Digital Cataloging Guidelines

The efficiency of Internet searches will ultimately depend on web pages providing consistent product descriptions of themselves. An increasing array of products are digitized and sold in electronic commerce, beyond digital versions of paper-based products. Product descriptions in these cases should be more than mere descriptions of physical appearance because digital products essentially consist of ones and zeros. Nevertheless, little effort is being exerted to set standards and guidelines for digital cataloging. Two aspects of digital cataloging are relevant for electronic commerce: content description and search interfacing.

Content Description

Catalogs list and describe items available for sale or for other purposes, such as in the case of library catalogs. A good catalog not only describes a product succinctly but also provides a useful classification. Once such catalogs exist for all web resources, the efficiency of Internet searches will be greatly enhanced.

No guidelines or agreed-upon standards exist for digital catalogs. Digital libraries are developing digital catalog standards but these are based on conventional methods (that is, digital library catalogs are based on non-digital library catalogs with a simple addition about file types). The catalog industry has been working on electronic catalog standards in connection with CommerceNet since 1994 (http://www.commerce.net/work/taskforces/catalogs). Electronic catalogs refer to electronic versions of product catalogs that producers and retailers offer consumers for ordering. Although one goals of its task force is to develop a framework to define products using taxonomies, the task force has focused narrowly on the question of search interfaces and architecture.

Because of the sheer number of web resources, it is easier for content producers to provide content descriptions when products are made than to rely on Internet search agents visiting web pages after they are made. When geographic data is collected, it is conventional to compile meta-data describing the data; for all physical databases, producers compile codebooks without which they are often useless. The same logic should apply to web resources and all digital products.

Search Interfaces

Once adequate product descriptions exist for all digital products, they must be presented on demand to searchers, who may use a variety of search methods or desire to access multiple catalogs for comparison. The CommerceNet Catalog Working Group is developing such an open and versatile electronic catalog system. Although the group is developing the framework for the catalog industry, such as virtual mail-order firms, it can be used for electronic commerce in general.

One of the group's proposed systems utilizes smart catalogs and virtual catalogs (Keller, 1997). Smart catalogs are product descriptions provided by producers. Virtual catalogs are maintained by intermediaries (retailers) and provide interfaces between consumers who seek information and producers who offer (smart) catalogs. Under the virtual catalog system, consumers need not interact with each producer to perform multi-vendor comparisons. Virtual catalogs allow producers control over their own catalogs, and offer dynamic and up-to-date catalog information. Precisely such a system is needed for Internet searches because of the large number of content vendors, the speed at which content changes, and the efficiency of intermediaries in maintaining quality and measuring and billing for usage.

11.3. Copyright Protection Standards

As mentioned in Chapter 5, electronic commerce requires not only a reexamination of basic business models and assumptions, as seen earlier, but also requires basic revisions of policy. Efforts are being made to amend or reinvent copyright laws to suit digital products and electronic commerce. The practicality and viability of any scheme will ultimately be determined by product characteristics, consumer usage behavior, and economic efficiency. Copyright enforcement efforts are needed when an author's market is eroded by unauthorized copies. But in some cases, the author's rights can be better protected by market-oriented mechanisms than by legal measures.

In general, current copyright debate revolves around the revision of existing laws to adapt to the new technological environment. However, the characteristics and usage pattern of digital products may be sufficiently different from paper-based products to require a fundamental shift in protecting the market for new, digital products. For example, the reproductive right features prominently in copyright law because reproduction via variant technologies of the printing press has been the primary mode of production, distribution, and usage in the paper-based world. In the digital world, however, reproduction often occurs for technical reasons, without the intention to duplicate and distribute. Sometimes, using a digital file may not even involve *reading* the document. For example, a user may want to obtain a graph summarizing a database; the database itself is never physically read or viewed except by the graphing program. Such differences must be considered as laying the foundation for the digital age begins with a fundamental shift in copyright protection. If current copyright law is a product of the invention of printing presses, the new digital copyright law should account for the changes that digital technologies bring into the paper-based world.

Important issues remain to be addressed. Missing in the current copyright debate is how the determination of copyright affects the pricing of digital products and government policies. A copyright payment is the royalty paid to the author to compensate for the cost of the production. Because copyright payment is made for each reproduction of the original, the copyright payment is the cost of reproduction. For this reason, variable costs for digital products will not be zero even when the costs of duplicating a digital file may come close to zero. As a result, the marginal cost of a digital product will vary with copyright payment, and the efficient price of a digital product will largely be a function of royalty payments, which account for a substantial portion of manufacturing costs. To see how the definition of copyright affects government policy, consider that, if a sale is made for a digital product, the income from the sale may be treated as an ordinary sale or as a royalty payment from a reproduction. The same income, then, will be governed by different federal income tax laws regarding sales income or royalty income, which are taxed at different rates.

The real impact of copyright modifications will be judged in the marketplace. Content owners' primary concern is the loss of revenue due to unauthorized reproductions and sales. Where revenue opportunities do not exist, copyright enforcement is only symbolic. Similarly, if there is no incentive to reproduce and distribute without authorization, the cost and effort expended to secure copyrights would not be economically justified. Products can be designed with this in mind. Many digital products can be personalized so as to make them useless for any other person. Highly time-sensitive information soon turns worthless, other than for archiving purposes. And finally, some products can be delivered interactively and in a secure manner, similar to stock market data distributed via private networks. Making products insensitive to reproduction and resale is an alternative to the vexing problem of securing digital copyright.

11.4. The Use of Consumer Information

Because there are sizable gains to be made from refining consumer demand information, collecting information about consumer preferences is widely promoted, and electronic commerce provides a unique opportunity for this.

But, although this information is clearly helpful to the sellers and researchers, a standard must be established to protect consumers. Presently, information collectors need only give notification and disclosure to consumers before using such consumer information.

Rather than relying on regulatory solutions, however, innovative concepts are being tested in electronic commerce. One new idea is to give consumers the right to sell information about themselves. As discussed in section 8.3, this market-based solution turns personal information into a marketable commodity. Many online services are offered in return for divulging personal information. In this case, the price for that information will be equal to the value of the service offered. Some consumers may use the service heavily, implying a high price for their information. Others may give out their information for a service they seldom use, signaling a low value for their personal information. Going beyond reporting names and addresses, consumers may be willing to sell all types of consumption data if the price is right. In a way, consumers will become information sellers by participating in market research or focus groups.

At least in one sense, selling personal consumption data may be detrimental to consumer welfare. In electronic commerce, such data will be directly linked to purchasing and price negotiation. With demand known, sellers may refuse to lower prices below a level that they think is a consumer's valuation. However, rather than going back to a market with imperfect demand and inferior product quality, the market may be able to produce an equitable and efficient result. For example, the potentially higher sale price can be partly compensated by a higher payment for personal information. This also demonstrates a reason consumer information may have to be priced and traded in the market. A slew of economic questions arise regarding prices and the efficiency in such a market. Perhaps the vigor evidenced in the debate on privacy and anonymity among legal scholars, government officials, and free-speech activists might guide economists to this task in the future.

11.5.   Digital Products and Pricing

In this nascent field of research in electronic commerce, economists already have developed multiple—often contradictory—theories of how digital products should be distributed, sold and priced. Some argue for bundling (a sort of flat fee) while others argue for micropayments (a sort of usage-based pricing). Each has some evidence for justification and mathematical as well as economic proofs (see Chapter 8 for more information on pricing and bundling). However, this section cautions against applying existing models of physical markets to the electronic marketplace. Those who see electronic commerce as simply an alternative marketing channel find spurious similarities between digital products and their physical counterparts, and argue that electronic commerce pricing will be no different from physical markets where vendors prefer bundling and subscription. Although some products and services will indeed be better served by bundling and subscription, this practice will be only a small part of how digital products will be sold in electronic commerce. Instead, the changing nature of information goods and market processes will demand more flexible distribution and pricing schemes, such as microproducts and micropayments.

Bundling and Subscription

In the physical world, information products are often bundled and sold on by subscription, and that observation has convinced many that the same practice may be adequately applied to pricing digital products. Witness the way a newspaper is delivered: all sorts of news and information in a one-size-fits-all package. Cable services, on the other hand, are priced as a tier instead of as a la carte options. Bundles of this type are convenient because precise information about consumer demand for each component or between components is not required; consumers can also average out the fluctuation in product quality and their own demand; and billing and payment are simplified. Bundling therefore appears to be an appropriate product selection strategy for many digital products, at least for digital information products. Consequently, some argue that information products should be sold just as newspapers and cable services are sold: bundled and by subscription.

Although these advantages do favor bundling, a more fundamental need for bundling newspapers and magazines is technological in nature. In the physical market, a payment mechanism suitable for purchasing a small portion of a newspaper simply does not exist. Also, the consumer's cost of disposing of the unwanted portion of the product is small. Therefore, the economic costs will also be negligible for any waste generated by bundling. For digital products, however, neither the disposal cost nor the delivery cost is zero. If a person subscribes to a digital newspaper but only reads a small portion of what is delivered, he is paying for the delivery and storage of something he does not consume. In addition, an indiscriminate broadcasting of digital newspapers will tax the delivery network, exacerbating congestion. Pricing digital products need not follow models used in physical markets when, in electronic commerce, microproducts can be produced according to demand and billed in an efficient manner based on usage.

Another questionable assumption is that physical newspapers and online newspapers are the same product. In fact, online newspapers may be totally different from their paper counterparts. Online newspapers offer consumers a different set of characteristics: interactivity, customization, search, links, and storage and reproduction mechanisms. These characteristics, in turn, result in different uses. An online newspaper may, for example, be linked to computer programs that input and analyze news items for investment decisions, automatic dissemination to colleagues, and so on. You can no longer assume that online and paper versions are indeed the same commodity.

The simple fact that consumers pay for a basic cable service, which is not much different from what is available for free, indicates that cable services are different from over-the-air television. In addition to better signal quality, cable television services offer more channels 24 hours a day and access to specialized programming. In the same way, Internet dissemination of television programs will exhibit further differences—perhaps even more fundamental ones. For example, cable television enables broadcasters to charge consumers directly for programs instead of relying on advertisers (for example, paid movie channels and pay-per-view services). Although cable operators have not fully exploited this possibility, online programming may indeed be sold a la carte, not by channel, but by unbundled program. Furthermore, advertising may be separated from content and sold as a separate product. As discussed in section 11.2, "Search Service and Its Market Implications," the peculiarity of over-the-air broadcasting necessitated inserting commercials into programs. But remote-control devices and split screens enable viewers to switch channels to avoid commercials. With VCR and digital television sets equipped with filtering devices, zapping through commercials will become even easier. Faced with a scarcely passive audience, advertising based on mass media is set for a wholesale revision.

Once formerly linked products are sold separately, proper prices for commercials and contents must be determined. Newspaper sellers claim that their advertising revenue helps lower the consumer price of their newspapers. Television networks claim that, without commercials, the quality of their programs would suffer. However, the value of a TV program is calculated by the advertiser's willingness to pay instead of the viewers' willingness to pay. Costs incurred by consumers are ignored, such as the disutility of watching commercials or flipping through advertisements as well as the waste of resources. What, then, is a direct price of a consumer watching an ad, or a 30-minute sitcom? Economists will have ample opportunity to ponder the prices of goods that were formerly considered public goods with no established market prices.

Buying a bundled digital product is similar to paying a flat subscription fee. Therefore, problems similar to those encountered with bundling exist for flat-fee subscription schemes used to sell digital products. Just as bundling does not account for variations in consumer tastes, charging a flat fee also ignores differences in usage, and often results in inefficient resource allocation. Since America Online, Inc. (http://www.aol.com) changed its fee schedule to a flat-fee system, its network has been severely congested, increasing consumers' average waiting time. One factor favoring a flat-fee system is that users often cannot control the amount of connection time. For example, if someone sends a lengthy e-mail or posts a long message on a UseNet newsgroup, the receiver must pay for the connection time required to download the files, which often turn out to be useless or unwanted. Under the new system, AOL's heavy users, who used to pay more than the new flat fee of $19.95 a month, reap the benefit of the new flat-fee billing system, whereas occasional users, whose payment used to be below the flat fee, are at a disadvantage. Besides this distribution problem, access time has increased by two to three times in the case of AOL, causing widespread congestion. A more efficient use of the resource can be achieved if fees reflect the actual cost of service or the usage (see Chapter 3 for more information on efficient infrastructure pricing).

Despite these inefficiencies, flat fees and subscriptions to bundled services are widely used because sellers can simplify billing and consumers can vary their usage without worrying about additional charges. This type of pricing strategy often works well with standardized products such as newspapers and TV programs. Consumers receive basically the same product, while disposing of the product's unwanted portions. But digital products can be highly customized based on revealed consumer information. Such differentiated products will, of course, require differentiated or non-uniform prices. Also, consumers with special tastes for only a small portion of the bundled product can be better served by unbundling, where there is a portion at a smaller fee. The subscription rate for cable television service, for example, is stagnant, around 60 percent, and is expected to remain under 70 percent. In other words, more than 30 percent of TV households find the subscription for bundled cable service unattractive. Offering a la carte channels is difficult due to the lack of sophisticated switching equipment and network for cable services. Similar difficulties, however, do not exist in electronic commerce. Thus, while bundling will be dominant for digital products—because any single digital document is a bundle of multimedia files—an excessive emphasis on bundling often leads to a misleading strategy of duplicating the inefficient pricing schemes used in physical markets.

To summarize, many similarities are shared by two forms of information products—digital versions (for example, online magazines) and physical versions (for example, paper-based magazines). Such outward similarities have encouraged many economists to conclude that pricing in electronic commerce will resemble the pricing of newspapers, magazines, and cable services. Although the current trend in today's electronic commerce supports such intuition, this has more to do with the characteristics of today's sellers and products than with the nature of digital products and the electronic marketplace. As long as sellers see electronic commerce only as a simple extension of their physical products, this trend may continue. However, tomorrow's electronic commerce, with numerous microproducers and information-based products, will certainly demand different economic models to guide business decisions.

Today, for example, a personal investment adviser or four years of college remain beyond the reach of many consumers who have no need for all their services or no funds for all the courses. In the virtual world, personal service providers will be available for multiple transactions as well as for one-time use. The enabling factor for these services to be provided is the lowered threshold, in terms of number and value of transactions. The fragmentation, or unbundling, of products and services will enable need-based transactions whereas today's investment advisers can justify only large clients because of the need to recoup fixed costs and operating expenses. By adding unbundled services and usage-based prices, service providers can increase sales while serving more consumers. Similarly, college education today consists of four years of continuous enrollment. When education is virtualized, need-based education and training will be available for specific topics and skills. Consumers will be able to enroll in a specific course to get a certificate of completion. As these examples illustrate, electronic commerce is indeed a new way of delivering products and services, which requires a more flexible pricing scheme than the familiar flat-fee subscription.

Unbundling and Micropayments

An important prerequisite of unbundling and mixed bundling is the designing of a micropayment system suitable for pricing the resulting microproducts and microbundles. Fees for bundled products often are large enough to be paid by credit cards and checks, and some economists argue that microproducts and micropayments discussed in connection with electronic currency will become largely unimportant. If transaction costs can be made low enough to handle even sub-dollar payments, why should digital product sellers be limited to accepting credit card payments and other large-scale payment methods? To justify a large bill, consumers are often required to purchase multiple products or a bundle with unwanted products. Micropayments are as essential to electronic commerce as product customization.

Micropayments and unbundling will be a natural response to a growing abundance of customized microproducts. You can see the potential sources and applications of microproducts in many different areas. Take, for example, traditional media. Newspapers, magazines, and TV programs are intermediary services that collect, edit, and distribute materials from various sources, often packaged in a bundled program or newspaper. However, there is no reason information should be distributed only via a centralized distribution system. In other words, the *New York Times* or CNN may not be the sole gatekeepers of news, ideas, information and knowledge. The Internet is a natural dispersed information channel for small, occasional sales. Its unique interactive capability also makes everyone a potential guest columnist on the net. Consumers will pay for these microproducts not by subscription but by micropayments.

Other sources of information microproducts exist because the pervasiveness of these information snippets—the new commodity of the 21st century—is the hallmark of the information age. Interactions among market agents generate new types of information goods. For example, each interaction between a consumer and a web page results in information about agents (for example consumer information). Product descriptions can be broken down into smaller components and sold individually. A market exists even for some of the millions of e-mail messages exchanged today. Finally, new commodities exchanged in the electronic marketplace will include many physical products made smart by applying intelligence and technology: smart automobiles, smart furniture, smart appliances, and so on. Just as you buy a can of motor oil or a replacement light bulb, consumers will want to purchase a new control routine for smart automobiles, an improved temperature diagnostic subroutine for smart boilers, and so on. If these smart products use open and interoperable standards, there will be no need to rely on proprietary, expensive, all-in-one software to install and update them. Instead, small shareware products will be readily available over the Internet. Microproducts and micropayments are essential in achieving such a vision.

Micropayments also play an important role in calculating equitable payments to component owners of a bundled product. In the physical world, the music industry has developed what is probably the most sophisticated copyright payment scheme through ASCAP and BMI (as discussed in Chapter 5). However, their payment schedule still depends on the estimated popularity of each copyrighted material played on radio and other media, and this popularity cannot be measured accurately. Some popular artists may be underpaid whereas others are overpaid. A bundled sale of digital products faces similar problems. Consumers may not view or use some components, while heavily using other portions or features. If the seller charges a flat fee for the bundled product, how would it distribute the revenue to the various copyright owners? Without actual usage data, a precise allocation will be difficult or inequitable. However, because the electronic marketplace has the technology to monitor usage, a more efficient revenue distribution will be based on individual sales—for which micropayments are needed.

Micropayments and Product Quality

Another motivation for developing microproducts and micropayments stems from the need to assure product quality. A long-term subscription of bundled digital products may be sufficient to guarantee quality based on the reputation of the seller. However, reputation has to be developed after repeated purchases. If sellers know, on the other hand, that the market will end soon, or they are short-run players it is profitable to cheat by selling low-quality products at high-quality prices. Knowing this, would consumers be willing to buy a product from unknown sellers? This problem is magnified if buyers are required to commit to a long-term subscription or to pay for a large bundle of unknown quality. It is unrealistic to assume that all sellers have reputation or to require costly mechanisms that verify and guarantee product quality.

Instead, as discussed in Chapter 4, recent research in contract theory offers some positive evidence that short-term sales based on micropayments may indeed produce higher quality than subscription and bundling. When products are homogeneous, it pays to learn about the product's quality because the cost of learning is spent only once. If consumers pay for learning, the benefits continue as long as the consumers buy the same product. An intermediary or a dealer can sample a product to find out its quality before committing to a contract to buy a large quantity. In electronic commerce, the problem is more complex for at least two reasons:

- Products are differentiated or customized such that quality may vary for each and every version of a product. Unlike the case of repeated purchases of a homogeneous product, the dealer or consumer must verify quality for all products. For example, the quality of timely information (a series of differentiated products) may change from time to time so that yesterday's quality does not guarantee today's or tomorrow's quality.

- The value of microproducts may not justify the cost of learning and verifying quality. In the case of high-value products, such as automobiles or jewelry, consumers spend time and effort to learn about quality. Intermediaries in these product areas often find it cost efficient to invest in the skills of recognizing quality (for example, expert knowledge of gemstones). However, if the product is of low quality, such cost may not be justified to the consumer. And intermediaries who deal with microdocuments in electronic commerce may not have any incentive to verify the quality of each microproduct.

With this in mind, will an intermediary or a consumer be willing to purchase a product online? What optimal payment scheme or contract will result in the highest possible quality? Subscription has been touted as a possible remedy for low quality because consumers discover the level of quality based on repeated purchases. But not all products can be sold by subscription; the market for information will be full of microproducts sold by microsellers who cannot use this mechanism. Bundling is also suggested as a solution, but it may actually lower quality if most consumers use only a portion of the product. An intermediary may be able to establish a selling procedure based on subscription and bundling by linking numerous microsellers and microbuyers, as discussed in Chapter 4. But the intermediary still is not able to determine quality and does not have sufficient incentive to investigate all products. An enforceable contract may be the mechanism that will establish an incentive for content producers to maintain high quality, as the following scenarios illustrate.

Suppose Alice is a digital product reseller who brokers hundreds of individual shareware programmers. These programmers send their products to Alice, who lists them on her web page. The following optional purchase arrangements are possible:

- *Commission*—Alice signs no contract with her suppliers and pays each programmer only after sales are made to consumers. Under this consignment scenario, if Alice accepts all potential shareware programmers and if many of their products are of low quality, she will soon lose her reputation as well as customers. She clearly needs some type of mechanism to ensure high quality.

- *Complete Contract*—Alice writes a contract with each shareware programmer that contains complete specifications regarding quality. Under this scenario, it is still costly for Alice to examine all products, and programmers have an incentive to cheat. This problem is magnified if the programmer is not a long-run player. Alice still faces the problem of losing customers. If the contract specifies only the quantity or the term for renewal, but not the quality, programmers still have an incentive to cheat because Alice is committed to buying the products while the contract lasts, regardless of quality.

- *Short-Term Option Contract*—Alice writes an incomplete contract that does not specify quality, and promises to purchase only one shareware program from each programmer. The contract stipulates that Alice will continue to represent the programmer as long as she does not receive a complaint from a customer. In essence, this type of contract establishes a short-term relationship with optional future transactions. The incompleteness is not in quality, which is difficult to define, but in quantity, because the contract leaves future sales unknown.

An incomplete, short-term contract forces Alice's suppliers to maintain high quality for fear of not being represented. Therefore, the contract works similarly to reputation: the seller (a programmer) is afraid of losing customers (Alice). Whereas reputation takes a long time to develop, however, a short-term option contract works more quickly because the term of sale is short-term. A subscription-based pricing scheme aims at building reputation over a long period while the possibility of terminating subscriptions encourages sellers to maintain quality. However, because quality can vary during the subscription period and subscribers are often unable to make immediate threats, this is inferior to a solution that does not require buyers any long-term obligation. For consumers, buying a microproduct is one such arrangement—which is similar to an incomplete short-term contract that enables Alice to impose quality on her suppliers.

Now, suppose Bob is a customer. From his point of view, an incomplete, short-term contract is the same as buying only what he needs from the array of products Alice offers. Bundling would mean that Bob is committed to buying a number of products, some of which may not be of high quality. Therefore, an efficient contract should allow Bob an option to terminate his patronage immediately if he is not satisfied with one product. In this way, microproducts and associated micropayments are essential for intermediaries and consumers to resolve the quality uncertainty in electronic commerce.

Incomplete contracts of this type occur frequently in real life. Traditionally, the incompleteness is explained by the cost in spelling out all possibilities of a transaction (transaction costs), or by the inability of the parties to predict or recognize all contingencies (bounded rationality). A third reason, recognized recently, is that an incomplete contract may be superior to complete contracts (strategic ambiguity) (Bernheim and Whinston, 1997). Often an incomplete contract results in a first-best outcome when some contract variables are non-verifiable, such as the quality of shareware in the preceding example. Although the literature on reputation asserts that quality can be maintained only if purchases are repeated over a long period between long-term players, strategic ambiguity hints at the importance of strategic, dynamic, short-term relationships. Micropayments and unbundling—and software applets—would then produce better-quality products than do subscription and bundling for digital products.

Information Products and Economics

When talking about digital or information products, economists typically focus on newspapers, magazines, and television programs. Although they are familiar commodities, information products have largely been neglected by formal economic analysts. To analyze a digital product market, the economics of information may have to evolve as a coherent body of models that specifically consider varied forms of information being converted to commodities, the production of such goods, and the valuation and uses of these products. Such a model can better guide producers and policy makers in, for example, determining a proper framework for digital copyright and pricing.

The ultimate question is whether we can treat information goods as we do physical goods. Already, information products appear to vex many economists trying to determine their production costs and consumer valuation. Currently, information and knowledge play an important role in at least two areas of economics. First, technology and research and development have been regarded as the engine of growth since the Industrial Revolution two centuries ago. Thus, information and technology appear to be the most important variables in growth theory. However, growth theory often takes technology as a given, neglecting the way it is created in the first place. Instead, it is customary to treat a technological development as an exogenous shock—something that just happens. When a model considers technology to be determined within the system (for example through R&D activities), it is concerned with the level of investments—the decision to allocate fixed investments. After the amount of investment is determined, the level of technological development is also determined. Therefore, technology plays a secondary role, although its importance is somehow recognized.

Information and knowledge also play an important role in the economics of information and uncertainty. In this area of economics, information is a signal that may improve the quality of knowledge about products, competitors, or buyers. Better information is a signal that has better quality—one that produces a finer partition of uncertain states of the world. The information, as a signal, merely helps to refine the process of transactions. Information in the sense of its everyday usage—as a commodity such as books, databases, newspapers and other intellectual properties—is often neglected by economists.

The primary difficulty in the economic analysis of information goods stems from an inadequate understanding of what information is and how we use it as a commodity. The way information and technology are used defies the normal, comfortable economic analysis in which a predictable and consistent result (a static equilibrium) is coveted. To obtain such a stable solution, a function, be it a cost function or a growth function, must exhibit a tendency to settle down, like a U-shaped average cost curve or the law of diminishing returns. On the contrary, the technological process often shows a sudden departure, or a cumulative or exponential growth, or an increasing return, making it difficult to predict the result of an R&D project. Another frustrating factor is that information and intellectual activities, once created, have no limit in reproduction; they are not a scarce resource whose allocation must be determined by a careful weighing of different uses and needs. Furthermore, many information goods fall under the category of public goods, whose producers are not adequately remunerated. To better understand the economic effects of information, future research must focus on how information is created and consumed. Electronic commerce presents an ideal environment for study because technology will make it possible to measure the use of information goods and enable an adequate compensation scheme.

11.6.   Taxation and the Future of Electronic Commerce

In the United States, taxes on Internet transactions have become the target of state and local efforts to increase revenues. Although federal governments prefer no new taxes in electronic commerce, a powerful argument for levying state and local taxes exists because transactions that are now taxed migrate to the Internet, leaving governments with a reduced tax base. To at least maintain the current level of tax revenues, state and local governments need to figure out how to apply existing rules of taxation to electronic transactions. Although discussion in this section mostly relates to the U.S. experience, similar situations are found globally.

Various governments' initial efforts to tax Internet commercial activities have resulted in numerous instances in which even the basic definitions of sales and use tax regulations have been found inadequate. Even the distinction between sales tax and income tax becomes unclear when business is conducted on the Internet. But most of all, the fluidity of online taxable entities makes it difficult to establish at any one time what is being taxed, who should be taxed, and who can impose taxes.

Taxable Item

If you attempt to apply existing tax laws to electronic commerce, the first task at hand is to determine which digital products are taxable under which tax mechanisms—sales tax, income tax, royalty tax, and so on. In the U.S., most state sales and use tax laws are based on the sale and sale price of some tangible personal property. Use tax is levied when the property is used to generate a service, such as when a building or a machinery is rented or leased. Tangible personal property is defined as "personal property that can be seen, weighed, measured, felt, or touched or that is perceptible to the senses in any other manner" (Texas Sales and Use Tax Definition, Sec. 151.005). If you adhere to this definition, most digital products, as well as many types of services, are excluded.

To extend taxation into the digital domain, some state laws specifically define computer programs and many types of services, for example information services, as taxable. But such ad-hoc measures become infinitely haphazard as electronic commerce grows and a typical transaction includes a wide range of products and services, such as software, hardware, and technical service. Digital files, although they all look similar, may be fundamentally different products—for example, electronic house keys, digital currency, weather information, computer programs, concert tickets, medical advice, and so on. Clearly, an adequate solution entails simplifying existing tax laws instead of complicating them further by extending them and applying them on an ad-hoc basis.

Taxes on Access

In the absence of clear definitions, the first stage of a potentially wide-reaching tax war is already being fought with Internet Service Providers (ISPs). ISPs may be subject to sales tax if they are defined as a service liable for such tax (for example, as information service providers). They also may be subject to telecommunications tax, which is applied to communication service providers. Whether the definition of sales tax applies will ultimately be tested in court. However, the levying of access fees on ISPs as telecommunications service providers has become a hotly disputed issue (ISA, 1996). Although the Federal Communications Commission (FCC) in 1983 exempted ISPs from paying access charges, the issue has not died. The FCC's argument was, in short, that ISPs are not common carriers like long-distance telephone companies (which pay access charges to local phone companies), but provide enhanced services, such as information provision, which are exempted from telecommunications tax under the Telecommunications Act of 1996.

Regional Bell operating companies, known collectively as local exchange carriers (LECs), hold a different opinion. They petitioned the FCC in 1997 to be allowed to levy local access charges on ISPs because, LECs argue, ISPs engage in the same type of business as long-distance carriers that pay per-minute access charges for each long-distance call that goes through an LEC's local network. Unlike long distance carriers, however, ISPs pay only per-line fees regardless of their total usage of the infrastructure. Internet connections by ISP subscribers occupy telephone circuits longer than do voice calls, increasing congestion in a network built to accommodate the lower average calling time for voice communication. The traffic generated by ISPs puts a strain on LECs' local exchange infrastructure, necessitating more investments to maintain a satisfactory level of service. Long-distance carriers share such investment costs by paying per-minute charges, and so should ISPs, LECs argue.

Complicating this picture is the growing popularity of Internet telephony, or using the Internet for voice, fax, and videoconferencing. Begun only in 1995, some 500,000 users have downloaded Vocaltec's software (http://www.vocaltec.com) for Internet telephony (Migdal and Taylor, 1997). Leading web browser vendors also have introduced client software to facilitate talking on the Internet (see "Internet Resources" at the end of this chapter). When national Internet access providers (see Chapter 3) offer voice and fax services on the Internet, they become long-distance carriers. In fact, the three long-distance carriers—AT&T, MCI, and Sprint—are the major backbone service providers for the Internet and also offer Internet services to consumers. If a voice call is transmitted through their Internet services, they need not pay access charges to LECs. But when the same call goes through the telephone network, LECs collect usage-based access charges, for example six cents out of the ten cents a minute for a typical long distance call (Migdal and Taylor, 1997).

Whether Internet traffic benefits outweigh the harm to LECs' business is in dispute. According to a study commissioned by the Internet Access Coalition (http://internetaccess.org)—whose members include Internet service providers, computer and software manufacturers, and information service companies—revenues in 1996 from Internet traffic far outstripped the spending required to accommodate that traffic (IAC, 1997). While revenues are growing for LECs and ISPs, both seem to have neglected necessary investments to counter congestion, making consumers and congestion their pawns in the game of access.

In February, 1997, the FCC solicited public comments regarding access charges on ISPs (http://www.fcc.gov/isp.html). Within a few weeks, the FCC received over 100,000 messages from the public (some of which came from spamming sites); again, this demonstrates the power of the Internet. Due to the huge response, the commission has extended the filing deadline, and will not make its ruling until later. However, the FCC has maintained its position against charges on ISPs, prompting its officials to voice the opinion that telephone companies, which wanted access charges, should be the target of mass e-mailing—not the FCC.

With state and local governments and competitors eyeing the Internet as a potential revenue source and the proposed Wyden-Cox bill (see the sidebar, "U.S. Congress and Internet Taxes" later in the chapter) trying to preempt all Internet taxes (Taylor, 1997), this nascent industry will face further struggles and the result will have a significant impact on the Internet's future. Unlike airwave spectra, which are finite, cable and fiber-optic conduits and communications equipment can be upgraded by increasing investments. Whether increased revenues from access charges will encourage telephone companies to invest to relieve congestion or how much fixed infrastructure costs ISPs should share with LECs is not entirely certain. While investment decisions and engineering solutions are being considered, usage-based prices will efficiently allocate limited resources. The key issue is to align Internet access prices with telephone charges in a model that recognizes the convergence in various types of communications infra-structure.

Taxes on Transactions

A separate taxing issue for electronic commerce relates not to the communications infrastructure but to goods and services. In the case of physical goods sold over the Internet, existing sales tax laws will apply with little difficulty. However, intangible goods (digital products) will necessitate new definitions. For example, while shrink-wrapped computer software is considered tangible property subject to sales tax, software downloaded over the Internet may not be subject to the same tax. Even when digital products are defined as tangible properties, the nature of the Internet network may require tax-code revisions or a new approach toward taxing transactions.

According to existing regulations, businesses must collect and pay sales taxes if they maintain a substantial presence in the taxing jurisdiction of a state. The U.S. Supreme Court set a guideline in a 1992 decision (*Quill v. North Dakota*, 504 U.S. 298) that mail-order firms are not required to collect sales taxes from customers in states where they have no physical presence—known as taxable nexus. Therefore, if a mail-order firm in New York sells a product to a customer in Texas, the firm is not required to collect and pay sales taxes to the state of Texas, unless substantial taxable nexus applies. What constitutes substantial nexus differs from state to state, and depends on court interpretation. For example, a nexus is established if an out-of-state business maintains an office or a representative, either permanently or temporarily. Here too, the definition of a representative has to be clearly determined. If a person lives in Oklahoma but commutes to his office in Texas, does he have an in-state presence in Texas? If a California firm has a web site in an electronic mall served by an operator in Texas, does the firm have sufficient presence in Texas to be subject to Texas sales tax? Identifying proper taxing jurisdiction is further complicated because a business may have no physical presence at all, but its virtual presence on the Internet may end up being interpreted as a presence in all locations. In this case, a web business will be required to collect state and local taxes (including sales, use, excise, transportation, telecommunications, and other taxes), all of which have rates differing from locality to locality.

To avoid double taxation, a simple tax structure would be based on either the seller (originator of sale) or the buyer (destination of sale). The U.S. Department of Treasury (1996), while discussing income taxes for global electronic commerce, recognized residence-based (originator of sale) taxation as the preferred method because the seller's residence is easier to identify and corresponds better to the economic activity. Because the originator's residence simplifies the number of tax rates to be applied, this method would be simpler than calculating different tax rates for customers, who may belong to different taxing jurisdictions. Complicated taxing schemes give sellers an incentive to circumvent them altogether by using offshore locations for business, which only requires establishing a computer server and managing remotely.

The Interactive Services Association (1996), whose members include America Online, AT&T, CompuServe, IBM, and Microsoft Corporation, prefers destination-based taxes. Under this scenario, as in the traditional mail-order business, out-of-state sales will not be subject to state sales tax. To simplify tax rates for multi-state operators, ISA also advocates setting a single tax rate for each state and basing taxes on the state to which sales are billed—thereby avoiding thousands of different tax rates levied by local governments. Such a system might be implemented without much difficulty if Internet commerce is deemed subject to interstate commerce regulations of the federal government, which is contemplating sweeping legislation addressing these issues. (See the following sidebar.)

U.S. Congress and Internet Taxes

Politicians and legislators know what's hot and what's not. A search at the Library of Congress using the keyword "Internet" produced 17 bills proposed in the 105th Congress. The bills cover a wide range of topics, including encryption technologies, the use of consumer information, and taxes. (See Bill Summary and Status site at http://thomas.loc.gov/bss/d105query.html.) The following three bills regarding Internet taxation have been submitted to Congress. H.R. 1054 and S. 442 aim to preempt local taxes on Internet transactions, and H.R. 995 addresses the issue of access tax.

(1) H.R.1054

- Sponsor: Rep. Christopher Cox (R-CA)
- Introduced 03/13/97

This bill's major objectives include the following:

- to amend the Communications Act of 1934
- to establish a national policy against state and local interference with interstate commerce on the Internet or interactive computer services
- to exercise congressional jurisdiction over interstate commerce on the Internet

- to establish a moratorium on taxes and other fees that would interfere with the free flow of commerce via the Internet

(2) S. 442

- Sponsor: Sen. Ron Wyden (D-OR)
- Introduced 03/13/97

S. 442's goals are similar to those of H.R. 1054; hence we call the Internet tax bill the Wyden-Cox bill. It proposes the following:

- to establish a national policy against state and local government interference with interstate commerce on the Internet or interactive computer services
- to exercise congressional jurisdiction over interstate commerce
- to establish a moratorium on taxes and fees that would interfere with the free flow of commerce via the Internet

(3) H.R. 995

- Sponsor: Rep. Dave Weldon (R-FL)
- Introduced 03/06/97

H.R. 995 proposes the following:

- to amend the Internal Revenue Code of 1986
- to clarify that fees for Internet and other online services are not subject to tax

The bottom line in all these proposals is that sales taxes will have to be simplified among thousands of local taxing jurisdictions. How this is accomplished will depend on the simplifying of existing tax structure. The ISA's approach toward Internet transaction taxes is ambitious in its need to reformulate a uniform sales tax regime. It is not clear whether such uniformity is required for transactions taxes to be levied on digital products. Also, because it advocates a buyer-based taxation, this will require consumers' revealing, at the very least, their addresses, whereas a seller-based system can support anonymous transactions. In the absence of federal preemption, the difficulty in rewriting local tax codes will favor adoption of a seller-based tax system.

Sales versus Transfer of Copyrights

Even more basic than the issue of how to apply sales tax is the question of whether many transactions in electronic commerce can be considered sales of tangible personal properties at all. As discussed previously, a digital product has almost zero reproduction cost after the first unit is produced. However, the variable cost of making a copy and selling it to a customer will not be zero because the cost of such a sale includes a copyright payment, often to many authors. Therefore, such transactions may not be considered sales that are transfers of physical goods, but rather transfers of copyright or the right to use a copyrighted material. In this case, royalty payments would apply as opposed to sales taxes.

In general, royalty—that is copyright—income is treated differently from business income. As a result, types and uses of digital products have to be considered when assessing state and local taxes, and when income taxes are levied (U.S. Department of Treasury, 1996). Income generated by a typical transaction involving software products can fall under any of the following three categories:

- Royalty income from the transfer of copyright
- Rental income from licensing the use of tangible property
- Sales income from the transfer of software products

Licensing software is generally considered an agreement to transfer copyrights, thus falling into the royalty income category. However, perpetual licensing is similar to an over-the-counter sale of a tangible product, and may be treated as a sale. If the contract is less than perpetual, the transaction may be considered equivalent to a rental or lease agreement. Finally, the sale of a digital book may be considered the sale of a physical product, similar to a printed book, or a transfer of copyrights, in which case the seller's income is treated as royalty income. Revisions in revenue codes will be necessary to avoid different treatment of these incomes, a situation that might result in double taxation or loss of tax credits applied to certain types of income. Furthermore, if states use different definitions for income generated on the Internet, it will complicate the decision to establish taxable nexus as businesses try to lower their tax liabilities.

Different treatments of the same income also cause problems when foreign taxing jurisdictions are involved. For example, income tax treaties between the U.S. and its partners treat business profits from sales and royalty payments differently in terms of withholding and adjusting foreign tax credits (Erickson, 1996). If the country where sales are made considers income subject to withholding, yet the country where the firm is located does not consider the income subject to withholding, the firm may face double taxation. Before such specific issues can be addressed, countries must first define how to treat sales of digital products and agree on a uniform application.

11.7. Anonymity and Legal Environment for Commerce

The future of electronic commerce depends on establishing adequate frameworks for commerce for the Internet. In addition to a workable tax regime, a consistent and effective legal framework will give content owners an incentive to market their products online while providing consumers and other market agents with a reference on what activities are acceptable or criminally liable. A legal framework is needed not only for copyrights but also for transactions that are the basis of commerce. For example, can contracts be signed electronically and sent over the Internet? Do these documents have legal enforceability? Can a third party act as a witness for an online signing of a contract or for completing a transaction? While governments are preoccupied with the possibility of money laundering, security breaches by hackers, and tax evasion, the ordinary aspects of commerce are neglected—even though these aspects constitute legal and commercial frameworks without which normal transactions cannot occur.

The biggest vacuum in the legal framework for electronic commerce is the lack of verifiable means for identities and transactions—aptly identified as the "weak correspondence between computer domain name and reality" by U.S. Department of Treasury officials. Often the anonymity of the Internet makes it more attractive and increases the level of communication, albeit between unknown parties. Flame wars are quite common in Usenet newsgroups. Dozens of messages are exchanged after users see a message that is offensive; if that message were printed in a newspaper, the response rate would be far less. Flames are even more common in newsgroups in which a lot of participants use anonymous identities. Even mass e-mail advertisers use anonymous sites, perhaps to avoid receiving angry protest e-mail or spamming sites, which generate and send multiple messages, even though common sense indicates that consumers will willfully disregard advertisements from unreachable sites. Nevertheless, you can send and receive communications more easily on the Internet than traditional media. Such a heightened level of activity should also help the future of electronic commerce. But the anonymity, suitable for political free speech, is often a hindrance for commerce.

The issue of anonymous transactions has been overblown and intermingled with privacy and free-speech issues. Anonymous transactions are possible, and sometimes needed, in physical markets. But developers of electronic payment systems and government officials are preoccupied with anonymity in electronic transactions for fear of behavior that can be easily corrected or dealt with by existing laws and a slew of technologies, such as money laundering, double spending, and credit card fraud. The possibility of large-scale online fraud is as rare, or as prevalent, as in physical markets. More mundane sorts of crimes are committed on the Internet where users, endowed with virtual identities, commit unacceptable behaviors, from flames to outright crimes.

Lack of identity leads to numerous crimes that may not be possible in physical markets. Although Jayne Hitchcock's experience (see the sidebar, "Anonymity and Internet Harassment") is a rare example of the abuse of anonymity on the Internet, many possible scenarios of identity crimes exist (Schneier, 1994). For example, in an old episode of the television sitcom *Cheers*, Sam plays a chess game with Robin, to whom Sam represents himself as a chess master. In reality, Robin is playing against a computer because every move Robin makes is related to Sam's friend, Norm, who is hiding in an adjacent room and entering the moves on the computer; the computer's move is then relayed secretly to Sam via earphone.

A similar but far more sophisticated fraud could be achieved on the Internet. For instance, suppose Sam claims that he is a grand master, and challenges both Kasparov and Karpov, but neither knows about the other challenge. Sam plays white against Kasparov and black against Karpov. Sam repeats every move Kasparov makes to Karpov, and vice versa. In this game, Kasparov is playing against Karpov, both of whom are impressed by Sam's chess-playing ability. This is all an innocent practical joke until economic transactions become involved.

Anonymity and Internet Harassment

As Internet usage increases, so does the Internet crime rate. Kids are sending death threats to the White House via e-mail from school computers; a dismissed employee of a large corporation forges e-mail messages to support her lawsuit against dismissal; and Internet deadbeats fail to pay required registration fees for their domain names. Finally, the anonymity of the Internet has also become the greatest tool for harassment.

The Woodside Literary Agency (WLA) posted advertisements in 1996, some 8,100 of them, in various UseNet newsgroups soliciting manuscripts from writers. The ad stated that the WLA would accept almost all submitted manuscripts, but asked a reading fee of $75 to $250. Although such a practice is unusual, the scam was aimed at writers who would appreciate any possibility to be represented by an agent and be published. A scam of this scale is not news. But when some writers began posting warnings against the WLA, the affair became a classic example of the dangers of Internet-scale crimes and retaliation.

Jayne Hitchcock sent her writing samples to the agency but became suspicious when the agency requested up-front fees. After she posted warnings about the antics of the agency, the WLA began posting numerous messages using her name:

"with her home address and phone number attached (the message read):

Female International Author, no limits to imagination and fantasies, prefers group macho/sadistic interaction, including lovebites and indiscriminate scratches. Stop by my house. Will take your calls day or night. . . ." (Mingo, 1997).

continues

continued

The resulting phone calls to Hitchcock's home were just the beginning. The WLA spammed her e-mail accounts with harassing letters; inundated various newsgroups with inflammatory messages using her name; sent her bosses insults and resignation letters with her forged name via e-mail; and sent similar attacks to her husband's and agent's e-mail accounts.

The WLA changed its e-mail addresses and service providers when complaints were lodged with its Internet service providers, and continued posting its advertisements using different names for originators. After almost a year of continued effort by a group of people, the identity of the WLA is still a mystery. The range of fraud and other criminal activities undertaken by the WLA runs the gamut of most problematic uses of Internet—fraud, e-mail spamming, misrepresentation, forged signatures, and forged messages—all perpetrated through the ease and speed of the Internet. On the other hand, the WLA's virtual identities are difficult to connect to real names and addresses. Even when a connection is established, law enforcement agencies are often clueless as to how to prosecute them.

Similarly, credit card frauds can occur even when merchants ask for proof that only the real owner can provide. Suppose Alice uses her credit card to buy an online book through a bogus bookstore. Alice orders a book online unaware of the bookstore's criminal intentions. When Alice presents her credit card online, the bogus bookstore operator simultaneously places an order to an online jewelry shop using Alice's identity. When the jewelry shop asks for proof to verify the credit information, the bookstore operator asks Alice the same question, and provides the answer to the jewelry shop. In this scheme, Alice is proving her identity to the jewelry shop, but the bookstore operator gets the jewelry at Alice's expense.

Such mundane crimes of identity can be undertaken quite easily on the Internet. Instead of building an elaborate office for scams, criminals and scam artists need only a web page, computer technologies, and virtual identities. While governments are preoccupied with primarily hypothetical crimes, they are neglecting adequate measures to prevent worldly crimes. A critical crime deterrent is the possibility of being identified. If the electronic marketplace were to mirror physical markets, a means to establish an identity, such as driver's licenses or Social Security numbers, would be needed. Verification services based on digital signatures are being offered, for example, by VeriSign (http://www.verisign.com), but there is little effort to make such services a common practice on the Internet. The fact that a commercial enterprise takes up such an important function is a clear indication of an inadequacy in governments' priorities.

11.8.   Global Framework for Electronic Commerce

The previous sections have emphasized the need for a new, cohesive framework within which electronic commerce can function. Complicated as that may be, a further staggering realization is that not many of the issues touched upon are local in the digital world. The internationalization of the Internet goes far beyond any expansion witnessed in the last century. For most of the 20th century, corporations have operated as multinational entities knowing no national boundaries. Literally, you can see free trade zones springing up in North America, Europe, and around the Pacific Rim. While these large economic blocks of countries represent the most recent achievement in fostering the free movement of goods, the Internet was created from its inception without borders. For goods and services that can be ordered and delivered over the network, the Internet is truly a global marketplace.

As political borders cease to block to trade, global electronic commerce has implications that reach far beyond mere economic gains from trading. For example, can nations control the movement of digital goods based on content or isolate themselves from the rest of the Internet? Can governments exercise their regulatory powers on the Internet? And how would the effort to set up a uniform legal and commercial environment for the global electronic commerce affect physical markets?

Convergence in Spatial Markets

It is easy enough to *say* that electronic commerce is global. The difficulty lies in identifying the effects of globalization on the economy—changes in income levels, jobs, domestic prices, and so on. An interesting exercise in international trade and finance economics is to observe how two previously closed economies are affected by subsequent interactions in human resources, materials, and capital. Even though the soundness of trade was proved via the theory of comparative advantages, in which trade makes sense even when one country has absolute advantages in all sectors, the advocates and opponents of free trade continue to debate other issues. Specifically, does international trade have an impact on domestic economies? And how would borderless electronic commerce change that?

By definition, a closed economy would not be affected by the international movements of goods and capital. The United States, for example, was considered relatively closed until the 1970s as its trade accounted for less than 10 percent of its Gross National Product (GNP). With the share increasing to more than 15 percent, opinions vary as to the impact of trade on the U.S. economy.

On one side, the flux of cheap imports into the U.S. is viewed as equivalent to a huge supply of cheap labor, which depresses low-skilled workers' income and increases income inequality. Exporting jobs overseas further creates an oversupply of unskilled labor and affects the laborers' income adversely. On the other side, competition from foreign labor is greatly discounted as a factor in the worsening of income inequality. Rather, the blame is put on domestic policies, especially the introduction of high technology, which raises the income level of skilled workers while nontechnical workers do not gain. The argument is that the flight of corporations abroad for cheap labor will not have a long-term effect because wages in those countries will eventually be driven up. Low productivity due to the low skill level of domestic workers is cited as the primary reason the income gap is worsening. For both sides, creating more jobs domestically will help to narrow the income gap. However, opponents to free trade argue that expanding job opportunities for low-skilled workers and perhaps encouraging more domestic investments by multinational corporations will raise wages for low-skilled workers. Advocates of free trade, on the other hand, argue that such policies will have no effect. Rather, the skill level and the productivity of low-wage earners have to be raised, perhaps through more job training and education, but not by restricting job exports by corporations.

The growth of global information infrastructure and its commercial use cuts through both of these arguments. Through electronic commerce, high-wage jobs—not just low-wage jobs—are being exported, that is high-value products are being imported. For example, software engineers in India work on projects via satellite networks linking directly with U.S. companies. High-skilled researchers and scientists in Eastern Europe can be linked via Internet for research purposes. This will depress wages for high-skilled laborers and should narrow income inequality. At the same time, education and training will become cheaper through electronic education services on the Internet, and technological skill and productivity in the electronic marketplace will level off among workers because the difference between high-tech and low-tech laborers is smaller than in physical markets. For these reasons, the income gap is expected to narrow as electronic commerce grows.

The global nature of electronic commerce will also change how corporations operate globally, making these corporations more mobile. Shifting manufacturing abroad is justified when wages are sufficiently different to account for the cost of relocation. With electronic commerce, that cost will be smaller, enabling corporations to exploit even small differences in wages. In essence, this will result in more open economies worldwide and a possible convergence in income levels.

Artificial Borders

Some governments are not discouraged by the prospect of a globalized network and believe that movements on the Internet can, as examples show, be controlled. Through content and access control, minors are protected from obscene and indecent materials (the Communications Decency Act of 1996 in the U.S.); consumers in some countries are protected from misinformation and other harmful effects of uninhibited exchange of information (Ang and Nadarajan, 1996); and a nation (China) can even prevent "spiritual pollution" by denying access to Internet sites that contain politically sensitive materials. In other cases, some European governments choose to be isolated by insisting on local languages as the communications standard instead of English, which has become the *de facto* language of the Internet. In this case, languages, not communications protocols, become the barrier to interoperability.

Imposing control on access and content on the Internet has been an important issue in terms of free speech. (See the *EFF Censorship and Free Expression Archive* at http://www.eff.org/pub/Censorship/and *Government Censorship: the Australian Case* at http://www.thehub.com.au/~rene/liberty/debate.html.) But what is the economic side of the debate regarding the free movement of ideas? Simply, substitute the word "ideas" with "goods." Thus, any regulation restricting the free flow of ideas will also restrict the free flow of goods. By setting up artificial control points on the Internet, governments can turn traders into smugglers.

This said, the case of cryptography software illustrates the futility of controlling movements on the Internet. Cryptography is the main technology for military intelligence and spying. As such, encryption technologies and software are designated as defense articles and services—listed on the U.S. Munitions List or the Commerce Control List—for which exporters need special licenses from the U.S. State Department or the Department of Commerce (from the latter for commercial software targeted for mass market). But when someone uploads such a cryptography program on a U.S. web site, he may be operating as an exporter without licenses because there is no way to identify and restrict access by foreigners. The alternative is not to put the programs on the Internet, or to set up controllable artificial borders. Neither option may be feasible, and both take away the benefits of an open network.

The European Union adopted in July, 1995 a Directive on Protection of Personal Data, which aims to provide a uniform regulatory setting for gathering and moving personal data such as names, addresses, and credit worthiness among its member states (http://www.privacy.org/pi/intl_orgs/ec/eudp.html). Although a uniform legal environment is desirable, the threat to control economic activities underlies the professed goal of consumer protection. When data is transferred outside the Union,

> "...the Directive includes provisions to prevent the EU rules from being circumvented. The basic rule is that the non-EU country receiving the data should ensure an adequate level of protection... The advantage for non-EU countries that can provide adequate protection is that the free flow of data from all 15 EU states will henceforth be assured, whereas up to now each state has decided on such questions separately" (European Commission press release, http://www.privacy.org/pi/intl_orgs/ec/dp_EC_press_release.txt.)

The down side to this is that when the level of protection is deemed inadequate, the European Union will have the authority to block exports of personal data. A resulting scenario may be the inability of U.S. corporations to access their own sales data compiled in Europe (Baker, 1995).

These and many other issues involving access and content control can be resolved through technology without resorting to making more rules and regulations. For example, many filtering programs, such as Net Nanny (http://www.netnanny.com/netnanny), allow total control over Internet browsing as well as application-level activities based on words, phrases, sites, and content. These programs enable parents stricter and more effective control over their children's access than legislation ever could.

Uniform Commercial Environment

The European Union's directive on personal data illustrates the need to have a global (not regional) perspective in securing a workable commercial environment for electronic commerce. A uniform commercial environment for the global information infrastructure (GII) has more to do with setting ground rules than erecting or removing artificial barriers.

However, a uniform commercial environment for the GII must represent international standardization and national interests to promote economic well-being. The question is whether a uniform law or regulation can avoid having differential impacts on individual countries. For example, using a closed-economy model of trade, countries leverage tariffs and income-tax policies to manipulate economic performance. However, a uniform import/export tax—such as no tax, making all Internet transactions duty-free—implies an open international economy that may result in the loss of policy control over domestic economy. Domestic industries are often protected by high tariffs, and a country's balance-of-payment position depends on selectively controlling exports and imports. Many countries may not accept simple uniformity if it means relinquishing this tool.

According to the U.S. and the European Union, the principal approach to achieving a healthy GII is to rely on the market (IITF 1996; European Council, 1994). However, a uniform commercial environment can only be achieved through widespread international negotiation and cooperation, of which there has been scant evidence. Several exceptions exist in the areas of copyright, key encryption, and electronic contract standards. But, even in these areas, the uniformity underlying these efforts is procedural rather than specific. That is, the goal is to lay a framework within which governments can verify, recognize, enforce, and promote international transactions.

In addition to the World Intellectual Property Organization's (http://www.wipo.org) worldwide conference on copyright (see Chapter 5), the Working Group on Electronic Commerce of the United Nations Commission on International Trade Law (UNCITRAL) (http://www.un.or.at/uncitral/mainindx.htm) published its Model Law on Electronic Commerce (excerpt available at http://www.un.or.at/uncitral/texts/electcom/english/ml-ec.htm), which establishes a uniform framework to establish the legal validity of electronic documents in commerce. The Model Law, adopted in 1996, sets standards for electronic equivalents to paper-based terms such as *writing, signature,* and *original.* Although UNCITRAL has been working on international standards for physical goods trading for more than three decades, such international bodies will need to take on an increasingly important role, and also will need to be taken more seriously, in global electronic commerce.

Another prime area of international policy interest is cryptography. As mentioned earlier, policies regarding encryption technologies are first and foremost affected by national security interests. Imagine, then, the Internet filled with private conversations, encoded with unbreakable encryption. Besides crimes and conspiracies that might be discussed, the normal process of information gathering by governments would be severely limited.

One method of managing encryption technology requires all keys to be archived or escrowed with a trusted third party. The archived keys would be used to break or recover encrypted messages. Managing such a key escrow system involves a certification authority that issues the keys, a trusted third party to archive such keys, and an infrastructure to provide the necessary confidentiality and accountability when governments want to access these keys on legitimate grounds. At present, the widespread use of encryption technologies is discouraged by the lack of technology to integrate encryption into applications, rather than by any impediments imposed by policy (Denning, 1997).

A global key escrow system is proposed mainly to balance law enforcement and national security concerns with the need to facilitate private communications and transactions on a global scale. Nevertheless, the OECD (http://www.oecd.org) adopted in March 1997 its Guidelines for Cryptography Policy without specifically endorsing such an international key escrow system. No matter what systems are supported in the market, however, continued international cooperation is imperative to achieve an interoperable encryption system because digital signatures, public keys, and encrypted digital currency are essential in providing identity, confidentiality, nonrepudiation, and other basic commercial requirements in the GII.

The global nature of the Internet is clearly one of its strengths, but a predictable international legal and commercial environment is lacking. Recent agreements negotiated by the World Trade Organization (http://www.wto.org) lay a solid foundation for global electronic commerce (see the sidebar, "WTO

Agreements"). The urgency to establish an international framework will grow as digital products become the commodity of the GII, which today remains largely a communications medium. While governments have some credible needs to control free exchanges of ideas—whether they be sociocultural or political reasons—restricting commercial transactions on the GII will have severe economic consequences.

WTO Agreements

Two recent agreements sponsored by the World Trade Organization have set up a global market in telecommunications, computers, and software—helping to remove tariffs and increase worldwide competition among high-technology firms.

(1) Basic Telecommunications Agreement

In February 1997, 69 WTO members signed the WTO Agreement on Basic Telecommunications Services, which will go into effect on January 1, 1998 as part of the General Agreement on Trade in Services. The Agreement concerns only basic telecommunications services, excluding value-added services such as online data services. Signing parties to the Agreement commit to

"negotiate on all telecommunications services both public and private that involve end-to-end transmission of customer supplied information (for example, simply the relay of voice or data from sender to receiver. They also agreed that basic telecommunications services provided over network infrastructure, as well as those provided through resale (over private leased circuits), would both fall within the scope of commitments. As a result, market access commitments will cover not only cross-border supply of telecommunications but also services provided through the establishment of foreign firms, or commercial presence, including the ability to own and operate independent telecom network infrastructure. Examples of the services covered by this agreement include voice telephony, data transmission, telex, telegraph, facsimile, private leased circuit services (that is, the sale or lease of transmission capacity), fixed and mobile satellite systems and services, cellular telephony, mobile data services, paging, and personal communications systems."

The basic telecommunications industry is a $600-billion-a-year industry. Table 11.1 shows the sizes and shares of the top 10 markets. In comparison, world trade in agriculture totaled $444 billion, automobiles $456 billion, and textiles $153 billion in 1995.

Table 11.1 World Trade Figures

	Revenues in Share of Millions (U.S. Dollars)	Percentage of Share
United States	178,758.0	29.70
EC (European Community)	170,166.0	28.27
Japan	93,855.0	15.59
Australia	11,403.0	1.89
Canada	10,689.0	1.78
Switzerland	8,889.0	1.48
Korea	8,728.0	1.45
Brazil	8,622.0	1.43
Mexico	6,509.0	1.08
Argentina	6,009.1	1.00

(2) The Information Technology Agreement

WTO's Information Technology Agreement aims at reducing customs duties on computer and telecommunications products beginning July 1, 1997, and eliminating them altogether by the year 2000. This agreement will also affect the $600 billion market that includes computers, software, telecommunication products, and semiconductors.

Categories of products covered by the agreement include:

1. Computers (including complete computer systems and laptops as well as components, such as CPUs, keyboards, printers, display units (monitors), scanners, hard-disk drives, power supplies, and so on)

2. Telecom equipment (including telephone sets, videophones, fax machines, switching apparatus, modems and parts thereof, telephone handsets, answering machines, radio-broadcasting and television transmission and reception apparatus, and pagers)

3. Semiconductors (including chips, wafers, and so on, of various sizes and capacities)

continues

continued

4. Semiconductor manufacturing equipment (including a wide variety of equipment and testing apparatus used to produce semiconductors, such as vapor deposition apparatus, spin dryers, etching and stripping apparatus, laser cutters, sawing and dicing machines, deposition machines, spinners, encapsulation machines, furnaces and heaters, ion implanters, microscopes, handling and transport apparatus, measuring and checking instruments, and parts and accessories)

5. Software (contained in diskettes, magnetic tapes, CD-ROMs, and so on)

6. Scientific instruments (including measuring and checking devices, chromatographs, spectrometers, optical radiation devices, and electrophoresis equipment)

Additionally, other main products of interest covered by the ITA include word processors, calculators, cash registers, ATM machines, certain static converters, indicator panels, capacitors, resistors, printed circuits, certain electronic switches, certain connection devices, certain electric conductors, fiber-optic cables, certain photocopiers, computer network equipment (LAN and WAN equipment), flat panel displays, plotters, and multimedia upgrade kits. The ITA does not cover consumer electronic goods.

11.9. Antitrust and Regulation Policies

In the interest of promoting competition and efficiency, governments often intervene in the marketplace. Antitrust laws and regulatory policies aim to promote market efficiencies, such as low prices and efficient resource allocation. Antitrust laws ensure efficient results by safeguarding the market from anticompetitive behaviors such as price-fixing conspiracies, predatory pricing, and competition-reducing mergers. Regulation focuses on markets in which the nature of a product or industry tends to favor a single firm and competition usually results in inefficiencies. In such markets, promoting competition would not be efficient, that is, would not bring about lower prices and more output. Such firms are called natural monopolies, and their regulation should be distinguished from other governmental regulations of wages, environments, safety, and so on.

Anti-regulation and anti-antitrust sentiment has been high since the 1980s. This sentiment stems from antitrust litigations that were largely ineffective or dragged on for decades without yielding clear guidelines for market participants. Also, it has been argued that regulated firms could subvert the regulatory process, for example, by influencing regulators, whereby firms were protected from competition with no apparent gain in efficiency. An alternative is to depend on market mechanisms. But the nature of digital products poses a severe problem in defining anticompetitive behaviors. For example, how do you determine that a digital seller is dumping or practices predatory prices when all products have essentially the same marginal cost? How do you distinguish the need for interoperability and standardization from monopolization? And should all digital products be regulated because they have economies of scale and allow only one firm to operate for efficiency reasons? Two factors seem to favor a single dominant firm in each digital product market: the economy of scale and interoperability.

Economies of Scale and Regulation

Economies of scale refer to gains or losses in production cost that occur as output is increased. Typically, production costs first decrease because fixed costs such as buildings and management expenses are shared. They then increase as inefficiencies kick in when the output level goes beyond the optimal level. For example, suppose a firm has ten permanent employees who can each produce ten widgets a day given the layout of the factory, materials, and so on. The salaries and other costs, such as office rent, must be paid whether the firm produces anything at all. The per-unit cost of the first widget produced is the sum of all these costs, which decreases until 100 units are produced a day. For the 101st unit, one employee may have to work overtime, the firm may have to pay special delivery charges to its material suppliers, or a new machine may need to be purchased. The average cost of a widget increases rapidly beyond the optimal level of production.

A simple case of decreasing average cost occurs when there is a high fixed cost but no (or constant) variable cost. Because the fixed cost is shared by more and more output, the average cost will decrease forever. It is commonly asserted that computer software costs nothing or little to duplicate. Development costs account for the majority of the software's production cost. Consequently, the average cost of a computer program will drop as more copies are sold. Similarly, most digital products appear to have economies of scale.

When a product has a decreasing average cost or an increasing economy of scale, the market often fails to achieve an efficient solution. Competition implies duplicated fixed costs, and no firm could recoup its fixed costs unless the market price equals the average cost. Without such guarantee, no firms will produce the product. Does this imply that all digital products should be regulated as natural monopolists?

Digital products may not have economies of scale for two reasons. First, computer software, and most digital products for that matter, may not have decreasing average costs. Although duplicating costs may indeed be relatively small compared to initial development costs, duplication costs are not the only variable costs for most products. Many physical products have low variable costs—for example, cereals, sneakers, and so on—but they do not have decreasing average costs, because variable costs (such as administrative, marketing, and distribution costs) increase at a faster rate as the number of sales increase (Liebowith and Margolis, 1995). For this reason, many digital products will have U-shaped average costs (see Chapter 8 for more detail about costs). Furthermore, for each copy of software or information sold, other substantial costs may exist, for instance, copyright payments and copyright enforcement costs, customer support expenses, and management and accounting costs. As a result, whether digital products exhibit decreasing average costs remains an empirical question.

Second, economy of scale is not as relevant when products are not homogeneous. The economy of scale simply indicates that having one producer is more efficient if you consider all varieties as essentially the same. For differentiated products catering to different segments of consumers, multiple products are desired. These products may be produced by one producer. However, the costs associated with differentiation and customization may indicate a lack of scale economies. For application software such as word processing and spreadsheet programs, differentiation is desirable. Any artificial means to standardize such programs will be contrary to competition and consumer satisfaction. Again, economy of scale will not be the primary concern.

Interoperability, Standardization, and Market Dominance

Some of the network effects often mentioned in computer-related literature concern interoperability rather than network externality. *Interoperability* means that two different products can communicate through some common interface to enable various functions such as swapping disks and files, or using third-party auxiliary equipment, macro programs, and extensions. Two interoperable computers can establish a connection with each other; interoperable word processors can exchange files; interoperable VCRs can read and play the same video tape; and most electric appliances can interoperate with the prevailing electric service and add-on equipment. Interoperability is achieved through standardization, the extent of which is determined by what needs to be exchanged. For e-mail messages, different operating systems (OSs)—Windows, MacOS, IBM's OS2, and Unix, for instance—may need to adopt standard communications protocols. Other features of an operating system need not be interoperable.

For example, Microsoft's dominant market position is explained by computer software tending to favor interoperability and standardization, with network externality thrown in as well. Microsoft Word files can be freely exchanged between those who use Windows and Macintosh operating systems, whereas WordPerfect files lose format when read with Microsoft Word, and vice versa, even when both programs are run on the same Windows OS. So, the interoperability has nothing to do with the compatibility of operating systems but rather is a matter of word-processing programs having interoperable features. To further illustrate the point, consider electric toasters. Toasters need at least two standardized features: they have to interface with the electric power source and they must be able to accept bread slices. Similarly, word-processing programs need two interface capabilities: they have to work with an operating system and must be able to accept different files. If word processors are interoperable, users will have minimal hassles in exchanging files created in one program into another. Today, such interoperability does not exist. In a way, the lack of interoperability among word-processing programs is akin to the inability to plug one hair dryer into another country's outlet—a problem anyone traveling from the U.S. to Europe has experienced. If the ability to exchange files is paramount in this age of information, some sort of interoperability among word-processing programs through standardization is necessary.

Standardization may be achieved either through standard-setting efforts or through competition. Standards may be established by defining features that need to be interoperable for everyone's benefit—for example, for interchanging files. However, a standard-setting session among competitors may be a disguised conference for collusion. Especially, the volume of exchanged messages on the Internet may prove to be a problem in detecting collusive behaviors among competing firms (Baker, J.B., 1996). On the other hand, vigorous enforcement to prevent industry collusion may discourage standard-setting activities (Lemley, 1996). Alternatively, through competition, one product becomes a *de facto* standard by dominating the market and forcing all others to comply with the product's standards. But, its producer is not obligated to reveal its specifications, unlike the case of industry-wide standard setting. Should governments require that all *de facto* standard products reveal their product specifications to competitors and producers of related products? This will necessarily involve a complex process of guaranteeing profits for the standard-setter, which is far from an improvement over government regulations.

Standardization does not mean that all competing products have to be abandoned. It only means that some interoperable features need to be based on the standards. How is this different from one product becoming a dominant product? Through standardization, consumers will have choices (for example, in programs) with interoperability, whereas left to markets they may have to face monopoly prices.

Videocassette competition between Betamax and VHS illustrates the market's ability to standardize products. Betamax versus VHS is similar to having two different sizes of floppy disks. When VHS became the industry standard, however, the result was not one firm producing VCRs. Under the interoperable standard, the healthy competitive market supports numerous competitors and lower prices for VCRs. The case of word-processing programs or operating systems is fundamentally different from Betamax and VHS standards because the competition in programs and OSs is not about standards. Instead, it often involves a variety of products that are vertically integrated—for example, microprocessors, computer hardware, OSs, and application programs and contents. You can witness vertically integrated monopolists in a wide range of product markets, although interoperability and standardization in no way imply that the computer industry will tend to be concentrated. Nevertheless, indiscriminate use of interoperability and standardization to excuse the vertical monopolization process has clouded understanding of the true nature of this market. Although market-driven solutions often encourage competition and efficiency without the follies of artificial government intervention, economists and market analysts need to provide clearer definitions and analyses of the effects of interoperability, standardization, and dominance on this multimedia computer industry.

Network Externality and Monopolization

In addition to scale economies and interoperability, network externalities are often cited to explain the emerging monopolistic market dominance of a few firms in computer and high-tech industries. As discussed in Chapters 2 and 3, some products, and especially communications networks, are more valuable if more people use the same product or network. Such an advantage results in market dominance after a product's market share surpasses a certain threshold. This section examines the effects of network externalities on market structure such as monopolization. A firm's monopoly power obtained by this process—that is, as a result of being a popular or superior product, must be distinguished from one amassed through anticompetitive behaviors. But, as in the case of interoperability, network externalities have become a catch-22 for government regulators.

Monopoly and Welfare Loss: The Problem

First, consider why monopolization is seen as harmful. A general result in the economic theory of firms states that the greatest economic sin of a monopolist is that it restricts output, and by doing so, raises the price above the marginal cost of production. Society's resources could be better used if the price equaled marginal cost, which usually means that more output is desired in the case of a monopoly.

Figure 11.2 shows a monopolist's pricing and output decision based on market demand and cost of production. To maximize its profit, a firm operates at the output level when its marginal cost is equal to its marginal revenue (Qm). The next unit will generate less revenue than its production cost, shrinking its total profit. By producing less, the firm misses the opportunity to increase its total profit. At the optimal output level (Qm), the market price is determined by demand (Pm), which is greater than the marginal cost (MC). The firm's per-unit profit is the difference between the price and the cost (Pm − MC), and the total profit is the shaded area in figure 11.2.

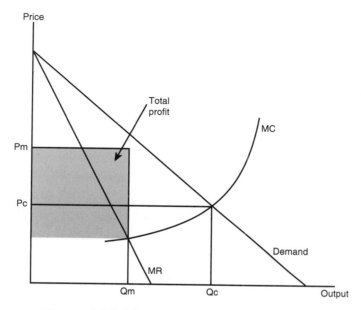

Figure 11.2 Monopolist's output decision.

At the Qm level of output, consumers' willingness to pay (Pm) is still greater than the cost of producing the product (MC). Thus society will be better off if more resources are allocated into this industry to increase the level of output until marginal cost and marginal benefit are equal. At Qc, for example, consumers are willing to pay Pc, which is equal to the marginal cost, but the firm will only break even because the price equals the cost. Comparing the zero-profit levels of output and price (Qc, Pc) with those of monopoly (Qm, Pm), the monopolist firm clearly produces too little and sells the product at a price higher than does a competitive firm.

For many physical products, this scenario's implications are straightforward. However, computer software and many digital products with network externalities do not allow ready applications of this monopoly model. For example, if Microsoft is a monopolist in the market for OS software, then Microsoft must be artificially restricting its output to raise price. A more competitive Microsoft would have produced far more units of Windows and other assorted operating systems. But, is Microsoft not selling enough products? That doesn't seem right. Rather, the problem, as far as regulators and its competitors are concerned, is that Microsoft dominates the OS software market—that is, the company sells too many.

This paradoxical result can be explained in several ways. Three explanations follow regarding the market position of Microsoft and its market impacts. These summaries also apply in general to most computer and high-tech industries.

- **No Market Power:** Output restriction occurs after the firm achieves market power. The firm in figure 11.2 is assumed to have monopoly market power. In other words, it can restrict output and raise price only because it does not face competition. Microsoft, on the other hand, still faces competition despite its dominance (producing roughly 80 percent of operating systems for desktop computers). Consequently, Microsoft's dominance does not result in lower output and higher price, as would be expected with a monopoly.

- **Scale Economies:** Figure 11.2 assumes that the firm has an increasing marginal cost. Instead, computer software generally has a decreasing marginal and average cost because of its high fixed cost and extremely low duplicating (variable) cost. In other words, the average cost of production decreases as more products are sold. An efficient level of product in such a case enables one firm to produce all necessary output to achieve the maximum economies of scale. Competing firms unnecessarily duplicate fixed costs and result in waste. Therefore, Microsoft's dominance in OS software is an efficient result owed to the characteristics of the software industry.

- **Network Externalities:** There are network externalities by which consumers benefit from having one standard product. With network externalities, the value of a product rises as more people obtain the same product. Therefore, the more the merrier. Microsoft's dominance simply is a manifestation of network externalities that relentlessly drive the computer software industry to standardization and dominance of a few successful firms.

The first argument of no market power proposes that Microsoft's market dominance does not have the problems associated with the standard monopoly. Despite its market share, Microsoft faces fierce competition from Apple's MacOSs, IBM's OS, and Unix-based OSs. Monopoly rents (higher profits) will be gained if no competition exists. But there is no evidence that Microsoft is in a position to raise prices because of present and future competition.

However, Microsoft's market power should be determined in the PC clone market rather than in OS software. OS software is useless without a platform on which to run. For that matter, a computer is also useless if it does not have an OS. Therefore, Microsoft is a player in the PC clone market. It may seem that fiercer competition exists in the PC market, in which no one firm commands more than 25 percent of the market. Because of competition, a PC's price is assumed efficient. This might be true in terms of hardware prices. However, PC buyers must also buy an OS, such as Windows 95, which commands a monopoly price. If this price were lower, more personal computers would be purchased. Consequently, monopoly problems exist in the PC market, in which the level of output may be well below the socially efficient level. Monopolistic components of a PC include the OS software as well as microprocessors dominated by Intel. Despite cost savings in many PC components, the PC's price is still prohibitively high for the majority of the population. The reason? Monopoly market power of Microsoft and Intel.

The second argument regarding economies of scale was discussed earlier. In short, the average cost of computer software may not be declining due to rapidly increasing nonproduction costs. Contrary to the assumption that software prices may be zero because of the scale economy, giving away these programs may very well be an act of dumping and predatory pricing.

Finally, network externalities, or economies of the network, seem to promote monopolistic computer software firms, which behave like telephone services. As more people use Windows on their computer, for example, its popularity feeds on itself, making Microsoft an unwilling monopolist. It is argued that Microsoft's market dominance is due to network economies of its products, and it is often more efficient to have only one firm producing such a product than to have many firms competing with similar products.

Analyzing this argument requires considerable effort because the term *network externality* is used indiscriminately in today's popular press and even in academic journals. The term is often used in connection with interoperability, standardization, and economies of scale. All these concepts relate to some type of market incentive that drives the market toward a single dominant product as consumers benefit from its dominance—leaving an impression that market positions of Microsoft and other computer-related giants are somehow due to the nature of products, not their anticompetitive behaviors. Network externalities seem to suffer the most abuse. Thus the following section focuses on this problem.

Externalities and Their Effects

To define network externality, we must begin with the term externality. An *externality* is a feature of a product that has no market price. Its price cannot be determined because there is no clear way to define ownership of the product, or sometimes to define the product itself. An example is air pollution from a factory. Because air is not owned, the price or cost of polluted air cannot be determined. Therefore, air pollution is an externality. Another example is shade associated with a large tree. The tree's owner cannot determine its shade as a product (because it is created by the sun), nor charge for it in any marketable way. Note that shade is *external* to trees, which have prices determined in the market. In a sense, an externality is a part of the characteristics of a product, which nevertheless cannot be priced in the market.

Externality is an important economic concept because it distorts the market result. An efficient market employs resources up to a point when their marginal costs equal market prices. Suppose that an air-polluting factory producing a widget has a marginal cost of $50 without considering the pollution. Suppose 10,000 customers want to buy the widget at $50. However, if the cost of pollution is included, say $10 per widget, the widget's cost becomes $60. At that price, fewer than 10,000 customers will buy the widget.

Therefore, widgets are overproduced—an inefficient resource allocation—if you do not consider its externality (negative in this case).

Again, suppose that a home-builder considers how many trees to plant. Suppose that the market value of each home increases by $3,000 if it has trees. At $100 per tree, the home-builder plants 30 trees. However, neighbors may benefit from the trees' shade and the neighborhood's increased home values; say these benefits are worth $500. Therefore, an optimal number of trees is 35 instead of 30 if the home-builder considers the externality of planting trees (positive in this case). Instead, trees are *underproduced* because the home-builder has no means of charging his neighbors the added cost of $500.

Because externalities bring about these inefficiencies, you need to counter externalities. For some externalities, the solution is to define property rights more clearly. If the cost of pollution is clearly defined, the widget factory may be required to pay $10 for each unit produced. If the home-builder can appropriate the benefit of tree planting, or be compensated for the cost, he will plant an optimal number of trees. If computer software has positive network externality (a benefit to its users), the program will be underproduced unless the producer can appropriate such benefit in terms of revenue. The economic concern stems from such solutions often being impossible through market processes.

On the other hand, if a market price already reflects the price of an external benefit or loss, no externality problem exists. For example, a computer OS may have a positive externality in that its value increases as more people use the same product. This can be represented by an upward sloping benefit schedule for consumers (see fig. 11.3), indicating that the average consumers' willingness to pay (WTP) increases with more users. Given the firm's marginal cost schedule, an optimal number of product is Q1, with the price of P1, if the firm can charge consumers for the benefit from network externality. If not, the output is reduced to Q2, with a lower price of P2, that corresponds to the willingness to pay without network externality. At P2, the marginal cost is below the true consumers' willingness to pay, indicating that the product is underproduced.

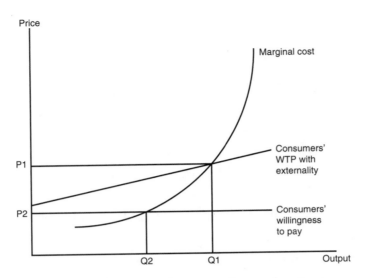

Figure 11.3 Network externality and output.

Network Effects versus Network Externalities

After you become clear about network externalities, you must distinguish simple network effects from network externalities. If market prices fully reflect the cost and benefit associated with an externality, no economic concern exists. For example, if market prices efficiently determine the level of air pollution or the number of trees planted, what we call externalities are no longer externalities. Still, market size has some sort of effect, and such effects are often called *network effects* to indicate that these effects do not result in market inefficiencies.

If the price of OS software or an application program is raised to extract most or all of the benefit associated with network externalities, the market needs no intervention. Similarly, the dominant position of such a product, or its desirability, should not be explained by network externalities. Instead, what appears to be the result of network externality may be due to economies of scale (Liebowitz and Margolis, 1995) or anticompetitive behaviors. When comparing prices in the computer hardware market, the OS market, and the applications software market, many perceive that network externalities are also behind the dominance of a player in all these markets. Simply put, prices for a PC drop as more people use the Windows OS. In addition, Windows has more application programs because more people use Windows, and so on. The market is invariably dominated by a vertically integrated firm or a multi-firm regime, such as the Windows-Intel platform. These arguments indiscriminately apply network effects to different industries. That is, network externalities between different products (often termed as *indirect* network externalities) are mostly network effects, not externalities (Liebowitz and Margolis, 1995). These network effects across different products are hardly distinguished from anti-competitive behaviors that impose artificial connections such as tie-ins, or exclude downstream competitors from accessing upstream products that one monopolizes.

Anticompetitive Behaviors

A dominant firm should not use its position in one market to influence other markets. For example, application programs need to interoperate with OS software, which may be dominated by one firm. Through anticompetitive behaviors, the dominating firm may extend its market power into the application software market. While governments cannot prevent the firm from entering related markets, this case may fall into the category of illegal tie-ins prohibited by antitrust laws. Often, such tie-ins are practiced as bundling of vertically related products. For example, Microsoft as a dominant firm in OSs tries to dominate the web browser market as well. If Microsoft uses its market power in OS to advance its interest in the web browser market, the company certainly appears to be a monopoly. However, enforcement efforts are often discouraged due to the need for interoperability, standardization, and network externality, which compound understanding of what constitutes anti-competitive behaviors in digital product markets. This section, provides an example of how interrelated digital markets may be analyzed to understand firms' behaviors in these markets.

Microsoft sells many application software products, including web browsers in addition to OS programs. By bundling this software with Windows OS, and using various means to make it difficult for consumers to use non-Microsoft applications, Microsoft tries to extend its monopoly market power of one market (OS software) into the applications market.

It is often argued that the scale economy in computer software, rather than monopolization, explains the bundling and the dominance of Microsoft. That will depend on the extent of the economy of scale in that product market, but is highly unlikely as was previously argued. Alternatively, some argue that a need for standardization and interoperability works to favor integrated software, such as Microsoft's bundles, which are also integrated with the Windows OS. But as argued earlier, there is no apparent reason why the need for standardization or interoperability between an OS and an application program should give one firm substantial advantages over others. In other words, Microsoft Word and WordPefect have equal opportunities in the market for word-processing programs, just as different VCR manufacturers have. If one program enjoys network externalities, its price must be higher than the other to reflect its true value. If one is more convenient with the Windows OS, it may indicate a lack of true interoperability and standardization. A monopolist in the OS market must provide all application software vendors equal access to its standards and specifications necessary to run any application on its OS. The monopolist is what is known as the *common carrier*.

Common Carriers and Microsoft

In telecommunications industries, the concept of common carrier is well-known and accepted by market players and regulators. For example, suppose Alice operates the only licensed magazine stand in Our Fair City. Suppose also that her stand is the only location all citizens can access. Bob and Charlie produce magazines that can be distributed only through Alice. Alice, in this example, acts as a conduit for contents created by the publishers. The selection of magazines on her stand is entirely up to her. She considers the number of magazines she can accommodate, and each magazine's popularity and profit margins. However, she cannot perform certain acts. For example, Bob may try to influence Alice not to carry Charlie's magazine by offering a higher commission. But Alice must also offer Charlie the same opportunity to pay a higher price before discontinuing his magazine. Bob may issue many versions of his magazine to fill up Alice's stand, but Alice must sell Charlie's unless she can prove that all Bob magazines are more popular than Charlie's—or Bob pays more money to carry his magazines.

The seemingly unreasonable restrictions on Alice and favors for Charlie stem from the city's inability to accommodate more magazine stands. When resources are limited, an equal and reasonable access by all publishers to the distribution medium becomes important. Besides First Amendment and free-speech issues, Bob's magazines may not be produced efficiently if the market process is interfered—for example, some consumers will never know the value of Charlie's magazine. Those who control limited distribution conduits are called common carriers. For example, local telephone networks are common carriers to long-distance companies because they cannot provide long-distance services without access to the local exchange monopoly.

Because of limited resources and often large investments needed to build and maintain common carrier services, common carriers are often regulated as natural monopolists. When regulations are abandoned, however, the market may produce inefficiencies. For example, suppose Alice decides to publish her own magazines (or merge with Charlie). If her magazine stand is no longer regulated as a common carrier, she has an incentive to sell only her magazines. Other publishers will have no distribution outlets. As long as Alice has the only magazine stand, therefore, other publishers must be guaranteed reasonable access to her stand.

Vertical Integration and Retail Wheeling

The point of the preceding example is that a monopolist selling OS software may be interpreted as a common carrier. Application software vendors are publishers who need access to the magazine stand—that is, an OS to run their programs. If Microsoft as a monopolist in OS also enters the application software market, what sort of behaviors are acceptable? Or what sort of fair and unfair advantages does Microsoft have over other vendors? The concept of common carriers, which is well researched in telecommunications economics, presents a framework that can answer these questions better than the jumble of interoperability and network externalities that seem to pervade today's analysis.

For example, suppose Alice, or Microsoft, is an upstream monopolist. Bob and Charlie, and application software vendors, are downstream competitors who depend on products and services monopolized by the upstream monopolist. When Microsoft enters the downstream market, it has an incentive to raise its downstream competitors' costs to expand its own downstream market share. Microsoft may sell its OS specifications to rivals at a higher price than its internal price, or restrict full access to the specifications. However, higher costs in the downstream market may reduce the number of Windows-based application programs and lower demand for Microsoft's OS. Therefore, Microsoft also has an incentive to lower, not raise, rivals' costs. Sibley and Weisman (1997) examine these incentives in the context of telephone services in which a local exchange monopolist enters long-distance call services whose providers must pay the monopolist access fees. Sibley and Weisman show that, as the monopolist begins its new service, its incentive is to lower rivals' costs, but as its share in the downstream market grows, it has more incentive to raise rivals' costs.

Sibley and Weisman also examine the effects of requiring the monopolist to enter the downstream market with a fully separate subsidiary, which is favored by government regulators. For example, should governments require Microsoft to spin off its application software business from its OS business? Although it is difficult to gauge how independent a subsidiary can be from its upstream owner, the upstream monopolist behaves differently if it does not consider the total profits from the two markets, as it does if it is a vertically integrated firm. In general, the separated monopolist has an incentive to lower rivals' costs because that will increase the overall market demand for its product.

The breakup of AT&T into regional Baby Bells and a long-distance company in 1983 was an effort to disintegrate or disaggregate a vertically integrated firm. AT&T's long-distance company subsequently found itself competing against numerous companies, such as MCI and Sprint. Regional

Bell companies, however, were granted a monopoly in the belief that they are natural monopolies. After only a decade, local exchange markets face competition from wireless networks, long-distance companies, and cable operators. This seemingly increasing competition has allowed the abandoning of regulatory constraints not only in the telecommunications industry but also in electric utility and natural gas industries.

Deregulation in the electric utility industry, for example, aims to provide more choices for consumers. How would consumers deal with competing electric power suppliers? Does this mean that consumers will have separate power connections or that they will have access to alternative power sources? The proposed electricity deregulation will result in neither scenario. Rather, the deregulation proposes a mechanism by which excess power supplies are routed—or *wheeled*—through existing power grids to reach final consumers. This *retail wheeling* requires an efficient means to connect various players in the market. For example, the electric utility industry consists of upstream power producers, power wholesalers who mediate excess power supplies and sell directly to industrial users, regional power grid operators, and electricity retailers who deal with consumers. If an excess power supplier is found in a remote area, a potential customer must be able to negotiate prices and arrange delivery, which may involve many intervening power producers and power grid operators. Wheeling costs are added to the final price.

Not surprisingly, electronic commerce on the Internet has become a critical ingredient in electricity deregulation. To facilitate intermediation in electricity wholesaling, the Federal Energy Regulatory Commission (FERC; http://www.fedworld.gov/ferc/ferc.html) in 1996 required each public utility engaged in interstate commerce to create an Open Access Same-time Information System (OASIS), also known as Transmission Service Information Network, or TSIN (see http://www.tsin.com for OASIS and TSIN), through which potential wholesalers can shop around instead of relying on personal contacts. A sample TSIN system is built on the Internet using secure web technologies. Again, the open, networked Internet environment is proving its superiority over proprietary bulletin board systems used by gas companies (Radosevich,

1997). Although today's TSIN is limited to wholesalers, electronic commerce will provide a crucial framework for further efforts to include consumer retailing in electricity as well as in natural gas.

Just as retail wheeling was unimaginable only a few years ago in regulated utility markets, the infrastructure convergence is opening an era of competition in numerous monopolistic markets with new types of firms. These include more specialized firms, a result of disaggregating formerly vertically integrated firms. On the other hand, regional monopolists are becoming national competitors through horizontal mergers (for example, SWB and Pacific Telesis; Nynex and Bell Atlantic) and through integration across different markets (for example, AT&T's entering regional Bell's markets and vice versa). In this shuffle, there is a danger of forgetting why society opted for disintegration and deregulation: to increase competition, lower prices, and raise economic efficiencies. To avoid a mishap, economic implications of these changes in market structure must be better understood. For example, if disintegration and retail wheeling make sense in the utility industry, why is it different to break up software companies into OS and application software units? If local exchange networks are common carriers, why would OS vendors not be treated the same way? Are network externality and interoperability the same forces that facilitate natural monopoly market structure in the communications and utility industries? And, should these forces be discarded as they are in the latter? This section answers some of these questions; others await more in-depth analyses.

11.10. The Economics of Electronic Commerce and the Internet

The economics of the Internet as an important use of telecommunications networks has become a fashionable area of research. The accumulated knowledge of telecommunications economics is beginning to be applied vigorously to classical economic problems of resource allocation as well as to policy issues for Internet communication. Electronic commerce is sometimes subsumed under this field because researchers erroneously assume that electronic commerce is just one of the many uses of the Internet infrastructure. This section clarifies the relationship between the Internet and electronic commerce, and in doing so, highlights the difference between the economics of the Internet and the economics of electronic commerce. In brief, the former emphasizes the nature of communications infrastructure whereas the latter focuses on issues of digital commodity markets. A further objective is to show the limitations in defining the economics of the Internet as a part of communications economics, in which regulatory policies are of paramount interest.

The Economics of Electronic Commerce

Research in the economics of the Internet is a subfield of communications economics. Communications economics deals with economic problems associated with limited resources, such as the telephone network, on which Internet traffic happens to travel. Although the Internet is based on different technologies, such as routing and packet switching, it is essentially an alternative use of the existing telephone network. Accordingly, Internet service pricing, taxation, and competition among service providers are important topics of research in determining efficient resource allocation, the profitability of investments in telecommunications, and proper government policies.

However, the very nature of Internet communications is changing. The next generation of Internet traffic may well bypass traditional telephone or cable networks and connect users via satellites that transmit data directly into personal computers. Such wireless communications are already beginning to dominate many business sectors, such as paging services, mobile telephones, and cable television. With low earth-orbiting satellite networks and infrared sensors in computers, the infrastructure for the future Internet may bypass the wired telephone infrastructure. After all these wired and wireless networks are converted into digital networks and become interoperable, today's wire-based Internet will be only a small portion of the information infrastructure. Regardless, the nascent interest among economists is focused on the wired Internet infrastructure.

In contrast, the economics of electronic commerce is concerned with a new market whose delivery and communication infrastructure happens to be the Internet. The distinction should be clearly made between digital product markets and digital delivery infrastructure. To use an analogy, the economics of the Internet focuses on the workings of the interstate highway system, and the telephone and mail networks, whereas the economics of electronic commerce focuses on markets whose transactions are facilitated by communications networks and delivery systems. The primary focus of the latter is on product choices, market strategies, prices, and other traditional subjects of economics within the context of digital products and, equally important, physical products whose production, marketing, and consumption processes are affected. Although transportation and communications economics is an important field, the economics of the Internet, as currently defined and researched, is only one small part of the economics of electronic commerce.

The confusion stems from the practice of regarding the Internet and electronic commerce as equivalent. The Internet, due to its openness and versatility, is the medium of choice for electronic commerce. However, any digital communications media will soon be capable of supporting virtual transactions in the electronic marketplace, including telephone wires, cables, microwaves, and satellites. Occasionally, commerce on the Internet is regarded as equivalent to electronic commerce. But the distinguishing characteristic of electronic commerce is in the way the market is organized and transactions are carried out: by virtual market agents, digital products, and electronic market processes. The economics of electronic commerce aims to analyze fundamental changes in market processes and products. Such an innovative market can exist and function regardless of the infrastructure on which it is based. The Internet, in essence, is only a transitory infrastructure on which the electronic marketplace has been launched.

The Economics of Information Infrastructure

The development of the information infrastructure, of which the Internet is one element, poses many technological and economic problems. To make the infrastructure a reality, technologies in varying and competing industries such as telephone, cable, private commercial information services, EDI, and various wireless communications will have to be interoperable. At the same time, simple equipment, such as cable modems, which enable Internet users to connect via cable, and digital switches, are taking more time and effort to develop than expected. Communications protocols and other product standards, such as video and audio compression, languages for web documents and applets, and digital currency have to be worked out among increasingly numerous and diverse participants. The dominance of the TCP/IP protocol as the communications standard was a happy consequence of its popularity among Internet users. The Internet's popularity made it the heavyweight in comparison with private online services, which first attempted to compete with the Internet and failed. As a result, the Internet has become synonymous with information infrastructure. But, as business interest intensifies, its future might not be as smooth as its past.

Numerous economic issues also pose threats to the future of information infrastructure. Flat-rate pricing for online services raised the specter of congestion and inefficiency. Local telephone companies and Internet service providers are fighting a battle over access charges. Governments are contemplating various forms of taxes and tariffs for Internet services and transactions.

Economists who are primarily interested in network economics are analyzing these issues because such issues arise naturally in telecommunications networks. While the information infrastructure is evolving from its dependence on wired telecommunications networks to a more diverse mixture of infrastructure including cable and wireless networks, the economics of Internet infrastructure remains focused on traditional problems of a wired telephone network, in which the economies of scale and regulatory efficiencies are of primary concern. The telephone industry is not only being deregulated but also faces competition from nontelephone infrastructure, which can carry all types of digital traffic. Future commercial potential and profitability determine investment decisions, and competition will be the driving force in achieving economic efficiency. The focus of economic analysis should also make a transition from regulatory economics to one of multiple infrastructure competition and related problems in resource allocation.

For example, the decision to exempt Internet service providers from paying access charges, despite their use of facilities owned by telephone companies, has a profound impact on the level of investment in the telephone network—or so it is claimed by telephone companies that will not invest if their fixed costs in cable and exchange equipment cannot be recovered. Such investment behavior is consistent with that of natural monopolists, and is the reason regulatory agencies allow a certain rate of return for these monopolists. However, in a competitive market environment, a telephone company will charge for its service based on marginal cost, not average cost, and access charges calculated to recoup fixed costs will be excess profits that cannot be expected. Whether access charges on ISPs are justified is an empirical question. The point here is that the information infrastructure needs to be analyzed not in the context of regulated natural monopolies—for example focusing on ways to recover fixed or stranded costs through market competition—but rather in terms of the market where various types of networks are converging to compete. Congestion-free pricing and competition may find new uses for stranded investments. The economics of information infrastructure goes beyond a simple extension of telecommunications economics. What its focus and emphasis should be is left as a future area of research.

11.11. Summary

This chapter presented some pressing issues in electronic commerce. Many of the issues discussed require applying a new perspective that commerce on the Internet represents a new type of market. Instead of treating commerce on the Internet as an extension of existing commerce or as an alternative distribution channel, the electronic marketplace should be perceived as a market in which players, products, and processes all undergo fundamental changes. Product differentiation, searches, copyrights, consumer privacy, micropayments, and other issues arise in physical markets as well. But because these factors take on different dimensions when players and products are virtual and market processes are networked and aided by computers, they can only be clearly understood if you put them in the larger context of electronic commerce as a market.

References

Ang, P.H. and B. Nadarajan, 1996. "Censorship and the Internet: A Singapore Perspective." *Communications of the ACM*, 39(6) pp.72–78.

Baker, J.B., 1996. "Horizontal Price-Fixing in Cyberspace." Presented at *The 1996 Antitrust Conference: Antitrust Issues in Today's Economy*. Available at http://www.ftc.gov/speeches/other/confbd4.htm.

Baker, S., 1995. "The Net Escape Censorship? Ha!" *Wired*, issue 3.09 (September, 1995). Available online at http://www.hotwired.com/wired/3.09/departments/baker.if.html.

Bernheim, B.D. and M.D. Whinston, 1997. "Incomplete Contracts and Strategic Ambiguity." *American Economic Review*, forthcoming.

Denning, D.E., 1997. "International Encryption Policy." In R. Kalakota and A.B. Whinston, eds., *Readings in Electronic Commerce*, Chapter 5, pp. 105–118. Reading, Mass.: Addison-Wesley.

Erickson, Elaine, 1996. "Software Royalty Income from Licensing Software: Is it Rental or Sales Income?" *HIGHTECH*, August, 1996. Available at http://www.wgl-hightech.com/0896/soft-text.html.

European Council, 1994. "Europe and the Global Information Society: Recommendations to the European Council." A copy is available at http://www.rewi.hu-berlin.de/datenschutz/report.html.

Information Infrastructure Task Force, 1996. *A Framework for Global Electronic Commerce*. Available at http://www.iitf.nist.gove/eleccomm/glo_comm.htm.

Internet Access Coalition, 1997. *The Effect of Internet Use on the Nation's Telephone Network*. Summary available at http://internetaccess.org/study.htm.

Interactive Services Association (ISA), 1996. *Logging on to Cyberspace Tax Policy White Paper.* Available at http://www.isa.net/about/releases/taxwhpap.html.

Keller, A.M., 1997. "Smart Catalogs and Virtual Catalogs." In R. Kalakota and A.B. Whinston, eds., *Readings in Electronic Commerce*, Chapter 11, pp. 259–271. Reading, Mass.: Addison-Wesley.

Liebowitz, S.J. and S. E. Margolis, 1995. "Are Network Externalities a New Source of Market Failure?" *Research in Law and Economics*, 17:1–22.

Lemley, M.A., 1996. "Antitrust and the Internet: Standardization Problem." *Connecticut Law Review*, 28(4): 1041–1094.

Migdal, J., and M. Taylor, 1997. "Thief or Benefactor?" *Telephony*, January 27, 1997, pp. 46–52.

Mingo, J., 1997. "Nowhere to Hide." *Los Angeles Times*, Feb. 10, 1997.

Radosevich, L., 1997. "Wired." *WebMaster*, February, 1997, pp. 26–31.

Schneier, B., 1994. *Applied Cryptography: Protocols, Algorithms, and Source Code in C.* New York: John Wiley & Sons.

Sibley, D.S., and D.L. Weisman, 1997. "Raising Rivals' Costs: The Entry of an Upstream Monopolist into Downstream Markets." Mimeo. Send correspondence to Weisman@ksu.edu.

Taylor, J.A., 1997. "Federal Lawmakers Plan Bill to Ban New Internet Taxes." *Investor's Business Daily*, Section A9, January 29, 1997.

U.S. Department of Treasury, 1996. "Selected Tax Policy Implications of Global Electronic Commerce." Available at ftp://ftp.fedworld.gov/pub/tel/internet.txt.

Suggested Readings and Notes

Law for the Internet

For a well-rounded discussion regarding legal aspects of electronic communications, see *The Law of Electronic Commerce* by Benjamin Wright, 1991 (Little, Brown & Co.).

For a case-oriented discussion on Internet crimes and their legal implications, see *CyberLaw: The Law of the Internet* by Jonathan Rosenore, 1997 (Springer-Verlag). Rosenore maintains CyberLex (http://www.cyberlex.com/cyxbar.html), which compiles notable happenings related to law and the Internet, and he writes for *CyberLaw* (http://www.cyberlaw.com), an online Internet law magazine.

Internet Resources

Online Commerce and Taxation

Steward A. Baker, 1996. "State Taxation of On-Line Transactions." Available at http://www.us.net/~steptoe/221277.htm.

Zak Muscovitch, 1996. "Taxation of Internet Commerce." Available at http://www2.magmacom.com/~dbell/tax.htm.

Laws Regarding Computers

Electronic Frontier Foundation Computer Law Archive:

http://ftp.eff.org/pub/CAF/law

Internet Spam/Harassment Site:

http://www.geocities.com/SiliconValley/6006/woodside.html

Internet Telephony

Voice on the Internet is based on the audio standard H.323 and other multimedia conferencing standards adopted by the International Telecommunications Union (http://www.itu.ch). See the ITU Standards site provided by the International Multimedia Teleconferencing Consortium, Inc., at http://www.imtc.org/i/standard/i_itustd.htm.

Today, Internet telephony consists mainly of PC-to-PC calls, but gateway software and hardware enable one to connect to the public network, making PC-to-phone or phone-to-phone calls via the Internet possible. See the following sites for gateways:

- Lucent Technologies at http://www.lucent.com/netsys/telephony.html
- Vocaltec at http://www.vocaltec.com

Both large and small companies have entered Internet telephony. See the following sites for examples:

- Netscape Conference from Netscape at http://www.netscape.com/comprod/products/communicator/
- NetMeeting from Microsoft at http://www.microsoft.com/netmeeting/
- GXC at http://www.gxc.com
- Delta Three at http://www.deltathree.com
- Net2Phone from IDT at http://www.net2phone.com

For news and commentaries regarding Internet telephony, see Pulver.com's web site at http://www.pulver.com or VON (Voice on the Net) at http://www.von.com.

CHAPTER 12

Future Directions for Economic Research

The first half of this book has detailed the characteristics of digital products, the behaviors of the players in electronic commerce—sellers, buyers and new intermediaries, and the market processes in the electronic environment—advertising, consumer searches, product choice, and payment. The electronic marketplace depicted here still resembles the familiar physical market in that it is organized around the transfer of products. After all, the basic function of a market, whether electronic or not, is to facilitate the transactions of goods and services. This resemblance, however, leads to the wrong conclusion as to what electronic commerce is about. Is electronic commerce simply an alternative channel for selling products, just as mail-order businesses and home-shopping networks are alternatives to traditional merchandising channels? For many sellers of physical products, the answer might appear to be yes.

However, unlike the mail-order industry or home-shopping networks, electronic commerce deals with fundamentally different—digital—products that are manufactured, delivered, and consumed unlike any physical product. In addition, producers and consumers actively interact to influence and determine product specification, quality, and price. More important, the enabling technologies of electronic commerce—computers and telecommunications infrastructure—are pervasive not only in product transactions but also in other everyday activities such as work, recreation, communication, politics, and so on. Electronic commerce, then, is one of the widespread changes caused by the pervasive use of technology, and a harbinger of yet more fundamental transformations to come in our economic life.

This new economic environment of the 21st century is alternately called a *digital economy*, an *information society*, or a *virtual economy*. The authors prefer *virtual economy* to emphasize that the new economy is driven by more than digital or information products. Instead, its decisive characteristics are the process innovations enabled by the networked, distributed, online environment. The words "virtual" and "virtual economy" are used loosely here to refer to technology-assisted online activities, of which electronic commerce is one. A popular Internet wisdom says:

If it's there and you can see it, it's real.

If it's not there and you can see it, it's virtual.

As discussed later in this chapter, the virtual world is as real as the physical world, because the former is rooted in the latter. Technologies enable us to interact with seemingly unreal persons and products online—the process called the "virtual" process. After first examining various views on the future economy, this section characterizes the virtual economy by focusing attention on three aspects of the new economy: virtual products, innovations in virtual processes, and the convergence in products, markets, and infrastructure. The following sections provide a frontier map of the new economy to help develop long-term business strategies as well as a meaningful research agenda.

As hindsight shows, the future is not easy to forecast, even for those experts who are in the midst of changing technology and market process:

- 1859: "Drill for oil? You mean drill into the ground to try and find oil? You're crazy!" Drillers whom Edwin L. Drake tried to enlist in his project to drill for oil.
- 1876: "This 'telephone' has too many shortcomings to be seriously considered as a means of communication. The device is inherently of no value to us." Western Union internal memo.

- 1920s: "The wireless music box has no imaginable commercial value. Who would pay for a message sent to nobody in particular?" David Sarnoff's associates in response to his urgings for investment in the radio.

- 1943: "I think there is a world market for maybe five computers." Thomas Watson, chairman of IBM.

- 1949: "Computers in the future may weigh no more than 1.5 tons." *Popular Mechanics*, forecasting the relentless march of science.

- 1968: "But what... is it good for?" Engineer at the Advanced Computing Systems Division of IBM, commenting on the microchip.

- 1977: "There is no reason anyone would want a computer in their home." A top executive of Digital Equipment Corp. (Selected quotes from the "Internet Grapevine: Wet Blankets Throughout History.")

- 1996: "The Internet is the CB radio of the 1990s." An Internet skeptic.

In this book's middle-of-the-road view, we neither believe that the Internet is only a fad nor that it will obliterate physical products and markets. The goal in this chapter is to construct a logical picture of the future economy based on how technological developments will be used for organizational and process innovations. Like any map describing a frontier, scales and distances may turn out to be incorrect. Nevertheless, a fairly adequate outline can be drawn because the new economy is no longer an unknown territory. On the contrary, signposts abound that point in all directions. Going off in these directions could lead us to some interesting places, or we could end up in a desert. To avoid such a calamity, this book will not predict what the killer application will be in 20 years or even which technology will nail the market next. Rather, the focus will be on market processes and the direction they will lead us into the next century.

Many terms are used to characterize the new economy being fashioned by the growing Information Superhighway:

- *An information economy*, because information is the new commodity
- *A knowledge-based society* in which added value comes from knowledge-based activities
- *An interactive and networked economy* where communications and market processes are interactive and immediate
- *A computer-mediated market* driven by computer technologies
- *A digital economy* in which digitization changes physical products into ones and zeros

These terms attempt to summarize various facets of the new economy, but boil down to three components. First, the future economy is distinguished by its product, alternatively described as information, knowledge, or technology. Second, the market environment consists of distributed network nodes connected by the telecommunications infrastructure. And third, computers and software are essential interface devices enabling people to interact with the networked environment and to create and process products (digitization).

To the extent that digitized products are mostly information, these three characteristics together seem to equate the future economy with the "interactive multimedia" industry of telecommunications (network), computer hardware and software (interface devices), and multimedia contents (product), which together define a market for producing, selling, delivering, and consuming contents online. Although the term "interactive multimedia" highlights the importance of the multimedia sector in the future economy, an industry-oriented view ignores critical aspects of an economic process where structural changes are effected in any or all of its market components of players, products, or processes. These changes include the ways people communicate, products are customized and sold, and firms and consumer groups are organized and interact with each other. The future virtual economy is differentiated from physical worlds by the way it is organized. The multimedia industries—computers, telecommunications, and (digital) publishing—are simply the vital infrastructure, or enabling technologies, on which these changes occur. Before delving into the definition and contents of the virtual world, the next section will examine what significance these enabling technologies hold for the future.

12.1. The Role of Enabling Technologies

Computers and related technological developments have become the hallmarks of a fast-growing, global economy in the midst of large-scale privatization, free trade, and cooperation among nations. In discussions about the world economy in the next 20 years, optimism is most apparent when talk focuses on the global information infrastructure and electronic commerce. Electronic commerce illustrates how technology will affect all aspects of economic life by combining computer technology, telecommunications, and market transactions into a seamless socioeconomic system. Not surprisingly, the future is often defined by various applications of computer-related high technologies.

These technologies and related industries are part of an integrated system just as automobiles and highways represented an economic system of the 20th century. To use the popular analogy, the Information Superhighway is the interstate highway; its contents are automobiles and their cargoes; the Internet service providers are the access roads; and transmission protocols are the traffic laws. Traffic congestion can occur on both interstate highways and Information Superhighways and can be alleviated by expanding highway lanes or using cables with larger capacity. Faulty planning and investments may fail to reduce congestion in access ramps to highways and in the last-mile access to the Information Superhighway. Tolls may be imposed on cars and more easily on messages moving on information highways.

This highway analogy is relevant and helpful in understanding what the Information Superhighway signifies and how it operates. Just as the automobile sector dominates today's economic activities with its associated industries of automobile manufacturers, new and used car dealers, parts suppliers and repair shops, motel and travel services, oil companies and gas stations, insurance services, and roads and highway maintenance and administration, the new economy will revolve around the many industries operating on the Information Superhighway—computer hardware, software, the communications industry (including telephone, cable, satellite, and wireless), and various content providers such as publishing, database, entertainment, and news organizations. In many ways, this new industrial sector—the interactive multimedia industry (Tapscott, 1996)—can be considered to be the automobile-related industry of the 21st century.

However, the highway analogy often fails to convey the importance of the infrastructure in the broader economic context. Just as today's economy adds up to more than an economy characterized by automobiles and the interstate highway system, the virtual economy supported by computers and the telecommunications industry is more than the sum of these industries.

For example, automobiles and highways triggered substantial changes in the urban landscape and social organization. We need only think of malls and suburban sleeper-towns, mobile single families, commuter traffic, and empty or declining inner cities. Similarly, the Information Superhighway will enable people to telecommute. This may reduce commuter traffic but may also encourage urban sprawl or the migration toward sun-belt and pollution-free rural states. In terms of business and market organization, structural changes will transform marketing methods into a close cooperation between producers and buyers, who can dictate what they want in a product and rapidly respond to changes in prices and product quality. Competitive strategies will see wholesale changes as market participants interact with each other in a technologically sophisticated and equitable environment. Accordingly, taxation must be revised to reflect ubiquitous online transactions, and government regulation must change to keep pace.

Granted, automobiles and highways play an important role in today's economy in terms of gross national product (GNP) and resource allocation. Still, the economy created and supported by these industries is more than an "automobile economy" or a "highway economy." Similarly, components of the interactive multimedia industry, however important, are simply tools by which products are produced and consumed and through which virtual players interact.

Still, it is of great interest to identify what technologies will become dominant in the future. Products will look different, depending on what software and encryption technologies are adopted; response time and prices will be affected by whether cable or satellite is used for delivery infrastructure; and market processes will change if push or pull technology is favored or if PCs or network computers with applets dominate the future computing platform. How will the market choose any one product over all the others?

The selection of a particular technology will depend on which market process is favored by users. For example, the push model of Internet advertising gives sellers control over marketing, but assumes consumers are passive—and too lazy to participate. The pull model, on the other hand, recognizes the incentive of consumers to actively participate in the market process and to reveal their preferences. For push models to succeed, virtual sellers need to restrict buyers' active participation, perhaps by promoting technologies that disable such features. However, sellers often ignore the extent to which virtual buyers are willing to participate in the market as well as the fact that available technologies can turn such willingness into action. Thus, to predict which enabling technology will be favored, consideration must be given to the objectives of virtual players and what market process will best support those objectives. The so-called web broadcasting and the new generation of push technologies are in fact variants of the pull model, because they enable consumers to select contents. Whether any given delivery scheme is called a pull or push model, its distinguishing feature lies in the way it interacts with recipients. In other words, the players and processes determine which of the enabling technologies will be most useful, not vice versa.

Some of today's nascent technologies are bound to be standards by the year 2015. Important features that will shape the future include computer processing, storage, communication, and presentation.

- **Computer Processing:** Computer processing power will continue to experience exponential growth, doubling in some 18 months. Personal computers with gigahertz clock speed will offer consumers the processing power to receive, select, and present daily news, e-mails, and various information available on the net. The human brain performs between 10 trillion and 1,000 trillion operations per second. By 2015, desktop computers will reach the low echelon of this human-like computational performance. With such computing power, a networked intelligence, and access to the depository of human knowledge, a computer will behave like an expert who assists in decision-making based on facts and knowledge.

- **Storage:** Read-and-write DVDs (formerly known as digital video discs) will become standard storage devices for digital documents, each disc holding over 10 gigabytes of data. These discs will replace CDs and video tapes when audio equipment, video players, digital HDTV, and computers are all linked together. For larger file storage and backups, magnetic tapes or hard drives will continue to hold an edge over optical disks, but files will be stored in central servers. Users will store their files on these servers and download when necessary. Original files on the server will be closely linked by icons and aliases to their copies on a personal computer or display device. Data integrity will be maintained through automatic updating without the chore of uploading or downloading.

- **Communication:** After a transitional popularity of ISDN networks, the last mile will demand more bandwidth and faster connection (see Chapter 3, "Internet Infrastructure and Pricing"). While optical fiber networks will make bandwidth a plentiful resource in the backbone, congestion in access ramps to the information infrastructure will call for efficient mechanisms for resource allocation. However, new products sent over fiber optic networks will be still larger and more complicated. As a result, bandwidth management will be important, but the challenge will be to devise products that take advantage of bandwidth rather than saving on bandwidth. Along with fiber optic cable networks, high-frequency non-cable networks using microwave and satellite communications will carry digital signals. There will no longer be differences between local switching telephone networks, mobile phone networks, long distance carriers, digital data services, and the Internet. All digital communications will become interchangeable and interoperable.

- **Presentation:** Presentation (display) devices will be integrated: it will be possible to move digital HDTV sets, computer monitors, security monitors, video phones, and various appliances' control screens wherever desired. Video, audio, data, and multimedia contents—today's video tapes, music CDs, multimedia CDs, and computer floppy disks—will be played by using one standard player. World Wide Web pages will present sophisticated visual simulations of web materials, instead of two-dimensional versions, using virtual reality languages. Virtual reality markup languages (VRMLs) will complete the progress toward a rich and real-life presentation that started with the launching of the World Wide Web 20 years ago.

These enabling technologies of the 21st century will support the activities of virtual businesses, governments, and consumer groups in their sales, research, recreation, and other activities. The goal of this chapter is to describe resulting changes in the economic and social sphere of the virtual economy, but it begins by describing the players and other components of this virtual economy, without which the enabling technologies have no value.

12.2. The Virtual World Is Built on the Physical World

Mainframe computers, before personal computers largely took over, used to present a "virtual" computing environment where a user interacted with the computer through a virtual monitor (dumb terminal), virtual memory, virtual storage space, and virtual computer—basically, shared CPU time on the mainframe. That virtual machine became today's desktop computer with its own CPU, memory, storage drive, and other peripherals, which are no longer virtual but real in the sense that the components are physical. Server-driven network computers, which rely on servers for programs and documents that are downloaded whenever they are needed, may be thought of as a reincarnation of the mainframe computer, with the help of Java and applets. Network computers, then, have the potential for combining the advantages of both the mainframe and PC computing environments—namely, easy network management and customization.

The virtuality of network computers stems from the fact that the memory, CPUs, and storage device are "representations" of physical machines. This in no way implies they do not exist, but only that what we interact with is a virtual representation of the real thing. If you interact with an *avatar*—a representation of an online person—on your computer screen, that online person is virtual, but the virtual personality is a representation of a real person. In the same way, the virtual economy is a particular representation of a physical economy. If you visit a store in your neighborhood by walking there, that is part of the physical economy. If you visit that store's online web storefront—its virtual representation—you participate in a virtual economy. Some virtual worlds might be created entirely out of imagination—for example, a virtual Mars colony for games or research. Even that virtual world, however, is a representation of our concepts. In short, the virtual world cannot be built without connections with the real world.

Despite this connection, the virtual world behaves differently from the physical world, because some physical constraints are no longer binding. For example, a person can be in several (virtual) places at the same time, collecting price information and conducting negotiations, for example. Everyone—not just mathematicians or economists—can be extremely smart in calculating costs and benefits of a project (actually, one's intelligent agent will do the computing). Changes we foresee in the future virtual economy are based on the idea that economic processes will look profoundly different as virtual processes are adopted.

One implication of the virtual world's connection to the physical world is the need to make that connection as real as possible. Although someone can have many online personalities, those personalities must represent a real person. More important, a means to establish a connection is needed. Without this, the virtual world will no longer be part of the physical world; therefore, any commercial, legal, or social interaction will become problematic—a cyberworld populated by autonomous, independent agents and bots. To make today's Internet a secure commercial medium, we need secure communications channels and secure payment methods. More important, virtual entities—

online buyers and stores—must have corresponding physical identifications to which orders can be shipped and payments can be billed.

Today's Internet world is transitory: e-mail addresses are temporary, host server names change, and web document URLs move faster than physical products and stores, leaving consumers stranded. This may be a growing pain but seems to be in line with the ephemeral nature of electric charges that are the basis of a digital world—like the electricity itself, virtual personalities don't lend themselves to permanence. Unlike messages engraved on a stone, messages stored as digital files can be changed, erased, or destroyed with the sweep of a magnet. Likewise, digital documents and contracts lack the reality and enforceability afforded by their paper counterparts. Somehow, virtual companies conjure up images of nonexistent, ephemeral entities.

By 2015, however, the virtual economy will be as thriving as today's physical economy. The key element that makes it a secure medium for business and other activities is the correspondence between the physical world and the virtual world. It is not the computers who inhabit the virtual world but the users, through their virtual identities and presence. When computers were said to have artificial intelligence, many envisioned a doomed world where computers and robots waged wars against humans. In the same way, the virtual world appears to some observers to be an autonomous world that will obliterate our physical existence. That vision is no more real than the idea of computers taking over our lives. Just as computers have made various tasks more efficient, the virtual world presents us with a better way of conducting our lives. Imagine the efficiency of computing power applied not only to word processing, spreadsheets, tax calculations, and drawings but also to essentially all human activities from communication to housecleaning and maintenance. Magnify that image by adding other technological innovations in communication equipment, household appliances, automobiles, and traffic control systems as well as process innovations in transactions, education, personal finance, and entertainment. In the end, what emerges is a virtual world as a medium on which human imagination, knowledge, and technology can flourish. The new economy is shaped by what we do with the medium.

To complete the correspondence between our physical world and the future virtual world, digital identities will be created around persons instead of around computers. Today, computers and servers are online personalities of the Internet, with humans attached to them. For example, a typical e-mail address is written as person@server.computer. Either the person's name or the server computer address can change. This e-mail address is similar to a postal address, in which building addresses are more or less fixed, while people move around. Each person, however, is distinguished by some distinct and permanent identification, such as a social security or driver's license number. A similar identification can be given to individuals to establish online identity.

In the physical world, a message cannot be delivered to a social security number. The difficulty is not in finding a way to deliver mail using social security numbers but in maintaining a database that links building addresses with social security numbers. In the virtual world, an elaborate and up-to-date name server will forward messages to appropriate online persons, no matter where they are. Likewise, businesses and other economic entities can establish online identities. This does not preclude people from using online equivalents of post office boxes or aliases if they choose to do so, but a permanent identity is essential for verification purposes.

Both governments and private entities will provide these permanent identities, just as identification cards are issued by governments, schools, and companies. Multiple identification cards will all point to the same person, which can be verified legally. Just as it is unlawful to assume multiple identities in legal and commercial transactions, multiple virtual identities must be prohibited in virtual transactions as well. As an extension to the physical identity, virtual identities will be based on legal, permanent, and verifiable identities. Legality need not be based on governments alone, however. Private certification authorities will also run a centralized registering system to provide varying levels of identity classes for different purposes. For the very reason aliases are accepted (for example, for authors), multiple virtual identities will also be useful.

12.3. Components of the Virtual Economy

The virtual economy has as its foundation the virtual market, where transactions occur in cyberspace. But nontransactional activities—such as advertising, consumer research, customer service, education, entertainment, and politics—are affected by the same Internet or online processes. With this in mind, let us define the components of the virtual economy:

- **Virtual players:** When buyers, sellers, or intermediaries establish their online identities, they become virtual market players. This process can be initiated simply by opening an e-mail account, being connected online, or setting up an online shop, such as a web storefront. Virtual players may be automated software agents, which—on behalf of their owners—can search, gather information, negotiate, and process orders. By using software agents, a person online can exist in many places at one time, or one person can have multiple online identities: thus, one person's multiple preferences can yield multiple online personalities. On the other hand, a group of consumers or sellers may act as a single entity. As we discussed in Chapter 1, "Electronic Commerce and the Internet," a virtual firm differs from a physical firm in both organization and structure, and a virtual consumer behaves differently online than offline.

- **Virtual products:** Product virtualization certainly includes digitization, which converts products of text, graphic, video, and audio components into digital files of ones and zeros; however, many non-multimedia products are also digitized. For example, concept- and process-based products, such as digital currency, tickets, and house keys, can have digital counterparts. In this sense, digitization or digitalization entails more than digital scanning or remastering to change the physical characteristics of a product; it also refers to a creative conversion based on the way a product is used. Products that cannot be digitized can be made into smart products by attaching suitable technological devices. Some examples are smart electricity meters, home security devices, traffic signals, and automobiles, which are networked via microwave and satellite links. By using online commands, home electricity usage can be controlled from office or hotel rooms or an e-mail message can be sent to the automobile to be picked up at work or the airport. Automobiles, house furnaces, and other smart products will have virtual interfaces that will interact with people—a process called *product virtualization.* Virtual products, therefore, include a far greater number of physical products than is conventionally assumed.

- **Virtual processes:** The term "virtual processes" refers to the way market players interact with products and other players, usually via interactive and real-time communications. Establishing online ordering and payment procedures is a necessary first step in enabling virtual market processes. But non-transactional interactions will become more important in such areas as the supply-chain management process, product development using direct consumer inputs, and advertising based on detailed consumer profiles and negotiations with consumers. The overall impact of virtual processes goes far beyond achieving a more efficient transaction; they will fundamentally alter production processes, consumption, and virtually all aspects of economic activities. Furthermore, online transactions are changing the way taxes are collected and government regulations applied. Worldwide transactions challenge not only the international system of tariffs and income taxes but also the very theory of international economic growth and cooperation. In sum, virtual processes mean more than interactivity or real-time communications, which are characteristics of underlying technologies. Instead, the importance of virtual processes lies in the transformation they cause in the relationship between the interacting parties.

Computers, software, and telecommunications infrastructures form the arena where virtual players interact with each other and exchange virtual products. The virtual economy is the game being played in that arena. The rules of the game are being refined from experience, while the layout of the court changes as the need arises. Some players are not even sure what game is being played today, while others are forming teams and establishing goals for the game to be played tomorrow. At the moment, the game seems deceptively similar to the one we have been playing all along; in other arenas, it is unclear to some why the game would ever change. Yet others point out fundamental differences, one of which is the convergence among products and industries.

12.4. The Convergence

The virtual economy, by its very nature, facilitates—and in some ways requires—convergence in products, processes, infrastructure, and market space. Convergence is a process by which products and producers considered to be in different markets suddenly find themselves in the same market. If very broadly defined, all digital products may be said to be competing with each other. Because their businesses all center around computer technology and information products, content providers such as television program producers and multimedia CD-ROM manufacturers are in the same market with network software and communications equipment vendors, but convergence cannot be defined so broadly. Telecommunications firms are not in the same market with online publishers, although their activities may depend on each other, just as mail-order booksellers depend on the services of post and parcel carriers. Similar intermarket dependence has often resulted in a mistaken belief that computer operating system software is in the same market with, for example, e-mail programs or Internet browsers (see section 11.9).

Convergence, even when defined rather narrowly, is still pervasive enough to characterize many aspects of the virtual economy. Four major types of convergence will appear by the year 2015:

- **Product convergence.** Digitization, for example, has made it unnecessary to distinguish among different forms of products. Audio CDs, pictures, and magazine articles all take the same digital format and can be edited or searched by the same processing software. This is sometimes called multimedia convergence. When a product exists in both digital and physical forms, the convergence may make one form obsolete. Whether a particular physical or digital form survives will depend on its usefulness in consumption. For example, computer catalogs in libraries have almost eliminated catalog index files. The former has undoubted superiority over the latter in terms of convenience, search capability, and save and print features. The same convenience factor may favor printed books over digital books, however, especially for books that should be read from cover to cover. For reference books, digital versions are decidedly superior in terms of consumption.

- **Process convergence.** One virtual process may be used for different purposes that used to be carried out by different processes. For example, a producer may solicit inputs from consumers regarding a feature of its product. That consumer-revealed information is then used for production (customization) as well as for marketing, sales, and negotiations with consumers regarding terms of payment. As a result, production, marketing, sales, consumption, and customer after-sale service are all converging into a seamless, integrated process of the virtual economy. The market-value chain can no longer be divided into stages and steps, and must not only be continuous but also concurrent. Such convergence cannot be expected with the broadcast mass media, which is why electronic commerce is more than an alternative marketing channel.

- **Infrastructure convergence.** Various types of communications infrastructure are converging as well. Infrastructure convergence is made possible by digitization of products and other technologies that support the transfer of digital signals. This convergence has made competitors out of telephone companies, cable operators, and microwave and satellite operators, which individually used to enjoy a natural monopoly status. For example, digital telephony on the Internet takes business from long distance carriers and access charges from local-loop providers. Satellite systems pose significant competition to Internet carriers and telephone operators by beaming signals directly to PCs and telephones, as they did with cable television programming. In these converging markets, the need for uniform fees and taxes is already highlighted by the struggle between local exchange carriers and Internet service providers. Beyond a common tariff structure, the convergence will demand new approaches in government regulation, competitive strategies, product development, transaction processes, and economic research and analysis.

- **Market space convergence.** Finally, globalization implies a spatial convergence of markets. A classic example of a monopoly is a geographically isolated firm—for example, the only gas station in an isolated town. In the virtual economy, there is no monopoly market power due to geographical isolation unless artificial borders are erected. Neither will there be the need to have franchise stores all over the virtual marketplace. One principle of franchising is to guarantee a monopoly market for each franchiser by not allowing two franchisers to locate next to each other. With only one market, there is no need for franchising, although mirroring—the practice of providing identical materials on different servers to lower the congestion problem—may eventually be considered to be a form of franchising.

Convergence brings about new opportunities as well as uncertainties. As products are digitized, they acquire new characteristics that increase their appeal. For example, a CD-ROM version of an encyclopedia provides search and link capabilities far exceeding the cross-indexing features provided by book versions. New products mean new uses, new customers, and new ways of doing business. Many focus on the opportunity to expand their business, but the novelty also creates uncertainty.

For example, as the telecommunications infrastructure converges, traditional boundaries among telephone companies, cable operators, and satellite operators become unclear. These companies are experimenting in such areas as video-on-demand services, interactive television, cable modems, online shopping, and video dial tone to gauge consumer response and future profitability in their widening playing field. Not knowing consumer demand and competitors' strategies, however, they are hesitant to plunge into the unknown. On the other hand, Bill Gates of Microsoft, Craig McCaw (who founded McCaw Cellular Communications), and other investors are willing to take a risk in the future of converging infrastructure. Their enterprise is called Teledesic Corp., which will invest almost $10 billion to place 840 low earth-orbiting satellites. The plan is to offer broadband connection, broadcasting, video conferencing, and other telecommunications services worldwide through Teledesic's satellite network. The project's possible payoffs may be as large as the size of necessary investments.

Convergence and the Market Structure

The success of Teledesic and similar projects hinges on convergence not only in telecommunications but also in networking technologies, computer interface, digital contents, and worldwide markets. As mentioned earlier, the Information Superhighway environment enables various products and services to be produced, distributed, and consumed. An efficient, worldwide information infrastructure will be useless if its usage is limited to a few activities such as voice communication or online newspaper delivery. If it entails all types of virtual activities, however, its economic impact will far surpass that of the modern telecommunications industry. Convergence is the key factor that will make or break an investment project that aims at leveraging the future information infrastructure. If successful, any company that controls the infrastructure is in a position to be a dominant firm in other areas of the virtual economy.

Suppose a firm is a dominant player in computer operating systems and many application program markets. It may also extend its dominance in the last mile from the computer to the information infrastructure through networking software and access services. By constructing the network itself, such a firm can integrate all aspects of the infrastructure necessary for virtual processes, establishing itself as a significant player in content provision as well by cooperating with other content providers. Virtual contents consist of more than information products and services. Online payment services, online banking, and digital currency services, for example, are necessary for the virtual market. A firm that can dominate the world digital currency market can take a lion's share of the seigniorage. Such a firm must possess the reputation and capital necessary to convince consumers to hold its currency, just as the wealth and credibility of the U.S. government is the sole guarantee to those who hold dollars. The process of vertical integration and monopolization in all these sectors of the worldwide economy has been unimaginable, but is becoming a reality driven by the convergence in markets and the relaxation in—or lack of—regulatory market interventions.

An alternative scenario is an efficient, competitive economy where decentralized markets support many players and allocate resources efficiently. The first step in promoting such an economy is to eliminate inefficient mechanisms for resource allocation, induce better quality for products and services, and guarantee a level playing field for all players. For example, as was discussed in Chapter 3, usage-based pricing in Internet access services will enhance quality and allocate resources efficiently. In the software market, the telecommunications economics, as we discussed in Chapter 11, "Business and Policy Implications of Electronic Commerce," can enlighten policymakers about what constitutes anticompetitive behaviors.

Electronic commerce, by its own efficiencies, will also be able to provide competitive and effective marketplaces for products and services often monopolized in physical markets. For example, differentiated and customized products will offer more choices than mass-produced goods, for which a firm with sufficient economies of scale has the cost advantage. Microproducts, applets, and microbundles enable short-term contracts between suppliers and intermediaries and between retailers and consumers. As we discussed in Chapter 4, "Quality Uncertainty and Market Efficiency," short-term contracts, in turn, reduce inefficiencies caused by quality uncertainty. Electronic payment systems based on micropayments and digital currency will facilitate selling microproducts in addition to bundling and subscription, for which existing payment mechanisms are adequate. Micropayments will also support a usage-based copyright payment system, enabling content sellers to meter and bill for small and large uses of their products. In short, electronic commerce enhances competition by its relentless drive toward efficiencies and open markets. Convergence is a two-edged sword, opening all markets for a single, powerful firm to dominate or for all firms to compete in each other's market.

Whether you believe the future economy will be monopolistic or competitive, various market forces are already in place to influence our economic lives in the next two decades. We can minimize the uncertainty by understanding the trends or processes that will be pervasive in the future economy. While specific business tactics must be based on actual, not forecast, data, recognizing the trend provides an invaluable insight about what business strategy will be needed. The remainder of this chapter highlights some fundamental changes in the way the virtual economy will operate, as we see it in the year 2015.

12.5.   The Virtual Economy in Action

Television has produced generations of couch potatoes shunning outdoor activities and contentedly receiving preprogrammed messages. The advent of the virtual world seems to be a more menacing threat than even television, as outdoor activities can now be played indoors and people have fewer reasons to get out of their houses to go to libraries, movie theaters, coffee shops, work, and schools. We become not only couch potatoes wearing virtual reality helmets, but our world itself is virtual where no real contact is needed. James Canton of 21st Century Online (http://21net.com/online/) offers this forecast of the virtual world:

> "Entire universes are synthetically generated by individuals, organizations, and groups designed to meet any need, desire, or fantasy. Total immersion with full neurosynaptic real-time stimulation that is preferable to reality emerges, as the majority of the global citizenry retreat into synthetically created virtual worlds."

An experiment in creating a virtual reality world was conducted by LucasFilm, a division of LucasArts (http://www.lucasarts.com), which started its Habitat project in 1985. Participants used online personalities called avatars to represent themselves in interaction with other users and objects. Habitat resembles a three-dimensional chat room where avatars replace text prompts in a chat group. Habitat's recent reincarnation is WorldsAway (see fig. 12.1), offered through the CompuServe online service. Here, users establish online identities they can change anytime at the Nu Yu shop. Users can build their own buildings, communities, and activities, including business, religion, and school.

Figure 12.1   A community scene in WorldsAway. Persons on this screen represent users, or dwellers, of this virtual community, who can interact with other participants and even objects, such as the door or toys shown here.

Virtual worlds such as Habitat or WorldsAway are very sophisticated entertainment platforms. But the fact that this form of entertainment mainly involves brain activities is perceived as menacing; in some way, virtual reality seems created the same way hallucination is induced by drugs. The real utility of such a virtual world, however, is its potential as a sophisticated and real presentation device. Instead of e-mailing or teleconferencing on telephones, net interactions can be made realistic by using the same technology. Entertainment is just one of the many uses that will become available as supporting technologies stop being a limiting factor.

Display devices and interactive platforms in the virtual economy may not be as sophisticated as WorldsAway's technology promises, but that is not a precondition to reaping the full benefit of the virtual economy. Two-dimensional screens and text-based e-mailing are sufficient to bring about the profound changes we envision in the future. Virtual products and virtual processes together will change the way we work, shop, entertain, travel, converse, and live. The convergence of both digital and physical products in the form of smart products and the pervasiveness of communication imply that we will be given tools for being in constant contact and control over our lives. Multiply the freedom afforded by the mobile phone a hundred times, and you begin to see what the virtual economy will do. The National Information Infrastructure initiative published by the U.S. government (http://sunsite.unc.edu/nii/NII-Agenda-for-Action.html) describes the potential as:

> "Imagine you had a device that combined a telephone, a TV, a camcorder, and a personal computer. No matter where you went or what time it was, your child could see you and talk to you, you could watch a replay of your team's last game, you could browse the latest additions to the library, or you could find the best prices in town on groceries, furniture, clothes—whatever you needed."

Imagine that this device is also connected to the Internet, to smart appliances in your smart house, and to your other worldly possessions. With virtual reality and sophisticated simulation technologies, not only words and text but also looks and "feels" will be experienced remotely—for example, you could feel the temperature in your house via the Internet. Even if future presentation and interface devices are not so advanced, the networked virtual environment will change our lives significantly.

Suppose Alice is away from her Austin, Texas, home vacationing in Los Angeles. If anything is out of order, her house alerts her instantly, reporting the problem and what it did to correct the problem within the parameters allowed, or asking for directions. Alice acknowledges—or sends instructions—and goes on vacationing.

One evening, Alice receives an e-mail message from Bob, who wants to use her empty house for two nights. Because her house uses a digital key, Alice sends the digital file—the house key—over the network, which Bob stores on his personal card. He goes to Alice's house, enters by using the downloaded key, and accesses the central computer. By inputting into Alice's computer a file that stores all his preferences about light, temperature, Internet news, and radio and TV stations—out of the hundreds of channels available—Bob makes himself at home. At the same time, Bob's intelligent agent, which connects itself with Alice's computer, begins notifying others of his whereabouts so messages can reach him without delay over the Internet.

The house key sent by Alice will expire in two days, at which time the computer will remove Bob's settings and restore Alice's. The key self-destructs by the same mechanism old computer hackers used to detonate computer viruses. If Bob refuses to vacate the house in two days, Alice can override his control of the house. (Perhaps she can send an e-mail message to her furnace to raise the room temperature to 100 degrees.)

There is nothing extraordinary in this scenario. In fact, the relevant technologies already exist:

- Digital keys are already used in hotels. It is a small step to convert the magnetic key into a digital file, which then can be transferred over the Internet.

- Smart cards are being introduced for transactions, including copying, transit payments, and digital coins, to be read by smart-card readers connected to computers.

- Smart houses and smart furnaces are being controlled by central computers. These smart products can monitor and store an immense amount of diagnostic data, with control and monitoring carried out remotely.

- E-mail is seen as the equivalent of modern letter-writing, but it is basically a file-transfer mechanism, which can handle letters as well as all types of files. Because of the familiarity and acceptance of e-mailing among Internet users, consumers will be ready to grasp its future functions.

- Permanent e-mail addresses are offered freely, which is based on the forwarding principle. A future virtual player will have a permanent Internet identity, much like a social security number. Messages will be forwarded to current servers based on dynamic updating of domain name servers or net identity servers.

The futuristic aspect in this scenario is in making all these technologies work in a seamless, interoperable system; therefore, when developing a component technology, businesses need to have a long-term perspective. For example, the analog HDTV standard has been abandoned by the Japanese government and corporations who introduced it early in the 1980s. Analog HDTVs will not operate with digital HDTVs and are thus unable to participate in the digital revolution. Going against such a trend will be a disaster. Likewise, smart products should adopt standard communications protocols so they can be controlled remotely via the Internet or other prevailing networks. Proprietary software will isolate the product and diminish its usefulness in the virtual economy. By visualizing how consumers use their products in the future, businesses can gain an insight into what features their products must offer as well.

The Alice and Bob example is decidedly not one of a market transaction involving sellers and buyers. Electronic commerce will be conducted in the same way Alice and Bob made contacts, exchanged their messages, and went about their everyday lives, but with added technologies and features of an economic system—payment mechanisms, product specifications, intermediation, and negotiation processes for trade, contracts, and delivery. The most significant lesson for product sellers in the above example is the need for interoperability that enables an integrated and seamless consumption process.

Future virtual markets invite speculation about what other general features can be detected to guide us during the next 20 years. The next section will delve into some market aspects of the future virtual economy.

12.6.   Growth of Virtual Intermediaries

Some people predict that intermediaries with a primary role of distributing products will no longer be needed in electronic commerce. This disintermediation hypothesis is based on the fact that the Internet offers instant transactions throughout the globe, with consumers able to contact producers directly. In fact, it isn't even necessary to go to an Internet shopping mall if a producer's web address is known. Intermediary services, however, include not only distributional services such as wholesale and retailing but also insurance, marketing, financial services, and other functions producers may prefer to delegate to intermediaries. As a result, the virtual economy will be populated by *cybermediaries* to provide such essential services as certification, payment services, quality assurance, copyright clearing, and royalty allocation, as well as distribution.

The necessity to support commercial transactions in the electronic marketplace has generated various types of new services and intermediaries, including cyberbanks, certification services, digital currency servers, electronic malls, and search services. Future virtual intermediaries, however, will do more than support transactions—they will also facilitate various market and non-market processes, such as the following examples:

- **Education brokers:** Schools and educational institutions perform intermediary functions as they organize the transfer of knowledge and skills by mediating transactions between teachers and students. Whether education is viewed as a collaborative or a transactional activity, the advent of flexible, distributed communications media and digital educational materials will demand a wholesale rethinking of how students learn or are trained for job skills. The new virtual educational service is not an electronic version of conventional classrooms or distance learning, but a customized, on-demand learning model that takes advantage of real-time interactions, flexible curricula, and immense amounts of materials provided by schools, teachers, authors, and so on. (Hämäläinen, Whinston and Vishik, 1996). While the tradition of liberal education will persist along with the unreplaceable value of a school or college, skills training and technical education will be better served by virtual education brokers.

- **Market organizers:** A virtual education broker is, in a sense, an organizer of a market for teachers, course material suppliers, students, performance or skill certifiers, and business clients who want their employees trained. Similarly, all types of markets will be organized and carried out by virtual intermediaries. Although stock-and-commodity trading floors will be preserved to remind us how physical markets in the previous century facilitated exchanges of these goods, electricity and gas will be purchased and delivered in the virtual market, movies and television programs will be auctioned off and delivered to individual homes, and political meetings will be held online, where political parties, influence peddlers, and interest groups will vie for attention. Intermediaries are those who organize markets or meeting places for existing products and services, but utilize virtual processes.

- **Personalized service providers:** Computers have already replaced personal secretaries who typed and edited your letters, organized appointments, and so on. Similarly, virtual entrepreneurs will be your personal shoppers, accountants, travel agents, investment bankers—all those personal assistants that only a millionaire can now afford. The enabling technologies are available today. Intelligent software agents can navigate virtual space, collecting and processing information, and desktop personal assistants that can learn about your tastes and act on your behalf are becoming more sophisticated. Although these technologies will make it possible to automate many tasks, specialists will continue to have better knowledge and expertise to complete some tasks, no matter how much information is fed into a software agent. Using these technologies, personalized service providers will maintain real-time contact with their customers, executing searches, orders, and negotiations based on personal preference profiles.

Education brokers and personalized service providers will not only offer old products in new bottles but will also change the way their services are sold in the marketplace. For example, instead of going through four years of college under a rigid curriculum, students will choose courses on the basis of which are needed—and when—for developing the critical skills employers demand or finishing an important research project. Individual professors will offer courses through education brokers, and a course's popularity will be determined by its usefulness. As a result, the virtual education market will consist of numerous fragmented course providers instead of a few colleges, customized and up-to-date products instead of set curricula, and short-term but continuous transactions, such as just-in-time learning instead of long-term (usually four-year), one-time transactions. The market process is need-based and decentralized. At the same time, products and services are fragmented, personalized, and flexible enough to be configured for a single sale or multiple sessions.

The market for information and knowledge, just as the education market, exhibits fragmentation and decentralization in products, content providers, and consumer uses. The beginning of such a decentralized market is seen in the World Wide Web, but many observers consider the proliferation of web pages in today's Internet to be only transitory and contend that they will ultimately find no market. Instead, electronic commerce awaits the entry of those who control valuable content, such as publishers, movie studios, and record companies.

What then is the role of publishers and movie studios? They are intermediaries who collect, process, and market products made by individual authors and directors. Newspaper publishers are information intermediaries who employ authors and reporters and deliver assorted stories in a printed medium. In the future virtual economy, columnists will sell their wares through a web site. Reporters will provide real-time accounts of an event on the Internet as well, and musicians will distribute demo recordings on the net. However, this model of direct sales will be limited by the sheer size of the market and the problem of quality uncertainty, and these products will instead be mediated by intermediaries. An electronic publishing or multimedia company will be in the business of buying and selling intellectual properties, but its editing and packaging function will no longer be affected by the limitations of its medium—channels, programming slots, or number of pages, for example—or by the need to appeal to the widest audience to maximize advertising revenues. Instead, the publisher's focus will be on customizing products and providing the best value for each customer.

12.7.   Customization and Smart Products

Customized products do what consumers want them to do. In the virtual economy, products will be differentiated to match consumer preferences, because products allow differentiation and necessary information about individual preferences is available. Products can be customized by the seller during the production process or by the buyer after the product is purchased. If the customization is not needed repeatedly, it will be more efficient to have producers customize the product. If the need to adjust the product is continuous, the product will be made smart, offering consumers the ability to customize it at the site of consumption. And if the product comes from many vendors, consumers will do the customizing themselves by using some filtering devices or will go through intermediary agents.

Producer's Customization and Market Research

To customize, producers need to learn about consumer preferences, but how will they learn about consumers in the future? The raging debate over the use of consumer information and privacy has given sellers a need to gather consumer information in an overt and direct way rather than covertly, but more sophisticated technologies will allow future sellers to gather information about their customers not only covertly but also effectively.

The most direct approach is to ask consumers to supply the information about themselves. This can be accomplished as part of the ordering process by presenting consumers with choices about product specifications. For example, consumers can build a personal computer or a mountain bike online by choosing among hundreds of styles and parts to suit their needs. If the product does not allow choices or has to be premanufactured, sellers often solicit product evaluations to improve quality and specifications. Consumers generally have an incentive to tell the truth, because misrepresenting their tastes will result in unsatisfactory products; thus, asking customers will be profitable in the virtual economy, where digital products, because of their transmutability, are conducive to customization. However, on some occasions, firms need information regarding planned products for which consumers' input may not be valuable because they do not have the same incentive to tell the truth. Expert analysis is often erroneous, as well, as shown in these examples:

- "A cookie store is a bad idea. Besides, the market research reports say America likes crispy cookies, not soft and chewy cookies like you make." Response to Debbi Fields' idea of starting Mrs. Fields Cookies.

- "I have traveled the length and breadth of this country and talked with the best people, and I can assure you that data processing is a fad that won't last out the year." The editor in charge of business books for Prentice Hall in 1957. (Selected quotes from the "Internet Grapevine: Wet Blankets Throughout History.")

Still, firms depend on market surveys and opinion research for strategic reasons other than product development. The virtual economy will present new opportunities to gather information through online market research and learning activities.

Online Market Research

Current methods of market surveys and focus groups leave much to be desired. Although open-ended questions usually accompany survey forms, both consumers and analysts focus on prepared questions, but the answers—ranging from "highly satisfied" to "not at all satisfied"—only provide insights into predetermined and preselected areas, which might not be the problem at all, and the answers themselves are questionable when consumers have no proven incentive to tell the truth. Furthermore, survey forms and techniques limit responses to verbal communication.

Logging and analyzing web access is an indirect method of observing consumer reactions, similar to watching through one-way mirrors. While this practice is under criticism, an online survey environment can be created to mimic many advantages of web log data. Using the virtual environment, this method will allow consumers to express their opinions not only verbally but through nonverbal actions and feelings. The key element in a virtual survey method is to overcome the restricting factors of survey forms that ignore nonverbal communications, yet it's difficult to interpret in a meaningful way these nonverbal forms of communication, which often consist of images, metaphors, and other cognitive expressions for which no interpretation consensus exists.

Experimental research focuses on consumer storytelling through images (Zaltman, 1996). Its premise is that most social communication is nonverbal and thoughts can occur as images. For example, when consumers are asked to bring images to describe their experience with a product, they may bring a picture of one of their pets or a rainstorm. A picture of a dog represents faithfulness, of course, while the storm hints at turmoil. Similarly, Internet users are asked to characterize the color of their e-mail messages. Low opinion about e-mail is represented by gray or black colors, while bright colors such as pink and yellow indicate more excitement.

While this approach to nonverbal communications touches on an important shortcoming in traditional survey methods, images and metaphors themselves are hard to interpret. To put them in words violates the very premise of "not being able to express in words." However, a less ambitious research environment can be constructed on the Internet. Instead of using worded questions and asking for ratings, consumers will be presented with images, games, and other interactive materials. By carefully constructing the experimental environment, researchers can capture subjects' natural behaviors and reactions by using cameras, audio inputs, sensitive mice, and so on to monitor actions, emotions, and feelings. Instead of inviting consumers to participate in experiments, advertisements and promotional free products will provide a research environment that feeds data back to the seller. In a sense, all potential customers will become focus groups, and the products themselves will offer opportunities to gain information about consumers.

Online Learning

Consumers form groups on the net to congregate with like-minded people and exchange opinions. UseNet newsgroups divide consumers by interest into hierarchical groupings. Thus, those who are interested in computers frequent groups in the *comp* hierarchy while art-inclined persons participate in *rec.arts* groups. Further divisions of interest result in *rec.arts.books* for book lovers and *rec.arts.books.hist-fiction* for those who favor historical novels. Along with numerous mailing lists organized to address specific interests, these online communities provide sellers a window for watching consumers learn from each other. The power of word-of-mouth marketing has induced many sellers to monitor messages and, if requested, provide relevant information as dutiful members of the interest group.

There is no indication that today's sellers actively analyze messages posted in these online communities. Even product-specific mailing lists managed by sellers disseminate information but do not allow postings or feedback from subscribers. The vast number of messages being exchanged may be a deterrent to any firm contemplating the mining of such data. Instead, sellers rely on traditionally mined data provided by web search operators, market research firms, or brokers of processed customer data. The future virtual economy, however, will consist of finely segmented online communities whose participants include the majority of potential consumers. By becoming an active member of these online groups, a seller will maintain contact with all its customers and find out about competitors' strategies as well as consumer responses.

As producers and sellers learn in a networked market environment, their product selection and pricing strategies will affect both their customers and their competitors. For customers, the issues will be the gains in better-matching products and the potential losses in discriminatory prices. For competitors, the strategic value of new information will depend on its availability to competitors. For example, if the data on the Internet is public, it will offer no competitive advantage, because all competitors will have the same information. However, if the data is made private, such information is strategically valuable; therefore, the cost of securing and processing such information will be weighed against the gains in the market share or the profit. In all likelihood, the profit potential will justify monitoring and analyzing public messages in some fashion.

Current economic and marketing models do not account for interactions between producers and consumers. The market somehow functions to match supply with demand. As the uncertainty about product quality and even about the identity of transacting partners grows in the virtual marketplace, however, market agents will no longer be passive. The availability of information and the technology to gather and process such information is the hallmark of an electronic market such as the Internet. Economic models, then, will have to incorporate the active learning by producers and the effects of such action on product choices, prices, competition, and consumer welfare. Just as researchers and corporate employees can collaborate and learn from each other on the Internet, firms and consumers will determine market choices through interacting and learning from each other. Such interactive learning will be pervasive in the future virtual economy.

Consumer Customization

Customization by consumers occurs in two stages. First, products are customized through a selection process in which consumers eliminate unwanted portions of a product. Second, products are modified to suit consumer tastes on receipt. For example, consumers may ask an online news service to send them news about a specific firm but not about others. Either the news producer or an intermediary personalizes the product and delivers it. The second stage of customization is not needed in this case. Alternatively, consumers may receive the news feed without selecting, but—after receiving all of it—discard unwanted parts. In terms of bandwidth efficiency, the second type of delivery is undeniably inferior, but it allows customers more control over the use of information.

The selection process by which consumers weed out unwanted products is called *filtering*. In the age of information overload, information filtering offers consumers not only the power to select products but also the means to automate repeated tasks by training filtering agents to recognize what is wanted and not wanted. For example, e-mail from unwanted sources can be filtered out by a software agent that recognizes the user's preference. The same preference profile can also be used to schedule meetings based on certain principles, such as no meetings between 9 a.m. and 10 a.m.; project A takes precedent over all other projects; or meetings should be based on the proximity of their location. Software agents are either fed such information by the user or programmed to learn by observing and analyzing the user's actions. The analysis typically consists of statistical score-keeping; that is, if a user repeats the same action twice or more, the agent recognizes it as the user's preference (Maes, 1994).

A logical extension of filtering agents in the future will be a smart product with the capability to learn and adapt to each user's preference. Instead of being endowed with this capability, all products will have an open interface to interact with any intelligent agent trained by a consumer. Thus, each consumer in the virtual economy will have an intelligent agent—a virtual alter ego—to monitor and sort incoming e-mail messages, search for product vendors, alert the user for new products of interest, interact with smart products to configure them to match the user's preferences, and so on. When you order an online article, negotiations will be conducted between your agent and the seller's. After you buy smart computer software, your agent will customize it for you. Your car, house security system, hot water boiler, coffeemaker, and centralized heating system will all be smart and configured and monitored by your agent, which will alert you and recommend a course of action when something is out of order. You will be able to display daily temperatures, gas and electricity consumption, boiler efficiency, and other data on your computer or HDTV screen, analyze the data, and exchange the information with others.

To accomplish this, smart products will have to be furnished with the capability to be customized and have an interface for interacting with smart agents. Such an interoperability requirement will not produce a single dominant product but will require some standardization for those features that need interfacing (see the discussion about interoperability in section 11.9). At a minimum, any smart product should adhere to a communications protocol in order to communicate or receive instructions through, for example, e-mail.

With filtering agents and smart products available to consumers, the debate between push-and-pull models of marketing will become pointless. Consumers may in fact prefer sellers to push all information to them so they can choose what is relevant, instead of leaving that decision to the sellers. When buyers have all the information, a seller's bargaining position will deteriorate accordingly; thus, sellers will choose what information to send, but buyers will have control over whether to receive that message. The effectiveness of the pull model will also be limited by the amount of information sellers are willing to provide. To market customized products, both sellers and buyers must communicate in a process of push-and-pull negotiation.

12.8. Globalization and Cybernations

While the virtual world will no longer have national boundaries, virtual communities and groups will abound. Instead of political boundaries, the virtual world will be divided by interests and preferences. In electronic commerce, globalization will afford sellers access to a larger market with regard to geographical area, but product differentiation and customization will mean a smaller market for each product.

Globalization is aided by the removal of tariffs and other regulatory measures based on geographical boundaries. The global telecommunications accord and the information technology agreement pioneered by the World Trade Organization during the last years of the 20th century have opened up a truly international trade in computers, telecommunications equipment, and software. A uniform commercial code and an income tax policy for international trade will further stimulate exchanges in digital products. Most important, a fully convertible digital currency will facilitate international transactions. As a result of these developments, a product's market will be defined not by geographical areas but solely by its customers.

Globalization, however, will not break down all market boundaries, as customers still have different tastes. While spatial convergence will remove geographical market boundaries, virtual communities will act as distinct and coherent groups, just as physical markets and nations do today. These cybercommunities or cybernations will be made up of like-minded consumers and businesses, congregating and interacting online. Sellers will want to know who participates in such virtual communities and how they interact.

In the virtual marketplace, consumers will learn about product quality from each other, while sellers will observe consumers' reactions to their products and marketing strategies. What will the implications be of such learning by agents in a market? For one thing, unlike today's emphasis on strategic interactions between firms, the electronic marketplace will make apparent the need for firms to interact with consumers and for consumers to interact with other consumers and firms. Specifically, consumers will not be myopic, but will become strategic players in the market. Cybernations and cybercommunities will become powerful instruments in influencing prices, product quality, and competitive behaviors. To counter this trend, firms will develop market strategies based on their interactions with consumers. Indeed, demand preferences can be manipulated, quality information (advertising) can be controlled, and reputation or brand loyalty can be cultivated, all by actively participating in virtual communities.

Cybercommunities are a natural outgrowth of today's Internet societies, where the process of word-of-mouth dissemination of information is greatly facilitated by personal e-mail, mailing lists, chat lines, newsgroups, and other discussion forums, which can occur concurrently and reach every corner of the globe.

Although we mentioned earlier that sellers are not yet actively gathering and processing information from messages posted in UseNet newsgroups, some recognize the value of doing so. Firefly (http://www.ffly.com) is an example of intelligent software agents observing, recording, and processing online data logged by users of various Firefly communities in an attempt to learn more about consumers. Processed or mined data results are then offered to producers, who use Firefly communities as avenues for targeted advertising. Software agents may even offer a review of a new product, using their knowledge about the preference of each community.

To succeed in this business venture, Firefly faithfully duplicates Internet communities. For example, there are newsgroups and chat areas for movie buffs, country music fans, or cartoonists. Such areas may be subdivided more finely by using a hierarchy of books, for example, and then fiction versus nonfiction, and so on. It is also possible to form groups based on different characteristics, such as authors or writing style. A list of an individual's membership, the intensity of participation, and such will provide a detailed preference profile of the person. A bookseller may find such a market segment and post a review directly or through Firefly's software agent, acting like a member of the group. By observing the message exchange and downloading pattern and correlating this with sales and other data, the seller may modify the product, change its advertising strategy, or find another target group. Knowing this, consumers may also engage in strategic behaviors to influence the seller's decisions.

The potential value of cybercommunities will be tempered by technical problems regarding the accuracy and usefulness of data gathered by software agents in cybercommunities. The window of time over which data is used to calibrate the preference profile of each community is an important consideration in a rapidly changing environment such as the Internet. Software agents need a substantial period of time to learn and match the preference of a group. In a rapidly changing market, however, the learning speed of agents may be too slow to be helpful. The group may change its composition and membership, or the group as a whole may undergo a shift in preferences. Such dynamic changes can perhaps be eliminated by requiring strict guidelines for join a group, but if there is such a guideline in the first place, there will be no need to "learn" about the consumers. On the other hand, too short a window of observation may yield very unreliable estimates about the preferences.

Despite these potential issues, marketing differentiated and customized products will depend on information gathered in cybercommunities. Mass market products are well suited for mass media advertising. On the other hand, niche market products often are too costly to advertise on such a scale, although the initial lack of people's knowing about and trying out the product will be detrimental to future sales (McFadden and Train, 1996). For niche products and experience goods consumers are wary of trying, a discussion group composed of people with similar tastes could become a major source of product information. If someone tries out a new product and posts an opinion of its quality, all other members will value the information, because they share the same tastes. And as we have seen earlier, the seller, as a business member or acting as a consumer, may offer a review to influence opinion or promote the product in an effort to induce some consumers to try it out.

12.9.   Market-Clearing Mechanisms

An efficient market leaves no excess supply or demand. In reality, most markets fail to match supply with demand at least temporarily, leaving some sellers with excess inventories and some buyers without desired products or services. One reason for this is the geographical distance that prevents the simultaneous participation of all sellers and buyers. Another reason may be the lack of information or the failure for a market to be coordinated. Still other reasons that prevent efficient market clearing include high transaction costs, and the bounded rationality of the agents—that is, sellers or buyers are not capable of transacting in the most efficient way.

A virtual market offers some reprieve to many of these sources of market inefficiency. An electronic market not only offers a cheaper, more cost-effective way to transact business, but also brings about a more efficient market-clearing mechanism, because it is not limited by spatial constraints or inefficiencies in conducting transactions. A typical electronic market consists of buyers and sellers, a commodity or commodities, and a price-discovering mechanism, such as a simultaneous ascending price auction or a sealed bid auction. An electronic market—unlike such physical auction houses as the New York Stock Exchange—removes the physical barrier for transactions. The long-run significance of an electronic market, however, will be its capability to create an efficient decentralized market, where the price-setting mechanism closely resembles the idealized process of *tatonnement*—a gradual or step-by-step market correction to match supply and demand—but in a fast automated fashion.

Already, pioneering electronic markets have been developed on the Internet, where such an enterprise duplicates many actions of a physical market. It offers a meeting place for buyers and sellers, a negotiation procedure, products, auxiliary services such as quality verification and payment clearing, and—sometimes—delivery service. Computers and electronic games are auctioned off on the Internet. Aucnet (http://www.aucnet.com) offers a clearing market among used-car dealers. Stock exchanges maintain online trading services for brokers. Governments auction off treasury bills electronically, and web advertising spaces are auctioned off to the highest bidders in real-time. Other interesting examples of clearing markets are given by McAfee and McMillan (1997).

Future electronic markets will be more than a simple use of technologies, whose impact is often in terms of cost savings. In some cases, an electronic market may open a new opportunity to trade a product that may not have been possible otherwise. In other words, an electronic stock exchange is more than an automated version of the New York Stock Exchange. As McAfee and McMillan (1997) illustrate, an electronic market can effectively replace a regulated market with a decentralized market. The result is often increased efficiency while avoiding many problems associated with bureaucratic administration and the lack of incentives. Regulation is often motivated because of the failure of the market to allocate resources. Nevertheless, in many cases, electronic markets succeed in overcoming the coordination problems observed in physical markets.

The railway industry, to give an example, is often a natural monopoly and is regulated as such. In such a market, one firm will be more efficient and thus able to provide the service at the lowest possible cost, while two or more competing firms may not survive. In Sweden, however, the central rail administration, who allocated the use of tracks centrally, was instructed to sell private firms access to these tracks. Opponents argued that, given the complexity of train routes and timing schedules, such a decentralized market allocation was impossible, not to mention a threat to train safety. Brewer and Plott (1995), through simulated experiments, demonstrated that not only was such a decentralized allocation possible but the result would be increased efficiency. The experiments consisted of several sessions of electronic bidding, where bidders did not know competitors' valuations of tracks. Nevertheless, the analysis of the results showed that actual bid winners—the final allocation of tracks— corresponded to the most desirable theoretical distribution. In this example, an electronic market was shown to be more than an automated physical market, as the former was able to achieve what the latter failed to do. In this sense, an electronic market is not just an application of new technology to existing markets—it is a new type of market.

Through electronic commerce, then, many goods will be allocated more efficiently, especially those regulated products and services now being targeted for deregulation. The trend toward deregulation is spurred by the belief that deregulated industries will result in better product choices, lower prices, and higher consumer welfare, but it is often unclear how these industries, which have been considered to be natural monopolies in which competition harms consumers, can be made competitive when resources are allocated efficiently. The answer will lie in virtual electronic markets by which a complex problem of resource allocation and price discovery processes can be coordinated. As discussed in Chapter 11, "Business and Policy Implications of Electronic Commerce," the web is already used to coordinate interstate electricity whole-sale and retail wheeling. In the virtual economy, different types of market-clearing mechanisms may be offered at the same time for the same product. Selling by posted prices may be more efficient than bid-based auctions if both sellers and buyers are fairly familiar with each other's values, that is, consumers' willingness to pay and the cost of production. On the other hand, auctions may be more efficient if there are many market agents and the supply and demand are somewhat uncertain. Market brokers may operate these mechanisms and compete through market experimentation and efficiency.

12.10.   Summary

This chapter looked at a broader picture of the future virtual economy—electronic commerce as a market with its unique market agents, products, and processes. Popular articles and movies on the subject of virtual reality conjure up a future where the physical world ceases to be important or is in a power struggle with the virtual world. A truly virtual world that can compete with the physical world only exists in a science fiction series such as *Star Trek*, where holodecks create real-life characters and an environment with which humans can interact. Even with their 24th century technologies, however, holodeck characters sometimes go awry—it was they, after all, who attempted to take over the ship itself in one episode. Luckily, the virtual world in the year 2015 will not be anything close to that vision.

The virtual world pictured here parallels our physical world in many respects. The most important change it will bring lies in the way we will interact with each other and with products—in other words, virtual processes. Technological developments in the next 20 years will be substantial, but the seeds of the virtual world—virtual players, products, and processes—are already here. The virtual world that knows no physical boundaries turns out to be cybercommunities and cybernations. While these interest groups exist only virtually, in one sense they are an extension of today's segmented markets. The difference, of course, is that these groups will have the means and reasons to be more coherent and will become a force to reckon with in the marketplace and in politics as well.

A hidden agenda in highlighting the features of the future world is to suggest some areas of interest for economic research. As a commodity market, the virtual marketplace presents fertile ground for research in all areas of economic theory. Aside from Internet economics (which deals with resource allocation and pricing for information infrastructure), cost structure and pricing models for information products have already interested many economists. More rigorous research is needed in digital products, product differentiation and customization, electronic search and advertising, copyrights, and digital currency. This chapter also emphasized the role of producer and consumer learning and the importance of consumer groups and actions, which is often neglected in firm-oriented theory of industrial organization. It is to be hoped that the virtual economy described here will guide both researchers and businesses in evaluating developments in electronic commerce in an appropriate and useful context.

References

Brewer, P. J. and C. R. Plott. "A Binary Conflict Ascending Price (BICAP) Mechanism for the Decentralized Allocation of the Right to Use Railroad Tracks." *Social Science Working Paper, #887*, California Institute of Technology, 1995.

Hämäläinen, M., A. B. Whinston and S. Vishik. "Electronic Markets for Learning: Education Brokerage on the Internet." *Communications of the ACM*, 39(6) 1996: 51–58.

Maes, P. "Agents That Reduce Work and Information Overload." *Communications of the ACM*, 37(7) 1994: 31–40.

McFadden, D. L. and K. E. Train. "Consumers' Evaluation of New Products: Learning From Self and Others." *Journal of Political Economy*, 104(4) 1996: 683–703.

McAfee, R. P. and J. McMillan. "Electronic Markets." *Readings in Electronic Commerce*. Ed. R. Kalakota and A. B. Whinston. Reading, Mass.: Addison-Wesley, 1997. 293–309.

Tapscott, D. The Digital Economy: Promise and Peril in the Age of Networked Intelligence. New York: McGraw-Hill. 1996.

Zaltman, G. "Metaphorically Speaking." *Marketing Research*, 8(2) 1996: 13–20.

Internet Resources

Smart Products

For home automation projects, see Electronic House Online at: http://www.electronichouse.com.

For appliance computerization, see 21st Century Boiler Controls at: http://www.facilitiesnet.com/NS/NS3mk5b.htm.

Habitat and Virtual Communities

Douglas Crockford's Habitat Page at: http://www.communities.com/people/crock/habitat.html.

WorldsAway at: http://www.worldsaway.com.

The 21st Century Technologies

Assorted articles and web sites that discuss the future in selected subjects include:

- Education: Vision 2010 at http://www.si.umich.edu/V2010/
- American embassy and the 21st century information technology: http://www.info.usaid.gov/faiig/wgrecs4.txt
- Workers and workplace: http://www.saigon.com/~vacets/articles/dungh1.html

- GIS: http://www.gatekeeper.com/stormwater/information/gis_full.html
- Medicine and healthcare: http://cfm.mc.duke.edu/chair/pcc/public/ahc/player.htm
- Court technology: http://www.ncsc.dni.us/ncsc/bulletin/future/future.htm
- Banking: http://www.grantthornton.com/gtonline/finance/currency/fall96c.htm
- Global economy: http://www.cgtd.com/global/gat-prs.html

INDEX

buyers
 connecting to sellers via
 intermediaries, 376
 as virtual players, 551

C

C-Net web site, 465

Cable News Network web site, 375

cable system operators (CSOs), 103

CAFE (Conditional Access for
 Europe), 410

call for votes (CFV), 46

capital, decreasing average cost of goods
 sold, 466

Career Path web site, 216

CAs (certification authorities), 394,
 397-398
 authorizing certificates, 395
 digital IDs, 395
 time-stamping services, 395
 transactional certificates, 395
 Verisign, 374

case studies, markets
 financial intermediaries, 382-385
 IPOs (initial public offerings), 383-385

cases (court)
 Church of Scientology v. the Net,
 39, 57
 Information Law Web: Copyright Court
 Cases
 Lotus v. Borland, 40, 57
 Quill Corp. v. North Dakota, 32
 U.S. v. Riggs, 178

cash (digital), 374
 CyberCash, *see* CyberCash
 non-cash payments in the U.S., 409
 see also currency; money

CASIE (Coalition for Advertising
 Supported Information and
 Entertainment), 219

catalogs, 472-473

categorizing digital products, 76
 externalities, 83-84
 intensity of use, 80, 82
 operational usage, 82-83
 timeliness, 78-80
 transfer mode, 76-78
 transfer modes, 86-87

CD (currency-deposit) ratio, 444

Center for Disease Control web site, 92

certificates, 394-399
 authorizing, 395
 CAs (certification authorities), 394,
 397-398
 Verisign, 374
 identifying, 395
 time-stamping services, 395
 transactional, 395

Certified Public Accountants (AICPA), 398

CFV (call for votes), 46

Chamberlinian monopolistic competition,
 319-320

chat groups, 293-294

CHIPS (Clearing House Interbank
 Payments System), 409

Christie's web site, 63

Church of Scientology v. the Net, 39, 57

Cisco Systems web site, 135

Clearing House Interbank Payments
 System (CHIPS), 409

clearing mechanisms, electronic markets,
 576-578

clearing procedures, 387

clickstream path attribute, 336

G

J-K

L

O

P

Q

W

Y-Z